MW01025454

PROVERBS AND
SONG OF SOLOMON

H. A. IRONSIDE

An Ironside Expository Commentary

PROVERBS AND
SONG OF SOLOMON

H. A. IRONSIDE

Kregel
Academic & Professional

Proverbs and Song of Solomon: An Ironside Expository Commentary

Originally published in 1933 and 1946. Reprinted in 2006 by Kregel Publications, a division of Kregel, Inc., P.O. Box 2607, Grand Rapids, MI 49501.

All rights reserved. No part of this book may be reproduced, stored in a retrieval system, or transmitted in any form or by any means—electronic, mechanical, photocopy, recording, or otherwise—without written permission of the publisher, except for brief quotations in printed reviews.

Unless otherwise noted, Scripture quotations are from the King James Version of the Holy Bible.

Scripture quotations marked RV are from the Revised Version of the Holy Bible (Church of England, 1885).

ISBN 978-0-8254-2916-3

Printed in the United States of America

10 11 12 13 14 / 6 5 4 3 2

CONTENTS

Part 2: Song of Solomon

PART 1

PROVERBS

PREFACE

To the general reader, the book of Proverbs, with its common-sense epigrams and sententious aphorisms, might seem to be the last portion of Scripture requiring any attempt at elucidation. But it is just because its chapters abound in pithy truisms that the marrow is often lost sight of by those who have been accustomed to hearing or reading them all their lives.

The present work is an attempt to press home upon the heart and conscience, with a view to the increase of everyday godliness, this distinctively practical portion of the Word of God.

The King James Version is used in the text, save where a uniform rendering of certain words seemed conducive to clearness, and where some other translation better expressed the thought of the original. Wherever changes have been made, the reader may rest assured competent authorities have been consulted, the marginal readings of the Englishman's Hebrew Bible being generally preferred. The poetical arrangement has been used, as it is more capable of clearly manifesting the contrasts, as well as the parallelisms, so abundant in this great storehouse of practical instruction.

Throughout, an effort has been made to bring to the reader's attention some scriptural examples of the proverbial statements. This feature of the work will, it is sincerely hoped, be a means of stimulating the reader to more careful, earnest Bible study.

H. A. IRONSIDE

INTRODUCTION

The royal preacher in the book of Ecclesiastes, after relating so graphically the story of his weary search for happiness "under the sun" and its disappointing result, leading to the often-repeated lament, "Vanity of vanities; all is vanity and vexation of spirit," directs those who would escape the devious paths he had himself trodden to the consideration of the collection of proverbs which he had "sought out, and set in order." The last seven verses of Ecclesiastes form a fitting introduction to the book which in our Bibles immediately precedes it.

> Vanity of vanities, saith the preacher; all is vanity.
> And, moreover, because the preacher was wise, he still taught the
>   people knowledge;
> Yea, he gave good heed, and sought out, and set in order many
>   proverbs
> The preacher sought to find out acceptable words:
> And that which was written was upright, even words of truth.
> The words of the wise are as goads,
> And as nails fastened by the masters of assemblies,
> Which are given from one shepherd.
> And further, by these, my son, be admonished:
> Of making many books there is no end;

And much study is a weariness of the flesh.
Let us hear the conclusion of the whole matter:
Fear God, and keep His commandments:
For this is the whole duty of man.
For God shall bring every work into judgment,
With every secret thing, whether it be good or whether it be evil.
—Ecclesiastes 12:8–14

In these words we have the divine reason for the book of Proverbs. God would save all who heed what is there recorded from the heartbreaking experiences and aimless wanderings of the man who was chosen to write them.

There are two ways of learning the emptiness of the world and the true character of sin. One, and by far the commonest way, is to tread the thorny path each for himself. To do so is to taste to the full the bitterness of departure from God. The only right way is to learn it all in His presence, accepting His word regarding it; and thus enabling the obedient disciple to say, "Concerning the works of men, by the word of Thy lips I have kept me from the paths of the destroyer" (Ps. 17:4).

The bitter disappointments, the skeptical darkness, and the weary heart of Solomon as a result of his trusting his own wisdom, so strongly delineated in the record of the tempests of his soul, need never be the portion of the child of God who orders his steps in the truth.

Human collections of wisdom and instruction are, after all, but the thoughts of men like ourselves. In the wisdom literature of the Bible, we have, as everywhere else in Scripture, the very breathings of the Spirit of God. And this is amazing grace: to think that He who spoke worlds into being, who wrought out redemption when man had fallen, who shall eventually bring in a new heaven and a new earth, wherein dwells righteousness; to think, I repeat, that He, the high and lofty One that inhabits eternity, should stoop in grace to give instruction for the very details of His creatures' lives down here, is cause for worship and admiration forever.

What an importance attaches to all that I do if the God who created me and redeemed me does not consider it beneath His notice to instruct me concerning my behavior in the family, my place in society, and my methods in business. All are under His eye; and if I act in accordance with the book of Proverbs, I shall "behave myself wisely, in a perfect way," in every relationship of life.

To some who prate much of heavenly truth while failing to enter into its intensely practical side, it may seem a far cry from Pauline nights to the commonplaces of Solomon; but to the Christian who would not be like Ephraim, "a cake not turned," but would hold the balance of truth, the precepts and warnings of Proverbs will have their place along with the precious truths of Ephesians.

The "ribbon of blue" on the border of the pious Israelite's garment set forth the heavenly character of the believer's habits. Such an azure ribbon is the book of Proverbs, when the light of the New Testament revelation shines upon it, making known the behavior suited to the one who is dead, buried, and risen with Christ. True, these glorious doctrines will not be found stated in the Old Testament: they belong to the special unfolding of truth revealed through the apostle Paul. But as "the righteous requirement of the law is fulfilled in us who walk not after the flesh, but after the Spirit," so the soul that most deeply enters into the reality of new creation will most appreciate the instruction of the great practical book of the Old Testament.

Like all other Scripture, it has been "written for our admonition, upon whom the ends of the ages have arrived."

To turn, then, to the structure of the book: it did not attain its present fullness until the days of Hezekiah; that is, though all equally God-breathed, it did not exist in the form of one book until that date, as 25:1 makes plain.

The main divisions would seem to be as follows:

- Chapters 1–9: Wisdom and Folly contrasted.
- Chapters 10–24: A collection of proverbs written by Solomon and set in order by him.
- Chapters 25–29: "Also proverbs of Solomon, which the men of Hezekiah king of Judah copied out."
- Chapter 30: The burden, or oracle, of an otherwise unknown sage named Agur, the son of Jakeh.
- Chapter 31: Instruction given to king Lemuel by his mother. This name was probably bestowed upon Solomon as a child by Bathsheba. In that case, the description of the virtuous woman given by one who had herself, at one time, been betrayed from the path of virtue, is worthy of the God of all grace. It is an acrostic poem, arranged according to the letters of the Hebrew alphabet.

Such is the arrangement of the book we purpose studying. As a part of "all Scripture," we may rest assured we shall find it "profitable for doctrine, for reproof, for correction, and for instruction in righteousness," helping to perfect the man of God unto all good works.

CHAPTER 1

PROVERBS 1

The first four verses would seem to justify the title long given to this
remarkable collection of sayings—"The Young Man's Book."

> ¹ The proverbs of Solomon the son of David, king of Israel:
> ² To know wisdom and instruction;
>   To perceive the sayings of intelligence;
> ³ To receive the instruction of understanding,
>   Righteousness, and judgment, and equity;
> ⁴ To give prudence to the simple,
>   To the young man knowledge and discretion.

There are ten words used in this brief introductory portion, which, inasmuch
as most of them recur again and again in the course of the book, should be well
weighed in beginning its study. None are mere synonyms used pedantically, and
therefore idly; but as "every word of God is pure," so these terms throughout are
employed with admirable precision.

The *wisdom* of verse 2 is "skillfulness"—the ability to use knowledge aright. It
occurs thirty-seven times in this one book.

Instruction in the same verse, as also in the one following, is used to translate
a Hebrew word which occurs twenty-six times in Proverbs, and is once rendered

"chasteneth," and once "chastening" (13:24; 3:11). It is so translated in Job 5:17 and in Isaiah 26:16. The meaning is "to teach by discipline."

Intelligence in verse 2, rendered "understanding" in the King James Version, has practically the meaning which in English we attach to the word *discernment.*

Understanding in the third verse ("wisdom," KJV) is a word seldom found in Scripture, and has the force of "to bereave" or "to miscarry." The "sayings of bereavement" might not exactly express the thought; but it conveys the idea of learning through the unhappy experiences of others, or of oneself.

Righteousness of verse 3 ("justice," KJV) refers to conduct and might be rendered "right behavior."

Judgment is equivalent to "decisions." It is the ability to "try the things that differ."

Equity refers to principles rather than conduct. It is uprightness or moral integrity.

Prudence ("subtilty," KJV) in verse 4 is in the original "craftiness." As used here it conveys the ability to detect that in others. "Wise as serpents" answers to it in the New Testament.

Knowledge is "information of a sound character."

Discretion is "thoughtfulness," a characteristic in which the young are generally lacking, but which becomes manifest in one who feeds upon the Word of God.

In these ten words we have the description of a well-rounded character, and it is important to remember that the study and practice of God's truth alone can produce it. To the young man this part of Holy Scripture especially appeals therefore, giving him needed furnishing for his path through the world.

> ⁵ A wise man will hear, and will increase learning;
> And a man of intelligence shall attain unto wise counsels:
> ⁶ To understand a proverb, and the interpretation:
> The words of the wise, and their dark sayings.

It is only the self-confident blusterer who considers himself superior to instruction. Readiness to learn is ever characteristic of the truly wise. That which is worthy of our contemplation is not always simply expressed; for God would have the senses exercised to discern both good and evil. It must be evident to any tyro that were it God's desire but to impart information to His creatures concerning the way to heaven and Christian responsibility, He could have done so in a much simpler way than that through which He has chosen to give us His truth. But this would have done away with that exercise which is both for our blessing and for His glory. Hence the exhortation, "study to show thyself approved unto God, a workman that needeth not to be ashamed, rightly dividing the word of truth" (2 Tim. 2:15). "Dark sayings" become luminous when the man of God studies them having eyes anointed with the eye salve of the Spirit of truth.

> ⁷ The fear of the LORD is the beginning of knowledge:
> But fools despise wisdom and instruction.

Thus on the threshold of this treasure-house of wisdom we are presented with one of the sharp contrasts with which the book abounds. There is no true knowledge apart from the fear of the Lord. All that pretends to the name, but ignores Him, is but folly. It is well for "the young man" to bear this in mind when meeting the many pseudo-scientific theories now abroad. Philosophers and savants have cast to the winds the fear of the Lord, and ruled Him out of His own creation. "Professing themselves to be wise, they became fools." Hence the abounding absurdities that are readily accepted by the ignorant as "science" and "true philosophy." Science means exact knowledge. To call by such a name the wild guesses of evolutionists and infidel biologists is but word prostitution. Hypotheses, however original and erudite, are not science. There never has been, and never will be, a conflict between the Bible and science. The conflict comes in between the Bible and unbelievers' vain theorizing; as, also, between religious notions unsupported by Scripture and scientific facts.

> ⁸ My son, hear the instruction of thy father,
> And forsake not the law of thy mother:
> ⁹ For they shall be an ornament of grace unto thy head,
> And chains about thy neck.

Throughout the Bible obedience to parents is coupled with subjection to God. Those expositors who see in the Ten Commandments four precepts Godward and six manward would seem, therefore, to have missed the mind of the Spirit. The view would appear unquestionably correct which gives five ordinances to each table. "Honor thy father and thy mother: that thy days may be long upon the land which the LORD thy God giveth thee" is the last of the first series. It is the recognition of divine authority and the subject place belonging to the creature.

Nor does responsibility as to this become less in the case of such as "are not under law, but under grace." In Ephesians 6:1 we read, "Children, obey your parents in the Lord: for this is right." And immediately attention is drawn to the preeminent character of this precept in the law. It is "the first commandment *with promise*."[1] Colossians 3:20 is similar: "'Children, obey your parents in all things: for this is well pleasing unto the Lord."

Believing children should be patterns of filial obedience, that thus they may adorn the doctrine of Christ. Young people professing allegiance to the Lord, who are impudent and not subject to those over them in the home, are a sad reproach to the name of Him whom they are supposed to serve. To hear a father's instruction and to cleave to a mother's law; these are the choice ornaments that beautify the young saint.

Disobedience to parents the apostle classes among the evidences of the last-day apostasy (2 Tim. 3:1–5). It is the crying sin of the present lawless times, and presages the awful hour of doom soon to strike. The scriptural "children, obey your parents" has almost universally been superseded by "parents, obey your children." It is a sowing of the wind. The whirlwind will yet have to be reaped. The human will disdains being brooked in any way. Terrible will be the outcome when, having cast off all parental authority, men will throw aside every vestige of allegiance to divine authority likewise, and will rush upon the thick bosses of the Almighty, as portrayed in the solemn chapters of the closing book of the Bible.

> [10] My son, if sinners entice thee, consent thou not.
> [11] If they say, Come with us, let us lay wait for blood,
> Let us lurk privily for the innocent without cause:
> [12] Let us swallow them up alive as sheol;
> And whole, as those that go down to the pit:
> [13] We shall find all precious substance,
> We shall fill our houses with spoil:
> [14] Cast in thy lot among us;
> Let us all have one purse:
> [15] My son, walk not thou in the way with them;
> Refrain thy foot from their path:
> [16] For their feet run to evil,
> And make haste to shed blood.
> [17] Surely in vain the net is spread in the sight of any bird.
> [18] And they lay wait for their own blood;
> They lurk privily for their own lives.

¹⁹ So are the ways of every one that is greedy of gain;
Which taketh away the life of the owners thereof.

Two things the young man is solemnly warned against here: evil companionships and "covetousness, which is idolatry."

The line of demarcation between the children of God and the children of wrath is sharply drawn in the inspired Word. "Come out from among them, and *be ye separate*," is the command of the Lord. If sinners entice, appealing to the lust of the human heart, turn away from them. Their entreaties are only defiling. Nothing pleases them better than to have the young man cast in his lot with them, all having one purse; but it is an ungodly fellowship, in which the believer can have no part. "O my soul, come not thou into their secret; unto their assembly, mine honor, be not thou united" (Gen. 49:6).

The only safe course is to part company at once. "Walk not thou in the way with them." Clean-cut separation from the world in all its forms is the path of blessing. Many a young Christian makes shipwreck because of dallying with the world on the plea, perchance, of improving it. Such a course is folly, and a great mistake. "Refrain thy foot from their path: for their feet run to evil"; and if you venture first to "walk" in their way, you will soon be "running" with them.

Nor can you plead ignorance in the day of your spiritual and moral breakdown; for God's Word had cast a light on your way, disclosing the net spread now in plain sight, and warning you against the treacherous wiles of the Devil.

In contrast to the entreaty of the wicked, the next section gives the voice of Wisdom, pleading that she be heard and heeded.

²⁰ Wisdom crieth without;
She uttereth her voice in the streets:
²¹ She crieth in the chief place of concourse,
In the openings of the gates:
In the city she uttereth her sayings,
²² How long, ye simple ones, will ye love simplicity?
And [ye] scorners delight in your scorning,
And [ye] fools hate knowledge?
²³ Turn you at my reproof:
Behold, I will pour out my spirit unto you,
I will make known my words unto you.

Throughout this first division, including chapters 1–9, Wisdom is personified. She is ever seeking to turn the steps of the young man from the door of folly and ignorance to the temple of knowledge and blessing. Here she is presented as one crying in public places, eagerly seeking to attract the attention of the passersby. In the marts of commerce, at the gates of justice, in the centers of population, among the idlers on the streets; everywhere she pleads and entreats, beseeching the simple to obey her voice. She is met by, not always positive refusal, but, what is far more common and equally as dangerous: procrastination. "Until when," she cries, "ye simple ones, will ye cleave to your folly?" But there is no response.

Others definitely refuse to listen to her voice. Scornfully rejecting her testimony, they delight in their fancied independence of mind, and manifest their true character by their hatred of knowledge.

To all such she addresses a warning of coming calamity, when it will be too late to heed her gracious invitation.

> [24] Because I have called, and ye refused;
>   I have stretched out my hand, and no man attended;
> [25] But ye have set at naught all my counsel,
>   And would none of my reproof:
> [26] I also will laugh at your calamity,
>   I will mock when your fear cometh;
> [27] When your fear cometh as a tempest,
>   And your destruction cometh as a whirlwind;
>   When distress and anguish cometh upon you.
> [28] Then shall they call upon me, but I will not answer;
>   They shall seek me early, but they shall not find me:
> [29] For that they hated knowledge,
>   And did not choose the fear of Jehovah:
> [30] They would none of my counsel:
>   They despised all my reproof.
> [31] Therefore shall they eat of the fruit of their own way,
>   And be filled with their own devices.
> [32] For the turning away of the simple shall slay them,
>   And the prosperity of fools shall destroy them.
> [33] But whoso hearkeneth unto me shall dwell safely,
>   And shall be quiet from fear of evil.[2]

It must be evident to all how like this is to the gospel call, with its attendant warning of coming judgment if despised. On the face of it, it is the Old Testament way of saying, "Be not deceived; God is not mocked: for whatsoever a man soweth, that shall he also reap. For he that soweth to his flesh shall of the flesh reap corruption; but he that soweth to the Spirit shall of the Spirit reap life everlasting" (Gal. 6:7–8). The principle abides whether applied to sinners or saints. But surely in Wisdom's cry the "ministry of reconciliation" may be readily recognized. It is

> God beseeching, man refusing
> To be made forever glad.

And what must the inevitable result be?

Ah, dear, unsaved reader, if into the hands of such a one these pages fall, remember there is not only a world in which you can say "No" to God, the God of all grace; there is also a world in which He will say "No" to you, if you meet Him as the God of judgment. There is not only a scene in which Wisdom's cry can be despised; there is also a scene where your cry shall be despised if you enter it a rejecter of the message of grace. There is not only a place where you, in your folly and carelessness of heart, can laugh at the entreaties of Wisdom; a day comes on apace when Wisdom shall laugh at your calamity and mock your bitter anguish.

Mark well; it is not God as such who will ever laugh at the grief of one of His creatures, however abandoned and iniquitous: it is Wisdom who speaks. That Wisdom which you now despise will then mock your hopeless wails.

What can be worse for a lost soul than to have to remember, in the abyss of woe, gospel messages once indifferently listened to, the Word of God once treated as a subject unfit for serious consideration; and then to have to cry in despair, "Jesus died, yet I'm in hell! He gave Himself for sinners. He provided a way of salvation for me, but, like the fool that I was, I spurned His grace until grace was withdrawn, the door of mercy was closed, and now I am to be on the wrong side of that closed door forever!" Thus will Wisdom laugh at your calamity, if you go out into eternity in your sin.

Nor can any blame God that it has fared so ill with them. All shall own that it was because they hated knowledge and chose not Jehovah's fear. Turning away with the simple, they are slain; prospering in their folly, they are destroyed. So shall it be with all who despise Wisdom and ignore her entreaties.

But all who hearken shall dwell safely, forever quiet from fear of evil. "Many sorrows shall be to the wicked: but he that trusteth in the LORD, mercy shall compass him about" (Ps. 32:10).

Nor must we think only of the warning to the unconverted. Even to those who are secure for eternity an apostle had to write, "See then that ye walk circumspectly, not as fools, but as wise, redeeming the time, because the days are evil. Wherefore be ye not unwise, but understanding what the will of the Lord is" (Eph. 5:15–17). It is true of saints as of sinners that we reap as we sow. The believer cannot take his own way with impunity. If he turns away from the house of Wisdom, to pursue the path of folly, he too must hear the mocking laugh at last of that Wisdom which he had dared to despise. The chastisement of the Lord must invariably follow departure from the ways that be in Christ. It is important to remember that the moment a poor sinner trusts the Lord Jesus as his Savior, his responsibility as a criminal having to do with the Judge is over forever. "There is therefore now no condemnation to them that are in Christ Jesus" (Rom. 8:1). But, that very moment, his responsibility as a child having to do with his Father begins; and that Father, "without respect of persons, judgeth according to every man's work" (1 Peter 1:17).

His new responsibility springs from his new relationship. Henceforth he is to "reckon himself dead indeed unto sin, but alive unto God through Jesus Christ our Lord" (Rom. 6:11). If he fails to do this, and allows himself to become indifferent to the will of God, he must know the rod of His discipline.

"The Lord knoweth how to deliver the godly out of temptation, and to reserve the unjust unto the day of judgment to be punished" (2 Peter 2:9). It is in *this* world that the Christian is dealt with for his failures. The unjust will be dealt with in that day of wrath; though even here sin brings suffering in their case as well.

Let us remember, then, that "the time is come that judgment must begin at the house of God: and if it first begin at us, what shall the end be of them that know not the gospel of God? And if the righteous scarcely be saved, where shall the ungodly and the sinner appear?" (1 Peter 4:17–18).

CHAPTER 2

PROVERBS 2

In the opening verses the secret that so many have sought in vain is made known: how to find the knowledge of God. After all, there is very little mystery about it. The Christian need not be scholarly and profound to understand the Scripture of truth. It is condition of soul, rather than a well-furnished mind, that is required. God has given His word. He exhorts us to search it in dependence upon His Holy Spirit, who is now come to guide us into all truth.

> ¹ My son, if thou wilt *receive* my sayings,
>   And *lay up* my commandments with thee;
> ² So that thou *incline thine ear* unto wisdom,
>   And *apply thy heart* to understanding;
> ³ Yea, if thou *criest after* knowledge;
>   And *liftest up thy voice* for understanding;
> ⁴ If thou *seekest* her as silver,
>   And *searchest* for her as for hid treasures;
> ⁵ *Then* shalt thou understand the fear of Jehovah,
>   And find the knowledge of God.

It is no careless reading of the Scriptures that is here indicated. The soul is exhorted to "receive" these sayings. This is something more than a cursory examination of them. The sayings of God must be received into the heart. And there they are to be "laid up," or "hidden." The ear must be inclined to wisdom; the heart applied to understanding; while the mouth cries after knowledge, and the voice is lifted up for that which will give spiritual intelligence. The whole being is thus devoted to the search for the truth. As men dig deep for silver and make diligent effort to locate hidden treasure, so the earnest seeker must dig into the Word of God, and be not content with surface findings. When thus esteeming the words of His mouth as more than one's necessary food, the result is certain: "Then *shalt* thou understand the fear of the LORD, and find the knowledge of God."

It is to be feared that even among those who hold and value much precious truth, diligent Bible study is on the wane. It is well to remember that reading books about the Bible is a very different thing to searching the Word for oneself. Notes and expositions may be helpful. If the writer did not so believe, he would not now be putting pen to paper. But if these works of uninspired men be permitted to take the place of the sure Word of the living God, the result can only be baneful in the extreme. The result of such one-sided study will be that men will draw their thoughts from one another, in place of from the great reservoir of truth itself. This will result in a dry intellectuality which is the very opposite of a fresh, vigorous spirituality.

> ⁶ For Jehovah giveth wisdom;
>   Out of His mouth cometh knowledge and understanding.
> ⁷ He layeth up sound wisdom for the righteous;
>   He is a buckler to them that walk uprightly.
> ⁸ He keepeth the paths of judgment,
>   And preserveth the way of His saints.
> ⁹ Then shalt thou understand righteousness, and judgment,
>   And equity; yea, every good path.

Intimately connected, ever, must be the search for truth and the walking in it when received. Where there is a single eye and a true heart, characterized by earnest desire to live in the power of the truth revealed to the soul, He whose truth it is will be a buckler, or defense, for His own, keeping them safely as they tread the paths of judgment; thus preserving their way. It is by so walking that one shall daily increase in the knowledge of righteousness, judgment, and equity; yea, every good path. Very different is this from mere mental adhesion to a certain theological system, or a particular school of biblical lore. It is not so much "holding the truth," as being held by that truth. Between the two states there is a vast difference. "Vain talkers and deceivers" abound, who speak "great swelling words," and boast of their knowledge and prophetic and dispensational teaching, or of ecclesiastical truth, whose unguarded ways and careless walk bring reproach upon the solemn and precious things they profess to glory in. They seem to chew the cud, but fail to manifest the divided hoof. Such a course persisted in sears the conscience and hardens the heart, until the most searching ministry fails to make any impression upon them.

The proper attitude for one who really holds the truth, and its blessed results, are set forth in the following verses:

> ¹⁰ When wisdom entereth into thy heart,
>   And knowledge is pleasant unto thy soul;
> ¹¹ Discretion shall preserve thee,
>   Understanding shall keep thee:
> ¹² To deliver thee from the way of the evil man,
>   From the man that speaketh froward things;
> ¹³ Who leave the paths of uprightness,
>   To walk in the ways of darkness;
> ¹⁴ Who rejoice to do evil,
>   And delight in the frowardness of the evil one;
> ¹⁵ Whose ways are crooked,
>   And perverse in their paths.

Wisdom and knowledge entering into the heart and becoming pleasant to the soul, give that discretion which preserves from evil; and the understanding, or discernment that keeps from false ways. Two enemies are seen besetting the feet of the young man. Here it is the evil man; in the next few verses, the strange woman. The evil man is the man who walks in the pride of his heart and in independence of God. This, to the young, seems very attractive, appealing to the natural mind. But to follow the evil man is to "leave the paths of righteousness" and to "walk in the ways of darkness." The truth of God possessing the reins will deliver from this, keeping the recipient of it from the self-willed ways of the evil one and pointing out his crooked and perverse paths. But this is not the only enemy seeking to beguile the simple. The Word of God is also given

> ¹⁶ To deliver thee from the strange woman,
>   Even from the stranger which flattereth with her sayings;

¹⁷ Which forsaketh the guide of her youth,
    And forgetteth the covenant of her God.

Again and again we catch glimpses of this strange woman flitting in and out in the pages of our book. Who is she? Does she speak of anything more than impurity and uncleanness? Unquestionably the primary meaning is clear on the face of the passages that concern her. She is the ensnaring enemy of morality and virtue, who today, as in Solomon's time, pursues her nefarious traffic in the bodies and souls of the young and unwary. Forsaking the guide of her youth, forgetting the covenant of her God, she gives herself up to impure pleasures and soul-destroying lusts.

¹⁸ For her house inclineth unto death,
    And her paths unto the dead.
¹⁹ None that go unto her return again
    Neither attain they to the paths of life.

So true is this that those who have been ensnared and fallen into ways of uncleanness go through life under a blight from which they never recover. The memory of unholy revels, of filthy pollutions, will abide and prove a source of shame and grief to the end. The more sincere the repentance, the more truly will this be the case.

But having considered all this, is there not another meaning also to be taken from these many warnings concerning the strange woman? In a secondary sense it seems evident that as in the evil man we have set forth independency of God— rationalism run riot; so in the strange woman we see false religion as eventually to be headed up in Babylon the Great, the mother of harlots and abominations that be upon the face of the earth. How devious are her ways! How subtle and deceptive her solicitations! And how truly can it be said that *"her* house inclineth unto death, and her paths unto the dead!" Only the Word of God can preserve the soul from her corruptions and keep the feet in the paths of life.

²⁰ That thou mayest walk in the ways of the good,
    And keep the paths of the righteous.
²¹ For the upright shall dwell in the land,
    And the perfect shall remain in it.
²² But the lawless shall be cut off from the earth,
    And the transgressors shall be rooted out of it.

It is not the heavenly but the earthly hope that here comes before us. The book of Proverbs, like all the rest of the Old Testament, speaks of earthly things. The heavenly things were as yet unrevealed. So it is the portion of the godly Israelite that is here presented to us. He shall dwell in the land in the day when the lawless Gentiles and the transgressors among the chosen people shall be rooted out of it. Ours is a far better portion. We have an inheritance reserved for us in heaven, whither Christ the Forerunner has for us entered!

How much greater is our responsibility to see that our steps are ordered according to the Word of the living God!

PROVERBS 3

¹ My son, forget not my law;
   But let thy heart keep my commandments:
² For length of days, and long life,
   And peace, shall they add to thee.

Here we are still on Jewish ground, but the exhortation is of all importance to us as well as to those who see in long life an evidence of the special blessing of the Lord. For there is that in the exhortation which should appeal to all. "Let thy heart keep my commandments" is a much-needed word. This is far more than submission to duty; it is loving devotion to the will of God. "Thy word," said the psalmist, "have I hid in my heart that I might not sin against Thee" (Ps. 119:11). And of Ezra it is recorded that he "prepared his heart to seek the law of the LORD, and to do it, and to teach in Israel statutes and judgments" (Ezra 7:10). This preparation of the heart in man which is so truly from the Lord is what is sadly lacking among many whose outward ways testify to the slight hold the truth they profess really has upon them. Love is the spring of true service to the Lord. "If ye love Me keep My commandments" (John 14:15) are His own words; and He goes even deeper when He says, "If a man love Me he will keep My sayings" (John 14:23). This is the heart delighting to run in His ways if His mind be but made known, whether there be positive command or not.

³ Let not lovingkindness and truth forsake thee:
  Bind them about thy neck;
  Write them upon the table of thy heart:
⁴ So shalt thou find favor and understanding
  In the sight of God and man.

"The law was given by Moses, but grace and truth came by Jesus Christ" (John 1:17). The law was truth, but it was truth without grace. This latter having come by Jesus Christ, the believer is exhorted to be speaking the truth in love" (Eph. 4:15) "Speaking the truth" is one word in the original, and is a participle. J. N. Darby suggested coining a word to express it—"truthing." It is not merely *speaking* the truth. It is being characterized by the truth; but all must be in love. A hard and fast intolerant spirit that makes the truth like a series of legal enactments, and is censorious toward those who see not eye to eye with oneself; this is far removed from the Spirit of truth. Loving-kindness will commend the truth, when an acrimonious, judging spirit will deter the timid from its reception. They are to be bound about the neck, in this way displayed in the sight of man; and written upon the heart, thus finding favor with God.

⁵ Trust in Jehovah with all thy heart;
  And lean not unto thine own understanding.
⁶ In all thy ways acknowledge Him,
  And He shall direct thy paths.

Solemn the admonition, and precious the assurance here for all who would be guided in the way of peace. "He that trusteth in His own heart is a fool" (28:26), but happy is the man whose trust is in the Lord. Confidence in self is like leaning on a broken reed. God has given His Word to guide in every detail of life that thus our sanctification might be by the Truth, and it is therefore inexcusable to lean upon our own poor finite intelligence.

If He be acknowledged in all our ways we shall not want guidance, for He is faithful who has promised to direct our paths. "If thine eye be single, thy whole body shall be full of light" (Matt. 6:22).

⁷ Be not wise in thine own eyes:
  Fear Jehovah, and depart from evil.
⁸ It shall be healing to thy sinew
  And moistening to thy bones.

To be wise in our own eyes is the very opposite to leaning not unto our own understanding.

Where the Lord is truly feared, evil will be hated and departed from. "Let every one that nameth the name of the Lord depart from iniquity" (2 Tim. 2:19). So shall strength and freshness characterize the soul. To go on with God while walking in that which His Word condemns is impossible. The path of blessing is the path of obedience. If He has spoken, the subject soul will not stay to question but obey implicitly.

> ⁹ Honor Jehovah with thy substance,
>   and with the firstfruits of all thine increase:
> ¹⁰ So shall thy barns be filled with plenty,
>   And thy presses shall burst out with new wine.

Having learned to depart from evil, the Lord becomes the object of the heart. It is not giving Him the *first* place merely. It is a poor thing when Christ has but the first place in the soul. He must have all if one is to go on with Him in holy joy and unhindered communion. The Israelite brought the firstfruits as a token that he acknowledged Jehovah's sole ownership of the land of Canaan. He had said, "The land shall not be sold forever; the land is Mine" (Lev. 25:23). The giving of the firstfruits was the recognition of this. So, as the believer honors Him with his substance, he gladly owns that all is the Lord's to be used as He directs.

But so great is His goodness that when He is thus honored, He pledges Himself to see that there is no lack in barn nor press for the one who owns himself His steward. Many a saint goes on in comparative poverty because of his indifference to the principle here laid down. All comes from God; yet He graciously receives from those He has redeemed, and delights to ever be Himself the greatest giver. None shall find Him in their debt.

> ¹¹ My son, despise not the chastening of Jehovah;
>   Neither be weary of His correction:
> ¹² For whom the LORD loveth He correcteth;
>   Even as a father the son in whom he delighteth.

These words form the text for the apostle's exhortation on the Lord's discipline in Hebrews 12. He has expounded them by the inspiration of the Holy Spirit; so to that precious portion of the Word we would turn. We need not trust our own thoughts, however much we seek to be subject to Scripture, when we have the mind of the Spirit fully revealed.

After having traced the path of faith down through the pages of the Old Testament, the apostle bids us lay aside every weight, everything that would hinder progress; thus enabling us to distance sin which ever would beset our steps, while we run with patience the race set before us. Christ himself is put before the soul as faith's Author and Perfecter. God would have the heart occupied with Him who, His own path of shame and suffering over, is now "set down on the right hand of God." To "consider Him" is the antidote for weariness and faintness.

He goes on to show that trial and difficulty must not be accounted a strange thing. All are but a part of our discipline. And thereupon he cites the passage we have now come to in the book of Proverbs. The difference of wording results from his quoting from the Septuagint, the Greek version generally in use at that time.

> My son, despise not thou the chastening of the LORD,
> Nor faint when thou art rebuked of Him.
> For whom the LORD loveth He chasteneth,
> And scourgeth every son whom He receiveth.

In the book of Job a similar word is found, credited to Eliphaz the Temanite, "Behold, happy is the man whom God correcteth: therefore despise not thou the chastening of the Almighty" (Job. 5:17).

It was no new truth that the Lord exercised discipline among His saints. In fact, it is because they are His own that He does chasten. This word has not necessarily the sense of "punish," though, unquestionably, chastening is often directly retributive. But the primary meaning is discipline. God is a God of order. His family must be under His discipline. Therefore the apostle says, "If ye endure chastening, God dealeth with you as with sons; for what son is he whom the father chasteneth not?" It is no evidence that the heart of God is not toward me that I am left to suffer affliction. All is but part of that discipline which an all-wise Father sees to be necessary. In fact, if I am not the subject of this disciplinary training, I am not one of His at all! "But if ye be without chastisement, whereof all (that is, all sons) are partakers, then are ye bastards, and not sons."

Nor is the Lord's discipline of the selfish or uncertain nature that ours often is, in regard to our own households. "We have had fathers of our flesh which corrected us, and we gave them reverence: shall we not much rather be in subjection to the Father of spirits, and live? For they verily for a few days chastened us after their own pleasure [or, as seemed good to them]; but He for our profit, that we might be partakers of His holiness." Not always have earthly parents the direct good of their children in view when they discipline them. How often we may be moved more by the disturbance of our personal comfort than by the sense of the child's need of correction! In such a case we chasten after our own pleasure. Our God and Father never so deals with us. He has our profit ever before Him. But though this is so, we are certain to prove that "no chastening for the present seemeth to be joyous, but grievous: nevertheless afterward it yieldeth the peaceable fruit of righteousness unto them which are exercised thereby" (Heb. 12:11; see also vv. 7–10). Thus we have briefly outlined the Scripture teaching as to the Lord's discipline.

May grace be given to reader and writer neither to faint beneath the chastening as though some strange thing happened to us, nor yet to despise it, thus ignoring the Lord's hand in it all; but rather to be exercised thereby, that it may indeed yield in us and in our ways the peaceable fruits of righteousness, and so we shall be partakers of His holiness. Thus shall we enter into the blessedness of the following verses:

> ¹³ Happy is the man that findeth wisdom,
>   And the man that getteth understanding.
> ¹⁴ For the merchandise of it is better than the merchandise of
>   silver,
>   And the gain thereof than fine gold.
> ¹⁵ She is more precious than rubies:
>   And all the things thou canst desire are not to be compared
>   unto her.
> ¹⁶ Length of days is in her right hand;
>   And in her left hand riches and honor.
> ¹⁷ Her ways are ways of pleasantness,
>   And all her paths are peace.
> ¹⁸ She is a tree of life to them that lay hold upon her;
>   And happy is every one that retaineth her.

Men will brave untold dangers and exhaust human ingenuity in their search for precious metals and sparkling jewels; but in following Wisdom's ways treasures are to be found which all the costly gems of earth could never equal in value. Length of days, riches and honor she offers to those who find her; and coupled with these, she gives what earthly stores often detract from: peace and quietness of soul. The ways of Wisdom are the ways that be in Christ; the ways into which the Word of God would guide the feet of the subject soul. Such ways are indeed "ways of pleasantness, and all her paths are peace." To thus find the true wisdom, is to feed on the tree of life. No happiness such as men in the flesh enjoy, is to be compared with this.

It is the same wisdom by which Jehovah founded the earth that He offers to us, to be our guide on our pilgrim pathway. Of this the next section reminds us.

> [19] Jehovah by wisdom hath founded the earth;
>   By understanding hath He established the heavens.
> [20] By His knowledge the depths are broken up,
>   And the skies drop down the dew.

Surely it is grace immeasurable that thus leads the One who upholds all things by the word of His power, to concern Himself about the steps of His creatures. The Word of God is but another expression of the wisdom that spoke worlds into existence, and it is "written for our learning, that we through patience and comfort of the Scriptures might have hope."

> [21] My son, let them not depart from thine eyes:
>   Keep sound wisdom and discretion;
> [22] So shall they be life unto thy soul,
>   And grace to thy neck.
> [23] Then shalt thou walk in thy way safely,
>   And thy foot shall not stumble.
> [24] When thou liest down, thou shalt not be afraid:
>   Yea, thou shalt lie down, and thy sleep shall be sweet.

Someone has said, "It is not enough that one hold the truth, if the truth hold not him." To so take hold of what God has revealed as to have it control the heart and life, is what is continually insisted on in this most practical of all books. Thus, to "keep sound wisdom and discretion," gives one to lay hold on what is really life, and ornaments the neck with grace. The foot, too, will be kept from stumbling, and the disciple will be guided in the way of truth. Rest and refreshment become likewise the portion of all who esteem the Word of God above all the thoughts of men.

²⁵ Be not afraid of sudden fear,
    Neither of the desolation of the lawless, when it cometh.
²⁶ For Jehovah shall be thy confidence,
    And shall keep thy foot from being taken.

It is the obedient soul who can lay hold of the precious promises of Scripture. The willful and lawless have no such title. If walking in subjection to the truth, neither sudden fear nor the desolation of the wicked need affright, for Jehovah, whose truth it is, will be the confidence of all who walk uprightly, and will keep the feet of His saints.

God thus being given his place, man will have what belongs to him. Of this the next portion speaks.

²⁷ Withhold not good from its owners,
    When it is in the power of thy hand to do it.
²⁸ Say not unto thy neighbor,
    "Go, and come again, and tomorrow I will give,"
    When thou hast it by thee.

To owe no man aught but love is a command that is binding on every child of God. To withhold another's due when able to pay, evidences the fact that covetousness is in the heart and is being permitted to gain ascendancy over the life. Often the poor are made to suffer by thoughtlessness in this respect. Payments looked forward to for the supplying of the necessaries of life are needlessly deferred by those more blessed with earth's goods than they; and real suffering results, often leading to bitterness and hatred. Such conduct on the part of a Christian is in every way to be deplored. Money owed to another is not mine. To use it for my own purposes is dishonesty. God's eye sees every such action, and He has said, "Be sure your sin will find you out!"

²⁹ Devise not evil against thy neighbor,
    Seeing he dwelleth confidently by thee.

The abuse of trust is, in the sight of the Holy and the True, an abominable thing. Confidence misplaced has ruined many. How dreadful the testimony if the one who has abused that confidence be a professor of Christianity! It is things like these that turn the ignorant to skepticism, and ruin the influence of those who might, if faithful, be used in blessing to many.

> ³⁰ Strive not with a man without cause,
>   If he hath done thee no harm.

And even if he have harmed me, One greater than Solomon has said, "I say unto you that ye resist not evil." Under law, it was a sin to strive with another without adequate ground; but under grace, as God has dealt with me, so am I to deal with my debtors.

> ³¹ Envy thou not the violent man,
>   And choose none of his ways.
> ³² For the froward is abomination to Jehovah;
>   But His secret is with the righteous.
> ³³ The curse of Jehovah is in the house of the lawless;
>   But He blesseth the habitation of the just.
> ³⁴ Surely He scorneth the scorners;
>   But He giveth grace unto the lowly.
> ³⁵ The wise shall inherit glory;
>   But shame shall be the promotion of fools.

Asaph was envious of the foolish when he saw the prosperity of the wicked, until he went into the sanctuary of the Lord, where he was given to understand their end. Then his heart was grieved, and he owned his folly (Ps. 73). Seeking to satisfy their souls with the evanescent things of earth, they remain in ignorance of the counsels of Jehovah, which are known only to the righteous. Their end will be anything but enviable, for the curse of the Lord is in their houses, and He scorns their haughty pretensions. His blessing abides upon the habitation of the just, and "He giveth grace unto the lowly." Those who are content to thus abase themselves and walk in the steps of Him who was ever the humble, dependent One down here will be despised by those who are wise in their own conceit; but they shall inherit true glory at last, when the false glitter of worldly fame has faded away forever, and "shame shall be the promotion of fools."

PROVERBS 4

¹ Hear, ye children, the instruction of a father,
And attend to know understanding.
² For I give you good doctrine;
Forsake ye not my law.
³ For I was my father's son,
Tender and only [beloved] in the sight of my mother.
⁴ He taught me also, and said unto me,
Let thy heart retain my words:
Keep my commandments and live.

Solomon's own early training is here touchingly alluded to. His mother's only son, tenderly loved and cared for; the object of his father's heart, he had been solicitously instructed in the law of the Lord and had profited thereby.

It is only necessary to read the unhappy history of his half-brother Adonijah, whose father had never displeased him in saying, "Why hast thou done so?" to realize how much Solomon was indebted to his mother's counsel and his father's instruction. The value of parental discipline cannot be overestimated. To be brought up in the nurture and admonition of the Lord is a blessing beyond our ability to appreciate. Strange that David could so differently treat two sons as in the cases instanced above!

But it is not the responsibility of the parents that is here dwelt on. It is that of the children rather, who are thus nurtured and cared for. He who, whatever his aberrations, knew so well the value of wise and godly instruction, says:

⁵ Get wisdom; get understanding:
  Forget it not; neither decline from the sayings of my
    mouth.
⁶ Forsake her not, and she shall preserve thee:
  Love her, and she shall keep thee.
⁷ Wisdom is the principal thing;
  Therefore get wisdom:
  And with all thy getting get understanding.

It is not knowledge merely which the soul needs, but the wisdom and intelligence to use knowledge aright. This is the principal thing, and this he impresses on the young. Wisdom will preserve from folly, and if truly loved will keep the feet of her disciple.

⁸ Exalt her, and she shall promote thee:
  She shall bring thee to honor, when thou dost embrace her.
⁹ She shall give to thy head a chaplet of grace:
  A diadem of beauty shall she deliver to thee.

In the previous chapter it is stated that "shame shall be the promotion of fools." Wisdom brings to honor and true promotion. Even in the world is this true, however much iniquity may abound; but among the children of God how valuable is a man of wisdom! Mere knowledge may puff up and render the possessor thereof contemptible; but the word of wisdom is always in season; and though oftentimes rejected, is at least appreciated: the conscience assenting to what the unspiritual man may be determined to refuse.

¹⁰ Hear, O my son, and receive my sayings;
  And the years of thy life shall be many.
¹¹ I have taught thee in the way of wisdom;
  I have led thee in right paths.
¹² When thou goest, thy steps shall not be straitened;
  And when thou runnest, thou shalt not stumble.

The book of Ecclesiastes, as already noted in our introductory chapter, portrays the wrong paths into which the royal writer had wandered when, for the time being, he forsook that Word which had been the guide of his youth, and gave himself up to commune with his own heart and to seek out a way of pleasure for himself. It is not necessary to follow him in paths of folly to learn their end. The book now before us marks out right paths, the way of wisdom. All who walk therein shall find their steps unstraitened, and shall be enabled to run without stumbling. How needful, then, to heed the exhortation that follows!

> ¹³ Take fast hold of instruction; let her not go:
>   Keep her; for she is thy life.
> ¹⁴ Enter not into the path of the lawless,
>   And go not in the way of evil men.
> ¹⁵ Avoid it, pass not by it,
>   Turn from it, and pass away.
> ¹⁶ For they sleep not, except they have done evil;
>   And their sleep is taken away unless they cause some to fall.
> ¹⁷ For they eat the bread of lawlessness,
>   And drink the wine of violence.

The principle here enunciated is of prime importance and cannot be too often insisted on. The child of God is called to separation from all evildoers. He who knows what is in the darkness has described their unholy ways. We need not mistake them. Called to holiness, we are to avoid their path. To trifle and temporize with them is most deleterious and will greatly hinder soul progress. The true pilot may not know every rock or reef, but his wisdom consists in taking the safe channel: so the Christian need not make himself aware of all the evils of the day. He is to simply take the safe path described in the verse that follows:

> ¹⁸ But the path of the just is as a shining light,
>   That shineth more and more unto the perfect day.
> ¹⁹ The way of the lawless is as darkness:
>   They know not at what they stumble.

Marked is the difference thus presented. The path of the righteous, leading onward and upward to that city where the glory of God doth lighten it and the Lamb is the lamp thereof, shines brighter and brighter as the uncreated glory from that city of bliss illumines it with splendor. Who would not cry, "Let me die the death of the righteous; let my last end be like his"? A far more exceeding and eternal weight of glory is at the end of that path.

Alas! how great the contrast when we turn to the way of the lawless. As their road nears the pit of woe, darkness begins to envelop it; the awful stygian smoke of the abyss obscuring even the light of nature and revelation alike: so that men stumble blindly on, knowing not what causes them to fall. The end we well know—eternal banishment from the presence of God.

With two such paths to choose between, the admonition that immediately follows may well be borne in upon the soul.

> [20] My son, attend unto my words;
>   Incline thine ear unto my sayings.
> [21] Let them not depart from thine eyes;
>   Keep them in the midst of thy heart.
> [22] For they are life unto those that find them,
>   And healing to all their flesh.

The Spirit of Christ in the psalmist could say, "Thy word have I hid in my heart, that I might not sin against Thee" (Ps. 119:11). It is the heart controlled by Scripture that assures a walk in the truth. God desires truth in the inward parts: the very reins of our being should be the seat of wisdom. When this is the case, the words of knowledge indeed become life and health to the one who keeps them.

The word that follows but emphasizes this all-important principle.

> [23] Keep thy heart above all keeping:
>   For out of it are the issues of life.

Here is displayed a scientific knowledge and accuracy far beyond the times in which Solomon wrote. The great discovery of William Harvey in 1628, the circulation of the blood, which revolutionized medical thought, is here calmly taken for granted and used to set forth, or illustrate, a spiritual truth. Just as the heart is the center of the physical system, whence flow the issues of life, so, in a moral and spiritual sense, the heart, used as a synonym for the soul, is that which must be jealously guarded, that thence may go forth that which is for the upbuilding of the child of God.

> [24] Put away from thee a froward mouth,
>   And perverse lips put far from thee.

As it is out of the heart's abundance that the mouth speaks, mouth and heart are here intimately connected. A froward mouth and perverse lips bespeak one who is not in subjection to God. Where His Word has its place in the soul, the lips manifest it.

> 25 Let thine eyes look right on,
>   And let thine eyelids look straight before thee.
> 26 Ponder the path of thy feet,
>   And let all thy ways be established.
> 27 Turn not to the right hand nor to the left:
>   Remove thy foot from evil.

It is not the mouth only that shows the state of the heart. The feet likewise will walk according to the condition of the soul. Forgetting the things behind, we are exhorted to press on to the prize of the calling of God on high. The eye is to be fixed on the goal, looking straight before. For us, this is Christ. As the plowman cuts a straight furrow when the eye is on a distant point directly before him, so the Christian's path will be that of the just, when the eye of the heart is fixed on the Lord Jesus, now ascended to glory. But this involves likewise earnest concern about one's ways, that all may be established in accordance with the truth. Evil is to be judged and departed from, the foot turning neither to the right nor the left. The mind of God once known is to be faithfully acted upon, irrespective of self-interest or the thoughts of others who discern it not.

To walk with God necessarily means to be misjudged and misunderstood by unspiritual persons who are ignorant of the power of God and the value of His truth. But if one has His approbation, there need be no consulting with flesh and blood, but implicit obedience to what He has said in His Word.

CHAPTER 5

PROVERBS 5

The warning of chapter 2 against the strange woman is in this portion reverted to, and additional instruction given. It is a subject of deep solemnity if this unholy siren be seen to picture false religion, with its snares and seductions; while, of course, looked at in its simple, primary meaning, it is of great importance. If any are entrapped, it is not for lack of warning, but for willful neglect of instruction.

> ¹ My son, attend unto my wisdom,
>   And bow thine ear to mine understanding;
> ² That thou mayest regard discretion,
>   And that thy lips may keep knowledge.

Throughout the book, the need of more than casual attention to the words of wisdom is enforced. To hear with no thought of heeding is not what is contemplated; but the bowing of the ear to understanding, in order that discretion may be regarded and knowledge kept. That servant which knew his Lord's will and did it not was to be beaten with many stripes. When God stoops to make known His will, it should be esteemed not merely as duty but as privilege to obey.

³ For the lips of a strange woman drop as a honeycomb,
  And her mouth is smoother than oil:
⁴ But her end is bitter as worm-wood,
  Sharp as a two-edged sword.
⁵ Her feet go down to death;
  Her steps take hold on sheol.
⁶ Lest thou ponder the path of life,
  Her ways are moveable that thou canst not know them.

Fair and plausible are the words of the stranger-temptress; dark and terrible the ending of association with her. She plies her awful avocation today as of old, and thousands are her victims. Like the harlot church of the closing book in our Bibles, she seduces and deceives, turning the heart away from the simplicity of the paths of truth, and leading to death and sheol. Many are her devices to delude the unwary; movable her ways, that their evil direction may not be known. Nothing is more attractive to the refuser of Wisdom's words than the specious pleas of this deceptive system. The only safety is in cleaving to the words of God; hence the admonition in the verses that follow.

⁷ Hear me now therefore, O ye sons,
  And depart not from the sayings of my mouth.
⁸ Remove thy way far from her,
  And come not nigh the entrance of her house:
⁹ Lest thou give thine honor unto others,
  And thy years unto the cruel ones:
¹⁰ Lest strangers be filled with thy wealth;
  And thy labors be in the house of a stranger;
¹¹ And thou mourn at the last,
  When thy flesh and thy body are consumed,
¹² And say, How have I hated instruction,
  And my heart despised reproof;
¹³ And have not hearkened to the voice of my teachers,
  Nor inclined mine ear to them that instructed me!
¹⁴ I was almost in all evil
  In the midst of the congregation and assembly.

To learn by painful experience, if the Word of God is not bowed to, is a bitter and solemn thing. God is not mocked; what is sown must be reaped. The unsteady hand, the confused brain, the bleared eye, premature age, and weakened powers; with days and nights of folly to look back on with regret that can never be banished from the memory: such are a few of the results of failing to heed the advice of wisdom in the natural world. And in the spiritual we have what answer to all these—inability to try the things that differ, weakened spiritual susceptibilities, unsteadiness of behavior, loss in time and loss at the judgment seat of Christ; such are some of the sad effects of refusing the path of separation from apostate religion in this day of Christ's rejection.

Throughout this collection of Proverbs, the strange woman is looked upon as an intruder from the outside, not a daughter of Israel who has been betrayed from the path of virtue. The law declared there was to be no harlot among the women of the chosen people. It was from the surrounding countries the temptresses entered to seduce the young men of the separated nation. Hence the "strange woman": not "strange" in the sense of peculiar; but the stranger woman who plied her meretricious arts to deceive those who should be holy to the Lord. But so low had become the moral state of Israel, that even the daughters of the people of God had fallen into the degradation of the heathen, as is evident from the words already noticed in 2:17. Though called a "stranger" or "foreigner," she had "forsaken the guide of her youth, and forgotten the covenant of her God." Hence she is viewed as an outsider, having no place in the congregation of the Lord.

Sanctified wedded love, in contrast to the loose and godless ways of what has been presented, we now have brought before us.

> ¹⁵ Drink waters out of thine own cistern,
>   And running waters out of thine own well.
> ¹⁶ Let thy fountains be dispersed abroad
>   And rivers of waters in thy streets.
> ¹⁷ Let them be only thine own,
>   And not strangers with thee.
> ¹⁸ Let thy fountain be blessed;
>   And rejoice with the wife of thy youth.
> ¹⁹ Let her be as the loving hind and pleasant roe;
>   Let her breasts satisfy thee at all times;
>   And be thou ravished always with her love.
> ²⁰ And why wilt thou, my son, be ravished with a strange
>   woman,
>   And embrace the bosom of a stranger?

For us, marriage represents the mystic union between Christ and the church. Every Christian home should be a little picture of the relationship of our glorified Head with the members of His body. How holy, then, is that earthly association which speaks of such exalted heavenly mysteries. "Marriage is honorable in all, and the bed undefiled: but fornicators and adulterers God will judge" (Heb. 13:4). How much precious teaching in the New Testament, particularly the epistolary portion of it, flows from this truth. Husbands and wives are urged to dwell together according to knowledge *that their prayers be not hindered.* (See 1 Peter 3:1–7). What a test is this! When husband and wife are so living before each other that with joy and confidence they can kneel and pray together, the home will be what God desires; but where the ways and words of either or both hinder such seasons of communion with each other and the Lord, there is something radically wrong.

> 21 For the ways of man are before the eyes of Jehovah,
>   And He pondereth all his goings.

This fact is just what the soul needs to keep in mind, to realize the solemnity of being in this world for God. His eyes are on all our ways. Nothing escapes that holy gaze. All is naked and open before Him with whom we have to do. He weighs and ponders every thought and word and action. Nothing is too insignificant for His notice; nothing too great for His attention. At the judgment seat of Christ He will make manifest His estimate of it all. In that day how many of us would give worlds, did we possess them, if we had only been more truly faithful in all our ways in this scene!

> 22 His own iniquities shall take the lawless himself,
>   And he shall be holden with the cords of his sins.
> 23 He shall die without instruction;
>   And in the greatness of his folly he shall go astray.

Certain retribution will follow the lawless. The very sins in which he now delights are the links he is forging to make the chain that shall bind him forever. Having refused instruction in life, he shall die without it, left to go astray in the folly his soul loved. Dying in his sins, he goes out into the darkness, where the light he refused in time shall never shine upon him again!

CHAPTER 6

PROVERBS 6

Even the unregenerate, did they but order their lives and their business methods in accordance with the instruction here given, would be saved many a failure and loss. Suretyship has been the downfall of many who, avoiding it, might have been comfortable and prosperous. Here the one so ensnared is urged to deliver himself if possible, before the penalty has to be paid.

> ¹ My son, if thou be surety for thy friend,
>   If thou hast stricken thy hand with a stranger,
> ² Thou art snared with the sayings of thy mouth,
>   Thou art taken with the sayings of thy mouth.
> ³ Do this now, my son, and deliver thyself,
>   When thou art come into the hand of thy friend;
>   Go, humble thyself, and make sure thy friend.
> ⁴ Give not sleep to thine eyes,
>   Nor slumber to thine eyelids.
> ⁵ Deliver thyself as a roe from the hand of the hunter,
>   And as a bird from the hand of the fowler.

Unlikely as it may seem on the face of it, pride is generally the incentive to suretyship. A desire to be thought well of, to be accounted in easy circumstances, has led many a man to "strike hands," or go on another's bond, who was quite unable to assume so serious a responsibility and yet discharge his obligations to those properly dependent on him. With others it is an easygoing disposition that leads one to thoughtless pledges, the performance of which would be ruinous. In either case, if thus entrapped, it is well if the command here given is heeded; and humbling though it may seem to be, the confession made that one has undertaken more than righteousness and foresight would advise. Far better a little temporary embarrassment and misunderstanding, even ill-will, than to find out later that others have to suffer for the maintenance of a foolish and sinful pride.

Prudence and forethought (not to be confounded with the anxiety of the morrow condemned by the Lord in His discourse on the mount) are commendable virtues, to teach which even so feeble a creature as the ant may well serve.

> ⁶ Go to the ant, thou sluggard;
>   Consider her ways, and be wise:
> ⁷ Which having no guide, overseer, or ruler,
> ⁸ Provideth her meat in the summer.
>   And gathereth her food in the harvest.

A lesson for eternity as well as for time is taught by the ant, which we reserve until we reach the thirtieth chapter, where it is again brought before us as one of four wise things, each of which teach spiritual truths. The temporal lesson is of grave importance. Improvidence is not faith; it is the grossest presumption to act the part of the sluggard and then to expect divine provision in the hour of need. In this as in all else sowing follows reaping. Diligence and carefulness are commanded and commended by the Lord, and both honor Him; while slothfulness on the part of one of His is a reproach upon His name. To arouse such to a sense of duty is the object of the verses that follow. In the spiritual, as in the natural things, "the diligent soul shall be made fat" (13:4).

It has become the fashion for certain wiseacres to sneer at "Solomon's grain-eating ant" who stores her food in the harvest for future use. Solomon is supposed to have mistaken the eggs of the ant for grains. But it is now fully demonstrated that he was wiser than his critics.

In Palestine there is a species of ant which is not carnivorous, but feeds on grain and does indeed store its food in harvest time as he declared. Scripture here, as always, is correct and exact.

How much more fitting it would be if, in weighing the words of the Omniscient, poor shortsighted man would own his limitations and at least take it for granted the Bible is right until proven otherwise!

> ⁹ How long wilt thou sleep, O sluggard?
> When wilt thou arise out of thy sleep?
> ¹⁰ Yet a little sleep, a little slumber,
> A little folding of the hands to sleep:
> ¹¹ So shall thy poverty come as one that travelleth,
> And thy want as a man with a shield.

Sleeping in time of labor is out of place in a scene where man has been commanded to eat his bread by the sweat of his face. No one has a right to count on God to undertake for him in temporal matters, who is not himself characterized by energy and wakefulness. Poverty and want follow slothfulness; as in a spiritual sense, endless woe must follow the one who sleeps on in this the day of grace, refusing to be awakened. "A little more sleep, a little more slumber," says Judson, "and thou shalt wake in hell to sleep no more forever!"

> ¹² A man of Belial, a wicked man,
> Walketh with a froward mouth.
> ¹³ He winketh with his eyes,
> He speaketh with his feet,
> He teacheth with his fingers;
> ¹⁴ Perverseness is in his heart,
> He deviseth mischief continually; he soweth [or, casteth
> forth] discord.
> ¹⁵ Therefore shall his calamity come suddenly;
> Suddenly shall he be broken without remedy.

The one who is careless as to his own affairs, is likely to interfere altogether too much with those of others. Having nothing to occupy his time, he becomes an idling busybody, every part of his being devoted to folly. His mouth is froward; his eyes belie the words his lips give utterance to; feet and hands are used to call attention to what were better left unnoticed; for in his heart is frowardness and mischievous devices. He becomes thus a sower of discord, scattering evil words as one might scatter thistledown, to bring forth a harvest of sorrow that can never be fully destroyed. There were such among the Thessalonian saints, against whom the apostle warns and bids the godly keep no company with them that they may be ashamed.

> ¹⁶ These six things doth Jehovah hate;
>   Yea, seven are an abomination of His soul:
> ¹⁷ Haughty eyes, a lying tongue,
>   And hands that shed innocent blood;
> ¹⁸ A heart that deviseth wicked imaginations,
>   Feet that be swift in running to mischief,
> ¹⁹ A false witness that speaketh lies,
>   And he that soweth discord among brethren.

In no uncertain terms Jehovah's judgment of the evil speaker is set forth. Seven things are abominable, six He hates in addition to the one already noticed. It is put in as though the worst of them all.

A proud look He ever detested. Haughty eyes belong not to the one who has been a learner at His feet who is "meek and lowly in heart." The twelfth Song of Degrees gives the utterance of one who has thus been discipled into His school. "Lord, my heart is not haughty, nor mine eyes lofty; neither do I exercise myself in great matters, or in things too high for me" (Ps. 131:1). This is the state that is well-pleasing to Him who has said, "To this man will I look, even to him that is poor [or, lowly] and of a contrite spirit, and trembleth at My word" (Isa. 66:2).

A lying tongue! How opposed to Him who is Himself the Truth, and who desires truth in the inward parts. False words bespeak a deceitful heart.

With these evidences of the activity of a corrupt nature He joins "hands that shed innocent blood." For he who would with his tongue destroy the good name of another is of one ilk with him who would with wicked hands take his brother's life.

"A heart that deviseth wicked imaginations" is the spring of all the rest. Out of the heart proceed all unholy words and doings. So "feet that be swift in running to mischief" are at once mentioned. They follow where the heart has already gone. The last two are often found together. "A false witness that speaketh lies, and he that soweth discord among brethren." Good and pleasant it is in the eyes of our God when brethren dwell together in unity. The talebearer who, by spreading abroad evil insinuations and accusations, mars that happy unity is abhorred of the Lord.

If we would, any of us, having all a common nature, be kept from these hateful ways, there must be an earnest cleaving to God and His Word that we may thus be sanctified by the truth.

> [20] My son, keep thy father's commandment,
>   And forsake not the law of thy mother:
> [21] Bind them continually upon thy heart,
>   And tie them about thy neck.

Subjection to parental discipline is subjection to God. If the parents are themselves godly and seek to bring up those committed to their care in "the nurture and admonition of the Lord," they are laying a solid foundation upon which all the superstructure of the afterlife can safely rest.

> [22] When thou goest, it shall lead thee;
>   When thou liest down, it shall keep thee;

Practical and precious will the instruction of wisdom thus become. Abroad or at home, in activity or in the place of repose, the word shall be alike sweet and shall keep from stumbling.

>   And when thou awakest, it shall be thy meditation;
> [23] For the commandment is a lamp;
>   And the law is light;
>   And reproofs of instruction are the way of life:
> [24] To keep thee from the evil woman,
>   From the flattery of the tongue of the strange woman.

Once more is the young man's particular snare referred to. The purifying influence of the Word of God will, above all else, be his protection from the flattering lips of the false stranger who would allure him from the path of truth and virtue to falsity and ruin. Earnestly is he warned to beware of her fascinations.

> [25] Lust not after her beauty in thy heart;
>   Neither let her take thee with her eyelids.
> [26] For by means of a harlot a man is brought to a piece of
>   bread:
>   And the adulteress will hunt for the precious life.

Again are we reminded that it is the heart which must be kept or guarded if the feet would be preserved from forbidden paths. Sorrow and poverty—spiritual and natural—will be the dread result if there is any tampering with uncleanness. With her fascinating glances the adulteress will endeavor to entrap. Unhappy then the one whose heart is not garrisoned by the sanctifying truth of God! To trifle here is to be overcome, as the next verses strongly urge.

> ²⁷ Can a man take fire into his bosom,
>   And his clothes not be burned?
> ²⁸ Can one go upon hot coals,
>   And his feet not be scorched?
> ²⁹ So he that goeth in to his neighbor's wife;
>   Whosoever toucheth her shall not be innocent.

How many a dreadful blot upon an otherwise upright and honored life has resulted from what at first was a thoughtless familiarity, which led on step by step to the awful overthrow of uprightness and virtue, culminating in lifelong sorrow. No other sin, unless it be the taking of human life which is often its fearful result, leaves so dreadful a stain behind, as witness David's case.

> ³⁰ Men do not despise a thief,
>   If he steal to satisfy his soul when he is hungry;
> ³¹ But if he be found, he shall restore sevenfold;
>   He shall give all the substance of his house.
> ³² But whoso committeth adultery with a woman lacketh
>   understanding:
>   He that doeth it destroyeth his own soul.
> ³³ A wound and dishonor shall he get;
>   And his reproach shall not be wiped away.
> ³⁴ For jealousy is the rage of a man;
>   Therefore he will not spare in the day of vengeance.
> ³⁵ He will not regard any ransom;
>   Neither will he rest content though thou givest many gifts.

How faithful is the God who thus condescends to point out in language severely plain and clear the awful consequences of the sin that brought the flood, and yet shall bring the fire! Other wrongs men may forgive and forget. This one is never forgotten. A thief stealing to satisfy his hunger excites no one's abhorrence.

Yet, if arrested, restitution is demanded. Jehovah's law said he should restore it in the principal and add the fifth part. Human law, according to verse 31, demands even up to sevenfold, and may indeed involve the culprit in utter ruin, causing him to forfeit "all the substance of his house." But at least it is possible to make amends, though it take all one has. But there is a sin for which amends can never be made, either to the wronged husband or the partner of the folly. Repentance toward God will not efface the reproach. The marks of the wound and the dishonor will remain to haunt one through the years. The rage of the rightly jealous man who has been so terribly incensed will not be appeased by gifts however great, or protestations however earnest and sincere.

He who, with warnings such as these before him, deliberately goes on trifling with sin is without excuse. The only safe course is to gird up the loins of the mind; to bring every sinful, wandering thought into subjection; that thus the truth of God may control the heart and reins. Only thus shall one be enabled to "flee also youthful lusts," which are elsewhere described as "fleshly lusts that war against the soul." In this way Joseph stood in circumstances far more tempting than those in which David fell. "Shall I do this great evil, and sin against *God*?" This was what preserved him. This alone will preserve any similarly tempted one.

CHAPTER 7

PROVERBS 7

God alone can estimate aright the depravity of the human heart. Knowing its perverseness and the need of continued warning, another entire chapter is devoted to the subject which we have already been considering. That there may be no stone unturned to save the youth from the strange woman's snare, her ways and behavior are graphically delineated. If he turn after her now, he does so with his eyes fully opened.

> ¹ My son, keep my words,
>   And lay up my commandments with thee.
> ² Keep my commandments and live;
>   And my law as the apple of thine eye.
> ³ Bind them upon thy fingers,
>   Write them upon the table of thy heart.

It is this constant dwelling upon the Word of God that preserves from sin. Notice how upon both hand and heart that Word is to be bound and written. This involves far more than cursory reading of the Scriptures. It is the making it one's own, the daily feeding upon it, that preserves the soul.

⁴ Say unto Wisdom, thou art my sister;
  And call Understanding thy kinswoman:
⁵ That they may keep thee from the strange woman,
  From the stranger that flattereth with her sayings.

Satan has no more powerful weapon for the overthrow of the young than flattery. Wisdom and understanding are needed to preserve from this snare. They will teach me to mistrust and to judge myself, and thus to estimate aright the lying words of any who would seek to effect my ruin by means of the vanity of my heart.

The balance of the chapter requires little comment. With the perspicuity of an eye-witness, a scene is brought before us which has been duplicated not only by the thousands, but millions of times, and is as true today as in the days of Solomon. The young man may well ponder it with care, and thus be warned of the dangers besetting one who, trusting in his own heart, departs from the living God and forsakes the counsel of his mother and the guide of his youth.

⁶ For at the window of my house
  I looked through my lattice,
⁷ And I beheld among the simple ones,
  I discerned among the youths, a young man void of
      understanding,
⁸ Passing through the street near her corner;
  And he went the way to her house,
⁹ In the twilight, in the evening of the day,
  In the black and dark night:
¹⁰ And, behold, there met him a woman
  With the attire of a harlot, and subtle of heart.
¹¹ (She is loud and stubborn;
  Her feet abide not in her house:
¹² Now is she without, now in the streets,
  And lieth in wait at every corner.)
¹³ So she caught him, and kissed him,
  And with an impudent face said unto him,
¹⁴ I have peace sacrifices with me;
  This day have I paid my vows.
¹⁵ Therefore came I forth to meet thee,
  Diligently to seek thy face, and I have found thee.

¹⁶ I have decked my bed with coverings of tapestry,
  With carved works, with fine linen of Egypt.
¹⁷ I have perfumed my bed with myrrh, aloes, and cinnamon.
¹⁸ Come, let us take our fill of loves until the morning:
  Let us solace ourselves with loves.
¹⁹ For the goodman is not in his house,
  He is gone on a long journey:
²⁰ He hath taken a bag of money with him,
  And will come to his house at the day of the new moon.

The reverent student of this solemn portion of the Word of God will see at once how apt an illustration this religious-appearing woman is of the false, apostate church. Loud and stubborn, movable too have been her ways, so that she might ensnare those who otherwise would never seek association with her. The vision of Revelation 17 may well be studied in connection with this chapter.

Returning to the narrative, we learn the direful fate of the youth who foolishly took the way to her house and weakly followed where she led.

²¹ With her much fair speech she caused him to yield,
  With the flattering of her lips she forced him.
²² He goeth after her straightway,
  As an ox goeth to the slaughter,
  Or as a fool to the correction of the stocks;
²³ Till a dart strike through his liver;
  As a bird hasteth to the snare,
  And knoweth not that it is for his life.

Such is the end of the path of sin and folly. Death, with shame unutterable, must be the sad result of refusing instruction and listening to the words of the flatterer.

²⁴ Hearken unto me now therefore, O ye sons,
  And attend to the sayings of my mouth.
²⁵ Let not thy heart decline to her ways,
  Go not astray in her paths.
²⁶ For she hath cast down many wounded;
  Yea, many strong men have been slain by her.

[27] Her house is the way to sheol,
  Going down to the inner chambers of death.

What enduring patience that thus continues to instruct all who have an ear to hear and who desire to have an understanding heart! In such a passage as this, as in all Scripture, we hear the very voice of God, and find every word profitable. Happy the youth who keeps the instruction here given, that he may be preserved from the bitterness of remorse which so many have proven!

CHAPTER 8

PROVERBS 8

W hat relief it is to the soul to turn from contemplation of the folly and sin against which the young man is warned in the previous chapter, to meditate now upon Wisdom's ways, especially when the anointed eye discerns under this name the Uncreated Word, our Lord Jesus Christ, the Wisdom of God! For though the feminine form is used throughout, it is nevertheless clear that in the latter part of the chapter it is He who is before us.

Wisdom is first presented as one seeking to draw the simple from paths of error to the temple of knowledge and understanding.

> ¹ Doth not Wisdom cry?
>   And Understanding put forth her voice?
> ² She standeth in the top of high places,
>   By the way, in the places of the paths.
> ³ She crieth at the gates, at the entry of the city,
>   At the coming in at the entrances.

Not for men to seek her does Wisdom wait. With yearning heart she takes her stand in the marts of commerce, the paths of pleasure, the courts of judgment, and the schools of learning. Anywhere and everywhere that men are to be found, there is she—her cry and entreaty sounding above all the bustle of life. (See 1:20–23.)

⁴ Unto you, O men, I call;
 And my voice is to the sons of man.
⁵ O ye simple, understand prudence:
 And, ye fools, be of an understanding heart.
⁶ Hear, for I will speak of excellent things;
 And the opening of my lips shall be right things.
⁷ For my mouth shall speak truth;
 And lawlessness is an abomination to my lips.

As Wisdom incarnate is to be found in our Lord Jesus Christ, the living Word, so are the instructions of Wisdom to be found in the written Word. It is by means of that precious volume which "holy men of God wrote as they were moved by the Holy Ghost," that the only true and lasting wisdom and knowledge are to be found. "Right things" and "truth" alone are there recorded. Even when the sins of men and women are sharply delineated in all their grossness and hideousness, it is that we may thereby be admonished.

Man may cavil; infidelity may sneer; pseudoscholarship may reject; but He who cannot lie has declared "the Scripture cannot be broken." There alone is perfect wisdom found. Unhappy the man who turns from it to the vagaries of the human mind!

⁸ All the words of my mouth are in righteousness;
 There is nothing twisted or perverse in them.
⁹ They are all plain to him that understandeth,
 And right to them that find knowledge.

This is faith's answer to the caviler who prates of contradictions and errors in the inspired Word of God. Modesty alone might suggest the thought that the fault might be in the reader—not in the Word. But man's vanity and pride will not brook such a conclusion. Yet so it shall soon be proven to be; for "not one yod or tittle [the smallest letter, or vowel-point] shall pass from the law till all be fulfilled." How soon difficulties vanish when faith is in exercise! Seemingly insuperable objections are swept away in a moment when the light of heaven shines into the soul and on the page of Scripture. Jesus, in resurrection, opened both the Scriptures and the understanding of the two with whom He walked to Emmaus. It is this double enlightenment that causes difficulties to vanish like mist before the rays of the sun. "They are all plain to him that understandeth," for "the secret of the Lord is with them that fear Him."

¹⁰ Receive my instruction, and not silver.
  And knowledge rather than choice gold.
¹¹ For wisdom is better than rubies;
  And all things that can be desired are not to be compared
    to it.

Alone in the sacred Scriptures, in our times so relentlessly assailed by supercilious egotists and unspiritual divines, is this treasure to be found. The best writings of the best men are not to be compared with it, for here we turn from all the reasonings of man's heart to the very breathings of God. In the twenty-eighth chapter of Job we have the account of the patriarch's search for wisdom. All the precious metals and jewels of earth are not to be compared to it, "for the price of wisdom is above rubies." He finds it when he turns from everything on or under the earth to God Himself.

¹² I Wisdom dwell with Prudence,
  And find out knowledge of witty inventions.

As noted above, wisdom here is looked at as an essential part of Deity; further down, as Him who has been now revealed as the "Wisdom of God, the Eternal Son."

¹³ The fear of Jehovah is to hate evil:
  Pride, and arrogancy, and the evil way, and the mouth of
    perversions do I hate.

It is thus wisdom is manifest. It is the very character of God—that character all told out in Christ. Evil, pride, folly; all are hateful to Him who is light, and cannot abide the darkness.

¹⁴ Counsel is mine, and sound wisdom:
  I am understanding; I have strength.
¹⁵ By me kings reign,
  And princes decree justice,
¹⁶ By me princes rule, and nobles,
  Even all the judges of the earth.

It is not that rulers always act according to understanding, but that none rule at all save by the appointment of infinite wisdom. "The Most High ruleth in the kingdoms of men, and He giveth them unto whomsoever He will." This gives perfect rest to the man of faith in the midst of all the changing political scenes of earth. Let the form of the government be what it may; the chief magistrate be of whatever character he will; faith can bow in obedience, owning that "the powers that be are ordained of God."

> ¹⁷ I love them that love me;
>   And those that seek me early shall find me.

Wisdom sought, as in Solomon's case, in early youth delights to reward the seeker. It is important to bear in mind that it is wisdom—and not God *as such*—that is here referred to. "He," too, "is the rewarder of them that diligently seek Him," but it would be very faulty to limit His love alone to those who return that love. It is love in activity on the part of Wisdom we have here before us. To the one who loves her she gives the treasures enumerated in the following verses:

> ¹⁸ Riches and honor are with me;
>   Yea, durable riches and righteousness.
> ¹⁹ My fruit is better than gold; yea, than fine gold;
>   And my revenue than choice silver.

Unspeakably precious, and beyond all human valuation, are the gifts bestowed by Wisdom with lavish hand upon the diligent seeker, who has learned to love her for her own sake. Apart from her the feet will stray in folly's paths. She can say—

> ²⁰ I lead in the way of righteousness,
>   In the midst of the paths of judgment:
> ²¹ That I may cause those that love me to inherit substance;
>   And I will fill their treasuries.

From this point on, the anointed eye loses sight of all else and is fixed upon Christ, for He it is who is now presented for the contemplation of our souls. It is Christ as the Uncreated Word, yet the Begotten Son by eternal generation; words admittedly paradoxical, but after all distinctly scriptural. Some there are who have supposed the term *only begotten* necessarily implied a period, however remote, when the Son was not. This John's gospel clearly refutes, for "the same was *in the beginning with God."* He was begotten, not in the sense of having beginning of life, but as being of one nature and substance with the Father. Never was there a moment in the past eternity when He reposed not in the bosom of Infinite Love.

To explain the mystery is impossible, as the apostle himself declares. "No man knoweth the Son but the Father." Hence the devout heart can rest and adore where the skeptic seeks in vain for rational explanations of a mystery beyond human understanding.

> 22 Jehovah possessed me in the beginning of His way,
>   Before His works of old.
> 23 I was set up from everlasting,
>   From the beginning, ere ever the earth was.

Far back of the beginning of Genesis 1:1, to that "unbeginning beginning" of John 1:1, does the Spirit here carry us. There, in the past eternity, "when anything that ever had beginning began, the Word *was,*"[1] and that Word was the eternal Wisdom of God. It is a scene of fellowship to which we are introduced— Jehovah *possessed* Him. "The Word was with God, and the Word *was* God"; and love ineffable was the enfolding robe of deity, for Wisdom was the object of Jehovah's delight from everlasting.

> 24 When there were no depths, I was brought forth;
>   When there were no fountains abounding with water.
> 25 Before the mountains were settled,
>   Before the hills, was I brought forth:
> 26 While as yet He had not made the earth, nor the fields,
>   Nor the beginning of the dust of the habitable world.

The figure of generation, as already noted, implies unity of nature. "God so loved the world, that He gave His only begotten Son." God's thoughts are above ours. Our best human language is a poor vehicle indeed for the expression of truths so wondrous. Christ is eternally the Son, yet truly the Begotten.

> 27 When He established the heavens, I was there:
>   When He set a circle upon the face of the depth;
> 28 When He established the skies above;
>   When He strengthened the fountains of the deep;

²⁹ When He gave to the sea His decree,
   That the waters should not pass His commandment;
   When He appointed the foundations of the earth;
³⁰ Then I was by Him, as one brought up with Him:
   And I was daily His delight, rejoicing always before Him;
³¹ Rejoicing in the habitable part of His earth;
   And my delights were with the sons of men.

Creation is elsewhere ascribed to the Son. "Without Him was not anything made that was made." "All things were created by Him and for Him, and in Him all things consist." He is "the firstborn of all creation," superior to all, because by Him the Father brought all things into being. Daily His delight, He shared in that manifestation of power "as one brought up with Him," "rejoicing always before Him." But, amazing grace! His delights were with the fallen sons of men. The love of His heart was set upon those who deserved it not. It is not of Adam unfallen He speaks, but of his sons—therefore sinners lost and guilty.

> Ere God had built the mountains,
>   Or raised the fruitful hills;
> Before He filled the fountains,
>   That feed the running rills;
> In Thee, from everlasting,
>   The wonderful I AM
> Found pleasures never wasting,
>   And Wisdom is Thy name.
>
> When, like a tent to dwell in,
>   He spread the skies abroad,
> And swathed about the swelling
>   Of Ocean's mighty flood,
> He wrought by weight and measure;
>   And Thou wast with Him then:
> Thyself the Father's pleasure,
>   And Thine, the sons of men.
>
> And couldst Thou be delighted
>   With creatures such as we,

Who, when we saw Thee, slighted
  And nailed Thee to a tree?
Unfathomable wonder!
  And mystery divine!
The voice that speaks in thunder
  Says, "Sinner, I am thine."
                    —William Cowper

³² Now, therefore hearken unto Me, O ye sons:
  For blessed are they that keep my ways.
³³ Hear instruction, and be wise,
  And refuse it not.

Upon the declaration of Wisdom's love for and delight in men is this entreaty based. To refuse instruction and spurn the ways of understanding is to trample on divine affection and to harden the heart against divine grace.

³⁴ Blessed is the man that heareth me,
  Watching daily at my doors,
  Waiting at the posts of my entrances.
³⁵ For whoso findeth me findeth life,
  And shall obtain favor of Jehovah.
³⁶ But he that sinneth against me wrongeth his own soul:
  All they that hate me love death.

How strong the incentives presented to heed the voice of Wisdom! Blessing and life, the loving favor of the Lord, are the portion of those who so do. The one who refuses to listen, sins against his own soul, for he seals his own destruction.

CHAPTER 9

PROVERBS 9

In concluding the section that has been hitherto claiming our attention, a final contrast between Wisdom and Folly is set forth. The figure of the previous chapter is still adhered to. Wisdom is likened to a prudent woman inviting the wayfarer to enter her home, where true knowledge is imparted to all who seek it in sincerity. Folly takes her stand in a similar way, urging all to turn in to her, offering "the pleasures of sin for a season" to those who yield to her entreaties.

> 1 Wisdom hath builded her house;
>   She hath hewn out her seven pillars:
> 2 She hath killed her beasts;
>   She hath mingled her wine;
>   She hath also furnished her table.

Abundant provision has been made for the instruction and blessing of all who will heed. Such a temple of Wisdom is the Word of God as a whole, and this book of Proverbs in particular. Here is to be found all that man requires for his guidance through the mazes of his life on earth. A well-furnished table, at which millions have feasted, but inexhaustible still, is that which is spread before all who desire spiritual sustenance and cheer.

Nor does Wisdom wait for men to seek her out.

> 3 She hath sent forth her maidens:
> She crieth upon the highest places of the city,
> 4 Whoso is simple, let him turn in hither:
> To him that wanteth understanding she saith,
> 5 Come, eat of my bread,
> And drink of the wine which I have mingled.
> 6 Forsake the foolish, and live;
> And go in the way of understanding.

In the present dispensation of grace God is by His ambassadors beseeching men to be reconciled to Himself; not waiting until they begin to pray, but actually deigning to pray them to turn from their sin to His beloved Son. So, here, the handmaids of Wisdom are found in the places of public concourse, entreating the simple and those who lack true character to turn in and partake of the bread that strengthens, the wine that cheers. Happy the man who obeys the gracious invitation and forsakes the way of the foolish, thus laying hold on that which is really life.

Only the truly exercised will heed, however. The scorner will be pleaded with in vain. Empty, pompous, and self-satisfied, he pursues his own way until the judgment, long derided, falls at last, and he is crushed beneath it.

> 7 He that reproveth a scorner getteth to himself shame:
> And he that rebuketh a lawless man getteth himself a blot.
> 8 Reprove not a scorner, lest he hate thee:
> Rebuke a wise man, and he will love thee.
> 9 Give instruction to a wise man, and he will be yet wiser:
> Teach a just man, and he will increase in learning.

So it ever is. The more shallow and empty a man is, the less willing is he to listen to godly counsel; whereas, the truly wise are glad to learn from any who can correct and instruct. The less a man knows, as a rule, the more he thinks he knows. The more he really does know, the more he realizes his ignorance and his limitations. Hence the value of counsel and help from those who seek to walk with God, and to be exercised by His Word. Reproof will only be wasted on the scorner. He will take delight in holding up to ridicule all who, actuated by the purest of motives, endeavor to turn him from his folly.

These three verses would seem to be parenthetical, explaining the reason why the invitation of Wisdom's maidens meets with such opposite responses.

Their cry is evidently continued in the three verses that follow:

> [10] The fear of Jehovah is the beginning of wisdom:
>   And the knowledge of the Holy is understanding.
> [11] For by Me thy days shall be multiplied,
>   And the years of thy life shall be increased.
> [12] If thou be wise, thou shalt be wise for thyself:
>   But if thou scornest, thou alone shalt bear it.

However the scorner may prate of advanced knowledge because of his freedom from godly restraint, true wisdom is only to be found in the fear of the Lord, and true understanding in the knowledge of holy things. (The word is in the plural.) This alone makes for what is really life. Apart from the knowledge of God, it is but a mere existence at the best, with eternal darkness beyond it.

Nor are men putting God in their debt when they attend to the call of Wisdom; as though it were condescension on their part so to do. If they be wise, it is for their own advantage—not His. He is seeking their happiness and blessing. True it is that, such is the love of His heart, He finds joy in the gladness of His children; but, nevertheless, it is for his own good that man should heed the call of Wisdom.

Neither will God be the loser if the scorner persists in his senseless and foolhardy course. He alone shall bear it. Both in this life and the next, his folly shall be made manifest to himself and others.

The unhappy contrast to the portion we have been considering is set forth in the remaining verses of the chapter. Folly, too, has her temple, and, alas, many are her devotees!

> [13] A foolish woman is clamorous;
>   She is simple, and knoweth nothing.
> [14] For she sitteth at the entrance of her house,
>   On a seat in the high places of the city,
> [15] To call passengers who go right on their ways:
> [16] Whoso is simple, let him turn in hither:
>   And as for him that wanteth understanding she saith to
>   him,
> [17] Stolen waters are sweet,
>   And bread of secrecies is pleasant.

¹⁸ But he knoweth not that the dead are there,
  And her guests are in the depths of sheol.

Alas, so ready are men to give heed to Folly, that she needs none to go about entreating them to enter her house. She is represented as sitting at the entrance, enticing those who go right on their way to turn in to her abode of sin and shame. Many are the guests who enter; few indeed the number that return: for her house is but an entryway to the pit. "The dead are there, and her guests are in the depths of hell." Illicit pleasures charm for a time, and ensnare the simple. The end is the wormwood and the gall, when the anguished soul, bowed in bitterness that shall never be alleviated forever, is forced at last to confess how dreadful has been the mistake of turning from the call of Wisdom to seek the deceitful allurements of Folly.

One who tried them to the full wrote before he died,

> My days are in the yellow leaf;
>   The flower, the fruit of life is gone.
> The worm, the canker, and the grief,
>   Are mine alone.
>   —Lord Byron

CHAPTER 10

PROVERBS 10

We now enter upon the second division of the book, which brings us to the strictly proverbial portion. Hitherto we have been listening to Wisdom's exhortation to enter the house and avail ourselves of the mass of instruction gathered together for our enlightenment as to suitable behavior in all circumstances. From this the siren voice of Folly would turn us aside.

Happy the man—particularly the young man (for again be it remembered this is the book for the direction and guidance of youth)—who refuses the latter, and, attracted by the former, enters and seeks conscientiously to make his own what is here recorded.

As Scripture itself abounds with illustrious examples of almost every proverb we are to have before us, a reference will generally be given in the notes to some person or circumstance manifesting the truth of the saying in question. By referring to these in connection with the reading of the pages that follow, it is hoped the reader will be impressed as never before both with the fullness and richness of the Word of God, and with the remarkable manner in which every part of it is linked up with the book of Proverbs.

¹ The proverbs of Solomon.
A wise son maketh a glad father;
But a foolish son is the heaviness of his mother.

In these words the keynote is struck to be again and again referred to throughout the book and returned to in the final chapter. The son who is characterized by wisdom causes his father to rejoice as in the case of Solomon himself (1 Chron. 22:12; 2 Chron. 1:7–12). On the other hand it is the mother who feels most keenly the folly of her child. See Esau in Genesis 26:34–35 and 27:46.

> ² Treasures of lawlessness profit nothing:
> But righteousness delivereth from death.

God has not abdicated His throne as the Moral Governor of the universe; hence sowing follows reaping, as surely as night follows day. "As the partridge sitteth on eggs and hatcheth them not; so he that getteth riches and not by right, shall leave them in the midst of his days and at his end shall be a fool" (Jer. 17:11). On the other hand righteousness, however much one may be called upon to suffer for it in a world like this, "delivereth from death," when that death, as in the case of the flood and many lesser incidents, is an evidence of God's judgment. In the book of Esther, Haman is the exemplification of the former and Mordecai of the latter.

> ³ Jehovah will not suffer the soul of the righteous to famish:
> But He casteth away the desire of the lawless.

Let the outward circumstances be as they may, the soul of the righteous is lifted above them all and finds cause to rejoice in the midst of tribulation. The lawless have no such confidence; their desire, when they seem just about to comfortably enjoy it, is often taken away in a moment. The triumphant song of Habakkuk (3:17–19) fitly illustrates the first clause, and the fate of the rich fool (Luke 12:16–21) the second.

> ⁴ He becometh poor that dealeth with a slack hand:
> But the hand of the diligent maketh rich.

Scripture never countenances slothfulness, but commands on the part of the Christian that he be "not remiss in zeal." This, the disorderly among the Thessalonians had evidently forgotten (2 Thess. 3:7–12), and the apostle has to write urging them "that with quietness they work, and eat their own bread." Faith and laziness do not mingle. What is sometimes miscalled faith is really presumption. Diligence is the fit companion of the former, as beautifully set forth by Ruth, the Moabitess, who takes the place of the poor and the stranger among the gleaners in the fields of Boaz, to be exalted in due time (Ruth 2–4).

> 5 He that gathereth in summer is a wise son:
> But he that sleepeth in harvest is a son that causeth shame.

The principle abides whether in relation to time or eternity. The hour of opportunity if improved bespeaks wisdom; if neglected tells of present folly and future shame. It is of the utmost importance that one set a proper value on the God-given present; "redeeming the time for the days are evil." Let the laborer in the harvest fields of the Lord heed the word here given. Now is the time to gather precious sheaves which will be cause for rejoicing in the day of the soon-coming "harvest home." He who sleeps in the present reaping season will suffer shame and loss at the judgment seat of Christ. What an example of the diligent laborer is to be found in Paul, throughout his life of ceaseless activity and concern for a dying world. Demas was one who, charmed by the love of the present world, went off to sleep and left the service for other hands. His shame abides to this day (2 Tim. 4:10).

> 6 Blessings are upon the head of the just:
> But violence covereth the mouth of the lawless.
> 7 The memory of the just is blessed:
> But the name of the lawless shall rot.

Not more different is the esteem in which the righteous and the wicked are held in life than is their memory after death. Of Paul we have just written above. In 2 Timothy 4:17 we find him standing for judgment before Nero, whom he there denominates "the lion," from whose mouth he was at that time delivered. Surely, despite his loneliness and his apparently despicable condition, blessings were even then upon the head of Christ's doughty servant. On the other hand, how truly did violence cover the mouth of his oppressor; leaving him without excuse before the bar of man and of God. Both have long since passed from this scene. Let the centuries witness whose memory has rotted, and whose is still cause for thanksgiving!

> 8 The wise in heart will receive commandments:
> But a prating fool shall fall.

Wisdom, as we have seen, begins with the fear of the Lord. Those so exercised are ready indeed to bow to His Word and to receive His commandments. For the Christian, this is the way in which his love for Christ is manifested. The prating fool, who is too wise in his own conceit to require instruction, must learn by coming to grief. In Nebuchadnezzar and Belshazzar we see the two contrasted. See Daniel 5:18–23.

> ⁹ He that walketh in integrity, walketh surely:
> But he that perverteth his ways shall be known.

To walk in integrity is to walk with God. Whatever misunderstanding there may be at times, the one who so lives shall be shown to have walked surely at last. Men of the world confess that "Honesty is the best policy." For the man of God, uprightness is not policy, but the delight of his heart; and by it he brings even wicked men to acknowledge that his ways are above reproach, as was manifested in Joseph after being so sorely tried (Gen. 40–41). On the contrary, he whose ways are perverse, though he may cover them for a time, must inevitably be discovered at last. (See Ziba's case in 2 Sam. 16:1–4; 19:24–27.)

> ¹⁰ He that winketh with the eye causeth sorrow:
> But a prating fool shall fall.

Winking with the eye, from time immemorial, has been construed as giving the lie to what the lips utter. He whose words and intentions are opposed is a source of grief to others, and shall fall himself. The kiss of Judas was an action of this nature. Note last clause here is as in verse 8.

> ¹¹ The mouth of a righteous man is a well of life:
> But violence covereth the mouth of the lawless.

When the life is ordered in accordance with righteousness, the words of the mouth will be for blessing and refreshment to others. It is by carelessness here that many who attempt to minister the gospel are powerless and barren in their service. The testimony of the lips is not backed up by the testimony of the life. Hence, power and usefulness are lacking. Mere "sound words" are not necessarily used in blessing. But if such come from a heart in touch with God, witnessed to by ways that be in Christ, then indeed shall they prove a well of life to the hearers who are truly athirst. Such was the ministry of Samuel in the dark days subsequent to the death of Eli. For last clause see verse 6.

> [12] Hatred stirreth up strifes:
> But love covereth all sins.

The latter part of this verse is quoted in the New Testament. In 1 Peter 4:8 it is written, "and above all things have fervent charity among yourselves: for charity shall cover the multitude of sins." It is not, as some have foolishly supposed, that kindliness and benevolence, on the part of one otherwise guilty before God, will atone for his transgressions, thus covering them in the day of judgment. Other's faults, not my own, I am called upon to cover. Not by indifference to evil, but by faithfully, in love and grace, showing my brother his sin and seeking to exercise his conscience in the presence of God, that confession may be made, and thus the sin be covered. Where love is lacking, it is a common practice to play the part of a talebearer, which only tends to add to the evil; for the repeating of sin is defiling, and often leads to lifelong un-happiness and misunderstandings. In Doeg the Edomite we have a sample of the hatred that stirs up strife; in Nathan's dealing with David, a lovely exem-plification of the love that covers (1 Sam. 22:9–19; 2 Sam. 12:1–14). See the notes on 11:13.

> [13] In the lips of him that hath understanding wisdom is
> found:
> But a rod is for the back of him that is void of heart.

None have, perhaps, exhibited in their own decisions the contrast of this verse so markedly as Solomon himself and his son Rehoboam. The former, hav-ing been under exercise before God, had been given a wise and understanding heart (1 Kings 3:5–28). The latter trusted his own wisdom and the counsel of the companions of his youth, and found a rod for his back in consequence (1 Kings 12:8–19).

> [14] Wise men lay up knowledge:
> But the mouth of the foolish is near destruction.

None perceive their own limitations so clearly as the truly wise. Humility and a willingness to learn from all who can instruct them is characteristic of such.

The conceit of the foolish knows no bounds. With their own mouths they proclaim it in the ears of all men of sound judgment. Their prating but invites destruction. Timothy "from a child" followed the ways of the first-mentioned (2 Tim. 3:14–15). The magician Elymas is an illustration of the last described (Acts 13:6–11).

> [15] The rich man's wealth is his strong city:
> The destruction of the poor is their poverty.

For time alone, and in an era of peace, does this apply; for "riches profit not in the day of wrath": neither does temporal poverty interfere with future glory. See the rich man and Lazarus (Luke 16:19–31).

> [16] The labor of the righteous tendeth to life:
> The produce of the lawless is sin.

It is an Old Testament way of stating the truth of Romans 8:6, "For to be carnally minded is death; but to be spiritually minded is life and peace." The righteous man is the spiritual man. His labor is in accordance with the mind of God, and consequently tends to life. All that the wicked produces is but sin in the sight of infinite holiness; because the sinner is polluted, like a poisoned well, which may give forth water cold and sparkling, but only to be dreaded after all. The first two offerers, Cain and Abel, exemplify the truth here stated (Gen. 4:5–8).

> [17] He is in the way of life that keepeth instruction:
> But he that refuseth reproof erreth.

It is only when man learns to mistrust himself and to rely alone upon the unerring Word of God, unfolded by the Holy Spirit, that his feet walk in the way of life. It is not a question of eternal life or final salvation. But the way of life is the divinely marked-out path for all the children of God. Such cannot afford to refuse reproof. It is the greatest kindness another saint can show me, to direct my attention to any portion of the truth of God which I am failing to practically own. Let me gladly, then, receive correction, that thus I may be preserved from dishonoring the One who has redeemed me to Himself. Saul refused reproof and lost his kingdom (1 Sam. 15:23). In David, whatever his failures at times, we see one who was characterized by keeping instruction, and who therefore trod the path of life.

¹⁸ He that hideth hatred with lying lips,
  And he that uttereth a slander is a fool.

Hypocrisy and talebearing are alike detestable. To dissimulate—feigning love and friendship while the fire of hatred burns in the heart—and to spread evil stories are most reprehensible.

It is a matter much to be deplored, that there is by no means the concern about evil speaking among the saints of the Lord that there should be. In His Word He has over and over again expressed His abhorrence of it in unmistakable terms. In the law it is written, "Thou shalt not go up and down as a talebearer among thy people" (Lev. 19:16). The tales might be true; but that could not excuse the bearer of them. If a brother or sister had sinned, there was a far different way to deal with the matter than in spreading the story of his or her shame through the camp of Israel. The following verse delineates the godly way to deal with such a case: "Thou shalt not hate thy brother in thy heart: thou shalt in any wise rebuke thy neighbor, and not suffer sin upon him" (Lev. 19:17).

This is most searching and solemn. If untrue, I am bearing false witness if I repeat evil. If true, I am defiling others and injuring the soul of the wrongdoer, who might be delivered from his error if I went to him in the spirit of meekness. It is an "ungodly man [who] diggeth up evil." A man of God will seek to cover it, by leading the sinning one to repentance and self-judgment.

Joab's dealing with Abner (2 Sam. 3:27) was of the character described in the first clause; the accusers of Jeremiah, in the last (Jer. 37:11–15).

¹⁹ In the multitude of words there wanteth not sin:
  But he that refraineth his lips is wise.

It is remarkable how large a portion of the Scriptures God has seen fit to devote to the subject of His creatures' words. Readiness of speech is seldom to be found where sin does not creep in. To refrain the lips is often difficult, but it is the part of true wisdom. In the epistle of James an entire chapter is devoted to "the tongue," that small but most unruly member. The man of God will weigh his words, remembering that for every idle one he must give an account, for it is written, "By thy words thou shalt be justified, and by thy words thou shalt be condemned." See Ecclesiastes 5:1–7.

²⁰ The tongue of the just is as choice silver:
  The heart of the lawless is of little worth.

Tongue and heart seem to be used here almost synonymously, for the one is controlled by the other. The tongue of the just bespeaks a heart in subjection to God. Therefore the words uttered are of value. The heart of the lawless is made known by his idle and perverse conversation. It was so in the case of Simon Magus, while his reprover displayed the opposite (Acts 8:23).

> ²¹ The lips of the righteous feed many:
>   But fools die for want of heart.

It is not only that the righteous man's conversation is without foolishness and slanderous statements, but it is positively for profit. When he speaks, it is for edification. Others are blessed; his lips feed many. Not so with the fool. His speech is worthless, and he lacks the heart to learn from those who could instruct. Samuel and Saul again come to mind. The words of the former were a means of blessing to thousands, but the unhappy man he had anointed failed himself to profit thereby. See also verses 31–32.

> ²² The blessing of Jehovah, it maketh rich,
>   And He addeth no sorrow with it.

How unspeakable the folly that would lead one to turn from "pleasures forevermore" and riches imperishable, untainted by sorrow, for the vain baubles offered by the world and Satan, which leave only pain and disappointment at last! The blessing of the Lord is found in the pathway of obedience. Even Christians often miss it by laxity and indifference to moral and doctrinal evil. Such can only blame themselves when, walking by the light of their own fire and the sparks that they have kindled, they lie down in sorrow.

It is not that the blessing of the Lord insures freedom from tribulation in a world like this; but whatever the trial, all can be received as from a loving Father's hand, and thus no sorrow will be known. Habakkuk and Paul, in large measure, had entered into the blessing here spoken of (Hab. 3:17–19; Phil. 4:11–13).

> ²³ It is as sport to a fool to do mischief:
>   But a man of understanding hath wisdom.

What the wise man would shrink from with horror, the fool will practice, not only with complacency, but with positive fiendish delight. The man of understanding, whose heart and mind are controlled by the fear of the Lord, will behave himself wisely in a perfect way. Such a fool was Balaam; and Phinehas was a man of understanding, whose wisdom stayed the vengeance of the Lord (Num. 31:16; 25:6–13).

> [24] The fear of the lawless, it shall come upon him:
>   But the desire of the righteous shall be granted.
> [25] As the whirlwind passeth, so is the lawless no more:
>   But the righteous is an everlasting foundation.

The two proverbs are really one, contrasting the expectation and end of the righteous and the wicked. The lawless, however bold his appearance, has ever a gnawing fear at his heart of impending calamity. He may well dread the future, for it has judgment unsparing for his portion. The desire of the righteous will as surely be granted—even blessing forevermore.

Soon, as the whirlwind passeth, will the wicked pass away and be no more, so far as this world is concerned. It is no question of extinction of being. He will be gone from earth into a dark and grief-filled eternity. An everlasting foundation is that of the righteous—even God's imperishable truth. Daniel and his accusers illustrate the two sides (Dan. 6:4–24).

> [26] As vinegar to the teeth, and as smoke to the eyes,
>   So is the sluggard to them that send him.

As a strong acid sets the teeth on edge, and smoke inflames the eyes, so is it beyond measure irritating to place confidence in a man who is really indifferent to the success or failure of his commission. How often have the Lord's sent ones proven to be sluggards, dallying with the world, turning aside for any trifle, instead of pursuing their path with purpose of heart! See the unfaithful servant in Luke 19:20–26.

> [27] The fear of Jehovah prolongeth days:
>   But the years of the lawless shall be shortened.
> [28] The hope of the righteous shall be gladness:
>   But the expectation of the lawless shall perish.
> [29] The way of Jehovah is strength to the perfect:
>   But destruction [shall be] to the workers of iniquity.
> [30] The righteous shall never be removed:
>   But the lawless shall not inhabit the earth.

Again, in all four verses, though each a distinct proverb, we have the righteous and the lawless in contrast, both as to the present and the future. Not greater will be the difference between the two classes in eternity than in time. Now, the fear of the Lord prolongs life; for the indiscretions and iniquities of the lawless break their physical constitutions and shorten their days. In eternity, gladness shall be the fulfilled hope of the righteous, while the vain hope of the wicked shall perish, and his portion be endless judgment.

Strength is found in the way of Jehovah; destruction and woe shall be to those who tread the paths of sin. In the age to come, the portion of the righteous shall abide; he shall never be removed: but the evildoer will have no inheritance in the glorious kingdom then to be established. For both worlds the lawless are not gainers, but losers, by their willful rejection of the Word of Life; while "godliness is profitable in all things, both in the life that now is, and that which is to come." A host of testimony-bearers on each side come up to confirm the solemn truths here enumerated so pithily. Cain and Abel; Noah and the antediluvian world; Abraham and his idolatrous kin; Isaac and Ishmael; Jacob and Esau; Joseph and his accusers; all in the first book of the Bible, with a vast number throughout its remaining books, witness the great contrast which the testimony of experience in all ages has but confirmed.

With two additional proverbs on the tongue the chapter closes. They are intimately connected and should be considered together:

> 31 The mouth of the righteous bringeth forth wisdom:
> But the froward tongue shall be cut out.
> 32 The lips of the righteous know what is acceptable:
> But the mouth of the lawless speaketh frowardness.

The way and end of the two classes we have noticed. Again we are instructed as to the difference in their speech, which but makes bare the state of the heart. Wisdom and acceptable words proceed from the lips of the righteous, like limpid streams from a pure fountain. Frowardness, like a filthy torrent, is poured forth by the tongue of the wicked, soon to be silenced in judgment. Jezebel is a solemn beacon, declaring the truth of this word in regard to the wicked. Elijah, whom she hated, may be cited as an instance on the other side.

CHAPTER 11

PROVERBS 11

R ighteousness and lawlessness in contrast is the subject of this chapter, as of the major part of the last. It is as though God would, in the wonders of His grace, use every opportunity to warn the young and inexperienced of the dangers and sorrows to be encountered when the heart rebels against His Word; and to put before them the blessings and delights, both temporal and spiritual, to be found in subjection to wisdom and truth.

> ¹ A false balance is abomination to Jehovah:
> But a perfect weight is His delight.

The balances of earth our God would have regulated by the balances of the sanctuary. Absolute integrity is His delight. A deceitful balance indicates lack of uprightness in heart. Man may never be cognizant of the error; but where the fear of God is before the eyes, He will be considered, and every transaction will be conducted in His presence. It is a solemn thing when Christians follow the world in the slipshod business methods of the day. How the name of Christ is dishonored when shams and false weights are discovered in the case of such! It is well to often call to mind what is written in the law, "Thou shalt not have in thy bag divers weights, a great and a small: thou shalt not have in thy house divers measures, a great and a small: but thou shalt have a perfect and just weight, a perfect and just measure shalt thou have: that thy days may be lengthened in the land which the LORD thy God giveth thee" (Deut. 25:13–15). Such was God's standard for an earthly people. How shameful when a heavenly people fall below it! It may seem a trifling thing that a yardstick is slightly short, or a pound weight not up to the standard; and one may try to ease his conscience by saying that it is customary, and that people know what to expect; but these are the things that indicate character and tell of a good conscience put away. A Zaccheus may well cause such to blush (Luke 19:8).

> ² When pride cometh, then cometh shame:
> But with the lowly is wisdom.

Nothing is more detestable in God's sight than pride on the part of creatures who have absolutely nothing to be proud of. This was the condemnation of the Devil—self-exaltation. In another, how hateful we instinctively see it to be; but in ourselves, how readily and almost unconsciously is it tolerated! In any case, it indicates a lack of brokenness and self-judgment before God. Lowliness of mind is an indication of true wisdom. It bespeaks the man who has learned to judge himself aright in the presence of God. In Nebuchadnezzar we have a striking illustration of the two opposite states manifested at different times in the same person (Dan. 4).

> ³ The integrity of the upright shall guide them:
> But the perverseness of the treacherous shall destroy them.

When there is purpose of heart to walk in the truth, the Spirit of God can be counted upon for guidance and direction. When the heart is treacherous, destruction will assuredly follow. The principle here laid down is far-reaching and of vast importance. It enters into every detail and ramification of a believer's path and service. It is not so much intelligence that is lacking among the mass of saints as real integrity of heart. There will often be found true devotedness to Christ coupled with very little knowledge of Scripture, and yet remarkable ability to try the things that differ, and to use what little one has for the glory of God. On the other hand, great intelligence has frequently been found coupled with gross carelessness and treachery of heart, leading to a moral and spiritual breakdown eventually. A tender conscience, subject to the guidance of the Word and Spirit of God, is the great *desideratum.* Contrast Obadiah and Ahab (1 Kings 18:3–4; 21:25).

4 Riches profit not in the day of wrath:
   But righteousness delivereth from death.

How empty and vain the confidence of the wealthy who trust in uncertain riches, in the day of wrath; whether it be when God suffers such a day to over-take men on earth, or whether we think of the full outpouring of His wrath upon the wicked dead! See Revelation 6:12–17 and 20:12–15.

Righteousness alone delivers from death: righteousness of which man in his natural state is bereft. Declared righteous by faith when God's testimony is believed, practical righteousness flows from the impartation of the new nature when born again. Noah, found righteous when the rest of the world had lapsed into violence and corruption, is an apt illustration of the truth here stated (Gen. 6).

5 The righteousness of the perfect shall make straight his
      way:
   But the lawless shall fall by his own lawlessness.
6 The righteousness of the upright shall deliver them:
   But transgressors shall be taken in their own naughtiness.
7 When a lawless man dieth, his expectation shall perish:
   And the hope of unjust men perisheth.
8 The righteous is delivered out of trouble,
   And the lawless cometh in his stead.

Retribution, a manifest law of God both for this world and the next, is the great lesson of these verses, which connect intimately with verses 27–30 of the preceding chapter. "God is not mocked: whatsoever a man soweth, that shall he also reap"; whether of the flesh unto corruption, or of the Spirit unto life eternal. "The Lord is a God of judgment, and by Him actions are weighed." Nothing escapes his notice. All shall receive a just recompense of reward. The path of righteousness leads to endless glory; that of lawlessness, to sorrow and woe. He who seeks to ensnare the upright will fall into the meshes of his own gin. No better example is to be found of the instruction of this section than the book of Esther in its entirety.[1] Daniel's experience with his accusers, as before noticed, emphasizes the same principle. God's retributive justice is swift and sure. It is in vain to seek to turn aside His holy and righteous governmental dealing.

9 A hypocrite with his mouth destroyeth his neighbor:
   But through knowledge shall the righteous be delivered.

The hypocrite has but one thought before his mind—to cover his own baseness, whatever the consequences to others: hence a readiness to falsely accuse and destroy the peace of the innocent in order to maintain the mask of righteousness for one's self. But the upright can afford to leave all in the hands of God, who in His own way and time will vindicate His servant. The case of Potiphar's wife and Joseph might have been in Solomon's mind as he penned the words (Gen. 39).

> ¹⁰ When it goeth well with the righteous, a city rejoiceth:
> And when the lawless perish there is shouting.
> ¹¹ By the blessing of the upright, a city is exalted:
> But it is overthrown by the mouth of the lawless.

Whatever may be the sins or evil propensities of men individually, collectively they realize, in some measure at least, the value of national and municipal righteousness. Therefore they hail with delight rulers who are wise and good; for through such, a city is lifted up; while evil rulers are detested because of the manifest unhappy results of their oppression. Thus men rejoiced over the downfall of Abimelech (Judg. 9:53–57), and, in a later day, upon the exaltation of David (2 Sam. 19:14).

> ¹² He that is void of heart, despiseth his neighbor;
> But a man of understanding holdeth his peace.

When another would stir up strife, it is well if he be met by one who has been instructed in the school of Him "who, when He was reviled, reviled not again; when He suffered, He threatened not, but committed Himself to Him that judgeth righteously." If railing and unkindness be met with contempt or anger, however well deserved, it is but adding fuel to the flame. To go quietly on, as David when cursed by Shimei, committing all to God, is the course of wisdom and blessing. See notes on 20:22.

> ¹³ A talebearer goeth about revealing secrets:
> But he that is of a faithful spirit concealeth a matter.

Talebearing, even though the tales be true, is most mischievous. If there be a fault, to lovingly admonish in private and then conceal from all others is in accordance with the mind of God.

There is an instructive word in this connection in Exodus 37. Verses 17–24, inclusive, relate to the making of the candlestick, or lamp stand, for the tabernacle. Among the accessories to it, we read in verse 23 that Moses "made his seven lamps, and his snuffers, and his snuff-dishes, of pure gold." There is that here that is intensely interesting, and unspeakably precious.

No lamp will long burn well without occasional snuffing. Hence God has made provision even for so apparently insignificant a matter as this. To the mind of man it might seem of trifling importance as to how a light was snuffed, and what was done with the black snuff afterward. In God's eye, nothing is trivial that concerns the glory of His Son, or the welfare of His people.

The snuffers were made "of pure gold"—that which symbolizes the divine glory, and speaks, too, of perfect righteousness. It may often happen that some saint of God is losing his brightness, and no longer shining for Him as he once did. It is the priest with the golden tongs to whom is entrusted the delicate task of "snuffing." "Brethren, if a man be overtaken in a fault, ye who are spiritual restore such a one in the spirit of meekness; considering thyself, lest thou also be tempted" (Gal. 6:1). Thus will the "snuffing" be accomplished according to God, and the restored brother's light burn all the brighter for it.

But what then? Is the evil to be spread abroad, and made a matter of common knowledge? Ah, there were not only the snuffers, but the snuff dishes; and they too were of pure gold! The priest was to put carefully away, in these golden receptacles, the black, dirty snuff which he had removed from the wick. To have gone about spreading the filth upon the spotless garments of other priests would have been to defile them all. It must be hidden away in the presence of God! Is not this where we often fail?

How much grief and sorrow might have been prevented in many an assembly if the golden snuff dishes had been more often used! On every hand we hear of strife and discord brought about through evil speaking; and it is remarkable how ready we are to listen to that which we know can only defile. Oh that there might be more "angry countenances" among us when the backbiter is out seeking to spot and blacken the snowy garments of God's holy priests! See 25:23.

In the New Testament the divine way of dealing with a brother's fault is clearly defined: "Moreover if thy brother shall trespass against thee, go and tell him his fault between thee and him alone: if he shall hear thee, thou hast gained thy brother" (Matt. 18:15). If brethren would sternly refuse to listen to complaints against others until this first condition has been complied with, it would go far to do away with evil speaking. Many a brother would be won if approached in priestly nearness to God by one who carried with him the golden snuffers and the snuff dish.

But if he refuse to hear? Then "take with thee one or two more"; and if still willful, as a last resource, "tell it unto the church." But this not until the other means have failed.

By thus acting in accordance with the Word of God, much shame and misery might be spared innocent persons, and many wandering ones recovered who, through backsliding, are driven deeper into the mire. God, too, will be glorified, and the Lord Jesus honored; for He has said, "If I then, your Lord and Master, have washed your feet, ye also ought to wash one another's feet. . . . If ye know these things, happy are ye if ye do them" (John 13:14, 17).

> [14] Where no management is, the people fall:
>   But in the multitude of counsellors there is safety.

To depend entirely upon one's own judgment is the height of folly. Even the wisest and godliest are often given to blunders and errors of discernment; for infallibility is a dream indulged in concerning one man alone. To weigh a matter in the presence of God; to invite the counsel of those whose experience and spirituality evidence ability to try the things that differ is the course of wisdom. Rehoboam lost the major part of his kingdom by neglect of this important truth; and many a one has suffered grievous loss for the same disdain of counsel and help.

> [15] He that is surety for a stranger shall smart for it:
>   And he that hateth suretyship is sure.

These words were written centuries before the Cross to warn men of what is still a very common ground for failure and ruin in business life. To go surety for a stranger is a most dangerous thing, as thousands have learned to their sorrow.

But there was One who knew to the full what all the consequences of His act would be, and yet, in grace, deigned to become "Surety for a stranger." "Ye know the grace of our Lord Jesus Christ, that, though He was rich, yet for your sakes He became poor, that ye through His poverty might be rich" (2 Cor. 8:9). He was the stranger's Surety.

A surety is one who goes good for another. Many a man will do this for a friend long known and trusted; but no wise man will so act for a stranger. But it was when we were "strangers and foreigners," "enemies and alienated in our minds by wicked works," that Jesus in grace became our Surety. He "died, the Just for the unjust, that He might bring us to God."

All we owed was exacted from Him when He suffered upon the tree for sins not His own. He could then say, "I restored that which I took not away" (Ps. 69:4). Bishop Lowth's beautiful rendering of Isaiah 53:7 reads, "It was exacted, and He became answerable." This is the very pith and marrow of the gospel.

How fully He proved the truth of the words we are considering when He suffered on that cross of shame! How He had to "smart for it," when God's awful judgment against sin fell upon Him. But He wavered not. In love to God and to the strangers whose Surety He had become, "He endured the cross, despising the shame."

His sorrows are now forever past. He has paid the debt, met every claim in perfect righteousness. The believing sinner is cleared of every charge, and God is fully glorified.

> He bore on the tree the sentence for me;
> And now both the Surety and sinner are free.

None other could have met the claims of God's holiness against the sinner and have come out triumphant at last. He alone could atone for sin. Because He has settled every claim, God has raised Him from the dead and seated Him at His right hand in highest glory.

There He sits—the glorified One, administering grace and blessing to all who see in Him the stranger's Surety, and trust Him for themselves.

> [16] A gracious woman retaineth honor:
> And strong men retain riches.

As strength of body enables a man to retain his wealth against those who would assail it, so strength of character is evidenced even in the weaker vessel by the ability to yield, in grace, rather than to stand for what might be thought her rights; and thus she retains honor. Many are fearful of forfeiting the admiration of others by kindliness and humility, and so wrap themselves in a haughty, chilling dignity which after all makes them but the objects of scorn, if not of disgust. Nothing is so truly lovely and admirable as a gracious, conciliatory spirit, whether in the home, the assembly, or in our dealings with the world. How brightly does this shine out in Abigail (1 Sam. 25)!

> [17] The merciful man doeth good to his own soul:
> But the cruel troubleth his own flesh.

It is the same kindly, forgiving spirit that is here lauded. Not only others, but one's own self, will be blessed and helped thereby; "while hardness and cruelty will inevitably come back on the one who so acts. He cannot but be unhappy in his own soul; and then, with what measure he metes, it shall be measured to him again. Joab was a man of this stamp (1 Kings 2:5–6); in Isaac we see the opposite (Gen. 26).

> ¹⁸ The lawless worketh a deceitful work:
>   But to him that soweth righteousness shall be a sure
>   reward.
> ¹⁹ As righteousness tendeth to life,
>   So he that pursueth evil [tendeth] to his own death.
> ²⁰ They that are of a froward heart are an abomination to
>   Jehovah:
>   But such as are upright in their way are His delight.
> ²¹ Though hand join in hand, the evildoer shall not be
>   unpunished:
>   But the seed of the righteous shall be delivered.

Sin and righteousness are set in sharp contrast again. Deceit and lawlessness go together. They shall be to the eternal undoing of those who practice them, because all such are an abomination to the Lord.

In the upright He delights, therefore their reward is sure. It is in vain for men to attempt to ward off the certain judgment coming by confederating together to defeat the justice of the Almighty. Vengeance will inevitably follow their iniquitous course; but deliverance shall come in due time to the righteous. Sennacherib and Hezekiah are the central figures in a solemn scene that sets forth the great and important principle of these verses (2 Chron. 32).

> ²² As a jewel of gold in a swine's snout,
>   So is a fair woman that is without discretion.

Utter incongruity! Beauty allied to virtue is incomparably lovely. Bereft of discretion, it is sad indeed. See Jezebel's melancholy history.

> ²³ The desire of the righteous is only good:
>   But the expectation of the lawless is wrath.

"Thoughts of peace and not of evil" fill the heart of the righteous. His desire shall be more than met; for "all things work together for good to them that love God, who are the called according to His purpose." The expectation of the wicked is only judgment. He heaps up wrath for himself against the day of wrath. Note 10:28, and see Jeremiah and Zedekiah (Jer. 17:16; 34:1–3).

> [24] There is that scattereth and yet increaseth:
>   And there is that witholdeth more than is meet, but it
>   tendeth to poverty.
> [25] The liberal soul shall be made fat:
>   And he that watereth, shall be watered also himself.

Bunyan's quaint rhyme, propounded as a riddle by Old Honest and explained by Gaius, is in itself a suited commentary on these verses:

> A man there was, though some did count him mad,
> The more he cast away, the more he had.
> He that bestows his goods upon the poor
> Shall have as much again, and ten times more.

It is the divine plan for increase and enlargement. Like the Egyptian farmer who scatters his seed upon the retreating waters of the Nile to reap a rich harvest "after many days," so the one who is in touch with the philanthropy of the heart of God will find true increase later by scattering now; while he who greedily seeks to keep all for himself will find his course has led to utter ruin. In 2 Corinthians 9:6–10 the Holy Spirit takes this up as a divine principle, and applies it to the grand subject of Christian benevolence. St. Paul there quotes the latter part of verse 24 and the beginning of verse 25. "But this I say, He which soweth sparingly shall reap also sparingly; and he which soweth bountifully shall reap also bountifully. Every man according as he purposeth in his heart, so let him give; not grudgingly, or of necessity: for God loveth a cheerful giver." And he goes on to assure them that He who notes all done for His glory will minister in abundance to them who thus freely use the substance committed to them for the blessing of others. The Philippian assembly had tasted of the joy of thus ministering to the Lord (Phil. 4:10–19). In Nabal of old we learn the folly of greed and self-occupation (1 Sam. 25:10–11, 38).

²⁶ He that withholdeth corn, the people shall curse him.
But blessing shall be upon the head of him that selleth it.

To hold in store that which would feed the multitude while people are dying for need of it, with a view to extortionate charges later, is conduct that deserves the curses it draws forth. The story of the medieval bishop of Rouen who so acted has made his name for centuries to be execrated and detested. We have just seen such a case in Nabal, who, living in prosperity himself, refused to share with David and his followers when persecuted by Saul. In Joseph, the husbander of Egypt's resources for the good of the famine-stricken world, we see behavior such as is commended in the last clause.

If in this world the curses of the dying shall fall upon the withholder of corn, what shall be said of him, who, being in possession of the bread of life, having the knowledge of the precious grace of God, is yet quite unconcerned as to the need of the vast multitudes on every hand who are going on to the second death, the lake of fire? It is in vain to plead that they know, and do not heed. The Christian is responsible to warn, to preach, to entreat the lost to be reconciled to God. We are debtors to all men because of the treasure committed to us. Sad indeed will be the accounting for such as live to themselves, withholding the corn which alone can meet the dire need of the spiritually famine stricken. Blessings shall be on the head of those who are as earnest in offering to men the free grace of God, as are the men of business in seeking sales for their wares.

²⁷ He that diligently seeketh good procureth favor:
But he that seeketh mischief, it shall come upon him.

It is again the retributive justice of God that is brought to our notice. The seeker after good shall be rewarded according to his faithfulness in endeavoring to bring joy and cheer to his fellows. But the mischief-maker, who rejoices in iniquity and desires the undoing of his neighbor, shall be undone himself. The confession of Adoni-bezek is a striking case in point (Judg. 1:5–7). Caleb well illustrates the first clause (Josh. 14:6–13).

²⁸ He that trusteth in his riches shall fall:
But the righteous shall flourish as a branch.

Those who prosper in the world are very apt to "trust in uncertain riches"; hence the need of being continually reminded of the evanescent character of all that this scene affords. See the rich fool of Luke 12:16–21.

The genuine riches are moral—not material. It is the righteous—not the moneyed man—who is truly wealthy. See the blessed man of Psalm 1.

> [29] He that troubleth his own house shall inherit the wind:
> And the fool shall be servant to the wise in heart.

To trouble one's own house is, I take it, to so walk as to leave an evil example for those coming after to follow. Jehovah visits the iniquities of the fathers upon the children to the third and fourth generation. It is not merely physical ills handed down in judgment, as in the case of the drunkard's child being born with an inherent tendency to disease; but the father's ways are copied by the children. This is what is so prominent in the case of Jeroboam the son of Nebat, "which made Israel to sin."

The fool, though superior in station, will be the servant to the wise in heart. It is not the outward trappings and insignia of office that make a man to be truly great. When Daniel and Belshazzar met face to face, or when Paul and Festus confronted each other, who were the superior persons?

> [30] The fruit of the righteous is a tree of life;
> And he that is wise winneth souls.

A tree of life to those who perish—such is the fruit of the righteous. Refreshment and gladness are shed forth, that those who languish may enter into blessing. Thus, "he that is wise winneth souls." It is not merely, as in the King James Version, that "he that winneth souls is wise"; but all who are truly wise according to God will be channels of blessing to others—winners of souls. Searching is the truth here stated.

Wisdom consists not in the knowledge of Scripture or divine principles, precious as such are and must be; but in the ability to walk in the power of these things, and to so minister to men and women, yea, and children too (preeminently, one might say), that they shall be won for Christ and His truth. Tested by this, how few are the wise! It is evident that soul winning is not the slipshod business many would make it out to be—the mere hit-or-miss ministry that is so common today. On the contrary, it is a divine science, requiring much earnest preparation of heart in the presence of God; careful study of the need of the souls of men and of the truth of the Scriptures as given to meet that need. Paul is again, of all merely human soul winners, the great example here, "made all things to all men, if by any means he might save some." This is the wisdom so much needed in turning men from the power of Satan unto God (1 Cor. 9:19–23).

> [31] Behold, the righteous shall be recompensed in the earth:
> Much more the lawless and the sinner,

This is the passage quoted by the apostle Peter (though from the Septuagint version) in the fourth chapter of his first epistle, where he says, "The time is come that judgment must begin at the house of God: and if it first begin at us, what shall the end be of them that obey not the gospel of God? And if the righteous scarcely be saved, where shall the ungodly and the sinner appear?" (vv. 17–18). By comparing this eighteenth verse, in its transposed form, with the proverb itself, much light is shed on the quotation as used by Peter. The righteous being scarcely, or with difficulty, saved, refers to their salvation on earth, not their entrance into heaven. Here, in this scene, righteous and wicked are subjects of God's government. If, then, the godly shall be visited and recompensed here for the evil they may do when the heart turns away from the Lord, what of the wicked and the openly profane? Dire indeed will be their judgment. In a national way, we see this in the case of Israel, the righteous nation, punished in measure for their sins; so was Edom, the proud, defiant persecutor, who had cast off all fear of God. See the prophecy of Obadiah.

God never spares His children when they willfully follow their own ways. "Whom the Lord loveth He chasteneth, and scourgeth every son whom He receiveth." How impious the thought that the wicked can defy Him as they please, and yet go unpunished at last! Judgment may linger, but it is certain to be executed eventually. "They shall not escape."

CHAPTER 12

PROVERBS 12

¹ Whoso loveth instruction, loveth knowledge:
But he that hateth reproof is brutish.

The man who loves instruction for its own sake values true knowledge, let it come through what channel it may. What he desires is the truth, not the ability to display his acquirements. The mere vain pedant hates reproof, and, like a brute beast, values not correction (10:17). He prefers his own unbridled will, however contrary his thoughts and ways may be to sound instruction. This was the great characteristic of the world before the flood (Job 22:15, 17). Josiah, the godly young king of Judah, is a fine example of the opposite (2 Chron. 34).

² A good man obtaineth favor of Jehovah:
But a man of wicked devices will He condemn.
³ A man shall not be established by lawlessness:
But the root of the righteous shall not be moved.

In the very nature of things, the face of the Lord cannot but shine upon the good man. His root shall be firmly established. "He shall be holden up, for God is able to make him stand." But that same divine character which makes Him delight in uprightness necessitates His condemnation of a man of wicked devices.

He shall never be established. "The ungodly shall not stand in the judgment, nor sinners in the congregation of the righteous." See Hushai and Ahithophel (2 Sam.15:32; 16:15–23; 17).

> 4 A virtuous woman is a crown to her husband:
>   But she that maketh ashamed is as rottenness in his bones.

It would be a grave mistake to limit the word *virtuous* to the thought of chastity. The virtuous woman is one in whom all noble qualities shine, as set forth fully in the last chapter. Such a woman is indeed a crown to her husband. One who by folly and slothfulness makes ashamed is like the sudden coming on of old age. Contrast Sarah (Gen. 18:12; 1 Peter 3:1–6) with Job's wife (Job 2:9–10).

> 5 The thoughts of the righteous are just:
>   But the counsels of the lawless are deceit.
> 6 The words of the lawless are to lie in wait for blood:
>   But the mouth of the upright shall deliver them.
> 7 The lawless are overthrown, and are not:
>   But the house of the righteous shall stand.

Right thoughts result in right words and right actions, and shall be rewarded by Him whose delight is in righteousness. But evil thoughts have their fruitage likewise in evil words and deeds, and they too shall receive a just recompense of reward. The judgment of God is according to truth, as every soul of man shall own at last. Contrast Absalom and David.

> 8 A man shall be commended according to his wisdom:
>   But he that is of a perverse heart shall be exposed to
>   contempt.

Even among natural men wisdom is a commendation, while a vain and foolish spirit but exposes to contempt. The world can appreciate sobriety and spiritual intelligence, though it may refuse or even persecute it. But to pretend to either, while bereft of both, is to draw forth the disgust of all reasonable men. Note the difference in the estimation formed by their fellows of Gideon and Abimelech (Judg. 7–9).

⁹ He that is despised, and hath a servant,
  Is better than he that honoreth himself and lacketh bread.

The Douay version renders the final line somewhat differently: "Better is the poor that provideth for himself." The thought evidently is that the one who is looked down upon as lowly, but whose needs are met, is far happier and more to be envied than he who delights in making a pompous display while feeling the pinch of hunger and distress. See Jacob and Esau (Gen. 25:27–34).

¹⁰ A righteous man regardeth the life of his beast:
  But the tender mercies of the lawless are cruel.

A truly righteous man cannot act inconsistently with his character even in regard to a dumb beast. The very dependence of the creature upon his consideration will but tend to stir his compassions, so that he will treat it with the kindliness proper to all noble souls. The wicked, or lawless, on the other hand, becomes only the more brutal as he recognizes his own title to control the lower creation. Cruelty and unrighteousness go hand in hand. Contrast Jacob with Balaam. See Genesis 33:13–14 and Numbers 22:23–31.

¹¹ He that tilleth his land shall be satisfied with bread:
  But he that followeth vain persons is void of heart.

The diligent husbandman is abundantly rewarded for his toil, while the trifling, idling companion of reckless coxcombs is but manifesting his lack of intelligence. This is a searching word for young Christians. God's Word is a field well worth our tilling. Those who obey the apostolic injunction conscientiously, "study to show thyself approved unto God, a workman that needeth not to be ashamed, rightly dividing the word of truth," are invariably repaid for every hour earnestly devoted to the consideration of this precious field. Many, alas, waste much time in idle folly, companying with empty, frivolous worldlings, and neglecting their Bibles, to the serious detriment of their spiritual life. Such often wonder how it is that other Christians can discover so much that is new and edifying in the Scriptures. They see no such lovely lessons and helpful suggestions. No; because they do not really "till the land." If they did, they too would be satisfied with bread.

Incalculable is the loss those who so act must suffer, both in time and eternity. This neglect of the Bible is the root of much backsliding, coldness of heart, and departure from God. Where the believer makes it a daily practice to "dig" into the Book for himself, and then seeks, by the Spirit's power, to walk in the truth learned, growth in grace and in the knowledge of the things of God soon becomes most marked. Timothy is a fine pattern for all young saints on this point (2 Tim. 3:14–17), while the ungodly Jehoiakim is a warning beacon for all in danger of taking the opposite course to that we have been outlining (Jer. 36:22–32).

> ¹² The lawless desireth the fortress of evil:
>   But the root of the righteous yieldeth fruit.
> ¹³ The evil is snared by the transgression of the lips:
>   But the just shall come out of trouble.

The wicked would surround his very soul with evil, while hoping to escape in the day of retribution; but he is snared with the words of his mouth, and worse are the calamities to which he is exposed than those which he sought to ward off. *Vide* Gehazi (2 Kings 5:20–27).

The righteous, with holy confidence, places his trust in God, and bears fruit to His glory. In the day of his trouble he has a Deliverer near at hand. See Elisha (2 Kings 6:17).

> ¹⁴ A man shall be satisfied with good by the fruit of his
>   mouth:
>   And the recompense of a man's hands shall be rendered
>   unto him.

We have seen over and over again in this book that it is a principle of the divine government, which no man may turn aside, that "whatsoever a man soweth that shall he also reap." To every man will recompense be made according to his doings. The Christian is not superior to this law of the kingdom of God. Rather he bows his head and owns its justice. See the parable of the unmerciful servant (Matt. 18:24–35).

> ¹⁵ The way of a fool is right in his own eyes:
>   But he that hearkeneth unto counsel is wise.
> ¹⁶ A fool's wrath is presently known:
>   But a prudent man covereth shame.

Two things are here stated as being characteristic of the man who is denominated a fool; that is, one who lacks divine wisdom. He is proud and self-confident, refusing to brook correction: on the other hand, he is intolerant of others' faults, manifesting his indignation readily, and making worse the wound instead of binding it up. The wise and prudent man is in every way the contrast to all this. He is hardest on himself; consequently readily accepts counsel, willingly owning that others may be wiser than he; and he is ever ready to cover the shame of another, rather than to tell it abroad. It is the same contrast that existed in the days of Noah, when Ham unblushingly related the tale of his father's shame, as though himself superior to his sire; while Shem and Japheth went backward to cover their dishonored parent (Gen. 9).

> [17] He that speaketh truth showeth forth righteousness:
> But a false witness, deceit.
> [18] There is that speaketh like the piercings of a sword:
> But the tongue of the wise is health.
> [19] The lip of truth shall be established forever:
> But a lying tongue is but for a moment.
> [20] Deceit is in the heart of them that imagine evil:
> But to the counsellors of peace is joy.
> [21] There shall no evil happen to the just:
> But the lawless shall be filled with mischief.
> [22] Lying lips are an abomination to Jehovah:
> But they that deal truly are His delight.

The six verses are all occupied with the same general theme—lips of truth contrasted with a lying tongue. The latter is an abomination to Him who is Himself the Truth. The former He delights in because it is in accord with His own nature.

Honest speech manifests integrity of heart: falsity declares unerringly the lack of truth in the inward parts. The one who hesitates not at deliberate lying scatters pain and sorrow on every side; his venomed words piercing like a sword the hearts of sensitive and gentle souls. To these the tongue of the wise is health and upbuilding. But the day of reckoning is coming, when the lip of truth shall be established forever, and the lying tongue go into oblivion.

It is well to remember that it is intentional deceit that is here in question. One is often pained to hear good men recklessly charge others with lying because they have uttered an untruth in the innocence of their hearts. A statement may be false as to fact, but true as to intent; just as a statement may be true as to fact, but uttered with the intent to deceive. It is the deceit in the heart that causes the lips to utter a lie. None should be so charged unless the evidence makes it clear there was intention to prevaricate.

The just shall be preserved from evil, even as they have sought the good of their fellows: but to the lawless, judgment without mercy shall be meted out; for God cannot but make manifest His hatred of that which is false, and His approbation of truth and righteousness. Contrast Nehemiah and Sanballat (Neh. 6:5–9).

> ²³ A prudent man concealeth knowledge:
> But the heart of fools proclaimeth foolishness.

The man who has the least worth saying is generally the man who says the most. The prudent man is not forever airing his knowledge; the fool loses no opportunity to proclaim his empty folly. See Jeremiah and Hananiah (Jer. 28:1–11).

> ²⁴ The hand of the diligent shall bear rule:
> But the slothful shall be under tribute.

It is not ability only that causes one to succeed and secures advancement. There must be earnest endeavor, otherwise talent and brilliancy count for nothing. The slothful, however much he may have the advantage of another in natural gifts and intelligence, will in the end be inferior to the patient plodder. This is what someone has called "the gospel of work." It is all-important, both in the natural and the spiritual sphere. Contrast Gideon and Barak (Judg. 6:11–12; 4:4–9).

> ²⁵ Heaviness in the heart of a man maketh it stoop:
> But a good word maketh it glad.

"How forcible are right words," bringing comfort, cheer and encouragement to those in grief of soul and bitterness of spirit! See Nehemiah and Artaxerxes (Neh. 2:2–8).

> ²⁶ The righteous searcheth out his neighbor:
> But the way of the lawless seduceth them.

The man whose own ways are clean, and whose conscience is free, will be able to sound and search his neighbor in a godly way to his edification and restoration to God, if his steps have gone astray. "He that is spiritual discerneth all things." The insubject, lawless man has not his brother's good at heart, but rather his undoing; hence his words are seductive and ensnaring. Nathan is an illustration of the first; the wise woman of Tekoa of the second (2 Sam. 12:1–14; 14:1–20).

> ²⁷ The slothful man roasteth hot that which he took in
>   hunting:
>   But the substance of a diligent man is precious.

Some men can bestir themselves for a time, but soon fall back into their customary slothful manner. Many are they who attend the ministry of the Word but fail afterward to meditate upon and make their own what they hear. Their course is like one who goes forth to the field or forest, and while the excitement of the hunt is upon him spares no pains, but turns his prey to no true account afterward. The way of the diligent is very different. He uses what he has, and thus more is given, as in the parable of the talents. Ruth, who gleaned all day and at even *"beat out* that which she had gleaned," is a striking illustration of this (2:17). The servant who hid his talent in the ground pictures the contrary spirit.

> ²⁸ In the way of righteousness there is life;
>   And in the pathway thereof there is no death.

The way of righteousness is that path of the just that shines more and more unto the perfect day. Passing through a scene of death, it goes on to the land of life; and that eternal life is now the precious possession of all who, by the straight gate, have entered upon it. What men call death, real and true as it is to every one who treads the path of sin, for the just is but the end of the way opening into the gladness and glory of the Father's house. "This God is our God forever and forever. He will be our guide even *over* (not, as in the KJV, *unto*) death." Happy the portion of all who tread the way of holiness, through a world of sin, up to the city of God!

CHAPTER 13

PROVERBS 13

In the first verse of this portion we are again reminded that it is the wise who are grateful for counsel and help; the foolish scorner will not accept rebuke.

> ¹ A wise son heareth his father's instruction:
> But a scorner heareth not rebuke.

It is the part of true wisdom to own that the more experienced may save me much by instructing me as a result of what has been learned on a road already trodden, and which to me is all new ground. The self-confident scorner will pass on, indifferent to the words of the wise, to learn for himself by bitter experience of the snares and pitfalls he might have been saved from, had he been humble enough to accept counsel from those competent to teach. Contrast Isaac (Gen. 26) with Simeon and Levi (Gen. 34:25–31).

> ² A man shall eat good by the fruit of his mouth:
> But the soul of the transgressors shall eat violence.
> ³ He that keepeth his mouth keepeth his life:
> But he that openeth wide his lips shall have destruction.

The evil speaker is but laying up trouble and sorrow for himself in the future; as the one into whose lips grace is poured shall surely find grace when in need himself. To control the lips is to keep the life. The perfect man is the one who has his tongue in subjection. He who lacks wisdom in this respect will bring sure destruction upon himself. Of this Shimei is a solemn warning (1 Kings 2:8); David, when tempted greatly to speak for himself, illustrates the opposite (1 Sam. 17:28–29).

> 4 The soul of the sluggard desireth, and hath nothing:
> But the soul of the diligent shall be made fat.

The New Testament reiterates the principle here declared, that "if a man will not work, neither shall he eat." It is as true in the things of the spiritual life as of the natural. The diligent seeker after the precious truths laid up in the Word of God is the one who is made to rejoice over that Word as one that finds great spoil. The sluggard's portion is leanness of soul and dissatisfaction continually. Contrast Ezra 7:10 with the returned captives (Hag. 1:2–6).

> 5 A righteous man hateth lying:
> But a lawless man is loathsome, and cometh to shame.
> 6 Righteousness keepeth him that is perfect in the way:
> But lawlessness overthroweth the sinner.

Truth in the inward parts is the secret of practical righteousness. That which is false is necessarily hateful to the one who is in the way of holiness. He has judged iniquity, and his concern is to so walk in secret before God as to glorify His name in this world, where it has been so terribly dishonored. The insubject man makes himself odious and is overthrown by his own sin, being put to shame even here, and whose future portion is to be cast into outer darkness for eternity. Contrast Jehoiada and Athaliah (2 Kings 11).

> 7 There is that feigneth himself rich, yet hath nothing:
> There is that feigneth himself poor, yet hath great riches.

It is the nature of fallen man to act the hypocrite. The poverty-stricken will pretend to wealth; the wealthy will feign poverty. He who has nothing desires to be esteemed as one who has much; and he who has great riches oftentimes considers his safety to lie in being considered one who has little or nothing. The first is proud and vain; the last, mean and miserly. The one is the spirit of Laodicea

(Rev. 3:17): the other we see carried out by the wily Gibeonites, to deceive Joshua and the army of Israel (Josh. 9).

> ⁸ The ransom of a man's life are his riches:
> But the poor heareth not rebuke.

The verse is confessedly ambiguous. Various renderings give little help. The thought seems to be that riches are the confidence of their possessor. He therefore can haughtily scorn the one who would reprove him. But the indigent is crushed by a rebuke, having no spirit left to enable him to stand against it. Both are natural men, apparently.

> ⁹ The light of the righteous rejoiceth:
> But the lamp of the lawless shall be put out.

Brightly burns the flame of testimony when fed with the oil of grace, which the righteous alone possess. The lamp of the lawless may flare for a moment, but the true state of affairs will soon be manifested. He lacks the oil, so the light must fail. Compare the ten virgins (Matt. 25).

> ¹⁰ Only by pride cometh contention:
> But with the well-advised is wisdom.

What a commentary on the subtle pride in all quarters are the many bitter contentions between individual saints and collective bodies meeting in the name of Christ! *Only* by pride cometh strife. It is well that this solemn word be kept in mind. If pride were judged, and the sin of it frankly owned before God, how soon would much that has been contended for be seen in its true light, as contrary to the Scriptures, and hence opposed to the spirit of Jesus Christ! It is an old saying, that "it takes two to make a quarrel." Where the effort to maintain a foolish dignity prevails, or covetousness leads the heart to desire what belongs to another, contention speedily is stirred. But if met by lowliness and grace on the part of the offended one, how soon must the strife cease! With the well-advised is that wisdom which enables him to give the soft answer that turns away wrath. In the matter of the strife between the herdsmen of Abram and Lot, we see how pride was at the root. Most effectually did Abram meet it, when he offered first choice to the man who had no title whatever to the land which Jehovah had given to the other (Gen. 13).

¹¹ Wealth gotten by vanity shall be diminished:
But he that gathereth by labor shall increase.

That which comes easily, easily slips away. It is treasure for which one has
toiled that he really values, and is careful in the use of. The principle abides
when applied to the true riches, the precious truth of God. Some, like a sponge,
readily absorb, but as readily give out under pressure. That which is valued is
what has been won by labor. *"Study* to show thyself approved unto God, a workman that needeth not to be ashamed, rightly dividing the word of truth." Wealth
such as this is surely worth the self-sacrifice and devotion required to obtain it;
and when so obtained, it shall abide, and increase. See Ziba (2 Sam. 16:4; 19:29),
as contrasted with Caleb (Josh. 14:6–14).

¹² Hope deferred maketh the heart sick:
But the desire that cometh to pass is as a tree of life

The ever unsatisfied longing of a hungry soul results in faintness of spirit and
sickness of heart. Such is the *hopeless* hope of the Christ-less. How blessed the
contrast in the case of the Christian! He, too, at times is sick with longing;
longing to behold the Beloved of his soul: but soon shall his desire be accomplished, and precious as the tree of life shall be its fulfillment. David once was
sick with yearning desire. He would taste the water of the well of his childhood.
But when his desire was met and the water was brought, it was too precious for
him to taste: he poured it out before the Lord (1 Chron. 11:15–19).

¹³ Whoso despiseth the word shall be destroyed:
But he that feareth the commandment shall be rewarded.
¹⁴ The law of the wise is a fountain of life,
To depart from the snares of death.
¹⁵ Good understanding giveth favor:
But the way of transgressors is hard.

To despise the word of instruction, which is the law of the wise (giving
favor with God and man, as so abundantly proven by both Joseph and Daniel,
and a host of others), is to expose oneself to shame now, and eternal ignominy
hereafter. But he that fears the commandment, recognizing in it a fountain of
life, will be preserved from the sorrows attendant upon the way of the trans-
gressor, and the dark outlook beyond. Pharaoh despised the word, and fell

beneath the avenging hand of the Lord. Saul despised the word, and was put to grief before the Philistines. The last three kings of Judah despised the word, and learned to the full, when too late, the terrible mistake made. Would that the solemn example of these, and many more whose lives are recorded in both sacred and secular history, would speak loudly to those bent on taking their own way and ignoring the commandment of the Lord, who has said, "To this man will I look, even to him that is poor and of a contrite spirit, and trembleth at My word" (Isa. 66:2).

> ¹⁶ Every prudent man dealeth with knowledge:
> But a fool layeth open his folly.

It is the part of ordinary prudence to lay to heart what we have been considering. Fools alone will refuse it, and thereby manifest their folly. Alas, that so large a number of those who as to this world are wise, should be fools as to the next! And yet, after all, true wisdom for the life that now is, is manifested by subjection to God and dealing with the knowledge His Word imparts. It is the sinfully foolish one who turns a deaf ear to the voice of truth. Contrast Moses and Aaron with Korah and his company (Num. 16).

> ¹⁷ A lawless messenger falleth into mischief:
> But a faithful ambassador is healing.

The messenger who runs unsent, waiting not for his commission from his master, will but fall into and produce mischief. The one who faithfully goes forth as the ambassador of another carries health and blessing. In the work of the gospel this is all-important. We live in a day of great restlessness and activity. But few are the servants who wait to get the mind of the Lord as revealed in His Word. The result is much mischievous teaching and faulty instruction that bewilders and perplexes the hearers. Precious is the message of the faithful ambassador as he goes forth beseeching men to be reconciled to God (2 Cor. 5:20).

> ¹⁸ Poverty and shame shall be to him that refuseth instruction:
> But he that regardeth reproof shall be honored.

Men may foolishly consider it beneath them to bow to instruction and learn from those competent to teach, but lasting honor comes to the one who is humble enough to receive help from whoever can impart true knowledge;

while ignominy and poverty shall be the portion of the self-sufficient soul. See Johanan and the captains (Jer. 42; cf. Prov. 12:1).

> ¹⁹ The desire accomplished is sweet to the soul:
>   But it is abomination to fools to depart from evil.
> ²⁰ He that walketh with wise men shall be wise:
>   But a companion of fools shall be destroyed.

When the heart's desire is attained, the soul rejoices. But the only desire of the fool is the gratification of his unbridled passions. He refuses to entertain the thought that iniquity is to be shunned. "Evil communications corrupt good manners." Association with the wise tends to wisdom. Companionship with vain persons is conducive to further vanity, and results in moral and spiritual ruin. Contrast Rehoboam with the young king Josiah (1 Kings 12:8; 2 Kings 22).

> ²¹ Evil pursueth sinners:
>   But to the righteous good shall be repaid.
> ²² A good man leaveth an inheritance to his children's
>   children:
>   And the wealth of the sinner is laid up for the just.

Again and again throughout this book the principle of retributive justice, even in this life, is insisted on. The sinner pursues evil, but only to find evil pursue him; while the righteous man who extends his goodness to others is repaid in kind. And when at last called away from this world, the good man, whether he leaves a fortune in material things behind him or not, yet bequeaths to his descendants an honored name and a holy example—an inheritance of incalculable value. That which the evildoer has laid up is soon dissipated, and passes into hands better able to use it aright. Contrast Jonadab the Rechabite (Jer. 35:6–11) with Coniah (Jehoiachin, Jer. 22:24–30).

> ²³ Much food is in the tillage of the poor:
>   But there is that is destroyed for want of judgment.

The poor husbandman will, if diligent, use every corner of his little plot, producing an amount and a variety of food that is often astonishing to his wealthier neighbor, many of whose broad acres are allowed to lie fallow, and much of whose crop may, through carelessness, be permitted to run to waste and be destroyed.

The man of small opportunities often makes the most of what he has, while the one of large privileges becomes slothful and neglectful.

We may see a needed lesson here as to spiritual things. Is it not frequently the case that a brother or sister with much leisure for study and prayer, boundless opportunities for the enjoyment of ministry, oral and written, and gifted in large measure, will be found to be taking his or her ease in a careless, lethargic spirit, gaining very little real food daily, and giving out little to others? On the other hand, how much more common a thing is it to find one whose daily toil occupies most of his waking hours, and whose talents and education are alike of a mean order, yet devoting himself earnestly to using what he has, letting scarcely a moment slip by wasted, and so gathering regularly much food for his own soul, and constantly imparting refreshment and blessing to his brethren!

The lack of spirituality is not the result of a lack of time to cultivate the things of God; but it betrays failure to use the opportunities presented.

We have heard of a blacksmith blowing a bellows, with a leaf of God's Word before him upon the wall, that he might glean a little for his soul as he attended to his forge; and of a cobbler pegging shoes with his Testament in front of him, from which ever and anon he snatched a precious morsel for his spiritual upbuilding. It was the tillage of the poor; but life and conversation proved there had been much food in it.

"No time for God" generally means "No heart for God," if the full truth were told. The diligent soul will make time, and often proves that a small portion of Scripture, or a few minutes of prayer, bear rich fruit, when heart and conscience are truly exercised. See the prayer of Jabez (1 Chron. 4:9–10).

> [24] He that spareth his rod hateth his son:
> But he that loveth him chasteneth him betimes.

Family discipline should be patterned after the divine discipline of Hebrews 12. It is not love, but the lack of it, that leaves a child to himself; to develop unchecked tendencies and propensities which shall result in future sorrow. Ours is a day of great laxity on this point. The coming generation will reap the bitter fruit of the absence of restraint and the evident aversion to chastening so manifest in the majority of homes. A sickly sentimentality, supposedly wiser and more compassionate than God Himself, has made it fashionable to decry the use of the rod, as a relic of a barbarous age; but the difference in the character of children and the home is certainly in the favor of Scripture, as any one may see who will.

It is even worse where, among Christians, government is ignored on the plea that grace is reigning. Grace never sets aside government. The two principles are not opposed or antagonistic. In the divine ways, they go on side by side, as they should in the home. Contrast Eli (1 Sam. 3:13–14) with Abraham (Gen. 18:19).

> [25] The righteous eateth to the satisfying of his soul:
>   But the belly of the lawless shall want.

The portion of the righteous may be small, but enjoyment is with it, for heart and conscience are at rest. But the lawless, though he riot in pleasure and plenty for a time, finds no real satisfaction; and his recklessness shall bring him to want at last. How much happier the portion of Lazarus at the gate of the rich man, with Abraham's bosom awaiting him, than that of the lawless prodigal of the previous chapter (Luke 15–16).

CHAPTER 14

PROVERBS 14

The wise and the foolish woman are brought before us in vivid contrast in the opening verse:

> ¹ Every wise woman buildeth her house:
> But the foolish plucketh it down with her hands.

The wise woman, by counsel and example, will lead her household in the right way, directing their steps in accordance with the word of the Lord. Thus her house is established on an immovable foundation of righteousness. The foolish, through her evil behavior and unworthy instruction, lays up sorrow for herself and grief for her offspring by her unholy influence. Contrast the mothers of Moses and of Ahaziah (Exod. 2; 2 Chron. 22:2–3).

> ² He that walketh in his uprightness feareth Jehovah:
> But he that is perverse in his ways despiseth Him.

It is the life that proves whether one is really walking before God or not. The testimony of the lips, if contradicted by the behavior, is of little worth. The one who fears the Lord will be characterized by godliness and faithfulness. "He that saith he abideth in Him ought himself also so to walk even as He walked."

If the ways are perverse and opposed to His revealed will, it is proof that God is really despised, and not feared: He wants reality. To talk of reverence while obeying the dictates of a selfish, carnal nature, is but hypocrisy. This was Saul's snare. Samuel declared the answer to it all when he said," Behold, to obey is better than sacrifice, and to hearken than the fat of rams" (1 Sam. 15:22). The testimony of the people themselves proves the prophet to have walked before them in the fear of God (1 Sam. 12).

> ³ In the mouth of the foolish is a rod of pride:
> But the lips of the wise shall preserve them.

Out of his own mouth the fool, by his vain boasting, condemns himself; but the words of the wise declare the state of their hearts. Able to give the soft answer that turns away wrath, slow to speak and swift to hear—their conversation manifests the wisdom that is in them. See Goliath and David (1 Sam. 17:41–49).

> ⁴ Where no oxen are, the crib is clean:
> But much increase is by the strength of the ox.

It would be a drastic measure indeed to slay the oxen in order to have a clean stable. The purpose would surely be attained, but at what a cost!

The strength of the ox adds to the wealth of the farm, and makes it well worth the use of a little time spent regularly in cleansing the stall. "Doth God take care for oxen, or saith He it altogether for our sakes? For our sakes, doubtless, it is written." It is cause for lamentation to notice the readiness with which assemblies sometimes resort to getting rid of troublesome saints, thus cutting off much increase and blessing which might have ensued had patience and grace but been exercised. Too often it is taken for granted that the great object of discipline in the house of God is to get rid of the offender; whereas the truth is just the opposite. Earnest endeavor to recover the erring one should be the first thing thought of. Much crying to God, and identifying ourselves with the sin of one who has misbehaved, will accompany this, if we are before Him about it as we should be. Finally, if all is in vain, and the evildoer persists in his sin, refusing to repent, excision is the last sad acknowledgment that the case must be left in the hands of God.

To bring the matter before the saints and take summary action before every available means has been used with a view to his recovery may indeed cleanse the assembly; but it will be to the loss of all. We need one another. It is when we have the effectual working of every part, by that which every joint supplies, that there is blessing and increase of the whole. How much better is it to cleanse by leading an erring brother to repentance, thus covering his sin, than by excommunicating him before all possible means have been exhausted in seeking his restoration to God! See Judges 20:35–48; 21:1–3.

> 5   A faithful witness will not lie:
>   But a false witness will utter lies.

The faithful testimony bearer gives forth words of truth and soberness. A false witness cannot be depended on, for he has committed himself to the declaration of what he knows is untrue. The Christian is called to be a follower of Him who is preeminently "the faithful and true witness." Refusing to handle the Word of God deceitfully, he is to speak what he knows on the authority of divine revelation. To give out the vaporings of the human mind, with its idle speculations, will be to utter lies instead of truth. See Paul before Festus and Agrippa (Acts 26:25); and note the sad contrast in the case of Peter in the corridor of the council room (Luke 22:55–62).

> 6   A scorner seeketh wisdom, and findeth it not:
>   But knowledge is easy unto the intelligent.

The scorner may inquire, but he sets not his heart upon the answer. Therefore wisdom he fails to find. But to the intelligent who are actuated by a sincere desire to know the truth, even if it means to be obliged to judge themselves and their ways thereby, knowledge is easy.

It is so, preeminently, with the attainment of the understanding of the Scriptures. The mocker is continually finding cause for objections and foolish quibbles in the Word of God. The devout and upright soul sees only light where the other sees darkness. If a man has difficulty in accepting the truth of the Bible, it will almost invariably be found that it is because he is clinging to and persisting in some unholy course that the Word condemns. When sin is judged and iniquity repented of, all becomes clear. Pilate was one who asked, "What is truth?" but was not concerned enough to tarry for a reply, though Truth Incarnate stood before him. Daniel, long before, had proven that all is plain to the spiritually intelligent.

> 7   Go from the presence of a foolish man,
>   When thou perceivest not in him the lips of knowledge.

8 The wisdom of the prudent is to understand his way:
But the folly of fools is deceit.
9 Fools make a mock at sin [or, at the trespass offering]:
But among the righteous there is acceptance.

When it becomes evident that a man is bent on folly, with no concern about righteousness, it is best to leave him to himself. To argue or reason with such a one is useless. It is defiling to the wise and gratifying to the pride of the fool. "From such turn away."

The prudent has wisdom given him to guide him aright. For this the fool has no desire. His heart is utterly false, and deceit is on his lips. At sin, and the offering for it, he mocks. He has never realized the heinousness of the one, nor the need of the other. Consequently it is in vain to try to turn him from his lawless course. The righteous find acceptance because they have judged themselves, and bowed to God's just and holy sentence. Owning their true estate, they find a better one. Walking in obedience to God, they are acceptable to Him.

Let none gather from this that Scripture teaches that acceptance, in the sense of salvation, is on the ground of legal works. Far from it. Not until a man is justified by faith, as Abraham, does he do the works of righteousness. Good deeds are not the procuring cause of justification and new birth, but the result of these great and important blessings.

For an example of the fools who make a mock at sin and refuse instruction, see Jeremiah 44:15–19, where the remnant in Egypt defy the word of the Lord spoken through His prophet.

10 The heart knoweth its own bitterness;
And a stranger doth not intermeddle with its joy.

Every heart has its secret of joy or sorrow that no other ever shares. Hidden deep down from the sight of the nearest and the dearest are, often, griefs too deep for utterance or joys too great for words. How truly was this the case with our blessed Lord Himself! Whoever sounded the depths of the anguish of His soul, or who can estimate aright His joys?

To such a High Priest we can go with our own heaviest sorrows, and with Him we can share our inmost thoughts of exultation and delight.

11 The house of the lawless shall be overthrown:
But the tent of the upright shall flourish.

¹² There is a way which seemeth right unto a man,
But the end thereof are the ways of death.
¹³ Even in laughter the heart is sorrowful;
And the end of that mirth is heaviness.

If the "young man" who gives his attention to the wisdom of Solomon perish at last, as a result of missing the path of life, it will not be for lack of warning and a paucity of instruction. Clearly and unmistakably, the two classes are again contrasted.

We read first of the house of the lawless and the tent of the righteous. The house might seem by far the more stable, but it shall be overthrown; for its foundations shall be destroyed because built upon sinking sand. The pilgrim's tent wherein the upright tabernacles as he journeys through a foreign scene—foreign to the new nature within him—will abide and flourish until tenting days are over.

Man naturally chooses his own way—a way that seems right unto himself. But it ends in death, for it is opposed to the truth of God. "The labor of the foolish wearieth every one of them, because he knoweth not how to go to the city" (Eccl. 10:15).

There is a city which the most sinful and vile, if believing in a future state at all, cannot but long to enter—that city discerned afar off by Abraham, and described by John as the New and Holy Jerusalem, of which the Lamb who died is the Center and Lamp from whom shines all the glory of God. He Himself said, while on earth, "I am the Way." By His name alone is salvation proclaimed to sinners lost and guilty. There is none other name, and no other way, that will lead to the city of light.

A way there is—yes, many such; but none can rightly be designated *the* way save Jesus only. The end of *a* way that seems right is death—death moral, death spiritual, death eternal, yet death conscious forever!

Those who refuse *the* Way, to tread *a* way of their own choosing, find no true joy or confidence. "They, being ignorant of God's righteousness, and going about to establish their own righteousness, have not submitted themselves unto the righteousness of God" (Rom. 10:3). Hence their way is one of doubt and uncertainty. Though they laugh, the heart is not at rest, and their mirth is destined to end in madness. See Micah in Judges 17 and 18:14–26.[1]

Happy those who refuse every way of man's devising, and turn to Him who is the Way, the Truth, and the Life!

¹⁴ The backslider in heart shall be filled with his own ways:
And a good man shall be satisfied from himself.

The word *backslider* occurs in this verse only. Elsewhere in the Bible it is never used. "Backsliding" is found a number of times in our English version, fifteen in all (generally as an adjective, though also as a participle, and several times as a noun), but only in the books of Jeremiah and Hosea. It is well to notice that neither form of the word occurs in the New Testament.

A backslider is one who has given up ground once taken for God. Many a soul gives up in heart long before it is manifested in the life. The conscience becomes defiled; and if self-judgment does not follow, the truth begins to lose its power over the heart. The sad result of a broken-down testimony soon follows, until he is filled with his own ways. It is important, however, to carefully distinguish between backsliding and apostasy. The backslider is one who fails in practically carrying out the truth. The apostate, on the other hand, gives up the truth entirely, even denying the Lord that bought him; thus proving his unreality, whatever his previous profession may have been. It is to such that John refers in his first epistle, 2:19, as also Paul in Hebrews 6 and 10. Needless to say, no true believer ever becomes an apostate.

The good man—that is, the man who is real for God—shall be filled from what is in himself. The testimony of the Lord controls the reins of his being. His life will be in accord therewith.

Peter was a backslider in heart long before he fell; so, we may rest assured, was David. In the faithful stand of Shadrach, Meshach, and Abednego, we see men whose hearts were under the sway of divine principles when in seclusion, and who therefore overcame in public (Dan. 3).

¹⁵ The simple believeth every word:
But the prudent man looketh well to his going.
¹⁶ A wise man feareth, and departeth from evil:
But the fool rusheth on, and is confident.
¹⁷ He that is soon angry dealeth foolishly:
And a man of wicked devices is hated.
¹⁸ The simple inherit folly:
But the prudent are crowned with knowledge.
¹⁹ The evil bow before the good;
And the lawless at the gates of the righteous.

Wise and simple are relative terms, referring not so much to mental condition as to the fear of the Lord on the one hand, and indifferent self-sufficiency on the other.

The simple are ready with amazing incredulity to believe anything given forth by men as foolish as themselves, while stumbling over the clearest truths of revelation. No one has such strong faith in the greatest absurdities as the very man who quibbles over the truth of God. The unbeliever can believe unhesitatingly that he is the descendant of a long line of lower animals ranging all the way from protoplasm to ape, while he sneers at the Christian who receives by faith the divine record that "God hath made man upright, but they have sought out many inventions." The prudent man mistrusts himself, and trusts the Word of the living God. Ordering his steps in that Word, he looks well to his going.

Fearing the Lord, the wise man departs from evil. The fool, heeding no one, led by his lustful desires, rushes on in vainglorious self-confidence to his own destruction. If opposed in his follies, he rages in anger, but finds himself the object of the hatred of his fellows, because of his wicked devices. In searching for lawless pleasures he shall inherit folly, and at the end, when his wild race is run and his years of recklessness are past, in his decrepitude and poverty he shall bow at the gates of the righteous, forced at last to own that they had chosen the better part. Having devoted themselves to the acquisition of wisdom, the good are crowned with knowledge, and honored, when the simple are despised. Contrast Saul and David.

> ²⁰ The poor is hated even of his own neighbor:
> But the rich hath many friends.
> ²¹ He that despiseth his neighbor sinneth:
> But he that is gracious to the afflicted, happy is he.
> ²² Do they not err that devise evil?
> But loving kindness and truth shall be to them that devise
> good.

In a world like this, where covetousness rules, the rich will always have many to laud and admire them; while the poor will be despised and oppressed. To so act is to greatly err, for hath not God chosen oftentimes the poor of earth to be rich in faith? The eye of God is beholding all, and He will reward those who are gracious and kindly in their dealings with the lowly. He will see that lovingkindness and truth are meted out to them in return. Contrast the princes of Judah with Ebed-melech (Jer. 38:1–14; 39:15–18).

²³ In all labor there is profit:
  But the talk of the lips tendeth only to penury,

Labor is profitable, both because of what is produced, and in that it fills the hands and occupies the mind, thus greatly lessening the danger of giving way to a corrupt nature. But mere talk, empty boasting, and foolish vaunting of oneself, results in material and spiritual poverty: How suited the prayer for fallen creatures, "Set a watch, O LORD, before my mouth: keep the door of my lips" (Ps. 141:3)! See the parable of the two sons, one of whom labored to profit; the other said, and went not: it was the talk of the lips alone (Matt. 21:28–31).

²⁴ The crown of the wise is their riches:
  But the foolishness of fools is folly.

Whether poor or wealthy in this world's goods, the wise are always rich, possessing treasure that can never fade away. The fool, whatever his possessions, is but filled with folly, and nothing shall profit him eventually. Of Nabal, Abigail had to say, "Nabal [a fool] is his name, and folly is with him." And the words are true of all his class. Amnon is a fit illustration of this unhappy company (2 Sam. 13:13). For the lasting portion of the wise, see Daniel 12:3.

²⁵ A true witness delivereth souls:
  But a deceitful witness speaketh lies.

In verse 5 we had a faithful witness; here, a true witness. Such a one will deliver souls. Our Lord presents Himself in the double character of the "Faithful and True Witness" to Laodicea. He it is, in a day of lukewarmness and laxity, who abides as the Faithful Testimony-bearer, maintaining the truth; and as the True Witness, delivering all who bow in repentance. A deceitful witness is in every way the contrary of this—playing fast and loose with the teaching of the Scriptures, to the eternal loss of those who credulously accept his unholy speculations. "If the blind lead the blind, both shall fall into the ditch." Contrast Moses with Jannes and Jambres (2 Tim. 3:8).

²⁶ In the fear of Jehovah is strong confidence:
  And His sons have a place of refuge.
²⁷ The fear of Jehovah is a fountain of life,
  To depart from the snares of death.

To teach the fear of Jehovah was the object of the Holy Spirit in inspiring Solomon to pen the Proverbs. He who has learned it finds strong confidence and a place of refuge. It is not the slavish fear of an abject bondman, but that filial reverence which all His children love to render Him. Such rejoice to have found a fountain of life, and instruction as to their path on earth, so that they may avoid the snares of death. "Sons," or "children" (KJV), is used here in a moral sense. Relationship to God, as we now know it, was not revealed before the coming of the Son of God into the world to make known the Father. But those who truly feared the Lord were manifested as His children though they had not received the Spirit of adoption, enabling them to cry, "Abba, Father." See Cornelius (Acts 10).

> [28] In the multitude of people is the king's honor:
> But in the want of people is the destruction of a prince.

Rank and title avail nothing if there be not those who own the authority of a monarch. When the Lord Jesus "in His own times shall show, who is the blessed and only Potentate, King of kings, and Lord of lords," all redeemed creation shall own His benign sway. David and Ish-bosheth illustrate the verse (2 Sam. 3–4).

> [29] He that is slow to wrath is of great understanding:
> But he that is hasty of spirit exalteth folly.

The man of God will have the ability to rule his spirit. Controlling himself, he manifests great understanding; for he who lacks self-control is little able to profit others. A hasty spirit but exalts folly and hinders the reception of what may be set forth, even though it be right and true. Bad temper is always a sign of weakness. The man who knows he has the mind of God can afford to quietly wait on Him. See Micaiah and Zedekiah, the son of Chenaanah (1 Kings 22:24–25).

> [30] A sound heart is the life of the flesh:
> But envy the rottenness of the bones.

A sound heart is the heart of one who is broken before the Lord, and has learned not to think of himself more highly than he ought to think. Envy manifests at once the lack of self-judgment, and, on the part of a Christian, bespeaks a coming breakdown of his discipleship if he fails to humble himself in secret. This was the hidden cause of Asaph's unhappiness, "until he went into the sanctuary of the Lord" (Ps. 73).

³¹ He that oppresseth the poor, reproacheth his Maker:
But he that honoreth Him, is gracious to the needy.

To deal harshly with those in poverty is to reproach God who made both rich and poor, and whose inscrutable wisdom permits some to be in affliction, while others have more than heart can wish. He who honors God will view the needy as left to test the hearts of those in more comfortable circumstances, and will value the privilege of ministering to them as far as able, thus showing them the kindness of God. See the case of Mephibosheth (2 Sam. 9).

³² The lawless is driven away by his evil-doing:
But the righteous is confident, even in his death.

The deaths of lawless and righteous stand out, like their lives, in vivid contrast. The wicked is taken away in and by his iniquities, and goes out into a hopeless eternity to face his guilty record at the bar of Omnipotent Justice. The upright in heart, who in life has faced his sins in the presence of the Holy One, dreads no judgment after death, so falls on sleep with trustful hope of coming joy and bliss. Balaam wished for such a death, but found the opposite (Num. 23:10; 31:8). Stephen knew the confidence referred to, and could kneel down and die with a prayer for the forgiveness of his murderers on his lips (Acts 7:59–60).

³³ Wisdom resteth in the heart of him that hath understanding:
But that which is in the foolish is made known.

The intelligence and sagacity of the man of understanding make known the wisdom that is in his heart; while the senseless behavior of fools tells all too plainly what is within. See note on verse 24.

³⁴ Righteousness exalteth a nation:
But sin is a reproach to any people.

History is but the perpetual illustration of what is here declared. Nations, like individuals, are judged according to their ways. No country has prospered long that forsook the path of national righteousness. When pride and vanity, coupled with greed and cruelty, have been in the ascendant, the hour of humbling was not far away. Israel will ever be the great object lesson for all people. When the Word of God was esteemed, and His will honored, they prospered. When sin and neglect of God triumphed, they became a reproach. He was right who said, "Israel is the pillar of salt to the nations, crying to all people, 'Remember!'"

> ³⁵ The king's favor is toward a wise servant:
> But his wrath is against him that causeth shame.

Nothing causes one in authority to set value upon the services of a minister of state so much as the display of wisdom and discretion; but let his counsel prove disastrous and evil result from accepting his advice, and the king's indignation will know no bounds. May those who seek to serve a greater King be characterized by that wisdom which shall make them of real value in the work He has committed to them. See Darius and Daniel, in contrast with Ahasuerus and Haman (Dan. 6:3; Esther 7:7–10).

CHAPTER 15

PROVERBS 15

It is impossible for man to estimate aright the power for good or evil that lies in the tongue. A kindly, gracious word will often disarm a most ill-tempered and wrathful man; while a sharp, cutting remark has frequently separated friends dear to each other for years, until some trivial circumstance arose which might have been turned to an occasion for grace and forbearance on the part of each had love been ruling.

> ¹ A soft answer turneth away wrath:
> But grievous words stir up anger.
> ² The tongue of the wise useth knowledge aright:
> But the mouth of fools poureth out foolishness.

It is considered unmanly by many not to resent an insult, and to allow wrathful words to pass unchallenged; but it takes far more true character to meet an angry man in quietness of spirit, and to return cool, calm words for heated, hasty ones, than it does to give railing for railing, or malice for malice. The latter bespeaks a man who does not yet know how to rule his spirit; the former, one who has his personal feelings in subjection. Grievous words but add fuel to the flame, while a gracious demeanor will go far toward cooling the angry passions of another.

The wise man knows how to use knowledge so that it shall be for profit; knows, too, when to speak and when to be silent. The fool is always ready with a retort, whether it be fitting or not.

In Gideon's answer to the men of Ephraim we have a precious example of the soft answer that turns away wrath and the wisdom that uses knowledge aright.

In Jephthah's reply to the same people we are given to see a sad illustration of the folly of using in such a case the grievous words that stir up anger (Judg. 8:1–3; 12:1–6).

> ³ The eyes of Jehovah are in every place,
> Beholding the evil and the good.

How comforting is this truth to the weary heart, who, like poor Hagar in the desert, feels abandoned by all save One, but can say with assurance, "Thou, God, seest me"! To know that His eyes are on all our ways is sweet indeed when there is confidence and hope in Him. But for the wicked to know that he can never hide from those all-seeing eyes is perhaps the most terrible thing he has to face. Nor need it be wondered at, when it is remembered that He who beholds all is the Holy and the True! It is sin unrepented of that makes it so dreadful a thing to be under the eye of God. He who acknowledges his guilt and bows in repentance before Him, need no longer fear, for sin confessed is sin removed through the atonement of our Lord Jesus Christ. David's musings in Psalm 139 form a precious commentary on this verse.

> ⁴ A healing tongue is a tree of life:
> But perverseness therein is a breach in the spirit.

How much more common is the tongue of perversity than the healing tongue! The one separates brother from brother, and makes breach upon breach; the other binds together, giving cheer and gladness, and is as a tree of life to those who meditate upon its utterances. The healing tongue is the tongue of the peacemaker. The perverse tongue belongs to him who sows discord among brethren. May it be ours to covet the former and flee the latter.

Abraham possessed the tongue of healing when he said, "Let there be no strife, . . . for we be brethren" (Gen. 13:8). Sheba the son of Bichri by his hasty tongue caused division and dissension in Israel and brought judgment on his own head (2 Sam. 20).

⁵ A fool despiseth his father's instruction:
But he that regardeth reproof is prudent.

The young man is very apt to consider his knowledge superior to that of his father, forgetting that you cannot leap over many years' experience. It is the part of folly not to learn from one who has been over the path before you. To regard reproof and thankfully accept correction is an evidence of true wisdom. Contrast Manasseh with his father Hezekiah (2 Kings 18–21).

⁶ In the house of the righteous is much treasure:
But in the revenues of the lawless is trouble.

See note on 14:24. The true riches are found in the house of the righteous. Whatever other revenue may accrue to the evildoer, he shall have trouble and sorrow in large measure. See Achan (Josh. 7:19–26).

⁷ The lips of the wise disperse knowledge:
But the heart of the foolish doeth not so.

In place of idle jests and unkind speeches, the lips of the wise spread abroad what is for profit and blessing—the true knowledge that edifies the hearer. The foolish can only utter what is in his heart and benefits no one, but really harms. Paul and Elymas at Paphos fitly illustrate both sides (Acts 13:6–12).

⁸ The sacrifice of the lawless is an abomination to Jehovah:
But the prayer of the upright is His delight.
⁹ The way of the lawless is an abomination to Jehovah:
But He loveth him that followeth after righteousness.

"They that are in the flesh cannot please God." The sacrifice of the wicked, together with all their ways, is but evil in His sight. Before He can accept aught from the sinner, there must be repentance—a bowing of soul before Him—seeking His face in sincerity. When there is integrity and uprightness of heart He will manifest His favor, for He delights in those who follow righteousness.

It is of all importance that the sinner be brought to realize that, having gone out of the way, he has become altogether unprofitable. The Lord asks nothing from him, can accept nothing from him, until he first receives the gift offered him from heaven—the Lord Jesus Christ. When He has been received by faith the whole life will be changed, and loving service to God will be most acceptable and very precious in His sight. But it will be the fruit of the new life, not the labor of one toiling for that life.

It will be seen at once, in the light of the verses before us, how contrary to Scripture it is to ask unconverted men to give of their means to support the work of the Lord, or to make sacrifices for Christ's sake. All they can do or give will be stained with sin and unfit for His holy presence. See Psalm 66:18.

> [10] Correction is grievous unto him that forsaketh the way:
>   And he that hateth reproof shall die.
> [11] Sheol and destruction are before Jehovah:
>   How much more then the hearts of the sons of men?
> [12] A scorner loveth not one that reproveth him:
>   Neither will he go unto the wise.

"All things are naked and open before the eyes of Him with whom we have to do," and "He is a discerner of the thoughts and intents of the heart." The unseen world, which to man is dark and hidden, is all open before Him. He alone searches the hearts of men, and tries the reins. When they refuse correction His eye is observing their perversity, and He will see that they are judged according to their works. It is only the scorner who resents correction and reproof, and hence avoids the wise, lest his evil ways be called in question. But One he cannot avoid. With Him he must have to do whether he wants or not. Solemn indeed will be the accounting for opportunities refused, instruction neglected, and grace despised. See the wise and foolish builders of Matthew 7:24–27.

> [13] A glad heart maketh a cheerful countenance:
>   But by sorrow of heart the spirit is broken.

The happy man is the one who has a heart at rest, and who can therefore rejoice at all times. Such a one is the soul who has found in Christ not only a Savior, but a daily portion. He who casts all his cares upon Him, who has learned to commit all his affairs into His hand, will ever have a glad heart and a cheerful countenance. A burdened heart is the portion of the one who tries to carry his own sorrows and daily cares, and fails to turn all over to Him who so delights to bear them for us. Nothing breaks the spirit like hidden grief; but such need not be the portion of any saint who will allow the Lord Jesus to be not only his Sin-bearer, but his Burden-bearer too. See Paul in Philippians 4.

¹⁴ The heart of him that hath understanding seeketh
    knowledge:
But the mouth of fools feedeth on foolishness.

Our food has much to do with making us what we are. The same is true of us
morally. We become like that on which we feed; and we feed on what our hearts
crave. The man of understanding values knowledge and devotes himself to its
pursuit. The fool cares not for that which would build true character and draw
him from his evil ways, but feeds on folly and vanity, thus becoming all the time
more empty and foolish than before.

Let the young Christian ponder this well. Have you learned to know Christ?
Then leave behind forever the flesh-pots of Egypt. Do not attempt to feed the
new life on the world's trashy literature and its sinful pleasures. If you do, there
will be no real growth, and a moral and spiritual breakdown is sure to follow.
But if you set the Lord before you and find your food in His Word and what is
for edification, you shall grow in grace and in the knowledge of the truth. Imitate David (Ps. 119:103–104), Jeremiah (Jer. 15:16), and Job (Job 23:12). Do
not allow yourself to fall into the ways of the mixed multitude (Num. 11:4–9),
who lost their appetite for angels' food by lusting after Egyptian dainties.

¹⁵ All the days of the depressed are evil:
But he that is of a cheerful heart hath a continual feast.

This connects intimately with the thirteenth verse. One who is depressed and
gloomy himself sees every day full of causes for grief and dismal foreboding. It is
a wretched way to live and indicates lack of confidence in God. When the heart
is cheerful, all days are bright, and the soul has a continual feast. This is not
frivolity, but that holy joy which results from tracing everything that is permitted to come upon me back to God. Habakkuk entered into it in large measure
(Hab. 3:17–18).

¹⁶ Better is little with the fear of Jehovah,
    Than great treasure and trouble therewith.
¹⁷ Better is a dinner of herbs where love is,
    Than a stalled ox and hatred therewith.

The one who has found his joy in the Lord can well understand the dear old
saint who spread upon his humble board a bit of bread, an onion, and a glass of

water, and then joyfully thanked God for "all this and Jesus." Better, far better, is it to have little on earth, and to know Him and abide in His fear, than to have great treasures and varied luxuries, coupled with trouble and hatred. So thought Daniel and his companions when they refused to defile themselves with the king's meat (Dan. 1).

> [18] A wrathful man stirreth up contention,
> But he that is slow to anger appeaseth strife.

Of this the first verse of our chapter has already reminded us; but we may well have it brought before us again, for we take so long to learn. A wrathful man is of necessity a proud man; otherwise he would not be so easily stirred by what touches himself. A lowly man will be slow to anger, for he has learned not to think of himself more highly than he ought to think, and therefore will not readily resent insults and offenses. Contrast the spirit displayed by Saul and David (1 Sam. 20:30–34; 24:8–22).

> [19] The way of the sluggard is as a hedge of thorns:
> But the path of the upright shall be made plain.

Difficulties abound in the mind of the slothful man. His way seems hedged up by thorns, and he has all manner of excuses for not acting at once according to what he knows is right and suited. The upright, learning his duty, presses on and finds his way made plain before him as he takes one step after another.

If God commands, I have simply to obey. He makes Himself responsible to clear the obstacles from my path, or to give me the ability to overcome them. Hear David's notes of triumph in Psalm 18:29 and 2 Samuel 22:30. How unhappy the contrast in the case of the ten spies (Num. 13.)

> [20] A wise son maketh a glad father:
> But a foolish man despiseth his mother.

Compare with 10:1. A wise son gladdens the heart of his father by heeding instruction and practicing virtue. A foolish man considers himself superior to his mother and ignores her loving advice and helpful counsel. See chapters 17 and 30.

> [21] Folly is joy to him that is destitute of heart:
> But a man of understanding walketh uprightly.

Delighting in iniquity, determined to have his own way despite every warning and entreaty, the fool plunges on, rejoicing in his folly. The man of integrity, subjecting himself to the fear of God, walks in uprightness, refusing to be decoyed by sinful pleasures and fascinations. See notes on verses 16 and 18 in the previous chapter.

> [22] Without counsel purposes are disappointed:
>   But in the multitude of counsellors they shall be
>   established.

See the note on 11:14 and compare 24:6.

He is a wise man indeed who cannot well afford to counsel with men of intelligence and experience concerning matters of moment, particularly where others are likely to be widely concerned. See Paul and Barnabas in Acts 15.

> [23] A man hath joy by the answer of his mouth:
>   And a word spoken in season, how good is it!

The answer that leaves no regrets will be a word spoken in its season. True words are not necessarily seasonable ones. Many a sorrow and heartache has been caused, both to the speaker and others, by repeating what in itself was true enough, but which should never have been passed on to a third party. But a word in season is precious and helpful, refreshing to the hearer and giving joy to the one who utters it. After the idle speculations of the three friends of Job, how seasonable was the answer of Elihu!

> [24] The way of life is above to the understanding,
>   That he may depart from sheol beneath.

Sheol is the world of spirits—the unseen. It refers not to the place of future punishment only, but to what was, even to the children of God before the Cross, a land of darkness beyond the grave. And, inasmuch as long life was a blessing promised to the faithful Hebrew, an early cutting off from this present life was a calamity to be dreaded. Hence the way of life could be said to lead away from sheol beneath. Those who trod it would be preserved to an honored old age in the land given by God to His earthly people. Hezekiah's case aptly illustrates the state of mind that was common among truly pious persons in the past dispensation in regard to death. See Isaiah 38 and 2 Kings 20.

²⁵ Jehovah will destroy the house of the proud:
But He will establish the landmark of the widow.

"Though the LORD be high, yet hath He respect unto the lowly: but the proud He knoweth afar off" (Ps. 138:6). His face is ever set against those who exalt themselves; but from of old He has been the support of the fatherless and the widow who confided in His love and care. He would have His needy people trust His grace more implicitly, assured that His heart is ever toward them. But the haughty and self-inflated have no title to His consideration and loving-kindness. Their house shall fall, and their pride be withered up. Contrast the judgment on Coniah's house (Jer. 22:30) with the Lord's care of the widow of Zarephath (1 Kings 17:10–16).

²⁶ The thoughts of the evil are an abomination to Jehovah:
But the words of the pure are pleasant sayings.

Already we have considered the Lord's estimate of the sacrifice and way of the lawless. We now learn that the very thoughts of the evildoer are also an abomination to Him "who is of purer eyes than to behold iniquity." But the conversation of the pure is pleasant in His sight, as being the outflow of a heart exercised unto godliness. We see both classes in John 6:68–71.

²⁷ He that is greedy of gain troubleth his own house:
But he that hateth gifts shall live.

Bribe-taking has been a snare to which those whose place it is to sit on the judicial bench, and those called as witnesses have always been exposed. Greed and covetousness have proven the undoing of many such, to the ruin of themselves and the shame of all who bear their name. The hater of gifts—that is, the one who resolutely refuses to be bought (for in such a case the "gift" is really his price)—shall live.

The soldiers who guarded the tomb of our Lord were silenced by bribes, to their eternal dishonor (Matt. 28:11–15). Samuel could challenge Israel to testify to his integrity on this very line (1 Sam. 12:3–4). See 29:4.

²⁸ The heart of the righteous studieth to answer:
But the mouth of the lawless poureth out evil things.

The man who walks in the fear of God will weigh his words, lest by a hasty utterance he dishonor his Lord and hinder where he desires to help. The wicked has no such consideration, and speaks whatever comes to his lips, let it do what harm it may. People often actually pride themselves on being, as they suppose, frank and outspoken, when in reality they are simply manifesting the unexercised state of their consciences: for, if truly aroused to the value of words, they would weigh them well before giving them out, and thus save much mischief and sorrow. Because a thing is true, it is not necessarily a fit subject to be discussed, and passed on from one to another. The righteous will consider carefully its bearing for good or ill before uttering what can never be fully recalled. Contrast Elisha with the sons of the prophets at Jericho (2 Kings 2:15–18).

> ²⁹ Jehovah is far from the lawless:
> But He heareth the prayer of the righteous.

The lawless have no title to expect anything from Jehovah; He makes no pledge to heed their cry. When the day of their distress comes they find none on whom to call. Of old, when idolatrous Israel turned to Him in their troubles, He refused to be entreated of them and referred them to the gods they had served, in order that they might realize what it meant to have turned the back upon Him.

But He has pledged Himself to hear the prayer of the righteous, and with Him, to hear is to answer. The man who delights himself in God when all is bright will find Him a Friend nigh at hand when darkness enshrouds the soul. But let him not forget that it is written, "If ye abide in Me, and My words abide in you, ye shall ask what ye will, and it shall be done unto you" (John 15:7). See Joshua at Gibeon (Josh. 10:12–14).

> ³⁰ The light of the eyes rejoiceth the heart:
> And a good report maketh the bones fat.

The gospel of the glory of the blessed God is such a "good report." "Faith cometh by hearing [by a report], and hearing [or, the report] by the word of God" (Rom. 10:17). Precious as light to the eye when one has been groping in darkness is this grand report to a soul that has been longing for deliverance from a burdened conscience.

The good report sent from heaven to men in their sins is concerning God's Son, Jesus Christ, "who was delivered for our offenses, and raised again for our justification." It is a Person who is presented to man in the gospel. When He is trusted and His work apprehended, it does indeed rejoice the heart, "making the bones fat." See the jailer of Philippi (Acts 16:29–34).

> ³¹ The ear that heareth the reproof of life
>   Abideth among the wise.
> ³² He that refuseth admonition despiseth his own soul:
>   But he that heareth reproof getteth understanding.
> ³³ The fear of Jehovah is the admonition of wisdom;
>   And before honor is humility.

See note on verse 10. He who is humble enough to be thankful for correction when going astray shall remain among those whom Jehovah esteems as wise.

The instructed of earth are often too proud to receive an admonition. Fancying themselves superior to him who would, in the fear of God, reprove them when in error, they disdainfully turn away; but in so doing show that they despise their own souls.

It is only those who hear reproof who get understanding. Abiding in the fear of the Lord they own it is the part of wisdom to acknowledge their mistakes and faults, and so to receive admonition as coming from Himself, for "before honor is humility." He who takes the lowly self-forgetful place will be lifted up in due time. See Joseph's remarkable history (Gen. 37–50).

CHAPTER 16

PROVERBS 16

The human proverb, "Man proposes, but God disposes," finds its far earlier counterpart in the first verse.

> ¹ The purposes of the heart are of man:
> But from Jehovah is the answer of the tongue.

"It is not in man that liveth to direct his way." He may plan and arrange, but when the time arrives to speak or act it is from Jehovah the answer comes. See Balaam (Num. 23–24).

> ² All the ways of a man are clean in his own eyes:
> But Jehovah weigheth the spirits.

Ever since the Fall it has been second nature with man to justify himself. Until brought into the light of God's holiness there is nothing of which he is generally so certain as the defensibleness of his own conduct. His ways are clean in his own eyes, but he is not to be trusted in his own judgment, for the heart is deceitful above all things and desperately wicked. Jehovah weighs the spirits. His balances are exact. His judgment is unerring; and He it is who solemnly declares, "Thou art weighed in the balances, and art found wanting!"

Thus man is shut up to the salvation provided through the finished work of the Son of God on Calvary's cross. Otherwise condemnation alone can be his portion. See Belshazzar (Dan. 5:25–30).

> ³ Commit thy works unto Jehovah,
> And thy thoughts shall be established.

The word *commit* might be rendered "roll." He who rolls his affairs over upon the Lord, will find Him ever ready to take charge of them all, and to carry them on to a proper completion and establishment. But it must be borne in mind that if I thus commit all to Him, I no longer choose for myself as to what the outcome should be, but say with confidence, "Thy will be done." He would have every desire told out in His ear, and then left in faith that He may act according to His love and unerring wisdom. See Hannah (1 Sam. 1:9–20).

> ⁴ Jehovah hath made all things for himself:
> Yea, even the lawless for the day of evil.
> ⁵ Every one that is proud in heart is an abomination to
> Jehovah:
> Though hand join in hand, he shall not be acquitted.

All things shall resound at last to the glory of God. Earth's long tale of sin and sorrow will only result in magnifying His love and His holiness eventually. Those saved by His grace will be to His praise forever; but the wicked will also own His justice in the day of their condemnation. He detests pride; and all who walk therein (let them endeavor by confederation to resist His power as they may) shall be broken before Him and brought in guilty when He sits on the throne of judgment. How much better now to bow in repentance, while He is on a throne of grace! See His word as to Sodom and Gomorrah (2 Peter 2:6; Jude 7).

> ⁶ By loving-kindness and truth iniquity is purged;
> And by the fear of Jehovah men depart from evil.

Atonement is made for iniquity by loving-kindness and truth—so far as putting things right with man is concerned. It is not a question here of expiating sin before God. No amount of kindly deeds and truthful words can purge the conscience of guilt and give acceptance with Him. But if man has been sinned against, the manifestation of repentance leading to putting right what was wrong as far as possible, and consideration and thoughtful care in the future, will go far toward clearing his mind of the past evil. It is the fear of Jehovah that leads to departure from what is unholy and contrary to sound doctrine. So when one is in the fear of God he will endeavor to have a conscience void of offense both toward Him and toward his fellow men. See the apostle Paul (Acts 24:16).

> ⁷ When a man's ways please Jehovah,
> He maketh even his enemies to be at peace with him.

This is a far-reaching statement, which is much less pondered over than it should be. It allows of no exceptions. If a man's ways are pleasing to the Lord, his enemies will be unable to say one word against his character. They may hate him, but they are compelled to own that God is with him.

If therefore my enemies are not at peace with me, is it not time I was asking myself, "Do my ways really please Him?" Doubtless I shall soon be reminded of something needing to be judged in His presence.

One thing that is very conducive to closing the mouths of enemies is just going on quietly "through evil report and good report," bent on pleasing One alone, wasting no time in self-vindication, but committing all to Him who judges righteously. A holy, humble walk must silence even my worst foes. See Daniel (Dan. 6:4–5).

> ⁸ Better is a little with righteousness
> Than great revenues without right.

Integrity of heart is better than thousands in silver and gold. How poor and mean is the man who piles up his millions, but sacrifices his conscience to do it! A bare living, with the mind and heart at rest and a walk in accordance with righteous principles, is infinitely to be preferred to a large income coupled with covetousness and unholy practices. See Naboth and Ahab (1 Kings 21).

> ⁹ A man's heart deviseth his way:
> But Jehovah directeth his steps.

Compare with verse 1. See note. People frequently think they are having their own way, when in reality the Lord is leading them with "bit and bridle" through strange paths for their discipline and blessing at last. See Naomi (Ruth 1:21).

¹⁰ A sure decision is in the lips of the king:
   His mouth transgresseth not in judgment.
¹¹ A just weight and balance are Jehovah's:
   All the weights of the bag are His work.
¹² It is an abomination to kings to commit lawlessness:
   For the throne is established by righteousness.
¹³ Righteous lips are the delight of kings;
   And they love him that speaketh right.
¹⁴ The wrath of a king is as messengers of death;
   But a wise man will pacify it.
¹⁵ In the light of the king's countenance is life;
   And his favor is as a cloud of the latter rain.

It is the ideal king that is contemplated. Occasionally have earthly monarchs been raised up who hated iniquity and loved righteousness, but this world still groans for the coming and reign of the true King, who shall judge the nations with equity, and in whose mouth the vile person shall be contemned.

It is God's Anointed alone whose throne will be established by righteousness, and to whom lawlessness of every kind is an abomination. In His lips is there a sure decision, for His mouth transgresses not in judgment.

For all human rulers He is the grand pattern. In the measure that they are imitators of Him do they properly maintain the kingly glory.

Whatever is right and true among men is from God. All baseness and dishonest trickery is detestable in His eyes. So we have the weights and balances introduced in the midst of this section, relating to kingly dignity. For it is the same integrity that directs the decision of the upright king and the measures of the poorest of his subjects.

The king delights in lips of truth and loves sound speech. His anger is as a death sentence, but wisdom will pacify it. In his favor is life and refreshing. If of the light of a man's countenance this can be said, how much more of the King of kings! "In Thy presence is fullness of joy." See David (2 Sam. 3:36).

¹⁶ How much better is it to get wisdom than gold!
   And to get understanding rather to be chosen than silver!
¹⁷ The highway of the upright is to depart from evil:
   He that keepeth his way preserveth his soul.

Compare 2:1–9, and see notes.

The man of wisdom and understanding has his fortune made for both worlds. But it is easy to be deceived by a counterfeit wisdom which descends not from above, being earthly, sensual, devilish. That which does not begin with the fear of the Lord and keep from the highway of iniquity, is but Satan's counterfeit, let it be vaunted as it may by wiseacres who know not to depart from evil. See Daniel (Dan. 5:11).

> [18] Pride goeth before destruction,
>   And a haughty spirit before a fall.
> [19] Better is it to be of a humble spirit with the lowly,
>   Than to divide the spoil with the proud.

Pride was an archangel's ruin, as it has been the destruction of untold myriads of men and women on earth. It is the sure precursor of a fall, for the High and Lofty One who inhabits eternity cannot permit self-exaltation on the part of a creature to go unchecked.

Far better is it to be little in one's own eyes and to find happy fellowship with the lowly, than to share the pursuits and treasures of the proud in spirit.

It is when one sees pride in another that its hideousness is clearly revealed. How often we will complacently tolerate in ourselves what, when we behold it in someone else, fills us with disgust. But God takes note of the least beginning of unjudged haughtiness in each heart. What mind can conceive how hateful it must all be to Him! May writer and reader look to it that this baneful sin be checked in His presence, before it master us to our lasting sorrow! See Haman (Esther 5–7).

> [20] He that handleth a matter wisely shall find good:
>   And whoso trusteth in Jehovah, happy is he.
> [21] The wise in heart shall be called prudent:
>   And the sweetness of the lips increaseth learning.
> [22] Understanding is a well-spring of life to him that hath it:
>   But the instruction of fools is folly.
> [23] The heart of the wise maketh wise his mouth,
>   And addeth learning to his lips.
> [24] Pleasant words are as a honeycomb,
>   Sweet to the soul, and healing to the bones.

The five verses form a series of epigrams on the value of applied wisdom in the various affairs of life. To proceed wisely in a case presenting difficulties not readily overcome is an earnest of coming good. Only those do so, in the full sense, who confide in Jehovah and find their happiness in His fear.

When wisdom possesses the reins the behavior will be discreet, and kindly lips will manifest a lowly heart and willingness to be instructed. This is true understanding; which, like a spring of living water, dwells in the possessor of it, and flows forth to bless others. Of fools the opposite is true. Their folly is manifested to any person of discernment.

It is the condition of the heart that is of prime importance. If all be right there, the words of the lips will accord therewith; so that in place of the speculative vaporings of the worldly pedant there will be the counsel of the wise, who knows how to give forth what is profitable as well as pleasant and cheering. Note the characteristics of the wisdom that is from above in James 3:17, and see the confession of the queen of Sheba (1 Kings 10:6–9).

> ²⁵ There is a way that seemeth right unto a man,
> But the end thereof are the ways of death.

This verse repeats the statement of 14:12, as though to emphasize the danger of refusing the path of wisdom for self-chosen ways which can only end in death. See the note on that verse.

> ²⁶ The soul of him that laboreth, laboreth for himself;
> For his mouth urgeth him on.

It is because of his desire to be satisfied with the fruits of his toil that the laborer pursues his occupation. His appetite craves it of him, and so he presses on in his service. This is as God ordained when the Fall had shut man out of the garden of delight, and in the sweat of his face he was commanded to eat his bread. Wealth gotten without labor is generally a very dangerous acquisition. He who knows the weariness of honest toil will be careful how he uses that which results therefrom. Ponder the cases of Ruth (Ruth 2) and of Gideon (Judg. 6:11–12).

> ²⁷ An ungodly man [or, a man of Belial] diggeth up evil:
> And in his lips there is as a burning fire.
> ²⁸ A froward man soweth strife:
> And a whisperer separateth chief friends.

See notes on 11:13 and 17:9. It would be well if every one addicted to the sinfully cruel habit of talebearing would ponder carefully these words. It is an ungodly man who digs up evil, whose lips seem to be set on fire of hell. Such a one will go about scattering the seeds of strife as one might sow thistledown or the pods of other noxious weeds, to result in a harvest of grief and anguish to many a soul.

There is no question that whispering and backbiting is one of the greatest curses among Christians. By means of this detestable vice the dearest friends are alienated, misunderstandings of all kinds are created, and many are defiled by the recital of tales which a godly person would seek to cover and forbear ever to repeat. See what mischief was brought about by the talebearing of Doeg the Edomite, and see that you follow not in the steps of so unsavory a wretch (1 Sam. 22:9–19).

> [29] A violent man enticeth his neighbor,
> And leadeth him into the way that is not good.
> [30] He shutteth his eyes to devise froward things:
> Moving his lips he bringeth evil to pass.

Many an otherwise kindly and gracious soul has been misled by the energy and apparent earnestness of a violent man, and led one to join him in things that were quite opposed to his own more mature judgment, had he not allowed his eyes to be blinded. But the other's fair speech, coupled with what men call a magnetic presence, have often won the day, and led one, who would never have gone if left to himself, into a way that was not good. It is well not to be too easily persuaded. Before making a decision, take time to get the mind of God, that thus you be not partaker of other men's sins. Neglect of this led Jehoshaphat, a most amiable man, into many a snare (2 Chron. 18:1; 20:35–37).

> [31] The hoary head is a crown of glory,
> [If] it be found in the way of righteousness.

Probably the last line should read simply, "It shall be found in the way of righteousness." The verse does not say the hoary head will never be found in the paths of wickedness; for, alas, often white hairs crown the sinner's head. But it is *characteristic* of the way of righteousness; and when found there, it is indeed a diadem of honor. Riotous living in youth generally means decrepitude in middle age, and premature death. Temperance and righteousness tend to strength of body and length of days. Hear the testimony of Caleb, who wholly followed the Lord (Josh. 14:11); and note what is written of Moses (Deut. 34:7).

> ³² He that is slow to anger is better than the mighty;
>   And he that ruleth his spirit than he that taketh a city.

Self-mastery is the greatest of all victories. Men have subdued kingdoms who were defeated in the effort to control themselves. A bad temper is often excused on the ground of natural infirmity, but it is rather the evidence of unjudged pride and impatience. "Learn of Me," said Jesus, "for I am meek and lowly in heart." The meek man is not a spiritless man, but he is slow to anger. He can be righteously stirred when occasion requires, but not when it is his own dignity that is in question. "Add to patience *self* control" is a word for us all. It is generally a sign of weakness when one allows himself to become angry and excited in the face of opposition. Note the calmness of spirit and dependence on God manifested by Nehemiah, throughout the book that bears his name, when meeting the irritating sneers and downright opposition of the enemies of Jerusalem.

> ³³ The lot is cast into the lap;
>   But the whole disposing thereof is of Jehovah.

There is no such thing as chance, though it seems so to the man who looks only "under the sun" (Eccl. 9:11). But a supreme Intelligence is over all things, controlling even when unseen and unrecognized.

Casting lots was a method frequently resorted to among the ancients for determining vexed questions. By this means Canaan was divided among the tribes, and it was used on many occasions to detect guilty persons. The last mention of its use in Scripture is in connection with the election of Matthias to the vacant apostleship of Judas. It would seem that, as of old, God gave judgment, and so the company of the Twelve was kept complete. Paul evidently was never numbered with them. He was the messenger of the glory of Christ to the nations, while the Twelve were connected primarily with the Jewish testimony.

For instances of God's giving judgment by the lot, see the cases of the two goats of Leviticus 16:8; the land (Num. 26:55; Josh. 18:10); Achan (Josh. 7:16–18); Jonathan (1 Sam. 14:41); and Matthias (Acts 1:26). In the book of Esther we find the lot (called Pur) used by Haman to determine a fortunate day for the destruction of the Jews.

CHAPTER 17

PROVERBS 17

We are carried back to verses 16–17 of chapter 15, as we take up the first of the wise sayings in the present section:

> ¹ Better is a dry morsel, and quietness therewith,
> Than a house full of sacrifices with strife.

It will be remembered that portions of the peace offerings were eaten by the offerer and his friends. These are the sacrifices referred to. Such a feast would be supposed to indicate great piety on the part of the host and his intimate associates; but if marred by discord and contention, it lost all its precious character. A dry morsel with peace and quietness was much to be preferred to such an unbecoming celebration.

In some such manner had the Corinthians misused the Lord's Supper, making it an occasion for a common feast, where strife and party spirit raged. The apostle, rebuking them, bids them eat their own meals in quietness at home, that they come not together to condemnation (1 Cor. 11:17–22).

> ² A wise servant shall have rule over a son that causeth shame,
> And shall have part of the inheritance among the brethren.

A dependable servant is better than a misbehaving son. The latter can only rightly blame himself if his wronged father give him but an insignificant allowance, or cut him off altogether; while the servant who has been faithful in the performance of his duties is remembered as one of the household. But after all no hired servant can give the joy to the heart of a father that is afforded by an obedient son. See Eliezer (Gen. 15:2–3).

> ³ The fining pot is for silver,
> And the furnace for gold:
> But Jehovah trieth the hearts.

Trials and afflictions are, for the saints of God, what the fining pot and furnace are in the purifying of precious metals. "Wherein ye greatly rejoice, though now for a season, if need be, ye are in heaviness through manifold temptations: that the trial of your faith, being much more precious than of gold that perisheth, though it be tried with fire, might be found unto praise and honor and glory at the appearing of Jesus Christ" (1 Peter 1:6–7).

The refiner of silver and the purifier of gold know just what heat is necessary to purge away all dross and will take care that just the right amount be permitted. So with our God and Father. He desires to free us from the base things of earth, and He allows us to pass through the fires of affliction for that end. But it is precious indeed to know that He sits by the fining pot, waiting until His own image be reflected in the soul; and He walks in the furnace with His persecuted children. See the sons of Levi and the three Hebrew children (Mal. 3:3; Dan. 3:19–26).

> ⁴ A wicked doer giveth heed to false lips;
> And a liar giveth ear to a naughty tongue.

When the heart hides iniquity, the ear readily gives heed to lying lips and an evil tongue. The upright in heart learn to know the voice of the deceiver and to refuse his words; but the unjust and false soul readily falls in with those who are like himself. See the people of Judah and the lying priests and prophets (Jer. 5:30–31).

> ⁵ Whoso mocketh the poor reproacheth his Maker:
> And he that is glad at calamities shall not be held innocent.

Compare with 14:21. The Lord has left the poor always with us that we might be stirred thereby to kindness and consideration for those in less agreeable circumstances than our own. To mock and lightly esteem them because of their poverty is to reproach Him who has permitted our circumstances to be so diverse.

When calamity comes upon another, if, in place of loving sympathy, we cherish gladness in our hearts because of their griefs, an impartial Judge is looking on who will see that we are visited in our turn. God's complaint as to Edom was his rejoicing over Israel's punishment. As a result, he too was to be dealt with in judgment. See Obadiah 12–16.

> ⁶ Children's children are the crown of old men;
> And the glory of children are their fathers.

God sets the solitary in families. The aged find their youth renewed in their children's children, while the young revere their fathers and honor them by obedience to their instructions. This is the ideal household, where government is administered according to God, and love rules all hearts. Happy the home where the divine pattern is exemplified. See Jacob and the sons of Joseph (Gen. 48:8–22).

> ⁷ Excellent speech becometh not a fool:
> Much less do lying lips a noble.

Good words from the mouth of an evil man are distasteful and out of place, for the life fails to back them up. There is a sense of dissimulation about them that is very repugnant to an upright soul. On the other hand, *noblesse oblige* (rank imposes obligation). Falsehood coming from one who is looked up to as a leader of the people is even more to be decried. Men feel instinctively that he who leads others should be real himself. They will overlook lack of ability, an absence of brilliancy, or of natural or acquired talent; but unreality they will never forgive. It was this sense of the fitness of things that made men ask in derision, "Is Saul also among the prophets?" when his lips uttered "excellent things" (1 Sam. 10:10–12). The same feeling has caused the unconverted to remember with scorn Abraham's denial of his wife. The very fact of his exalted position causes his sin to be the more marked (Gen. 20:1–13).

> ⁸ A gift is a stone of grace in the eyes of him that hath it:
> Whithersoever it turneth, it prospereth.

A gift presented as a token of pure affection and esteem will be highly valued by its possessor and will pave the way for much that is of value. He who would find love should be a giver—not a mere receiver. But see verse 23. Jonathan's gifts to David cemented their friendship by expressing the love that was in his heart (1 Sam. 18:3–4).

Spiritually, we are reminded that Christ has ascended on high and given gifts unto men—not to be used for self-aggrandizement, but to be of service to the church. Rightly employed, however, the gift truly will be a store of grace, giving acceptance to him who has it, among those who value what is of God.

> ⁹ He that covereth a transgression seeketh love;
> But he that repeateth a matter separateth friends.

See remarks on 10:12; 11:13; and 25:23. He who covers transgression is an imitator of God and will be loved by all. He who repeats a matter to the detriment of another, takes for his pattern that evil spirit who is called "the accuser of our brethren."

To cover a transgression, however, does not mean to make light of sin and allow iniquity to go unrebuked in another. It is, on the contrary, to go to the erring one personally in tenderness and brotherly kindness; to seek to exercise his conscience as to that in his course which is bringing dishonor upon his Lord. If such a mission is successful, the sin should never again be mentioned. It is covered, and none other need know of it.

Alas that this is so seldom carried out among us! Evil is spread abroad; backbiting goes on in secret; and thus many are defiled, love wanes, and fellowship is destroyed.

The one who goes about repeating things for which there is no real necessity, is in a wretched business indeed. He separates true friends by his detestable practices and casts reproach upon the name of the Lord. It is a pity the people of God are not more awake to the evil character of the talebearer. He should be shunned as a polluted leper who will defile all who listen to him.

God alone can safely hear the sad story of a brother's shame. Into His ear it can all be poured, coupled with earnest prayer for the restoration of the one who has gone astray. To persist in retailing accounts of evildoing to fellow saints is but to distress and injure those who are persuaded to listen. Few indeed are the men who can eat the sin offering in the holy place, and who, hearing of a brother's wrongdoing, will take it to heart, and make it an occasion for self-judgment and confession on their own part to the Lord.

Someone has said that if tempted to relate unsavory things of an absent person, it is well to ask mentally three questions: Is it true? Is it kind? Is it necessary? To these a fourth might well be added: Have I told him about it personally? We fancy the effect of this would be to shut off an immense amount of sinful gossiping.

Nathan was one who could reprove in the fear of God, and cover when repentance was manifest (2 Sam. 12). In Sanballat we see the typical whisperer endeavoring to separate Nehemiah and his brethren by shaking their confidence in his integrity (Neh. 6).

> [10] A reproof entereth more into a wise man
> Than a hundred stripes into a fool.

Chastise the fool severely, and he maintains his self-complacency still; but gently reprove a wise man, and he will take it to heart. The one is so thoroughly enamored of his own poor judgment that he can conceive of none more capable than himself. The other realizes his own limitations, in measure at least, and is thankful for advice and correction. Contrast Abimelech and Herod (Gen. 21:25–26; Luke 3:19).

> [11] An evil man seeketh only rebellion:
> Therefore a cruel messenger shall be sent against him.
> [12] Let a bear robbed of her whelps meet a man,
> Rather than a fool in his folly.
> [13] Whoso rewardeth evil for good,
> Evil shall not depart from his house.

Nothing galls a haughty, insubject man more than to be held in restraint by lawful authority. He breathes the air of treason and rebellion; therefore he must be dealt with in severity. To contend with him is like battling with an enraged beast that has been robbed of its offspring. He will repay good with evil; therefore evil shall not depart from his house. "He that doeth wrong shall receive for the wrong which he hath done: and there is no respect of persons."

Note the ways and doom of Joab when he became lifted up in his own eyes (1 Kings 2:28–34).

> [14] The beginning of strife is as when one letteth out water:
> Therefore leave off contention before it becometh
> vehement.

A leak in a dike that could be stopped with a pebble, if noticed at the beginning, will, if neglected, grow greater and greater until, at last, the inrushing waters will carry all before them. So it is with strife. How many a lifelong contention has begun with a few hasty words, which, if repented of and apologized for at once, would have been healed immediately, and years of sorrow averted. The Spirit of God has said, "Be ye angry, and sin not: let not the sun go down upon your wrath" (Eph. 4:26). If this simple rule were literally obeyed, what untold heartaches would be avoided! Happy the man who lays his head upon his pillow nightly with the knowledge that there are no hasty actions or angry words unrepented of and unconfessed to any who have been offended, and who might have been alienated forever if the breach had not been made up at once in the fear of God. When days and weeks of charges and countercharges are succeeded by months of crimination and recrimination, reconciliation is a hard and difficult matter to bring about. Far better is it to humble oneself and take wrong, if need be, at the beginning, than to grieve the Holy Spirit of God and lacerate the hearts of beloved saints by a long period of un-Christlike wrangling which will leave wounds that never can be healed; or, if healed, scars that never can be effaced. See Paul and Barnabas (Acts 15:35–40).

> [15] He that justifieth the lawless,
>   And he that condemneth the just,
>   Even they both are abomination to Jehovah.

To justify the wicked and to condemn the righteous is to call evil good, and good evil (Isa. 5:20). Jehovah would have judgment according to truth. What is opposed to this is an abomination. Observe that to justify necessarily means to clear, or to declare righteous; not, as some theologians would have it, to *make* righteous. God justifies the ungodly on the basis of Christ's finished work; that is, He clears guilty sinners of every charge when they trust His Son, turning to Him in repentance. Making such to be practically upright in their lives is a different thing. It results from justification, but it is not that in itself. This is a distinction of vast importance if we would understand aright the Christian doctrines of grace as set forth in the letters to the Romans and the Galatians.

Here, to justify the lawless is to wink at sin and to pass by iniquity without a suited atonement; while to condemn the just is to impute evil where it is not found. To so do is intolerable in the sight of Him who is the righteous Judge. This was Pilate's dreadful sin, when, in order to please the people, he released

Barabbas and condemned Jesus, albeit declaring His innocence a few moments before (Matt. 27:24–26).

> ¹⁶ Wherefore is there a price in the hand of a fool to get
>   wisdom,
>   Seeing he hath no sense [lit., heart]?

It is useless for one who does not set his heart upon the acquisition of wisdom to endeavor to learn it by rote. No price can purchase it, if the senses be not exercised to discern between good and evil. A fool may grasp certain forms of knowledge, by dint of study and intellectual application; but this is a very different thing from having the reins of the being possessed by understanding. We only know truth as we walk in it. See Simon Magus (Acts 8:18–19).

> ¹⁷ A friend loveth at all times,
>   And a brother is born for adversity.

Involuntarily the Christian's heart turns from any human example, however true and devoted, and calls up one Friend whose love the many waters of judgment could not quench, neither could the floods of wrath drown it. Our Lord Jesus Christ is that Friend, whose love changes not, and who is preeminently a Brother born for adversity.

In thus writing of Him, one would not for a moment countenance the mawkish sentimentality which so forgets the dignity of His person as to call Him our "Elder Brother," and apply to Him similar unscriptural titles. But as a devoted brother can be depended on in the day of adversity, so can He be ever counted upon in the hour of need and trial. "Having loved His own which were in the world, He loved them unto the end" (John 13:1).

> His is an unchanging love,
> Higher than the heights above;
> Deeper than the depths beneath,
> True and faithful, strong as death.

It is unspeakably precious for the soul to abide in His love. If one doubt come in to obscure the full splendor of His undying affection, joy and peace will give place to gloom and foreboding. But when nothing is permitted to hinder the enjoyment of that perfect love that casts out fear, life is sweet indeed, and communion with Him dearer far than any human friendship can afford.

There is no question but that many saints have trusted Him as their Savior, who do not really know Him as a living, loving Friend—One who enters into all their griefs and would share all their joys. It is when He is known in this character that the difficulties of the pilgrim path can be faced with equanimity, and the heart can confide in Him in every hour of trial. See 18:24.

> [18] A man bereft of heart striketh hands,
>   And becometh surety for his friend.

See notes on 6:1–5; 11:15. It is the lack of sound judgment that leads one to go surety for another in the light of the repeated warnings of the Word of God; unless, indeed, he is quite prepared to lose, and can well afford it. "Heart" is used throughout this portion of the Scriptures very much as, in everyday language, we speak of common sense. It must be so understood here. (See v. 16 above.) Paul went surety for Onesimus, as Judah did for Benjamin; but each had counted the cost and was ready to pay the uttermost farthing (Philem. 18–19; Gen. 42:37; 44:32).

> [19] He loveth transgression that loveth a quarrel:
>   And he that exalteth his entrance seeketh destruction.
> [20] He that hath a froward heart findeth no good:
>   And he that hath a perverse tongue falleth into mischief.

There are those who delight in contention, and who thereby manifest their love for their own ways, being impatient of restraint. In their haughtiness, they make high their gates, thus inviting destruction; for, exalting themselves, they are near to a fall. Having a froward heart, they find only evil, their perverse tongues continually stirring up mischief. Hanun, proud and defiant, had to prove this to the full, as narrated in 2 Samuel 10.

> [21] He that begetteth a fool doeth it to his sorrow:
>   And the father of a fool hath no joy.

Such a verse requires no comment. It is an unhappy fact; so patent, that all may realize it. David's grief over Absalom is proof of its truthfulness (2 Sam. 18:33). See also verse 25.

²² A merry heart doeth good like a medicine:
But a broken spirit drieth the bones.

See 15:13, 15. Nothing breaks the system like gloom and melancholy. When the heart is filled with joy, the whole being is refreshed thereby. The merriment of the Christian is far more real than the mere frivolity of the worldling. He is able in all circumstances to rejoice in the Lord, and thus be lifted above what would depress and weigh down the soul. Then, in place of manifesting his happiness in the empty ways of the world, he can sing and make melody in his heart unto the source and object of his gladness. "Is any merry? Let him sing psalms" (James 5:13). The man of the world has to resort to various expedients to relieve his uneasiness and rouse his spirits. Hence his eager participation in all kinds of diversions, the object of which is to enable him, for the time being, to *forget*. On the contrary, it is when the child of God *remembers* his place and portion in Christ that his joy overflows. Contrast the different states of the unknown writer of Psalm 116 when occupied with himself, and when faith soared up to God.

²³ A lawless man taketh a bribe out of the bosom,
To pervert the ways of judgment.

Secretly the lawbreaker, conscious of his evildoing, would endeavor, by a gift, to bribe those who are called to sit in judgment on his crimes. Such a course is a tacit acknowledgment of guilt. It is hard indeed to deal faithfully with a man to whom one is indebted for a favor. Therefore the need of sternly refusing ought from those who are bent upon a sinful course. It was when the king of Babylon sent letters and a *present* to Hezekiah that even so godly a king as he was taken off his guard, and acted without seeking counsel of Jehovah, as he had so readily done when it was a letter of blasphemy he had received (Isa. 39:1; contrast 37:14).

²⁴ Wisdom is before him that hath understanding:
But the eyes of a fool are in the ends of the earth.

Concentration of mind upon the one great object of gaining the knowledge of the Lord and walking with Him—this is the wisdom that absorbs the man of understanding. The fool, with no settled purpose, wanders aimlessly here and there, tasting of various theories, getting a smattering of everything, but all to no purpose. Of such are those against whom Paul warned Timothy, men who "heap to themselves teachers, having itching ears," but who, after all, have no heart for the truth of God (which alone is wisdom), so are turned unto fables, "ever learning, and never able to come to the knowledge of the truth." The very opposite was that which characterized the great apostle himself, who could say, "One thing I do!" (See Phil. 3:13.)

> ²⁵ A foolish son is a grief to his father,
>   And bitterness to her that bare him.

See 10:1, and notice verse 21, above. The young man is not the only, nor by any means the greatest, sufferer when he throws discretion to the winds and plunges into folly and vice.

The poignant grief of his father's heart and the bitter disappointment of his mother are sorrows too deep for words to express. To have brought into the world one who despises their love, and overleaps all restraint, is terrible indeed. Alas, that it so little affects the haughty, stubborn heart of the wayward youth who plunges recklessly on, adding grief to grief, and woe to woe! See the stubborn and rebellious son of Deuteronomy 21:18–20.

> ²⁶ Also to punish the just is not good,
>   Nor to strike nobles because of uprightness.

The perversion of justice on the part of the prince who punishes the good man, or on the part of the subject who strikes the noble because of his uprightness, are alike evil. Neither is rare in this world, for it has been a common thing to take vengeance on innocent men in order to shield guilty ones, and to revolt against God-fearing princes because their peaceable ways were opposed to the lawless, restless spirit of the age. See the account of Ishmael's assassination of the upright prince, Gedaliah, and then his massacre of the fourscore men from Shechem, Shiloh, and Samaria, lest they make his crime known (Jer. 41:1–7).

> ²⁷ He that hath knowledge spareth his words:
>   And a man of understanding is of a quiet spirit.
> ²⁸ Even a fool, when he holdeth his peace, is counted wise:
>   And he that shutteth his lips is esteemed a man of
>   understanding.

See notes on 12:23 and 15:2. It is the simpleton who is always babbling. The man who has knowledge will not be continually airing his acquirements. He is of a quiet spirit and can bide his time. A man who must always be talking is generally one whose grasp of things in general is very slight; and, among Christians, an ever-running tongue certainly is no commendation to the discerning. He whose knowledge is limited is esteemed wise when his words are few. One who lives in the fear of God sets a value upon words that the careless soul cannot understand; for he remembers that "for every idle word that men shall speak they shall give account thereof in the day of judgment." Even that which he has experienced of God's love and favor is not always to be told lightly to others. Paul seems to have kept for fourteen years the secret of his having been caught up to the third heaven, until a seasonable time came to relate it (2 Cor. 12:1–7). Note the self-control of Elisha in this respect when going out after Elijah (2 Kings 2:3).

CHAPTER 18

PROVERBS 18

Nothing is more clearly taught in the Scriptures than the need of a separation between the clean and the unclean, between those who love the truth and those who walk contrary to it. Separation from evil is imperative, and he who would honor God must bow to it, whether it be to separate from evil friends, from ecclesiastical evil, or from evil in a business way. The word is plain: "Come out from among them, and be ye separate, saith the Lord, and touch not the unclean thing; and I will receive you" (2 Cor. 6:17). To walk apart from all that is unholy, and to refuse fellowship to those who by their endorsement are partakers of the sins of others, is the only proper course for a Christian who desires the Lord's approbation above all else.

But there is a separation that is very different from this and which the same Scriptures unqualifiedly condemn. Of this we now learn.

> ¹ A man having separated himself for his own pleasure,
> Rageth against all sound wisdom.

There is a vast difference between one who in lowliness and subjection to God separates himself from evil, and another who, through pride and self-importance, separates himself from those who refuse evil, in order to do his own pleasure. This is the heretic of whom we read in Jude's epistle: "These be they who separate themselves, sensual, not having the Spirit" (v. 19). Men of this stamp are "murmurers, complainers, walking after their own lusts; and their mouth speaketh great swelling words, having men's persons in admiration because of advantage" (Jude 16). It is most unhappy indeed when, as is sometimes the case, real Christians fall into the same ways as these false professors.

How often do we find men who are no doubt born of God and unquestionably gifted by Him, but in whom nature is strong, who are unbroken and willful. Men like these go on with their brethren as long as their mandates are bowed to and their authority owned. But let there be an unwillingness to follow their advice implicitly, and their pride will brook no refusal. Either they must have their way, or they will leave the assembly and begin something more to their own taste. These are the class who separate, not for the Lord's glory, but for their own pleasure; and having so done, storm and rage against all wisdom, railing against those who will not have their dictum to be supreme.

To separate from apostasy is right and scriptural. To separate from what is of God is schism and heresy. It is the human will setting itself up to choose—and ignoring the authority of the Word and Spirit of God.

Even where there are unhappy things among those who seek to be guided by Scripture—things which are hard to get at and which make cautious, godly men move slowly—to turn the back on what God has formed is very wrong. It is an egregious blunder to excommunicate myself because I fancy another should be disciplined. Where one is of a lowly spirit, such occasions will but furnish opportunities for waiting patiently upon God and seeking to exercise the consciences of fellow saints. It is only the headstrong and willful who will take matters into their own hands, and, if unable to override tender consciences, will separate themselves and rage against their brethren. Alexander the coppersmith was evidently a man of this stamp, if, as seems likely, he is the companion of Hymenaeus mentioned in 1 Timothy 1:20. Having given up the truth, he became the bitter opponent of those who stood for it (2 Tim. 4:14–15).

> ² A fool hath no delight in understanding,
> But that his heart may discover itself.

See note on 15:14. Nothing is more characteristic of the fool than his contempt for instruction and his lack of concern about intelligence. He reveals to the most casual observer the folly that is in his heart by the trifling words that trip lightly from his lips. Consider our Lord's rebuke to the Pharisees who had no delight in understanding (Matt. 23:17–19).

³ When the lawless cometh, there cometh also contempt,
And with ignominy reproach.

The casting off of restraint and acting in self-will results in shame and re-proach. He who would have the confidence of his brethren and be esteemed by his friends must manifest a spirit of subjection, on his own part, that bespeaks a sober-minded, thoughtful man, and one who values integrity. The opposite spirit results in ignominy at last, however high the head may be carried for a time. See Pashur (Jer. 20:1–6).

⁴ The words of a man's mouth are as deep waters,
And the well-spring of wisdom as a flowing brook.

The heart is the well, or fountain, whence these waters flow forth. In our Christian dispensation the Holy Spirit dwells in every believer and forms a more wondrous well-spring of wisdom than the wisest could have in the past age. He it is of whom our Lord spoke when He said, "If any man thirst, let him come unto Me, and drink. He that believeth on Me, as the Scripture hath said, out of his belly shall flow rivers of living water" (John 7:37–38). Commentators have searched in vain for the Scripture referred to; but may it not be that the very passage which we are considering was (perhaps with others) in the Lord's thoughts when He spoke? The thirsty soul finds in Christ the Wisdom of God, and, trust-ing in Him, receives that divine indwelling which causes wisdom, as a flowing brook of living water, to go out from his being for the refreshment and joy of other needy ones.

It was the general testimony of the Scriptures to which Jesus called attention; but in this proverb we find the very same figure used that He took up to picture the truth He was declaring. See Stephen (Acts 6:8, 10).

⁵ It is not good to accept the person of the lawless,
To overthrow the righteous in judgment.

How constantly the righteous Judge insists on impartial justice on the part of those set to represent Him in the tribunals of men! And if He so plainly declare His abhorrence of false and biased decisions in the courts of the world, how doubly jealous must He be concerning the judgments of His saints! See His word through Moses and the later revelations through Paul (Deut. 1:16–17; 16:18–20; 1 Cor. 6:1–7).

⁶ A fool's lips enter into contention,
And his mouth calleth for strokes.
⁷ A fool's mouth is his destruction,
And his lips are the snare of his soul.
⁸ The words of a whisperer are as dainty morsels,
And they go down into the depths of the soul.

See 26:20–22. The fool is ever ready for strife, and his mouth utters hasty and bitter words on the slightest pretext. His contentious lips call for severe rebuke, and shall be his own destruction, if he be not brought to repentance. In slander and scandal he delights, rolling evil tales as choice dainties under his tongue and filling his heart with what is unholy and perverse. To the whisperer he readily gives ear, and as readily imitates his ways. Of this spirit were Korah, Dathan, and Abiram (Num. 16).

⁹ He also that is slothful in his work,
Is brother to him that is a great waster.

The latter wastes his goods, the former wastes his time. Both come to poverty, as did the prodigal of Luke 15; and the disobedient son of Matthew 21:30 was clearly on the same road.

¹⁰ The name of Jehovah is a strong tower:
The righteous runneth into it, and is safe.

The name of Jehovah stands for the Lord Himself. To run into it, as into a strong tower, is therefore to confide in Him in the time of trouble. Such is the blessed privilege of every true saint. "Be careful for nothing; but in everything by prayer and supplication with thanksgiving let your requests be made known unto God. And the peace of God, which passeth all understanding, shall keep [i.e., garrison] your hearts and minds through Christ Jesus" (Phil. 4:6–7). All that perplexes and oppresses the spirit can be poured into His ear. Then the soul can leave it all with Him and can confide in His love. Thus the heart shall be at peace, protected as in a garrisoned tower, let the enemy rage as he may. See a lovely picture of this in the tower of Thebez (Judg. 9:50–57).

¹¹ The rich man's wealth is his strong city;
And as a high wall in his own conceit.

How different from what we have just been considering is the fortress of the man who, knowing not the name of the Lord, trusts in his wealth, fondly fancying in his conceit that he is forever secure. Riches soon vanish away and leave him, who had made them his confidence, desolate and forsaken. How often did the Savior, when on earth, have to rebuke those who trusted in uncertain riches! See especially Luke 6:24 and Mark 10:24.

> [12] Before destruction the heart of man is haughty;
> And before honor is humility.

See note on 16:18. It is needful that creatures so given to pride be again and again reminded of its dire result. It is a sure precursor of destruction. Humility, on the other hand, is the forerunner of honor. God delights to exalt the lowly.

The Hindu word for humility is said to be "the dust"; for it is a proverb among them that "you can walk on the dust forever and it never answers back." Humility is self-forgetfulness—the spirit of meekness, that, in the sight of God, is of great price. Weigh well His word to Barak (Jer. 45:5), and notice how the first clause of the verse before us is exemplified in Uzziah (2 Chron. 26:16), and the latter in his son Jotham (2 Chron. 27:6).

> [13] He that answereth a matter before he heareth it,
> It is folly and a shame unto him.

Rash judgments, founded on one-sided evidence or formed by jumping at conclusions, expose the unwise one to shame when the case is thoroughly investigated, and he is found to have spoken without proper proof. Such judgments have not been uncommon, even among Christians, who may well learn from this verse. But it is perhaps the young man who is especially exposed to this snare, particularly where there is boundless self-confidence. See David's erroneous judgment as to Ziba and Mephibosheth, already referred to (2 Sam. 16:1–4; 19:24–30).

> [14] The spirit of a man will sustain his infirmity;
> But a broken spirit who can bear?

It was when Jehoshaphat put the singers in the forefront of the army that victory hovered over his host. When the spirit of praise fills the soul, one is enabled to rise above the infirmities of the body and the trials of the way. But let the joy be lost and the spirit be broken, then defeat is certain. The saint can rejoice in the Lord, whatever his circumstances, if the line of communication is unbroken, and the conscience is free. This will make a victor of the feeblest. See Nehemiah's word to the returned remnant (Neh. 8:10).

> [15] The heart of the prudent getteth knowledge;
> And the ear of the wise man seeketh knowledge.

Emphasize the "getteth" and the "seeketh." It is because he *seeks* for knowledge that the wise and prudent man *gets* it. It is no haphazard accumulation of varied lore, but an earnest, daily search for true science—that is, absolute truth as revealed in the Word of God—that results in the enlightenment of the man of godly probity. See Ezra (Ezra 7:10).

> [16] A man's gift maketh room for him,
> And bringeth him before great men.

Contrast 25:14. We may consider this verse from two standpoints: the natural and the spiritual. Looked at from that of the first, its meaning is plain. A man, by bestowing favors upon subordinates, easily works his way into the presence of their master. This is a common method of procedure on the part of those who desire audiences where they are themselves unwanted. We need not dwell on it.

If, however, we think of gift in the way it is used in the epistles, as that which the ascended Christ bestows upon His servants for the edifying of His mystical body, it brings before us an important lesson. A gifted man needs not to force himself forward. His gift will make room for him as truly as in the world of nature and in the case of a material gift. In other words, the man who has had a ministry committed to him by the Lord Himself need never be a timeserving truckler to the present age: let him go on quietly in faithfulness, and the Master he serves will bring him to the front in due time if He would have him there at all. Self-assertiveness is the last thing that should be found in a servant of Christ. Lowly obedience to his Lord, coupled with the loving desire to serve in His name and for His sake, should distinguish the gifted man above all else. See the prophet Amos (Amos 7:14–15).

> [17] He that is first in his own cause seemeth just;
> But his neighbor cometh and searcheth him.

See verse 13 above. It is most unwise to hear but one side of a story (particularly when it is a matter that is troubling the saints of God) and give judgment upon what has been presented. Even with the most conscientious there is always the likelihood of but a partial account having been told. Therefore the wisdom of hearing not only both parties, but, if possible, of having them face-to-face. Most men can make out a good case for themselves, if left alone; because it has been natural for fallen man to justify himself since the day that Adam sought to throw the blame of his sin back upon God. Therefore, to decide a case on one-sided testimony is almost certain to result in a miscarriage of justice. See Saul and Samuel (1 Sam. 15:13–14).

> [18] The lot causeth contentions to cease,
> And parteth between the mighty.

See note on 16:33. When argument was in vain and differences seemed irreconcilable, the lot was resorted to as a final settlement. This was in a time when the written Word of God was not completed, nor the Holy Spirit abiding in His children. It is that word, ministered in the power of the Spirit, that is given us for a court of final resort in this dispensation of grace. Because of her sin Jerusalem was left with none to cast a lot to determine matters of controversy. Justice had been trampled on and would no more be found (Mic. 2:5). There is a warning for us in this, lest, if our ways be unrighteous, we turn to the Word of God in vain for guidance. "The *meek* will He guide in judgment; the meek will He teach His way."

> [19] A brother offended is harder to be won than a strong city:
> And their contentions are like the bars of a castle.

See note on 17:14. No tangles are so hard to straighten out as those in which brethren are concerned who once were knit heart-to-heart in true affection. To win back a brother who has been offended is more difficult than to subdue a walled city. Each is likely to view all that the other does with suspicion and mistrust once a lack of confidence possesses the soul. Entrenched behind the bars of wounded pride and unwilling to view the matter in relation to God, it will be impossible for either party to be overcome by grace and lowliness.

How much easier is it to humble oneself at first than after months or years of strife! There are few quarrels that could not be settled in a very short time, were both parties ready to meet quietly before the Lord to look into their differences; but the opportune hour, passed by, may not recur for a long season. Remember,

when tempted to perpetuate strife the dishonor that must thereby accrue to
the name of the Lord, and be warned by the unbrotherly example of contention between the men of Judah and of Israel, with its sad consequences (2 Sam.
19:41–43).

> ²⁰ Man's being shall be satisfied with the fruit of his mouth;
>   And with the increase of his lips shall he be filled.
> ²¹ Death and life are in the power of the tongue:
>   And they that love it shall eat the fruit thereof.

He who sows with his lips shall reap an abundant harvest, whether of sin unto
death or of righteousness unto life. Words seldom fall idly to the ground. Uttered often in thoughtlessness, they take root in congenial soil and come to
fruition most unexpectedly. Often has a chance word, dropped casually to a
stranger, been the means of untold blessing, rejoicing the soul of the one who
uttered it when at last he is apprised of its blessed result. The man of God may
well be encouraged to steadily pursue his way, sowing beside all waters the precious gospel of God, assured that "with the increase of his lips shall he be filled."

But if the words be evil, the harvest is just as certain; and it is well known that
weeds and noxious plants will flourish where nourishing fruits and grains cannot come to perfection. The man of unholy lips shall find abundant result from
his reckless words and shall as truly as the other "eat the fruit thereof."

Contrast the false teachers of 2 Peter 2 with the ambassadors for Christ of
2 Corinthians 5. Both shall yet be rewarded according to their sowing.

> ²² Whoso findeth a wife findeth a good thing,
>   And obtaineth favor from Jehovah.

It is not blind chance that unites congenial partners in the bonds of holy
matrimony. A wife (not merely a woman) is from the Lord and is an expression
of His loving favor. This being so, it is of gravest importance that the young
man, before he permits his affections to go out to a maiden, should seek to be
guided as to the proper object of his attention by the Lord Himself. There would
be fewer incompatible marriages if His mind was more often sought, and mere
fancy less frequently allowed to direct. Let the young Christian consider well
whether such a marriage as he is contemplating is likely to prove an unequal
yoke or a hindrance to soul-progress in place of a help. See Boaz and Ruth (Ruth
4:9–12). Note 19:14 (last clause).

²³ The poor useth entreaties;
  But the rich answereth roughly.

There is an evil genius in connection with great wealth that, if it be not closely watched against, dries up the milk of human kindness and hardens the heart against the needy. Let those whose temporal riches place them in the position to succor the poor remember that the ear of God notes every unheeded cry of the poverty-stricken, and His eye beholds every ungracious action on the part of those who could relieve, but do it not. See the parable of the implacable servant (Matt. 18:23–35).

²⁴ A man that hath friends must show himself friendly:
  And there is a friend that sticketh closer than a brother.

None complain so loudly of the lack of love and friendliness on the part of others as those who manifest very little of either themselves. He who busies himself to show love will receive it back again. He who is himself a friend will find friends to reciprocate his kindness. But the true Friend, as we saw in 17:17, is ever such. His heart is unchanged by the slights of the objects of his devotion. "There is a Friend that sticketh closer than a brother." He always manifested love and grace in a world where all by nature were estranged from Him.

Let those who complain of lack of love on the part of fellow saints imitate His holy example. Be concerned, not about receiving kindness, but about manifesting it, and "good measure, pressed down, shall men repay into your bosom." See the good Samaritan (Luke 10:29–37).

CHAPTER 19

PROVERBS 19

The first three proverbs are intimately connected, and we therefore consider them together.

> ¹ Better is the poor that walketh in his integrity,
> Than he that is perverse in his lips, and is a fool.
> ² Also, that the soul be without knowledge, is not good;
> And he that hasteth with his feet sinneth [or, maketh false
> steps].
> ³ The foolishness of man perverteth his way:
> And his heart fretteth against Jehovah.

It is the contrast between the path of truth and the way of self-will and ignorance. Far better is it to be poor and unknown, and yet walk before God in uprightness and integrity of heart, than to be loud in speech but given to folly and perverseness.

Ignorance is not to be admired. The worldly axiom, "Where ignorance is bliss, 'tis folly to be wise," is false and foolish. To be bereft of knowledge is undesirable. Mere zeal will not suffice to keep one right. One may be in earnest, but earnestly wrong, as was Saul of Tarsus before his conversion (Acts 26:9). He who runs on without learning the will of God adds sin to sin. His foolishness leads him astray, and his deceitful heart is irritated against the Lord. He is bent on his own way and can brook no correction. Compare Jonah when acting in self-will (Jonah 1:3; 4:8–9).

> 4 Wealth maketh many friends;
> But the poor is separated from his neighbor.

The well-to-do will always have many to claim friendship with him, while the indigent will often find his poverty a means of separating his neighbors from him; for, though a glamour may be thrown about it by the easily satisfied optimist, this is a cold, feelingless world after all.

But there is a legitimate sense in which friends may be made by means of wealth. Our Lord has bidden His disciples "make to yourselves friends by the mammon of unrighteousness, that when ye fail they may receive you into everlasting habitations." Riches, if used for the alleviation of misery and in reference to the coming age, may be the means of much blessing. When at last the one who has so used them passes away, he will find a host of friends who have been the objects of his Christlike benefactions on earth, waiting to welcome him into the everlasting home of the redeemed. Notice verses 6–7 and 17. The just man will not regard the rich more than the poor. See Job 34:19 and James 2:1–9.

> 5 A false witness shall not be acquitted;
> And he that breatheth out lies shall not escape.

The judgment of God is according to truth. He will see that every transgression and disobedience shall receive a just recompense of reward. A lie may seem to triumph for the time being, but the truth shall be eventually supreme. See the witnesses against Naboth (1 Kings 21:8–13). Note verse 9.

> 6 Many will entreat the favor of a prince:
> And every man is a friend to him that giveth gifts.
> 7 All the brethren of the poor do hate him:
> How much more do his friends go far from him?
> He pursueth them with words, yet they are wanting to him.

See note on verse 4 above. There are always multitudes to wait upon a noble and to play the part of friends to one who can be their benefactor. How different the spirit of Him who was charged with receiving sinners and eating with them;

who sought not the smiles of the great, nor feared their frowns! By His Spirit He has bidden those who would follow in His steps to be characterized by "minding not high things, but going along with the lowly" (Rom. 12:16).

It is like the world to prefer the rich and great to the destitute and outwardly ignoble; but let the Christian remember that his Lord appeared on earth as one of the poor whom His brethren despised and whose friends went far from Him, though He pursued them with tender entreaties. Surely those who are now, by grace, linked up with Him in blessing must ever cherish a loving concern for the needy.

> 8 He that getteth heart loveth his own soul:
> He that keepeth understanding shall find good.

The King James Version reads "wisdom" where we have used the literal rendering, "heart." The word so used is a Hebraism, standing for sound judgment, or common sense. See 15:21.

To follow after moral probity and to cleave to understanding bring true peace and lasting happiness. See Timotheus (2 Tim. 3:14–15).

> 9 A false witness shall not be acquitted;
> And he that breatheth out lies shall perish.

The passage is not exactly a repetition of verse 5. There, we are reminded that the liar shall not escape. Here, we are told what his doom shall be. He shall perish. He shall be destroyed. That is, his hopes shall be cut off, and he shall go out into the darkness, broken beneath the judgment of God to endure the unspeakable woes of the liar's eternity (Rev. 21:8).

> 10 Luxury is not seemly for a fool;
> Much less for a servant to have rule over princes.

Both are out of place. The servant ruling over princes and the fool nursed in the lap of luxury bespeak conditions that are opposed to what is right and orderly. Circumstances may arise in which a prince is helpless, and obliged to rely upon the judgment of one of lesser place; but the wise servant will use his powers with discretion, and keep the place of the subject, though all be under his hand. See Joseph (Gen. 47:14–20).

¹¹ The discretion of a man deferreth his anger;
    And it is his glory to pass over a transgression.

See note on 14:29. An uncontrolled temper, manifested in hasty anger unjudged, bespeaks a man who has never learned, in the school of God, the great lesson of self-government. It is the pompous, conceited pedant who cannot overlook an injury done to him, but must vent his wrath upon the offender whenever an occasion presents itself. A man of sound judgment and discretion has learned to pass lightly over offenses and seeming insults which would goad the one who is bereft of wisdom to intense indignation. In this, whatever his failings otherwise, even Esau proves himself when he greets his brother, Jacob (concerning whose transgression there could be no question), with such grace and magnanimity (Gen. 33:4–9).

¹² The king's wrath is as the roaring of a lion;
    But his favor is as dew upon the grass.

Because "in the word of a king there is power," his wrath is to be dreaded, and his gracious favor eagerly sought. How much more fully may the words be applied to the coming King, the Lion of the tribe of Judah! When the great day of His wrath has come, how wretched will be the estate of all who know not His grace, which to the repentant soul is indeed like dew upon the grass! Both aspects are illustrated in Pharaoh's dealing with his chief butler and his chief baker (Gen. 39).

¹³ A foolish son is the calamity of his father:
    And the contentions of a wife are a continual dropping.

The first line connects with 17:25. How unhappy the home where both a foolish son and a contentious wife are found! They are very likely to be together; for where the wife disputes her husband's authority and takes sides with the children in opposition to his proper discipline, the effect upon them will be anything but good.

It is a very common thing to see parents disputing and wrangling before their household, with the baneful result that the sons and daughters learn to despise the father's authority and to defy the mother's correction, when she does attempt it; thus growing up in a lawless, insubject spirit, bent upon having their own way and persisting in their refusal to submit to proper discipline. Christian parents may well ponder the instructions given to each in Ephesians 5; Colossians 3; and 1 Peter 3. The contentious wife has her unhappy illustration in Michal, the daughter of Saul (2 Sam. 6:16–23; 1 Chron. 15:29).

> [14] House and riches are an inheritance from fathers:
> But a prudent wife is from Jehovah.

See 18:22. One may inherit house and wealth, but none can give a prudent wife but the Lord. It is God who joins together, and therefore forbids man to put asunder. He who said at the beginning, "It is not good for man to be alone; I will make him a help meet for him," is still concerned about His people's happiness. Therefore the man of faith can safely trust Him to give a suited life partner. It is when, unwilling to wait on God, one chooses for himself, relying alone on his poor human judgment, that bitter mistakes are made, which are often irremediable. To marry in Christ is not necessarily to marry in the Lord. Any marriage between Christians would be in Christ. Only when the will is subject, and the mind of God has been learned, will marriage be in the Lord. See Rebekah's case, and note how markedly Jehovah ordered all (Gen. 24).

> [15] Slothfulness casteth into a deep sleep;
> And an idle soul shall suffer hunger.

See notes on 12:24 and 13:4. Many of us fail to realize that idleness is sin. Time wasted is time to be accounted for at the judgment seat of Christ. Needed rest is, of course, very right and proper. Jesus Himself had to say to His disciples, "Come ye yourselves apart, and rest awhile." But idleness is quite different. Slothfulness is trifling away opportunities that will never return. It is failing to appreciate the value of time. In a natural sense, the sluggard is made to feel the pinch of want; and spiritually, the same is also true. He who, for lack of godly energy, does not bestir himself to procure suited sustenance for his soul will come to want and know the pangs of famine. See Paul's words to both the Ephesian and Colossian saints (Eph. 5:16; Col. 4:5).

> [16] He that keepeth the commandment keepeth his own soul;
> But he that despiseth His ways shall die.

This is a truth frequently presented in Scripture. It is, so to speak, a kindness to oneself to obey the commandment of the Lord. The Word is a word of life. To forsake it is to die. Therefore he is short-sighted indeed who despises the ways of God and chooses for himself. He is but sealing his own destruction and bringing down well-merited wrath upon his own head. See Shimei (1 Kings 2:36–46).

> ¹⁷ He that hath pity upon the poor lendeth to Jehovah;
>   And that which he hath given will He pay him again.

It is truly precious to contemplate Jehovah as the patron of the poor. He has left such in the world to test the hearts of those who are better provided for, and He accepts what is done with compassion, to relieve the needy, as so much done for Himself. Money and goods bestowed with loving pity on those in distress are not gone forever. He takes note of every mite and makes Himself responsible to see that all shall be repaid; and we may be sure the interest will be greater far than could be realized in any other way. Genuine philanthropy is the result of true love to God. When His love is shed abroad in the heart by the Holy Spirit, there will be a corresponding concern for all men. To do good and to communicate is well-pleasing to the Lord, and shall in no wise lose its reward, even though it be the giving of but a cup of cold water in His name. The widow of Zarephath was none the poorer for ministering to Elijah in his distress, but found instead an unfailing cruse of oil and an unending supply of meal (1 Kings 17:10–16).

> ¹⁸ Chasten thy son while there is hope,
>   But set not thy soul upon slaying him.

Discipline, firm but gracious, should characterize the home. Brutal punishments, even to endangering the life of the one chastised, are very wrong, and opposed to the Spirit of God. Conduct such as this can only harden, in place of recovering, a wayward son. "Ye fathers, provoke not your children to wrath," is a needed admonition in many families. Unreasonable demands, and punishments all out of proportion to the offense committed, should be sedulously avoided. Many a child who might have been saved by careful, godly training in his earliest years has been left to grow up in untrammeled freedom until the father, at last, thought he was old enough for chastisement, when he has become the subject of severe treatment that has filled his heart with anger and alienated him for life from his well-meaning but exceedingly unwise parent. "The iron hand in the velvet glove" has long been the symbol of strict discipline administered in grace. To leave a child to himself is to manifest a cruel indifference to the fate of one committed to our care. To be heartless and unnecessarily severe in correcting him is to err on the other side. The happy medium is what the Word of God teaches and brings the desired results. It is well if the child is made to realize that it is his good which is sought, not the venting of an irate father's emotions, which has caused many a one to lose the respect of an observing youth. See Saul's unwise treatment of Jonathan, thereby alienating his heart in place of winning his confidence (1 Sam. 20:30).

> [19] A man of great wrath shall suffer punishment:
> For if thou deliver him, yet thou must do it again.

It is useless to shield a man given to uncontrolled anger; for though by the intercessions of his friends he may be again and again delivered from the unhappy consequences which would naturally have followed his ebullitions of temper, he is likely at any time to be as bad as ever, and to draw down righteous retribution on his own head, and involve those who undertake to defend him in common trouble and perhaps ruin. See 22:24. Such a man is manifestly unbroken, and lacking in the grace of self-judgment. He should be left to himself until he learns by punishment what he would not receive otherwise. Samuel found it hard to bow to this lesson, and only gave Saul up at last when the Lord distinctly called upon him to separate himself from him (1 Sam. 16:1).

> [20] Hear counsel, and receive instruction,
> That thou mayest be wise in thy latter end.
> [21] There are many devices in a man's heart;
> Nevertheless the counsel of Jehovah, that shall stand.

To despise counsel is to play the part of the fool. He who is wise values instruction, especially when it is of authoritative character. He knows that whatever man may plan, and however wisely he may scheme, the counsel of the Lord is certain and shall be duly carried out. God has said, "My counsel shall stand; I will do all My pleasure." How vain the man who would dare to set himself in opposition to it! Happy is he who, waiting on God for instruction, obeys implicitly His counsel, and therefore works for and with Him. See Joshua's commission (Josh. 1:5–9).

> [22] The charm of a man is his kindness:
> And a poor man is better than a liar.

A kindly, benevolent spirit appeals to all men, and charms by its unselfishness and thoughtfulness for others. But to promise large things while unable to perform them is reprehensible. It is far better to be poor and frankly admit one's inability to do what the heart might desire than to promise largely and be at last proven untrustworthy. To be what you are and not to pretend to be what you are not is a sound principle, the carrying out of which gains the esteem of any whose good opinion is worth seeking. See Peter and the lame man (Acts 3:6).

> ²³ The fear of Jehovah tendeth to life:
> And he that hath it shall rest satisfied;
> He shall not be visited with evil.

It is a synoptic statement of the precious truth unfolded in Psalm 91—the portion of the man who dwells in the secret place of the Most High, abiding under the shadow of the Almighty. Resting in the enjoyment of His omnipotent power and unchanging love, he who fears the Lord has no anxious concern as to his affairs. He can rest satisfied, knowing that he cannot be visited with evil, for all things must work together for the good of one in such a case. What seems to be evil will become but a means of blessing, by causing the heart to cleave more truly to the God of all grace. See Paul's song of triumph in Romans 8:28–39.

> ²⁴ A slothful man burieth his hand in the dish,
> And will not so much as bring it to his mouth again.

Having the very means of sustenance before him, the sluggard is too lethargic to avail himself thereof. The figure used may seem almost absurdly hyperbolic, but it is meant to picture a most extreme case; where, though seated at the table with nourishing food in his hand, the eater is overcome by drowsiness and prefers to abandon himself to ease and sleep rather than bestir himself to take his meal. The Word of God is such a dish; but, alas, many are the sluggards who, with abundant opportunity to feed upon its precious things, are too indifferent to search and find its treasures for themselves. Eglon, king of Moab, appears to have been largely a man of the stamp described (Judg. 3:17–25).

> ²⁵ Smite a scorner, and the simple will beware:
> And reprove one that hath understanding, and he will
> understand knowledge.

To allow the scorner to go unrebuked would often be to put a snare before the feet of the simple, who might conclude that the gainsaying was irresistible because unanswered. It is therefore right and proper to punish him who opposes the truth by exposing before all the fallacies of his position. If a wise man, it will be no hardship to be reproved; for the truth itself is of greater value in the eyes of him who has understanding than his own dignity. See Paul's word to Timothy regarding those who are perverted (1 Tim. 5:20).

> ²⁶ He that ruineth his father, and chaseth away his mother,
> Is a son that causeth shame and bringeth reproach.

See verse 13 above. Bitter indeed are the sorrows brought upon his parents by a rebellious son. Such a one is a very incarnation of selfishness. He will ruin his father, spending all his substance for self-gratification; and will in his stubbornness even drive his mother from him, refusing all correction. Ignominy and obloquy are thereby brought upon their name; but to all this he is supremely indifferent. Determined to be free from all restraint, he recklessly plunges on to his doom. It is a sad, sad picture, often duplicated in this unhappy scene, and is especially characteristic of the last days, in which we now live (2 Tim. 3:2).

> ²⁷ Cease, my son, to hear the instruction
> That causeth to err from the words of knowledge.

This is a far-reaching command of vast importance. It is an evidence of youthful pride for one to suppose he can listen to all kinds of theories, good and evil, but be defiled by none. Spiritual eclecticism may seem to savor of breadth of mind and liberality; but it generally ends in making shipwreck of the faith. You can only recognize and avoid error when the truth of God is known and delighted in. Therefore the need of earnest, diligent study of the Scriptures. When another gives out what is contrary to God's revealed word, it is time to refuse him and his teaching. You cannot afford to trifle with unholy doctrine.

Remember that what is opposed to the teaching of the unerring word of the Lord is directly from Satan. To dabble with it is to expose yourself to its powerful influence. Therefore refuse to hear it.

One simple question is all that needs to be propounded to any one taking the place of an instructor in divine things in order to detect the bias of his doctrine. It is this: "What think ye of Christ?" He who is unsound here is wrong throughout. If the true deity, or divinity, of the Lord Jesus be denied; if the atoning efficacy of His blood be explained away; if the sinlessness of His spotless humanity be in any way clouded, the system is wrong at the foundation, and it will prove to be unsound in all else.

> What think ye of Christ?" is the test
>   To try both your state and your scheme.
> You cannot be right in the rest,
>   Unless you think rightly of Him.
>   —J. Newton

For a Christian to continue to hear, or to support, a man who blasphemes his Lord, is treason of the darkest hue. If any bring not the doctrine of Christ, he is to be refused and no fellowship shown him, because he abides in the darkness; and "what fellowship hath light with darkness?" See the spiritualists of Isaiah's day (Isa. 8:19–20), and the Judaizers and Gnostics of the apostolic period (Col. 2:8; Titus 1:10–11; 2 John 9–10). All these classes are to be found in our times, multiplied a thousandfold. "From such turn away."

> [28] A witness of Belial scorneth judgment:
>   And the mouth of the lawless devoureth iniquity.
> [29] Judgments are prepared for scorners,
>   And stripes for the back of fools.

Belial seems in a veiled way to stand for Satan. It really means that which is worthless, but is generally used as that which is opposed to God. So that a witness of Belial would be one who is ungodly, and who therefore scorns judgment and correction. His mouth devours iniquity. It is his food; he lives upon it.

But a solemn accounting is before him. Independent though he may be now, he will at last have to learn that judgments have been by God prepared for such as he, and stripes for his back. Deceit and transgression may seem to go unchecked for a time, but the blow will soon fall that shall give the worthless witness to realize that God cannot be trifled with forever. See Ananias and Sapphira (Acts 5:1–11).

CHAPTER 20

Proverbs 20

W ho can tell the woes, the broken hearts, the blasted lives, the lost souls, that have been the result of failure to heed the warning of the verse with which this chapter opens?

> ¹ Wine is a mocker, strong drink is raging:
> And whosoever is deceived thereby is not wise.

No other vice has so cursed the world, and caused such awful misery and suffering, as intemperance. Those who sneer at the lurid tales of a Gough or a Murphy have only to go about after nightfall through the dark courts of our large cities to find the most dreadful pictures human eloquence have painted many times outdone. The wretched victims of the wine cup have been numbered in hundreds of millions, and yet Satan has no difficulty in persuading thousands of reckless youths to daily start upon the same fearful road that has lured these untold hosts to ruin.

Like every other creature of God, wine has its place. Scripture recognizes its medicinal virtue and a lawful use of it also when needed (1 Tim. 5:23). But how easily it becomes a snare that destroys the will and wrecks the life.

"Wine is a mocker," tempting the youth to his undoing, and deceiving him who with rashness supposes he can indulge as he pleases, and then, when he desires, set it aside. Even godly men have been deluded thereby to their shame and grief. See Noah and Lot (Gen. 9:20–21; 19:30–36). Consult notes on 23:29–35.

> ² The fear of a king is as the roaring of a young lion:
>   Whoso provoketh him to anger sinneth against his own
>   soul.

See note on 19:12. "The powers that be are ordained of God." Hence the necessity of recognizing their authority and submitting to every ordinance of man for the Lord's sake. To resist the power is to resist Him who appointed it, and is to provoke the king to anger, and thus to sin against one's own soul; for his wrath will be poured out upon the rebellious.

We may apply the words to the King of whom every other should be a type. Who can measure the power of *His* wrath when all His grace has been despised and He sits on His royal throne to execute judgment?

Hanun had to prove "the wrath of a king" when he refused his kindness (2 Sam. 10).

> ³ It is an honor for a man to cease from strife:
>   But every fool will be meddling.

See note on 17:14. How strange the pride that makes a man dread to own he has been wrong, or unwilling to back down graciously for the sake of peace, even though he may feel he is in the right—providing no divine principle is at stake. "Let your yieldingness be known unto all men" (Phil. 4:5) is a needed word. A man of God will be ready to give up his fancied rights rather than to prolong strife; but a fool will persist in contention and meddle with matters in which he should have no part. Even so devoted a man as Josiah failed for lack of having learned this lesson (2 Chron. 35:20–24).

> ⁴ The sluggard will not plow by reason of the winter;
>   Therefore shall he beg in harvest, and have nothing.

Ready upon any pretext to abandon his labor, the sluggard neglects the cultivation of his fields when others are at work. Therefore when harvesttime arrives, his fields are bare, and he is found begging of (as he would put it) his more fortunate neighbors. The fact is, fortune has nothing to do with it. Their diligence has brought its own reward, and his slothfulness its natural consequence. Compare 19:15, 24.

> ⁵ Counsel in the heart of man is like deep water;
> But a man of understanding will draw it out.

See note on 18:4. We have already been reminded more than once that it is only the fool who blatantly pours forth a stream of words upon every occasion (see 17:27–28; 18:7). With the prudent man it is quite otherwise. His words are few, unless there be occasion for them; and this not because of his lack of sound knowledge and the ability to instruct; but he prefers to bide his time. Deep in his heart, as in a well, he hides counsel and wisdom. Because of his sobriety, the simple may think him inferior to themselves; but a man of understanding will be able to draw forth what shall be for profit, at the suited period. See Joseph and Pharaoh (Gen. 41).

> ⁶ Most men will proclaim every one his own goodness:
> But a faithful man who can find?
> ⁷ The just man walketh in his integrity;
> His children are blessed after him.
> ⁸ A king that sitteth in the throne of judgment
> Scattereth away all evil with his eyes.
> ⁹ Who can say, I have made my heart clean,
> I am pure from my sin?
> ¹⁰ Divers weights, and divers measures,
> Both of them are alike abomination to Jehovah.
> ¹¹ Even a child is known by his doings,
> Whether his work be pure, and whether it be right.
> ¹² The hearing ear, and the seeing eye,
> Jehovah hath made both of them.

There is evidently a moral connection between each proverb in this section, all being more or less occupied with the question and the test of purity. Most men are ready to declare their own uprightness and kindness, as was Job before he saw the Lord. But faithful men, who will justify God though all others be found liars, are few indeed. In Elihu we see such a one as he speaks on God's behalf. See Job 29–31 for Job's defense of himself. In 32–37 we get Elihu justifying God.

The man who is really just (made such by grace) manifests it by his walk; not by the declarations of his lips. The children of such a man are blessed after him. Abraham is a shining example of this (Gen. 17:1–9).

If any are righteous, it should surely be the king who sits on the throne of judgment, and scatters away evil with his eyes. But even among such (or among men at large), who is there who will dare to say, "I have made my heart clean. I am pure from my sin"?

Unequal measures testify to the lack of integrity on the part of many. All such are evil in the eyes of the Lord (see 16:11; note v. 23 below).

Even in the case of a child, his ways and doings declare what he is, as in the instance of little Samuel in the tabernacle (1 Sam. 3:18–21). What shall be said of those older in years, with added responsibilities?

Manifestly, then, no man is pure in himself. But Jehovah gives to those who wait upon Him the seeing eye and the hearing ear, that they may behold and do His will and hear His voice. When all pretense to purity in oneself is given up, it is found in Christ for those who receive Him.

> [13] Love not sleep, lest thou come to poverty:
> Open thine eyes, and thou shalt be satisfied with bread.

See verse 4 above, and note 6:9–11; 24:33–34. Abundant are the warnings against slothfulness and self-indulgence. "Drowsiness shall clothe a man with rags." It is the active and diligent who are rewarded for their toil. "Awake, thou that sleepest, and arise from among the dead, and Christ shall shine upon thee." Such are the stirring words addressed by the Holy Ghost to Christians who are sleeping in a world where all should be aroused to a sense of the value of time, so rapidly passing away. "See then that ye walk circumspectly, not as fools, but as wise, redeeming the time, because the days are evil" (Eph. 5:15–16).

It was by taking his ease that David fell into his grievous sin (2 Sam. 11:1, last clause).

> [14] Bad! bad! saith the buyer;
> But when he is gone his way, then he boasteth.

How common is the deceit here mentioned! It is the characteristic falsehood of the bargainer. Depreciating the article his heart desires in order to procure favorable terms, when at last his price is acceded to, he goes his way rejoicing in his shrewdness and boasting of his ability to purchase at low rates. But a holier eye than that of man was looking on, noting every action, word, and thought; and the day of accounting draws rapidly nearer. See Ephraim (Hos. 12:7–8).

¹⁵ There is gold, and a multitude of rubies:
But the lips of knowledge are a precious jewel.

Gold and gems are of no value as compared with the lips that keep knowledge. No price can be set upon the precious truth of God, the wisdom that cometh from above. See 2:1–5 and consider Psalm 119:72.

¹⁶ Take his garment that is surety for a stranger:
And take a pledge of him for a strange woman.

See notes on 6:1–5; 11:15. Ruin and disaster dog the steps of him who unwisely goes surety for another, or who has any traffic with a strange woman. To keep clear of both is the only path of safety. To temporize is generally to invite defeat. The man who can say "No," and stand by it, when tempted to one side or the other, alone is secure. He who will not heed must learn for himself in bitterness of soul. See Judah (Gen. 38).

¹⁷ Bread of deceit is sweet to a man;
But afterwards his mouth shall be filled with gravel.

It is only for the passing moment that deceit seems to prosper and to promise well. The full result is far otherwise. In place of a sweet and delectable dainty, the mouth will be filled with gravel, hard and disappointing. Compare 9:17–18 and see Matthew 26:14–16 and 27:3–5.

¹⁸ Every purpose is established by counsel:
And with good advice make war.

Rashness and unthinking precipitation are to be deplored. Before beginning what may not readily be ended, it is well to count the cost and to counsel with some who are known to be wise and prudent. Our Lord expands and amplifies this proverb when He says, "What king, going to make war against another king, sitteth not down first, and consulteth whether he be able with ten thousand to meet him that cometh against him with twenty thousand? Or else, while the other is yet a great way off, he sendeth an ambassage, and desireth conditions of peace" (Luke 14:31–32). See Rehoboam and Shemaiah (2 Chron. 11:1–4).

¹⁹ He that goeth about as a talebearer revealeth secrets:
  Therefore meddle not with him that flattereth with his lips.

See notes on 11:13; 18:8; and 25:23. He who flatters to the face will as readily scandalize behind the back. By soft, sinuous words and ways he will gain the confidence of his victim, appealing to his pride and love of approbation, and thus loosening his tongue, until he relates things far better left unsaid. When he has thus lured him on to baring his heart, he will go to others and pour into their ears what he has just learned, flattering them in the same way and giving them to suppose that they alone are the recipients of his favor. No character is more detestable. Utterly lacking in moral principle and destitute of godliness, when such a person gets in among a Christian assembly, he can do untold mischief. The safe plan is to refuse altogether to listen to "him that flattereth with his lips." By so doing, much sorrow may be averted. The one who praises his listener while he backbites another, deserves to be treated in the spirit that David manifested toward the Amalekite who brought him news of Saul's death (2 Sam. 1:1–16).

²⁰ Whoso revileth his father or his mother,
  His lamp shall be put out in obscure darkness.

See note on 19:26. No parents are perfect in all their ways, but, like civil authorities, they are to be honored because of their position. They stand to children in God's stead. To honor the father and mother is to honor Him who has created us and established the home, setting the solitary in families. Therefore he who reviles his parents shall find his light put out, and be left in the darkness. Even though a father or mother fail grievously, a son whose spirit is as it should be will seek to cover and hide their shame. Only an ungrateful and foolish child will spread it abroad. This was the error of Ham (Gen. 9:22).

²¹ An inheritance may be gotten hastily at the beginning;
  But the end thereof shall not be blessed.

See 21:6 and 28:20. Treasure rapidly accumulated at the expense of conscience and honor will yield little comfort; for "the blessing of the Lord that maketh rich and addeth no sorrow with it" cannot be upon it. "As the partridge sitteth on eggs, and hatcheth them not; so he that getteth riches, and not by right, shall leave them in the midst of his days, and at his end shall be a fool" (Jer. 17:11).

They who set out with the determination to gather wealth at all cost will learn in bitterness of soul that they have missed the true and lasting treasure which would have given heart-satisfaction and joy in its possession. See God's word to the rich who have gained their fortunes by oppression of the poor (James 5:1–6).

> [22] Say not thou, I will recompense evil;
> But wait on Jehovah, and He shall save thee.

No lesson is harder for some of us to learn than that of confiding all our affairs to the hands of the Lord, especially when we feel we have been wronged and ill-treated. Yet it is plain from Scripture that the saint can make no greater mistake than to take charge of his own affairs in such a case. Nothing could be clearer than the injunction, "Recompense to no man evil for evil. . . . Dearly beloved, avenge not yourselves, but rather give place unto wrath: for it is written, Vengeance is Mine; I will repay, saith the Lord" (Rom. 12:17–19). To set about meting out evil for evil in the face of words like these is to act in direct disobedience to God, and we need not wonder if we make a terrible botch of it all. He who, owning that all has been allowed by the Lord for his good, bows his head and bends before the blast, will find God ever ready to interfere at the needed moment. To look away from the human instrument of our grief, however vindictive he may be, and to see, behind it all, the purposes of our Father working out, gives rest and comfort to the sorely-tried soul. It was this that sustained David when Shimei cursed and stoned him. The whole passage is so tender and striking, I cannot forbear quoting it in full:

> And when king David came to Bahurim, behold, thence came out a man of the family of the house of Saul, whose name was Shimei, the son of Gera: he came forth, and cursed still as he came. And he cast stones at David, and at all the servants of king David: and all the people and all the mighty men were on his right hand and on his left. And thus said Shimei when he cursed, Come out, come out, thou bloody man, and thou man of Belial: the LORD hath returned upon thee all the blood of the house of Saul, in whose stead thou hast reigned; and the LORD hath delivered the kingdom into the hand of Absalom thy son: and, behold, thou art taken in thy mischief, because thou art a bloody man. Then said Abishai the son of Zeruiah unto the king, Why should this dead dog curse my lord the king? let me go over, I pray thee, and take off his head. And the king said, What have I to do with you, ye sons of Zeruiah?

so *let him curse,* because *the Lord hath said unto him, Curse David.* Who shall then say, Wherefore hast thou done so? And David said to Abishai, and to all his servants, Behold, my son, which came forth of my bowels, seeketh my life: how much more now may this Benjamite do it? Let him alone, and let him curse; for *the Lord hath bidden him.* It may be that the LORD will look on my affliction, and that the LORD will requite me good for his cursing this day. (2 Samuel 16:5–12)

It is doubtful if, in all David's spiritual history, he ever reached a higher height of holy confidence in God than at this time of deep, deep trial. Shimei's spiteful cursing in so public a manner and at so sorrowful a time, must have deeply lacerated his already wounded spirit. But he bows his head in submission; and instead of executing vengeance on Shimei and seeking self-vindication from the charges made, "through evil report and good report" he holds on his way, in submissive confidence, saying, "Let him curse," and taking all from the Lord Himself.

Shimei was but an instrument, inspired by Satan, yet really permitted of the Lord, for David's chastening and discipline. As such he views him and looks not at second causes, but at the great First Cause Himself. This is most blessed! Would that every tried saint could follow his example!

The day came that Shimei was a cringing suppliant at the feet of the man he had cursed; publicly owning that he had acted perversely, and confessing "thy servant doth know that I have sinned" (2 Sam. 19:16–23). David's royal clemency was extended in forgiveness—a far greater victory than vengeance would have been. Afterward, in God's righteous government, he was put to death for the treachery that ever characterized him, in the reign of Solomon. "He that doeth wrong shall receive for the wrong which he hath done: and there is no respect of persons" (Col. 3:25). With judgment I have not to interfere. Be it mine to bow in submission to all God's ways, owning His hand in everything that would otherwise disquiet me.

> [23] Divers weights are an abomination to Jehovah;
> And a false balance is not good.

See verse 10 above. Divers weights are different tests for different things, according as they relate to oneself or not. One standard of righteousness, a true balance, with honest weights, should characterize the Christian. Frequently one finds these various weights applied in estimating the conduct of certain persons.

We excuse in one, particularly in ourselves, what calls for severe judgment in the case of another. But in the scales of the sanctuary both are tested by the same weights. God would have our balances patterned after His, and the opposite is an abomination in His sight. See the half shekel (Exod. 30:15).

> ²⁴ Man's goings are of Jehovah;
>   How can a man then understand his own way?

The prophet Jeremiah attests the same solemn truth. "O LORD," he says, "I know that the way of man is not in himself: it is not in man that walketh to direct his steps" (Jer. 10:23). So he adds, "O LORD, correct me, but with judgment; not in Thine anger, lest Thou bring me to nothing" (Jer. 10: 24). Concerning every one of us, it can be said, "Ye have not passed this way heretofore." This is true every step of our journey through this world. Each day we enter upon new scenes and new experiences; therefore the folly of depending on our poor, finite wisdom in order to understand our way. One alone knows the end from the beginning. With Him, all is one eternal Now. Who else but He can direct our steps? Happy the soul who can commit all his ways unto Him, and say with confidence and holy restfulness, "My times are in Thy hand." To such He has said, "I will instruct thee and teach thee in the way which thou shalt go: I will guide thee with Mine eye" (Ps. 32:8). But this daily guidance is only the portion of the subject, obedient believer. Others must know the bit-and-bridle direction of circumstances and tribulations. See Israel at the Jordan (Josh. 3:4).

> ²⁵ It is a snare to a man rashly to say, It is hallowed;
>   And after vows, to make inquiry.

Two things, yet very closely connected, seem to be here referred to, with a keen, underlying touch of irony that is meant to go home to the conscience. To say rashly of anything that it is holy, before one has investigated, or to make a vow concerning some matter which has to be inquired into later; these are foolish and dangerous things, and may result in much sorrow and trouble. Elsewhere Solomon speaks of the same blunder. "When thou vowest a vow unto God, defer not to pay it; for He hath no pleasure in fools: pay that which thou hast vowed. Better is it that thou shouldest not vow, than that thou shouldest vow and not pay. Suffer not thy mouth to cause thy flesh to sin; neither say thou before the angel, that it was an error: wherefore should God be angry at thy voice, and destroy the work of thy hands?" (Eccl. 5:4–6). The practice of making vows seems to be clearly contrary to the spirit of the Christian dispensation in which grace is reigning. Under law, when God was asking something of man, it was quite in keeping to make such particular pledges. The vow of Paul was evidently that of a Nazarite, taken prior to his conversion (Acts 18:18). It would therefore be of all-importance to make sure that such a promise was according to the mind of God before making it. See Jephthah's rash vow and its terrible consequences (Judg. 11:30–40).

> [26] A wise king scattereth the lawless,
> And bringeth the wheel over them.

No throne is established in peace when lawlessness and violence are rampant among the people. It is necessary, for the preservation of society, the peace of the righteous, as well as the stability of government, that those who oppose it be destroyed. So, before the millennial kingdom shall be set up, the wicked will be rooted out of the earth. See Isaiah 63 and Revelation 19.

> [27] The spirit of man is the lamp of Jehovah,
> Searching all the depths of the soul.

The spirit of man is not mere breath or some impersonal idea. God "formeth the spirit of man within him" (Zech. 12:1). It is by the spirit he is enabled to think and plan, to weigh evidences, and to understand things both material, moral, and spiritual. "What man knoweth the things of a man, save the spirit of man which is in him?" (1 Cor. 2:11.) Here it is evident that the spirit is the seat of intelligence. How would it sound to substitute "breath" for "spirit" in either of these Scripture verses, making them declare God formed man's breath as an entity within him, and that by his breath he apprehended the things that concerned him? Spite of all that casuists and sophists may allege to the contrary, the Bible clearly teaches the true individuality of the spirit.[1]

It is here called the lamp of Jehovah. Notice, it is not the light of Jehovah. The lamp is the vessel that holds the light, which itself is divine, proceeding from God. But man's spirit can be a light receiver and light retainer, illuminating every part of his moral being. This it is that gives him preeminence over all the lower creation. "What an immeasurable gulf there is between the lowest type of man, with all his capabilities of divine enlightenment, and the highest type of brute, who must be forever insensible to spiritual instruction![2]

The most degraded savage gropes after God, for his spirit is the lamp of

Jehovah, dimly though the light may shine. But take the beast and train him to the highest point of brute-intelligence, he manifests no recognition of responsibility to a Creator, no sense of spiritual conceptions. This fact alone is enough to forever destroy the agnostic theory of evolution as taught by Darwin and Huxley, and eagerly received by so many who are ever ready to run after what seems to be new and novel, particularly if it appears to eliminate God from His own universe.

Through the spirit God has His say to man. Thereby He pours His light into every chamber of his being. This it is that produces a sense of need, a yearning after Himself. For in his natural state "there is none that seeketh after God." When His testimony is received and the soul is bowed before Him in repentance, His Holy Spirit, through the Scriptures of truth, witnesses with our spirits that we are His children. See Elijah and the still small voice (1 Kings 19:11–13).

> ²⁸ Loving-kindness and truth preserve the king:
> And his throne is upheld by loving-kindness.

In verse 26 we saw that it was the king's wisdom to execute judgment upon his foes. Here we are reminded of the other side of his character. His throne rests on righteousness, but it is upheld by loving-kindness. The two are essential—loving-kindness and truth. "Grace and truth came by Jesus Christ." When He reigns, both shall be displayed in perfection (Isa. 32).

> ²⁹ The glory of young men is their strength:
> And the beauty of old men is the gray head.

See note on 16:31. In the economy of nature, as of grace, there is a time and season for all things. Youth delights in deeds of prowess and glories in physical strength. Age is the time for meditation and sobriety, and of this the gray head is a reminder, beautiful indeed in its place. In his first epistle, the apostle John takes up the same thoughts in a spiritual sense. The young men are those who are strong in the faith, in whom the Word of God abides, and who have overcome the wicked one. To the fathers, he simply writes, "Ye have known Him that is from the beginning." It is that experimental knowledge of Christ which is enlarged and deepened by the passing of the years (1 John 2:13–14).

> ³⁰ The blueness of a wound cleanseth away evil:
> So do stripes the depths of the soul.

Added suffering is often required to purge the system of poisonous matter; therefore the skillful surgeon is not always concerned to immediately heal a wound. There is often a probing, and consequent inflammation, that is very painful, but good in result. So it is with God's dealings when unholiness has been tolerated by His children. Stripes and sorrows may be laid upon them, but only that the inner parts of the being may be purged of all hidden evil by self-judgment and full confession in His presence. The unnamed author of the psalm of the laver is not the only one who could say, "Before I was afflicted I went astray: but now have I kept Thy word" (Ps. 119:67). As he would be an unwise patient who objected to the pain caused by the surgeon while he endeavored to free the wound from impurities that might effectually hinder healing, and which, if unremoved, might poison the whole system, so is the saint foolish indeed who repines under a Father's chastening hand and seeks to free himself from the stripes rather than to "hear the rod, and Him who hath appointed it."

CHAPTER 21

PROVERBS 21

The great truth that the prophet Daniel sought to bring to bear upon the conscience of the impious Belshazzar on the last night of his reign at Babylon is that which the opening verse presents, in a slightly different way. Daniel endeavored to impress the Chaldean king with his duty to acknowledge "the God in whose hand thy breath is, and whose are all thy ways"; but he would not be humbled. Here we are told that

> ¹ The king's heart is in the hand of Jehovah, as the rivulets of
> water:
> He turneth it whithersoever He will.

See 20:24. There is no monarch so great that he can act in independence of God. Whether he owns it or not, Jehovah is controlling him as He controls the flow of the water-brooks. He who "hath His way in the whirlwind and the storm" can make the wrath of man to praise Him, and restrain the remainder thereof. As already noted, the book of Esther is the fitting illustration of this, especially 6:1–10 (see remarks on 11:8). Jehovah's word to Cyrus, written long before that ruler was born, is another striking case in point. See Isaiah 45:1–7.

² Every way of a man is right in his own eyes:
But Jehovah pondereth the hearts.

See 20:6. Self-righteousness is perhaps the most human of all sins. Men will excuse and explain away in themselves what in others would be censured with severity. The Lord beholds the heart and takes notice of the pride gnawing like a worm at the root. Not he who commends himself, but he who is commended by God, is approved. See Paul (1 Cor. 4:4).

³ To do righteousness and judgment
Is more acceptable to Jehovah than sacrifice.

It was a common thing for men to forget that sacrifices and offerings were not pleasing to the Lord when uprightness was lacking. He ever placed righteousness and equity above ceremonial observances, as, we may rest assured, He does to-day. The Lord witheringly rebuked the Pharisees when He was on earth, for their attention to ritualistic details while justice and integrity were lacking. "I will have mercy, and not sacrifice" was His word. Isaiah sets forth the same truth, of the supreme importance of the execution of righteousness, when contrasting the ceremonial fasts with what Jehovah really delighted in (Isa. 58:5–14). See Samuel's word to Saul (1 Sam. 15:22).

⁴ A high look, and a proud heart,
And the tillage of the lawless, is sin.

As long as man persists in rebellion against God, he can do nothing that will be acceptable in His sight. Not only are lofty eyes and a proud heart evil, but even what might otherwise be meritorious is sin while man refuses to bow in repentance before Him.

Let a province rebel against its lawful ruler, the inhabitants may carry on many useful occupations and labor diligently in them, but all are tainted with sedition, so cannot be considered profitable or right. When they ground their arms at the feet of the king and own his sway, these same occupations become pleasing and proper in his sight. So it is with man away from God and with those who turn to Him in contrition of heart. See the Holy Spirit's estimate of Israel while God's Anointed is rejected (Rom. 10:1–3).

5 The thoughts of the diligent tend only to plenteousness;
  But of every one that is hasty only to want.
6 The getting of treasures by a lying tongue
  Is a vanity tossed to and fro of them that seek death.
7 The robbery of the lawless shall destroy them;
  Because they refuse to do judgment.

Riches accumulated by means of honest, wholesome toil give pleasure and a measure of satisfaction to their possessor. But the hasty gathering of wealth by lying and deceit, often coupled with downright robbery, will bring sorrow and shame in their wake. One may possess boundless stores of gold and silver, and yet be as needy as the Arab lost in the desert, who, when almost dead for want of food, found in the track of a caravan a package, which he opened with trembling eagerness, hoping it might be dates. He dropped it in dire disappointment, as he groaned, "It's only pearls!" Those pearls were worth thousands of dollars, but they could not feed a starving man. So with wealth illegally gotten. It cannot satisfy. He who possesses it will be in deepest and most abject poverty after all. Life will be a weary round of vexation and disappointment, and he will be left to groan at last, "All is vanity, and pursuit of the wind." See Ecclesiastes 5:10–17.

8 The way of a guilty man is very crooked:
  But as for the pure, his work is right.

Like the trail of the serpent are the ways of a guilty man. It is invariably a sign that something is radically wrong at bottom when a person's path is crooked, and he has to be continually excusing and explaining. He who walks with God will be above reproach; for he will shun every form of evil. The work of the pure is right. His life is like an open book, which explains itself, and shuts the lips even of enemies. Daniel was of this character; so that when the presidents and princes sought to find occasion against him concerning the kingdom, "they could find none occasion nor fault; forasmuch as he was faithful, neither was there any error or fault found in him" (Dan. 6:4). Ahab's history is a solemn illustration of the crooked ways of a guilty man (1 Kings 16–22).

9 It is better to dwell in a corner of the housetop,
  Than with a brawling woman in a wide house.

See note on 19:13. Happy must the family be where the lovely order of God's Word is recognized as to the various relationships of each one. If the husband render unto the wife due benevolence, and the wife be adorned by the ornament of a meek and quiet spirit, the children are likely to be in godly subjection, and the home a sweet foretaste of that eternal one for which we wait. But where a brawling woman seeks to rule and will not be content unless she has things her own way, it is most unpleasant. A quiet corner on the housetop is better far than to dwell in a palatial residence with such company. Both Job and David found it so at times (Job 2:9–10; 2 Sam. 6:20–23). See verse 19 below.

> [10] The soul of the lawless desireth evil:
>   His neighbor findeth no favor in his eyes.

We generally find in others what we look for. The man who seeks in his neighbor goodness and virtue is almost certain to find something worthy of praise; but he who goes about looking for evil can readily find that in most people which he can gloat over. None find favor in his eyes, even though he have to admit their superiority to himself. Of this ilk was Sanballat of old (Neh. 6:5–9).

> [11] When the scorner is punished, the simple is made wise:
>   And when the wise is instructed, he receiveth knowledge.

When he who resists the truth is permitted to go unrebuked, it strengthens his position in the eyes of the ignorant. For this reason, we are told, "Them that sin rebuke before all, that others also may fear" (1 Tim. 5:20). They are likely keenly to feel and bitterly to resent the correction; but this only emphasizes their need of it; for a wise man would profit by instruction, and receive knowledge. See the result of Paul's rebuke to Elymas the sorcerer, as contrasted with his withstanding of Peter and Barnabas (Acts 13:8–12; Gal. 2:11–16).

> [12] The righteous man wisely considereth the house of the
>   lawless:
>   He overthroweth the lawless because of their evil.

It is the final triumph of the righteous over the lawless that is referred to. The just man will not be unduly depressed, and certainly not anxious, when he sees the present prosperity of the wicked. He knows their joys are empty indeed, and their days of boasting few at the best. Soon he shall tread them down; for so has God ordained it. The verse might be easier understood by a Jew than a Christian; but in either case it abides true. Iniquity cannot flourish long. The just shall overthrow the house of those given to evil. Even a Jehu can thus be an instrument in God's hand (2 Kings 9).

> [13] Whoso stoppeth his ears at the cry of the poor,
> He also shall cry himself, but shall not be answered.

In 19:17 we had a positive statement regarding the Lord's assurance that he who had pity on the poor should be richly repaid. The negative is equally true. He who heeds not the bitter cry of the needy shall in due time cry himself, and be unheard. The destitute and afflicted have a faithful Friend in the God who created them. His concern is very real, and He takes note of all done for or against them. Especially is this so when they are of the household of faith. See the premillennial judgment of the nations of the earth, as pictured by our Lord Himself in Matthew 25:31–46.

> [14] A gift in secret pacifieth anger:
> And a reward in the bosom, strong wrath.

Nothing so readily vanquishes hatred and wrath as doing good to one who cherishes ill-will, providing it be done quietly and unpretentiously, so that others are not made aware of it. For there is danger that well-meant kindnesses, done openly in the sight of all, may be mistaken for unreal acting, designed to deceive onlookers. But what passes between two parties in private cannot be so construed, if mention be not made of it afterward. It was thus that Jacob sought to turn aside the assumed wrath of Joseph (Gen. 43:11–14).

> [15] It is joy to the just to do what is right:
> But it is ruin to the workers of iniquity.
> [16] The man that wandereth out of the way of understanding
> Shall abide in the assembly of the dead.

When a man is himself righteous, he delights in righteousness; whereas, in the mind of the unjust, moral rectitude seems to be the certain road to ruin. Take a business man who has learned to order his ways in public and private in integrity and honesty: to depart from principles such as these, would be, in his eyes, painful, and cause for grief and sorrow. But with too many it is accepted as an axiom that one cannot prosper in a business way and maintain the right. To attempt to do so seems to them to foreshadow certain and speedy failure. The young man launching out in life is very apt to be leavened with this unholy and utterly false idea; whereas the experience of multitudes has but confirmed the testimony of Scripture that the only true and lasting success results from righteous dealing.

He who wanders away from the paths of sound wisdom will remain in the congregation of the dead. "She that liveth in pleasure is dead while she liveth" (1 Tim. 5:6). That which is really life is only enjoyed by the upright who set the Lord always before them. Contrast Judas (Acts 1:18).

> [17] He that loveth pleasure shall be a poor man:
> He that loveth wine and oil shall not be rich.

The spendthrift and the self-indulgent are not in the way to future wealth and comfort. It is the frugal and self-denying who, by present carefulness, pave the way to easier circumstances in years to come. The young man who spends his time in folly, seeking dubious pleasures with unwise companions, is laying up misery and want for his afterlife. He who pampers his appetite with costly dainties in youth is likely to be brought to coarse fare in old age; while those who were wise enough to forego present indulgences, which would only have been baneful in their early days, will be in a position later on rationally to enjoy what, by dint of labor and carefulness, they have been enabled to lay by. The intemperate lover of folly and pleasure is likely soon to reach the depths to which sank the prodigal of Luke 15.

> [18] The lawless shall be a ransom for the righteous,
> And the treacherous for the upright.

This is intrinsic justice. But when grace was being made known in Christ Jesus, the Righteous became a ransom for the lawless, and the Upright for the treacherous! Justice demands the punishment of the guilty, in order that the guiltless may be delivered; but love gave the Guiltless to die that the guilty might be justified. An illustration of the proverb is seen in the siege and deliverance of Abel of Beth-maachah (2 Sam. 20:14–22).

> [19] It is better to dwell in a desert land
> Than with a contentious and an angry woman.

See verse 9 above. No creature is more lovely than a woman who exhibits the precious graces of the Spirit of God. Even natural graces adorn and beautify her beyond all that the foolish fripperies and vanities of her oftentimes artificial life can do. But a woman bereft of thoughtfulness and kindliness seems almost to be a misnomer. A contentious and angry woman is beyond all words disagreeable, and can by her tongue and her wretched ways produce untold misery. A tent in a wilderness alone is to be preferred to a palace in her company. Athaliah was evidently of this unhappy class, who, violent and treacherous, would stop at nothing to accomplish her unholy ends (2 Kings 11). See 27:15–16.

> ²⁰ There is desirable treasure and oil in the dwelling of the
>   wise;
>   But a foolish man swalloweth it up.

See verse 17 above. The wise man does not live for the present but prudently considers the coming years when strength will fail, and he will be unable to labor as in his youth and prime. Therefore when his days of rest from toil come, he has costly store laid by for the sustenance of those dependent still upon him. The foolish thinks only of the passing moment and spends with a lavish hand; but shall come to want at last. Consider Paul's word as to parents providing for their children (2 Cor. 12:14).

> ²¹ He that followeth after righteousness and loving-kindness,
>   Findeth life, righteousness and honor.

To steadily pursue righteousness and loving-kindness, exemplifying both in the walk and ways, this is the sure road to what all men desire—life and honor. They are linked together by uprightness. The empty glory of this world, the plaudits of the carnally-minded, are worth little after all. But to be honored by God, and by those who love Him—this abides forever. He delights to bestow His blessing upon those who esteem His Word and yield obedience to His truth. For the truth was not given to be a source of intellectual enjoyment alone, though it is that; but that it might be manifested in the life, as it was to the full in our Lord Jesus Christ. Coupled with moral rectitude He would have that gentle loving-kindness which commends the truth to those who might, by severity on the part of its adherents, be driven therefrom. When grace and truth thus together control the being, life, righteousness, and honor must be the happy result. See Asa, king of Judah, and note how he ever prospered as he sought what was pleasing to God. His only recorded errors but emphasize this (2 Chron. 14–16).

> [22] A wise man scaleth the city of the mighty,
>   And casteth down the strength of the confidence thereof.

Brute force and heavy fortifications are of no avail against superior wisdom. It is not might alone that counts, but science and ability. Seemingly impregnable positions have often been taken by the exercise of sagacity and stratagem. Jebus and Babylon were supposedly proof against every assault, but both fell before men of wisdom and sagacity (1 Chron. 11:4–6; Jer. 51:27–33). The lesson is important when it is against spiritual foes we are called to fight. For the overcoming of the powers of evil, that wisdom is greatly needed which comes from acquaintance with God and His Word. See Ephesians 6:10–18.

> [23] Whoso keepeth his mouth and his tongue,
>   Keepeth his soul from troubles.

Again we are directed to the subject that is so often brought to the fore in this book: the control of the tongue. Unwise words, however true they may sometimes be, are often the cause of grave trouble and disaster. To keep the mouth and the tongue as with an armed guard is to avoid many a grief and bitter memory. See James 3:2–12 and compare the notes on 11:13; 15:1; 17:20; and 18:6–8.

> [24] Proud and haughty scorner is his name,
>   Who dealeth in proud wrath.

An arrogant, self-willed spirit is manifested by unbridled words and uncontrolled anger. A humble man is a gentle man; he will not be given to ebullitions of wrath or outbursts of indignation. Of course the "dealer in proud wrath" is to be distinguished from one who on extreme occasions loses control of his temper and utters hasty words under strong provocation. Such a one may afterward be plunged in deepest sorrow and humiliation over his sin; but it is otherwise with the proud and haughty scorner. He has no compunction of conscience because of his wrong spirit, but persists in a course of action that is in every way contrary to meekness and forbearance, forgetting that the wrath of man works not the righteousness of God. See Simeon and Levi (Gen. 49:5–7).

²⁵ The desire of the slothful killeth him;
    For his hands refuse to labor.
²⁶ He coveteth greedily all the day long;
    But the righteous giveth and spareth not.

Like a drone in the hive, the slothful man covets the fruits of labor but detests
the work which produces them. He is occupied with himself, full of desire, but
opposed to effort. Selfishness is his strongest characteristic. The righteous man is
a producer. He loves to acquire, but only in order that he may "provide things
honest in the sight of all men," properly meeting the needs of those dependent
upon him, and having plenty to give to any who are in need. In this he is an
imitator of God "who giveth to all men liberally and upbraideth not." Contrast
the spirit manifested by Achan (Josh. 7:21) and the Philippian assembly (2 Cor.
8:2). See notes on 12:27; 13:4; 19:24; 20:4.

²⁷ The sacrifice of the lawless is abomination:
    How much more, when he bringeth it with a wicked
        purpose!

See notes on 15:8–9, 26 and 21:4. The sacrifice of the lawless is ever detestable and unacceptable in the eyes of God; but especially so when it is but a cover
for hypocrisy. To carry on so-called religious duties to be seen of men and to hide
a life of wickedness, is iniquity of the most revolting character. It was this that
caused our Lord so sternly to rebuke the scribes and Pharisees of His day. They
were punctilious in observing the law and the added directions of the Talmud in
regard to the temple offerings; they made broad their phylacteries; they loved to
pray standing on the street corners to be seen of men; but meantime they profited at the expense of poor widows and were characterized by covetousness and
wickedness of the vilest description. Their moral descendants are many in our
own day, who can put on a devout expression, use pious words, and ostenta-
tiously give of their wealth to public charities; but whose inner lives are black
and iniquitous. For a time they may cover from the eyes of men their true condition, but in God's sight their sacrifice is abominable.

²⁸ A false witness shall perish:
    And a man that heareth shall speak constantly.
²⁹ A lawless man hardeneth his face:
    But as for the upright, he establisheth his way.

The false witness may carry his point for the moment but his destruction is certain to come. He who testifies according to his hearing and knowledge will be able to maintain consistently his position, and speak constantly, or unchallenged. Such was the good confession witnessed before Caiaphas and Pontius Pilate by our Lord Jesus Christ, when the testimony of the lying witnesses agreed not one with the other (Matt. 26:59–64; 27:11–14).

He who has no regard for law, human or divine, will harden his face and persist in his false words and ways; but the upright by his consistent speech and actions establishes his purpose.

> ³⁰ There is no wisdom, nor understanding,
>   Nor counsel against Jehovah.
> ³¹ The horse is prepared against the day of battle,
>   But safety is of Jehovah.

The trusting soul rests on the fact that the counsel of the Lord will never be defeated. Therefore he fears not the wisdom or understanding or the plots of his foes. What can man do to harm the one who is covered by the wings of Jehovah? "Though a host encamp against me," said David, "yet will I not fear."

It is not numbers or superior accoutrements that ensures victory, but to have the God of our salvation going before us. This was the confidence of Asa when confronted by the vast army of Zerah the Ethiopian at the battle of Mareshah. "Asa cried unto the LORD his God, and said, LORD, it is nothing with Thee to help, whether with many, or with them that have no power: help us, O LORD our God; for we rest on Thee, and in Thy name we go against this multitude. O LORD, Thou art our God; let not man prevail against Thee" (2 Chron. 14:11). This is delightful to contemplate. With Asa it was not a question of the relative strength and prowess of the hordes of Africans and the army of Judah; but it was simply a question of the power of God and the puny ability of weak, mortal men. "Let not man prevail against Thee," was his plea. He chooses a word for man that emphasizes his insignificance and lack of strength.

In the Hebrew language there are various words which he might have used. *Ahdahm* is the ordinary term which links man with his first father, from a root meaning red clay. *Geber* is man in his might, from a root meaning to be strong. *Ish* is man in his dignity; whereas the word used by Asa is *Enosh,* from a root signifying frail and incurable. It is man in his low estate as fallen and mortal.

This then was all the great Ethiopian host meant to Asa. All were as nothing in contrast to the mighty power of the God who was leading on the army of

Judah and Benjamin. The result was certain, "The LORD smote the Ethiopians before Asa and before Judah; and the Ethiopians fled . . . for they were destroyed before the LORD, and before His host; and they carried away very much spoil" (2 Chron. 14:12–13).

May each tried saint cast himself upon the same Omnipotent Savior-God in every time of apparently overwhelming trouble, and thus prove for himself that "safety is of the Lord."

CHAPTER 22

PROVERBS 22

There is that which is far to be preferred to earthly treasure, though often it is forfeited to obtain the other.

> ¹ A [good] name is rather to be chosen than great riches,
> And loving favor rather than silver and gold.

The adjective *good* does not occur in the original text. But "a name" is used in the sense of a character of renown, as elsewhere in Scripture, notably in Genesis 11:4, "let us make us a name"; Deuteronomy 26:19, "make thee high . . . in name"; 2 Samuel 7:9, 23; 8:13; and many other passages. In this sense then a name is far preferable to vast wealth, and to be kindly esteemed than immense revenues. It is a great mistake for the young to suppose that such an honored name is most easily found on the battlefield, in the halls of government, the ranks of great writers, or in the marts of worldwide commerce. No name is more lasting and enduring than that won by him who lives for God, and for the sake of the Lord Jesus Christ counts all earth has to offer as dung and dross. It was devotion to David that caused Abishai and Benaiah to win immortal names (2 Sam. 23:18, 22) and devotion to Christ has caused many to be remembered forever who otherwise would long since have fallen into oblivion. Who would have heard of the twelve apostles, had they not left all and followed Jesus? What

185

would have been the glory of the name of Saul, the rabbi of Tarsus, compared with that of Paul the missionary of the cross?

> ² The rich and poor meet together;
> Jehovah is the maker of them all.

The fatherhood of God and the brotherhood of man is a scriptural doctrine if rightly used. In fact, it is alone from Scripture that men are given to know that God "hath made of one blood all nations of men for to dwell on all the face of the earth" (Acts 17:26). Human reason, apart from divine revelation, would never have discovered this wonderful secret. Universal brotherhood, the union of all the races and nations of men in one great family, springing from one common stock despite manifest physical and ethnological differences, was never dreamed of by philosophers until enlightened by the inspired Word of God. The fraternity of the higher races was more or less proudly owned by the sages of old; but to see in a despised and ignorant slave of inferior caste a brother was something that the human mind revolted against. But the Hebrew Scriptures testify throughout to the fact that all men sprang from one common father, Adam, and are linked together by ties that cannot be dissolved. This, the Christian Scriptures emphasize; and seeing in Adam the son of God, declare that God is "the Father of spirit," therefore in a creatorial sense, the Father of all men.

But let it be remembered that universal fatherhood in this aspect is a very different thing to the precious truth of the family of God as made known by our Lord and His apostles. Man by the fall lost the divine likeness and became a sinner ruined and alienated. Hence the need of redemption and regeneration. By new birth those who by nature were children of wrath and by practice sons of disobedience, are made children of god and partakers of the divine nature. A new life, eternal life, is imparted and the Holy Spirit given. Thus they cry, "Abba, Father." It is such persons alone who form the new creation brotherhood, because possessors of a common life and nature.

The distinction here made needs to be kept in mind in our day of looseness and laxity, when men rebel against the truth of the fall, and would fain call God their Father apart from new birth, and link up saint and sinner in one great family.

The Christian unhesitatingly and freely owns that Jehovah is the maker of all, and that His heart goes out to every creature He has called into being; but he sees two families throughout Scripture, "the children of God . . . and the children of the devil" (1 John 3:10). These are characteristic terms. Of course none is definitely called a child of the Devil until he manifestly proves himself to be such by opposing the truth and rejecting Christ.

> ³ A prudent man foreseeth the evil, and hideth himself:
> But the simple pass on, and are punished.

These solemn words are designedly repeated in 27:12. It is an evidence of God's exceeding love that He has so faithfully warned us of the terrible consequences that follow the refusal to bow before Him in repentance, and to receive the grace He offers through Christ Jesus. The wise man sees the evil afar off and hides himself in the refuge God has provided. But the simple harden the heart and refuse to hearken, thus ensuring their own destruction.

"A man shall be as a hiding place from the wind, and a covert from the tempest; as rivers of water in a dry place; as the shadow of a great rock in a weary land" (Isa. 32:2). Faith sees the fulfillment of these precious words in "the Man Christ Jesus"; and fleeing to Him exclaims, "Thou art my hiding place" (Ps. 32:7). If He be rejected and His grace despised, certain and eternal judgment must follow. Contrast the Philippian jailer with the Roman magistrates (Acts 16:25–40).

> ⁴ The recompense of humility and the fear of Jehovah
> Are riches, honor and life.
> ⁵ Thorns and snares are in the way of the perverse:
> He that doth keep his soul shall be far from them.

How different are the paths and the ultimate rewards of the godly and the perverse. Heaven and hell are not more diverse than the roads leading thereto. The godly man is marked out from his fellows by a meek and contrite spirit, and the fear of the Lord. The ungodly is insubordinate and self-willed. The way of the former leads to true riches, the honor that cometh from God, and life everlasting. The steps of the latter soon became entangled amid thorns and snares from which he who keeps his soul, by obedience to the word of Jehovah, shall be preserved. Contrast Hezekiah and his son Manasseh, before he was humbled (2 Chron. 29–33).

> ⁶ Initiate a child concerning the way he should go:
> And when he is old he will not depart from it.

To start the child right is of all importance. The saying of the Jesuit, "Give me your child till he is twelve, and I care not who has charge of him afterward," has passed into a proverb. The tree follows the bent of its early years, and so with our sons and daughters. If taught to love the world, to crave its fashions and follies in childhood, they are almost certain to live for the world when they come to mature years. On the other hand if properly instructed as to the vanity of all that men of this present evil age live for, from the beginning, they are in little danger of reversing that judgment as they grow older. Parents need to remember it is not enough to tell their little ones of Jesus and His rejection, or to warn them of the ways of the world; but they must see to it that in their own lives they exemplify their instruction. This will count above all else in the training of the young. To speak piously of separation to Christ while manifesting the spirit of the world in dress, the arrangement of the home, and the company sought and kept, will readily be set down by observing little ones as dissimulation and hypocrisy; and we need not then wonder if they grow up to cast all our *words* behind them, and to love what our *ways* proclaimed to be the real object of our hearts.

But where a holy, cheerful atmosphere pervades the home and godly admonition is coupled with godly living, parents can count on the Lord to keep their households following in the right way. See Timothy (2 Tim. 1:5).

> 7 The rich ruleth over the poor,
> And the borrower is servant to the lender.

He who heeds the scriptural injunction to "owe no man anything, but to love one another" (Rom. 13:8), will escape the awful bondage of the debtor. The rich almost invariably lord it over the poor, save where grace comes in to check the latent pride of the human heart. Therefore it is but natural that he who lends should consider himself superior to the borrower. The latter destroys his own freedom by his neglect of the divine command. It is better far to be in straightened circumstances and cast upon God, than to have plenty for the time being but to know that it belongs to another. Nothing so crushes the spirit of a man as debt, if he have any conscience about it at all. The Christian should fear it and flee from it as from the effort of the enemy to subvert his peace and destroy his sense of dependence upon the Lord.

There is by no means the concern about this matter among saints that it demands; people think little or nothing of running bills and borrowing money without proper security, which afterward may cause them deep grief and bring dishonor on Christ. He who would be alone the Lord's servant and in bondage to no man will shun debt in every form. Many a one by carelessness as to this, has left his family in as dire distress as did the son of the prophet whose decease is mentioned in 2 Kings 4:1.

> 8 He that soweth iniquity shall reap vanity:
> And the rod of his wrath shall fail.
> 9 He that hath a bountiful eye shall be blessed;
> For he giveth of his bread to the poor.

The two verses are in striking and intentional contrast; again reminding us of the certainty of a harvest like unto the character of the sowing.

He who sows iniquity will reap a dreadful crop of vanity; and though he take a lordly position and vent his anger against what is of God, his rod shall fail and his rule come to a derisive end, as in the case of the unhappy Pharaoh of the Exodus.

But the kindly, benevolent soul who plants the seed of thoughtfulness for others will reap a bountiful harvest of consideration and of blessing for himself. Bread cast upon the waters returns after many days. See Ebed-melech (Jer. 38:7–12; 39:16–18).

> 10 Cast out the scorner, and contention shall go out;
> Yea, strife and reproach shall cease.

See note on 21:11. The scorner of this book is practically the same as the railer of 1 Corinthians 5. Such a man can work untold mischief among a company of the Lord's people. His wretched evil speaking coupled with his contempt for all godly restraint, like the leaven placed in the meal, will, if unchecked, go on working until the whole is leavened. Therefore the necessity of obeying the Word of God, "Put away from among yourselves that wicked person" (1 Cor. 5:11–13).

The Law knew no mercy for such a character. One who scorned the God of Israel and troubled His people was, at the mouth of two or three witnesses, to be put to death that the evil might be put away from among them (Deut. 17:2–7).

In this dispensation of grace such an extreme measure is not commanded; but the saints are called upon to put him away from their company, in order that the rest may be saved from falling into his unholy ways, and thus the name of Christ

be kept from further dishonor. Outside, he is in the place where God can deal
with him. Inside, he is a source of grief to the assembly and a reproach to the
Lord. See Hymenaeus and Alexander (1 Tim. 1:20).

> [11] He that loveth pureness of heart,
>   Upon whose lips is grace, the king is his friend.

A righteous ruler delights in a man of pure heart and gracious words. And to
such a one the King of kings is indeed a Friend. It is the pure in heart who see
God, and they who are truly such will manifest it by obedience to the word, "Let
your speech be always with grace, seasoned with salt." A bitter, acrimonious, and
fault-finding tongue belongs not to the pure-hearted man of God, but is generally the evidence that one is far from being right himself. Note what is said of
Mordecai (Esther 10:2–3).

> [12] The eyes of Jehovah guard knowledge,
>   But He overthroweth the words of the treacherous.

The Lord's eye is upon His own truth, which is the only real knowledge. He
guards it day and night, and will never let it fall to the ground. When spoken by
His servants, His eye is beholding and He will see that it shall accomplish that
whereunto He sends it.

But the false words of the unfaithful shall come to naught. The Lord Himself
will overthrow them. Error cannot always prosper. It may seem to thrive for the
moment, but it shall be destroyed eventually. Contrast Micaiah and the prophets of Baal (1 Kings 22).

> [13] The slothful man saith, There is a lion without,
>   I shall be slain in the streets!

See notes on 12:27; 15:19; 19:24; 21:25. Many are the excuses devised by the
sluggard to account for his supineness and utter lack of energy. Where no dangers or difficulties exist he imagines them; and where they really are he exagger-
ates them to such a degree that they appear to be insurmountable. He who goes
forth in the strength of faith finds the lions have been rendered powerless to
destroy. Contrast with the slothful man of this verse, Benaiah the son of Jehoiada,
one of David's mighty men (2 Sam. 23:20). See 26:13.

¹⁴ The mouth of strange women is a deep ditch:
    He that is abhorred of Jehovah shall fall therein.

See notes on 2:16–19; 6:23–35; 7:4–27. It is with her flattering words that the strange woman allures him who stops to listen, to his destruction. None who walk with God will be taken by her; but he whose ways displease the Lord will readily fall a victim to her seductions, stumbling into sin and its fearful consequences as a blind man into a deep pit. Of this, Judah becomes a terrible example in Genesis 38.

¹⁵ Foolishness is bound in the heart of a child;
    But the rod of correction shall drive it far from him.

See notes on 13:24 and 19:18. To leave a child to himself is to ensure his ruin, for folly is bound up in his heart. Discipline, properly administered, will correct the natural tendency to go astray. The rod is, of course, not necessarily strictly such. Corporal punishment is not always required, and might at times be very unwise. But firm, yet kindly, discipline is what the passage declares the importance of. The rod, throughout Scripture, speaks of authority and power; in this case, that parental restraint to which the child owes so much. It was the lack of this that was responsible in large measure for the evil ways of both Absalom and Adonijah (2 Sam. 14; 1 Kings 1:6).

¹⁶ He that oppresseth the poor to increase his riches,
    And he that giveth to the rich, shall surely come to want.

The one is as foolish as the other. To seek to accumulate wealth by oppression of the needy, or to endeavor to curry favor by gifts to those who need them not because of their riches; both courses are precursors of want instead of solid increase.

For the moment, he who practices what is here condemned, may seem to prosper and flourish; but his end will manifest the truth of God's Word. He shall not be able to find the happiness he sought, and will at last be obliged to own that his purpose has been utterly defeated because of the iniquity of his heart. See what is said in James 5 of the rich who oppress the poor and withhold their wages.

¹⁷ Bow down thine ear, and hear the words of the wise,
    And apply thy heart unto my knowledge.

[18] For it is a pleasant thing if thou keep them within thee;
   They shall withal be fitted together in thy lips.
[19] That thy trust may be in Jehovah,
   I have made known to thee this day, even to thee.
[20] Have not I written to thee excellent things
   In counsels and knowledge,
[21] That I might make thee know the certainty of the words of
      truth;
   That thou mightest answer the words of truth to them that
      send unto thee?

We now have a challenge reminding us of that seven times repeated in Revelation 2–3, "He that hath ears to hear, let him hear." Many have been the words of wisdom to which we have been listening; many more are to follow. The soul may become so used to them as to fail to discern their excellent character. What is needed is that the heart be applied to the knowledge thus imparted. For it is of all importance that they be kept within and fitted to the lips of the hearer, whose trust must be in Jehovah, if he is to exemplify them in his life.

The expression, "Have not I written to thee excellent things," is a peculiar one. In the original, it is literally "have I not set them before thee in three ways" or, "a third time." This is evidently in a superlative degree. "The excellent things in counsel and knowledge" are things of the highest value, beyond mere human wisdom. It is God Himself marking out the safe and right way in which His children should walk. Thus will they "know the certainty of the words of truth," and be enabled to use them aright in reply to all who inquire. Blessed it is, in a day of doubt and skepticism, to be able to rest the soul on the very words of the Living God, knowing their true and precious character.

In the New Testament we find four inspired apostles quoting unhesitatingly from this book as that which, like all other Scripture, was God-breathed. Paul quotes from it in Romans 12:19–20 and Hebrews 12:5–6; James in 4:6 of his epistle; Peter twice in his first, and once in his second letter, namely 1 Peter 4:8, 17–18; 2 Peter 2:22; and Jude, in the twelfth verse of his trenchant arraignment of the false teachers already creeping in among the saints.

But what is of deepest interest to the believer, our Lord Himself in His address at the table of the Pharisee, as recorded in Luke 14, uses this treasury of proverbial truth as His textbook, and quotes approvingly from three verses of its twenty-fifth chapter (vv. 6–8). Added to this we find allusions and references to its teaching throughout the later books of the Old Testament and all parts of the

New. God has linked this plain and intensely practical portion—these "words of truth"—inseparably with all the rest of His holy book. As we pursue our study, may it be with a fuller sense of the sacred character of the homely admonitions and hints as to daily life which are to come before us.

> ²² Rob not the poor, because he is poor,
>   Neither oppress the afflicted in the gate;
> ²³ For Jehovah will plead their cause,
>   And spoil the soul of those that spoiled them.

This is a warning word to those who sit in the place of judgment, to which the gate refers. If the ways of justice are perverted, let him who renders a false and oppressive sentence, remember that the supreme Judge is looking on, and He will render to every man according as his work has been. Righteous judgment is precious in His sight because it then reflects the integrity of His own throne—a great *white* throne, unsullied by iniquity. If wrong is perpetrated upon the needy now, Jehovah Himself will appear as their Advocate in that highest court of all, when dreadful indeed will be the portion of those who have used the judgment seat on earth for the furtherance of iniquity. What will be the state of the Herods and Pilates when dragged before that bar of infinite holiness?

> ²⁴ Make no friendship with an angry man;
>   And with a furious man thou shalt not go:
> ²⁵ Lest thou learn his ways,
>   And get a snare to thy soul.

A man is known and formed by the company he keeps. "Evil communications corrupt good manners." Therefore the importance of considering carefully the question of intimate association and companionship, not to say fellowship. To keep company with a man given to wrath and fury is to be contaminated by his hasty ways, and to bring a snare upon one's own soul. Anger and malice are the works of the flesh. With such the Christian should have no association, for we are too easily defiled by such things; and to go on with one displaying such evidences of unjudged carnality is to endanger one's own walk and testimony. A Saul is no fit friend for a David. See 21:24.

> ²⁶ Be not thou one of them that strike hands,
>   Or of them that are sureties for debts.

²⁷ If thou hast nothing to pay,
  Why should he take away thy bed from under thee?

See notes on 6:1–5 and 11:15. Some there are who will never learn by precept. Therefore they must be taught by bitter experience. It would not be difficult to find numerous examples of persons who have read Proverbs all their lives, but who, despite its many warnings as to suretyship, have lost nearly all they had through endorsing notes or going on the bond of men who turned out unworthy of their confidence. How much that is painful, and shameful too, might have been avoided had such a passage as this been heeded!

When grace was reigning, they who "had nothing to pay" were frankly forgiven all their debt (Luke 7:40–43); but when stern justice has to be dispensed, he who has not the means to meet his self-imposed obligation is in danger of losing his very bed from under him.

²⁸ Remove not the ancient landmark
  Which thy fathers have set.

This is almost a repetition of that which the Lord of old had spoken through Moses: "Thou shalt not remove thy neighbor's landmark, which they of old time have set in thine inheritance, which thou shalt inherit in the land that the LORD thy God giveth thee to possess it" (Deut. 19:14).

Each Israelite had received his portion directly from Jehovah. Its bounds were marked out by clearly indicated landmarks, which all were commanded to respect. He who removed them forcibly, or in secret, would have to do with God for his transgression.

In this dispensation of grace the portion of the people of God is heavenly, not earthly. Their inheritance is in the precious truth which He has committed to us. To remove the landmarks—the great distinguishing doctrines of Scripture—will be to incur the divine displeasure. Yet, alas, this is the wretched business in which many learned doctors and wiseacres are engaged today. Nothing is too sacred for their irreverent handling. Precious truths like those of atonement and justification by faith—yea, even the mystery of the Holy Trinity and the Person of the Lord Jesus Christ—are, in their eyes, but common things which they may dismiss or ignore as they please. But a day of reckoning is coming, when God will judge them in righteousness, and when those who have been misled by their removal of ancient and venerable landmarks will curse them for the loss of their souls. Terrible will be the accounting of men who, while posing as instructors of the flock of Christ, have all the while been Satan's instruments for overthrowing the saving truths of Scripture. See Paul's warning word to Timothy (2 Tim. 1:8–13; 4:1–5). Compare 23:10–11.

> [29] Seest thou a man diligent in his work?
> He shall stand before kings;
> He shall not stand before mean men.

Reward is sure for the diligent. He who applies himself with earnestness to his appointed labor will work his way into notice, and be recognized because of his ability. How much more when it is unto the Lord he labors, seeking His approbation, rather than that of his fellows! "Not slothful in business; fervent in spirit; serving the Lord," is the canon for the ordering of the believer's daily service (Rom. 12:11). Often, one fears, we act as though it read, "Fervent in business; slothful in spirit; serving yourselves."

He who would stand before the King, and enjoy the sunshine of His approval by and by, must labor now to be well-pleasing to Him. In this the faithful life of Daniel may well speak to us. He was a man who, whatever the changes of government, always came to the front, standing before kings.

CHAPTER 23

PROVERBS 23

Nothing that concerns His creatures is of too small an interest for the Creator to take note of. Therefore, in the opening words of this chapter we have a section devoted to the suited behavior of a man who dines with one of higher station than himself.

> ¹ When thou sittest to eat with a ruler,
>   Consider well who is before thee:
> ² And put a knife to thy throat,
>   If thou be a man given to appetite.
> ³ Be not desirous of his dainties;
>   For they are deceitful meat.

Self-restraint at the table of one in power who has invited is what is here inculcated. To presume on the lasting favor of one in high station and to accept privileges accorded by him, as though deserved, is unwise on the part of one of lesser rank. There is a quiet deference which is consistent at such times. A blasè manner soon excites disgust, and readily draws down indignation and ill-will. Daniel and the Hebrew children manifested a commendable spirit when honored with the king's dainties. Though not sitting with him exactly, yet they may fittingly be referred to in this connection (Dan. 1).

⁴ Labor not to be rich:
  Cease from thine own wisdom.
⁵ Wilt thou set thine eyes upon that which is not?
  For [riches] certainly make themselves wings;
  They fly away as an eagle toward heaven.

Many are the warnings in Scripture against making the accumulation of wealth the object of the heart. The man who, trusting in his own wisdom, ignores divine instruction as to this, will find, when too late, that he has set his eyes upon that which is fleeting and evanescent; for earthly treasure is often dissipated far more easily than collected. Riches seem possessed with wings. Like eagles, they fly away, leaving him whose mind was set upon them disappointed and heartsick.

But, though God has thus faithfully set forth the folly of the mad chase after wealth, how slight has been the impression produced thereby upon the mind of saint or sinner. In the world, men will strain every nerve and exhaust every scheme to become possessed of money which they can never enjoy; and it is plain that many of the children of God are contaminated by the same covetous spirit. We are slow to learn, therefore the need of the Lord's discipline which many of us have to experience all our days. See Paul's word as to the dangers of making haste to be rich (1 Tim. 6:6–10, and note vv. 17–18).

⁶ Eat thou not the bread of him that hath an evil eye,
  Neither desire thou his dainty meats:
⁷ For as he thinketh in his heart, so is he:
  Eat and drink, saith he to thee;
  But his heart is not with thee.
⁸ The morsel which thou hast eaten shalt thou vomit up
  And thou wilt have wasted thy sweet words.

Eating and drinking are once more reverted to. Here the warning is against accepting the hospitality of an insincere person. He may speak fair and profess to delight in your company; but safety consists in shunning him and refusing his advances. If entrapped by appetite, depend upon it, all his delicacies will prove unsatisfying, and pleasant agreeable words will be wasted: for in one way or another he will see that his favors are returned. To do good and give, "hoping for nothing again," is not his thought. He will seek to use for his own advantage those who, by accepting his pretended kindnesses, put themselves under obligation to him. However bland his smile, "as he thinketh in his heart, so is he." Covetousness and self-seeking are there, and his ways are shaped accordingly. See the old prophet of Bethel (1 Kings 13).

> ⁹ Speak not in the ears of a fool,
> For he will despise the wisdom of thy sayings.

To seek to instruct him whose heart is set on folly and waywardness is but wasting one's breath, or like casting pearls before swine. When there is no desire for wisdom, but knowledge and understanding have been deliberately trampled under foot, it is useless to waste words. See 26:4. Jotham's remonstrance with the followers of Abimelech is a case in point (Judg. 9:7–21).

> ¹⁰ Remove not the old landmark;
> And enter not into the fields of the fatherless:
> ¹¹ For their Redeemer is mighty;
> He shall plead their cause with thee.

See note on 22:28. He who, because of their apparent helplessness, invades the field of the widow or the orphan in order to enlarge his own possessions will learn to his sorrow that they have a *Goel,* or Kinsman-Redeemer, in Jehovah Himself. He will espouse their cause and manifest His power on their behalf. Let those who are wronged commit their affairs to Him, knowing that He cannot fail any who trust His love and count upon His intervention. It is refreshing and uplifting to see how David referred all his concerns to this mighty Pleader, when misjudged and oppressed. See Psalm 35.

> ¹² Apply thy heart to instruction,
> And thine ears to the words of knowledge.

This is another reminder of that which was set before the young man so fully in the nine opening verses of chapter 2. Only when the heart is applied to instruction, and the ear bent upon hearing right and profitable words, will there be progress in divine things. A careless learning by rote will never profit. It is when the whole being is occupied with the truth that Wisdom makes her abode in the soul of him who seeks her. An aged Christian was said to have *"meditated the Bible through three times"* in his life. This is very different from merely *reading* the Scriptures. It implies patient, careful study of each portion perused.

Only by some such means will there be true spiritual growth. Listen to Jeremiah (Jer. 15:16).

> ¹³ Withhold not correction from the child:
>   For if thou beatest him with the rod, he shall not die.
> ¹⁴ Thou shalt beat him with the rod,
>   And shalt deliver his soul from sheol.

See note on 19:18. Discipline, administered seasonably (not in harshness, or undue severity), is for the profit of the child. In this way, by means of present suffering, he will be preserved from the ruin and wretchedness which are bound to follow a life of self-seeking and unsubdued, perverse will. Sheol is not exactly hell. It is the world of spirits; here used as that to which a vicious life will soon lead. Chastisement will correct these evil tendencies. It would be well if all parents had the concern as to the ordering of their children that Manoah manifested (Judg. 13:8–12).

> ¹⁵ My son, if thy heart be wise,
>   My heart shall rejoice, even mine.
> ¹⁶ Yea, my reins shall exult,
>   When thy lips shall speak right things.

We may hear, in these words of a father addressed to his son, the desire of our Father, God, that His children walk in the truth. It is precious indeed to be thus afforded the holy privilege of giving joy to His heart by loving wisdom and speaking right things. See 3 John 3–4.

> ¹⁷ Let not thy heart envy sinners;
>   But be thou in the fear of Jehovah all the day long.
> ¹⁸ For surely there is a latter end [or, a reward];
>   And thine expectation shall not be cut off.

To envy those who seem to prosper in wickedness is not wise, for their day of retribution is coming. However righteousness may suffer in the present age, it will be proven at last that they had the better part who daily lived in the fear of the Lord. It seems certain that in the latter verse of this pair the doctrine of future retribution is more than hinted at. Newberry suggests "Verily there is a hereafter" as an adequate rendering of the original. The thought appears to be that there is a time coming when present conditions shall be reversed, and righteousness shall triumph. Then he who has walked in integrity and the fear of God will be rewarded for all his sufferings here. See the last two beatitudes in our Lord's so-called Sermon on the Mount (Matt. 5:10–12).

> [19] Hear thou, my son, and be wise,
>   And guide thy heart in the way.
> [20] Be not among winebibbers;
>   Among riotous eaters of flesh:
> [21] For the drunkard and the glutton shall come to poverty;
>   And drowsiness shall clothe a man with rags.

Intemperance in eating and drinking bespeaks a heart uncontrolled by wisdom. The Christian is bidden to be temperate in all things, that by sobriety and careful behavior he may commend the gospel of God, keeping under his body and bringing it into subjection, not being ruled by its carnal appetites. He who heeds not words like these must bear his just punishment. This was the sin of the stubborn and rebellious son of Deuteronomy 21:20. See verses 29–35 below.

> [22] Hearken unto thy father that begat thee,
>   And despise not thy mother when she is old.

Exuberant youth, self-confident, and resourceful, is likely to forget the reverence due to parents when age enfeebles the once bright and active mind. Let the young give them that filial consideration which they will desire for themselves when years have destroyed early vigor and mentality. Esther's obedience to her aged cousin Mordecai is a lovely sample of what is here inculcated (Esther 2:20).

> [23] Buy the truth, and sell it not;
>   Also wisdom, and instruction, and understanding.

See note on 4:7–9. An important word this for our Laodicean and latitudinarian age. We may well cry, with the prophet, "Truth has fallen in our streets." But he who desires the approval of God above the praise of men will value it nevertheless, and be ready to purchase it at the cost of friends, reputation, possessions, yea, life itself. Nor will he part with it whatever the suffering that may result from contending earnestly for the faith once for all delivered to the saints. Rationalists may sneer, and the superstitious persecute; but he who possesses the truth will find with it wisdom, instruction and understanding such as all the wise men after the flesh are strangers to. Who exemplified what is here inculcated more than the one-time rabbi of Tarsus? See Philippians 3:7–11.

> [24] The father of the righteous shall greatly rejoice:
>   And he that begetteth a wise son shall have joy of him.
> [25] Thy father and thy mother shall be glad,
>   And she that bare thee shall rejoice.

See second clause of 10:1. Righteousness and wisdom in their children fill the hearts of parents with a joy beyond telling. To see those for whose salvation from folly and iniquity they have toiled and prayed, walking in uprightness and prudence through a world of abounding snares, cannot but gladden and greatly cheer. How little the young at times reflect upon the effect of their ways for good or ill upon their fathers and mothers. Many will declare that they love tenderly those who have lavished such unremitting affection upon them all their lives, while yet by their actions they are wounding their spirits and breaking their hearts. Consider verses 15–16 above. See Jacob and Joseph (Gen. 46–48).

> [26] My son, give me thy heart,
>   And let thine eyes delight in my ways.

It is again, as in verse 15, a greater than Solomon who speaks. To the lawless the words are not addressed. Such have no heart for God, nor can their eyes find in His ways anything in which to delight. But to His sons, He says "Give Me thy heart." It is His right, and surely the child of His grace will rejoice in thus being able to give Him what He craves. It is not mere service as in Martha's case, but heart occupation with Himself that he yearns for, as illustrated in Mary. Who that has known the preciousness of redemption by the blood of Christ will not gladly say,

> Take my poor heart, and let it be
> Forever closed to all but Thee.
> Take my love, my Lord; I pour
> At Thy feet its treasure-store.

He is worthy of the best we have to give. To Him we rightly yield the citadel of our deepest affections. It is only when He possesses the heart that His ways will be delighted in. See the living sacrifice of Romans 12:1–2.

> ²⁷ For a harlot is a deep ditch;
>   And a strange woman is a narrow pit.
> ²⁸ She also lieth in wait as for a prey,
>   And increaseth the transgressors among men.

Compare chapter 7; see the notes. If the young man would be preserved from impurity and ensnarement of soul, God must have his heart. None are safe who allow their affections to be fixed on objects "under the sun." Everywhere are there to be found those who would decoy from the paths of truth and virtue. In the Lord alone is there strength and deliverance. Like a deep ditch, hidden until one has stumbled into it, is the unholy woman who has been so frequently warned against. He who pleases God shall escape from her. How terribly was Samson made to suffer through one like this! (Judg. 16).

> ²⁹ Who hath woe? who hath sorrow?
>   Who hath contentions? who hath anxiety?
>   Who hath wounds without cause? who hath redness of
>   eyes?

Six questions are now asked, to be answered in the verses that follow. Woe, sorrow, contentions, anxiety (or perhaps, mutterings), needless wounds, and inflamed eyes are characteristic of him who is about to be described.

The abrupt inquiries fix the mind and focus the attention upon the terrible and vivid description of the drunkard that is at once presented in reply.

> ³⁰ They that tarry long at the wine;
>   They that go to seek mixed wine.
> ³¹ Look not thou upon the wine when it is red,
>   When it giveth its color in the cup,
>   When it goeth down smoothly.
> ³² At the last it biteth like a serpent,
>   And stingeth like an adder.
> ³³ Thine eyes shall behold strange women,
>   And thy heart shall utter perverse things.

³⁴ Yea, thou shalt be as he that lieth down in the heart of the
   sea,
   Or as one that lieth upon the top of a mast.
³⁵ They smote me [shalt thou say], and I was not sick;
   They have beaten me, and I knew it not:
   When shall I awake? I will seek it yet again.

Indulgence in the pleasures of the wine cup to inebriation is a prolific cause of human sorrow. Drunkenness is one of the greatest curses of the ages, yet it is a sin that seems ever seductive and attractive to the convivially inclined. Throwing to one side all restraint, such a one is allured by the sparkle of the bubbling liquor. But the results beggar all description. What seemed so delightful and innocent becomes like a venomous reptile taken into the bosom, whose bite sets the veins on fire. Immorality is linked with drunkenness, as effect with cause. All self-respect goes when the brain is controlled by the deadly poison. Lust and license possess the being.

The inebriate is like a man endeavoring to lie down in the heart of the waves of the sea, or like one who tries to sleep upon the mast head. Recovering a measure of consciousness there is the sense of bruising and wounding, but after all no determination to flee the cause that has, in a great measure, destroyed the will. The unnatural craving which possesses the being leads him to seek again the means of his destruction. See Nabal (1 Sam. 25:36–38).

It becomes the child of God to flee these things, and by sobriety and self-control to be an example to those who are weaker. "It is good, neither to eat flesh, nor to drink wine, nor anything whereby thy brother stumbleth, or is ensnared, or is made weak. Hast thou faith? have it to thyself before God. Happy is he that condemneth not himself in that thing which he alloweth" (Rom. 14:21–22). To play fast and loose with what has ruined so many myriads of our fellow men is certainly not to walk charitably. "We that are strong ought to bear the infirmities of the weak, and *not to please ourselves*" (Rom. 15:1). Careless indulgence in that which is to others like the poison of the adder is most inconsistent and thoughtless.

CHAPTER 24

PROVERBS 24

This chapter completes the first part of the book; the proverbs arranged directly by the wise king, and evidently put into circulation before his death.

The first one here is a warning against falling into the snare that so distracted the godly Asaph, until he went into the sanctuary of the Lord (Ps. 73).

> ¹ Be not thou envious of evil men,
> Neither desire to be with them.
> ² For their heart studieth destruction,
> And their lips talk of mischief.

See note on 23:17–18. It was when he saw the end of the wicked that Asaph felt every envious yearning vanish from his bosom. How could a saint of God begrudge the poor worldling his evanescent pleasures when judgment, like a dark and gloomy cloud, is lowering over their heads!

Nor is that the only thing that makes their lot wretched. Their hearts and lips are alike concerned in destruction and mischief. Who could be happy when so engaged? Disappointment and grief must ever be their portion, who hope through iniquity to find happiness. See, out of many instances with which Scripture abounds, the wretched life of Jehoram, king of Judah (2 Chron. 21).

³ Through wisdom is a house builded;
  And by understanding it is established:
⁴ And by knowledge shall the inner-chambers be filled
  With all precious and pleasant riches.

Storing the mind and heart with wisdom, knowledge, and understanding is like building a mansion on a solid foundation, and beautifying and enriching it with costly treasures that gratify the beholder and add to the enjoyment of the occupants. He can never be poor who has the wisdom that cometh down from above. See James 3:17–18.

⁵ A wise man is strong;
  Yea, a man of knowledge increaseth strength.
⁶ For by wise counsel thou shalt make war for thyself;
  And in the multitude of counsellors there is safety.

See notes on 20:18. Intimate is the connection between these verses and those just preceding. Wisdom makes strong its possessor, however inferior he may be in other respects to his adversaries.

The sense of the expression "make war for thyself" is evidently "make successful warfare," or "war to thine advantage."

⁷ Wisdom is too high for a fool:
  He openeth not his mouth in the gate.

The wise man is not rash. As he goes out to meet the enemy, he avails himself of the counsel and experience of others. He is not an egoist. His safety is in his willingness to hear what others soberly present. Our Lord may have had these words in mind, as also those of verse 27, when He instructed His disciples as to the importance of counting the cost before beginning to build or going forth to a conflict (Luke 14:28–32). See the poor wise man of Ecclesiastes 9:14–16.

Unable to attain to wisdom, because unwilling to repent of his evildoing, the fool will be speechless "in the gate," that is, when the hour of his judgment has come. See the man who ignored the wedding garment (Matt. 22:11–13).

How rich the grace that led the Eternal Wisdom to be as a lamb, dumb before the shearers, when He stood "in the gate," that judgment for His own might be exhausted upon Him (Isa. 53:7).

⁸ He that deviseth to do evil
   Shall be called a mischievous person.
⁹ The thought of folly is sin;
   And the scoffer is an abomination to men.

Evil thoughts, says our Lord, come from the heart, indicating therefore the moral pollution of the entire being. He who allows his mind to riot in evil devices is full of mischief. His thoughts of folly, whether put into execution or not, are sinful; for thoughts as well as deeds shall be judged when the secrets of men's hearts are laid bare. For them, as also for words and actions, men shall give account. The scoffer is one who permits the foolishness of his heart to control his lips. He rails at holy things, as did Pharaoh when he asked, "Who is the LORD that I should obey His voice" (Exod. 5:2).

¹⁰ If thou faint in the day of adversity,
   Thy strength is small.

It is the hour of trial that manifests whatever strength one really has. To faint, or become disheartened then, is to show that one has not been truly counting upon God for deliverance. The hour of trial and opposition will only find the trusting soul more confident still, for he knows where the source of all power is to be found. Contrast Elijah when threatened by Jezebel with David when the people spoke of stoning him (1 Kings 19:2–4; 1 Sam. 30:6).

¹¹ If thou forbear to deliver them that are drawn unto death,
   And those that are ready to be slain;
¹² If thou sayest, Behold we knew it not;
   Doth not He that pondereth the heart consider it?
   And He that keepeth thy soul, doth not He know it?
   And shall not He render to every man according to his
      works?

In these solemn questions reference seems to be made to a mode of execution, once prevalent in Syria and Palestine. Muenscher says, "When a criminal was anciently led to execution, a crier went before, who proclaimed the crime of which he had been convicted, and called upon any one who could say anything in behalf of the condemned culprit, to come forward; in which case, he was led back to the tribunal and the cause was re-heard." To have the information, which, if declared, would save the condemned man, but to selfishly withhold it and allow him to be slain, would be to take common ground with Cain and ask, "Am I my brother's keeper?" But the great Judge of all, who ponders the heart, would be witness against the one who acted so perfidiously and would assuredly render accordingly.

What shall be said of Christians who can see thousands daily of their fellow men passing on to eternal woe, and hear of millions more, yet scarcely ever bestir themselves to make known God's message of justification for guilty sinners through the Lord Jesus Christ?

Appalling is the thought that, albeit nineteen centuries have almost gone since Jesus said, *"Go ye* into all the world, and preach the gospel to every creature," we have today to face the fact that over five hundred million members of the human race are still awaiting the *first* proclamation of the gospel; and this, not because these millions live in inaccessible regions, but because there is so little heart, on the part of those so richly blessed, to carry the word of reconciliation to the regions beyond where Christ has not been named.

Even in instances where men have been ready to go, so amazing is the lethargy among those who could well afford to assist them, that it is only by exercise of the greatest self-denial they can get to, and remain in, the needy fields, white already to the harvest.

Let us not forget that for all these things we shall yet have to say to God. He will not lightly pass by the self-seeking, the worldly-mindedness, the positive indifference of His people which has led them to neglect to so large an extent the carrying of His gospel "into all the world."

The cry of those who are ready to be slain is going up into His ear day and night while they wait for a deliverer. Be it ours, then, not to say "we knew it not," but to rise to our privileges, and, in every way we can, help to spread abroad the saving word. See Ezekiel, the watchman to Israel (Ezek. 33:1–12).

> [13] My son, as thou eatest honey, because it is good;
>   And the honeycomb, because it is sweet to thy taste:
> [14] So shall the knowledge of wisdom be to thy soul;
>   When thou hast found it, then there shall be a reward,
>   And thine expectation shall not be cut off.

As honey is delightful to the palate, so shall Wisdom be to the soul of her devotee. In 5:3 we found the strange woman simulating this; but though her lips "drop as the honeycomb," they who follow her pernicious ways shall have bitterness in the latter end. On the contrary, Wisdom promises an assured re-ward—an expectation which shall not result in disappointment. The earnest seeker after understanding shall never be put to shame. See Cornelius (Acts 10).

¹⁵ Lie not in wait, O lawless man, against the dwelling of the
     righteous;
   Spoil not his resting place.
¹⁶ For a righteous man falleth seven times, and riseth up
     again;
   But the lawless shall be overwhelmed with mischief.

The wicked rejoice in iniquity, and are glad at the calamities of the righteous. But though the just man stumble frequently, he shall be lifted up again, for "God is able to make him stand." The sevenfold fall may refer, I judge, either to what are commonly called misfortunes, or to moral lapses brought on through unwatchfulness; for let the saint of God become careless, and he is as weak as other men. But where grace has wrought in the soul, there will be recovery; while as for the mere empty professor, he will return like a dog to his vomit or like a sow to her wallowing in the mire, thus becoming overwhelmed with evil. Contrast Peter with Judas (Matt. 26:75; 27:3–5). Compare Psalm 34:18–22.

¹⁷ Rejoice not when thine enemy falleth,
   And let not thy heart be glad when he stumbleth;
¹⁸ Lest Jehovah see it, and it be evil in His eyes,
   And He turn away His wrath from him.

Love does not gloat over the sorrows of others, even though richly deserved and although the one who is suffering has been a bitter foe. Remembering that he is himself a subject of grace, the humble contrite soul walks softly, having tears, not sneers, for the afflictions of his enemies. When it is otherwise, the eye of Jehovah will note it; He will see that he who is glad at calamities shall not be unpunished. This was what provoked His wrath against Edom (Obad. 12–16). Therefore His anger turned away from Jacob to Esau. See notes on 17:5.

¹⁹ Fret not thyself because of evil men,
   Neither be thou envious of the lawless;
²⁰ For there shall be no reward to the evil man:
   The lamp of the lawless shall be put out.

See verse 1 above. There is no reason to be either disquieted because of evil men, or to envy their present estate. They have no power or might, unless it be for a brief space delegated by the God of the righteous: and as for their wealth and prosperity, it is only for a moment and will soon vanish away forever, leaving them poorer than the poorest. No reward for all their toil on earth awaits them in eternity. Their lamp shall go out in darkness as they go down beneath the awful judgment of the God whose holiness they have despised, and whose grace they have refused. See Herod (Acts 12:20–23).

> 21 My son, fear thou Jehovah and the king;
>   And meddle not with them that are given to change:
> 22 For their calamity shall rise suddenly;
>   And who knoweth the ruin of them both?

Subjection to God, and therefore to the powers that be by Him ordained, should be characteristic of all who know the Lord. To meddle with them who are given to change would be to associate with or assist men who by rebellion and intrigue disturb the peace and order of society, delighting in revolutions and plots against the established government. In the church too such men arise, who would subvert all godly order and disquiet the minds of the saints. If left severely alone, their capacity for evil is greatly hindered. In worldly commonwealths, Christians are subjects, not rulers. Therefore it becomes all such to render to Caesar what belongs to him, not interfering with political changes and social upheavals. To fail thus to obey the Word of God will involve the unwise saint in many a snare; and when the overthrow of the revolutionary leader comes suddenly, "who knoweth the ruin of them both?"—that is, of the upstart and his followers. See Theudas and Judas of Galilee (Acts 5:36–37).

> 23 These things belong also to the wise.
>   It is not good to have respect of persons in judgment
> 24 He that saith unto the lawless, Thou art righteous;
>   Him shall the people curse,
>   Nations shall abhor him:
> 25 But to them that rebuke him shall be delight,
>   And a good blessing shall come upon them.
> 26 All shall kiss his lips who giveth a just sentence.

From verse 23 to the end of the chapter seems to be a kind of appendix to the book as originally sent forth. This is indicated by the introductory sentence, "These things belong also to the wise." Four subjects are taken up in this additional section, all of which have been previously treated, but are now, in two instances at least, somewhat amplified. The topics are the evil of respect of persons in judgment; counting the cost; prejudiced witness; and slothfulness.

Of the first, the verses quoted treat. He who justifies the wicked makes himself rightly abhorred. He will draw down upon his head the indignation of the upright. But he who rebukes or condemns the guilty will earn the esteem of the people and receive their blessing. All will "kiss his lips" who gives a right sentence. The kiss, among Eastern nations, was a symbolical act, denoting affection and esteem.

Solomon himself is perhaps the best illustration in Scripture of the righteous judge, until "He shall come whose right it is to reign, and to execute justice throughout the whole earth" (1 Kings 2; 3:16–28).

> ²⁷ Prepare thy work without,
>   And make it fit for thyself in the field;
>   And afterwards build thy house.

We have already noticed that the discourse of our Lord recorded in Luke 14:28–30 seems to have had reference to the principle enunciated in verse 6 above. This twenty-seventh verse appears to have been also before Him. The one was illustrated in His words about the king going out to battle. This finds its counterpart and fuller explanation in the warning drawn from the account of the man who began to build and was not able to finish. It is the part of wisdom to count the cost, lest the undertaking be too great, and prove but a monument of folly in the end. Such a reminder was the Tower of Babel, which overconfident men began sacrilegiously to build, but were unable to complete (Gen. 11:1–9).

> ²⁸ Be not a witness against thy neighbor without cause;
>   And deceive not with thy lips.
> ²⁹ Say not, I will do so to him as he hath done to me:
>   I will render to the man according to his work.

See note on 20:22. To appear as a witness against one's neighbor, with the deceitful purpose of accomplishing his ruin, because of real or fancied wrong, and in order to procure revenge, is opposed to the holiness that becomes a saint of God. The man of faith need not be concerned about defending his good name and certainly will not be found falsely accusing his neighbor, however much he may have suffered through him. He can quietly leave all in the hands of Him who will ever vindicate His faithful servants.

It is an important point reached in the experience of a believer when he learns to look behind all second causes to God Himself. Only then can he say, "I have learned, in whatsoever state I am, *therewith* to be content" (Phil. 4:11). The translators' addition of the italicized word *therewith* really mars the beauty of this lovely expression of subjection to the will of God. Content to know His will is being carried out, despite all efforts of the enemy to thwart it; such is the condition of mind and soul described by the apostle. This is a wonderful victory gained over the natural propensity to see in persons and things around us cause for complaint and dissatisfaction, and to be goaded on with a desire for revenge.

See the remarks as to David's behavior toward Shimei, in the notes on 20:22.

> [30] I went by the field of the slothful man,
>   And by the vineyard of the man void of understanding;
> [31] And, lo, it was all grown over with thorns,
>   And nettles had covered the face thereof,
>   And the stone wall thereof was broken down.
> [32] Then I saw, and considered it well;
>   I looked upon it, and received instruction:
> [33] Yet a little sleep, a little slumber,
>   A little folding of the hands to sleep:
> [34] So shall thy poverty come as one that travelleth,
>   And thy want as an armed man!

See notes on 6:10–11 and 20:4. Graphic is the portrayal of the sluggard's field, as by an eyewitness who stood sadly gazing upon it, and pondered as he viewed its desolation. Thorns and nettles flourishing, but fruit absent; the wall broken down; and everything speaking of lack of care and slothful indifference. May we too gaze upon it, and consider it well!

Verses 33–34 are the musings of his heart as he meditated upon the unhappy scene. Sleeping when he should have been laboring, the hour draws nigh when, aroused by poverty coming like a man on a journey, and want like a soldier in full armor, the sluggard will be awakened too late to realize that his wasted opportunities have gone beyond recall.

The spiritual lesson has already been discussed in the notes on the portions referred to above.

With this warning against sloth and laziness, the book, as first set forth, was brought to a close, unless the chapters attributed to Agur and Lemuel were then part of it. If so, the next section was inserted in its present place, by divine guidance we cannot doubt, when the work was issued in its final complete form.

CHAPTER 25

PROVERBS 25

¹ These are also proverbs of Solomon, which the men of
Hezekiah king of Judah copied out.

As already intimated, we now enter upon a portion of this book which did not form any part of it until the days of Hezekiah, nearly three centuries after the death of Solomon himself. Certain unnamed scribes, called in the Septuagint, "the friends of Hezekiah," rescued from oblivion the maxims which form the next five chapters. We know from 1 Kings 4:32 that the wise king "spake three thousand proverbs: and his songs were a thousand and five." Of the latter we know little. We have the Song of Songs, the dirge of Ecclesiastes, and it seems likely that Psalm 127 and perhaps others were from his pen. The rest of his songs God has not seen fit to preserve. In the book of Proverbs we have already had before us over four hundred sayings which he collated and handed down to future generations.

In the portion we now take up we find many additional proverbs; but whether transmitted orally or in writing, from his days to the times of Hezekiah, we are not able to definitely decide. The rendering "copied out" would be in favor of the latter thought, but as the word is as correctly translated "collected" (according to well-informed Hebraists), we cannot be positive as to either position. All the Christian needs to enable him to be certain of their divine inspiration is the well-known fact that they formed part of the Old Testament Scriptures when Jesus authenticated all of the three great divisions of the Law, the Prophets, and the Psalms.

> ² It is the glory of God to conceal a thing;
>   But the honor of kings is to search out a matter.
> ³ The heaven for height, and the earth for depth,
>   And the heart of kings is unsearchable.

More than once is our attention called, in the Bible, to the inscrutableness of God's counsels and designs. See Deuteronomy 29:29 and Romans 11:33–34. As the heavens are high above the earth, so, we are told, are His thoughts above ours. It therefore becomes Him to conceal from prurient curiosity His wondrous purposes.

But though He so acts, He would have those in authority search earnestly His Word that they may find out His mind and will. This is good and profitable exercise.

As they delve into His hidden things, so He also searches out the secret chambers of their hearts which to their subjects are unknown. He keeps His own secrets, even as they theirs, revealing the same only to a chosen few.

Now all saints are kings unto God. Therefore He would communicate His mind to each one who studies to show himself approved unto Him. May it be ours to be manifestly kings in this happy sense! See the words of the angel of the Lord to Manoah and his wife (Judg. 13:17–18).

> ⁴ Take away the dross from the silver
>   And there shall come forth a vessel for the finer.
> ⁵ Take away the lawless from before the king,
>   And his throne shall be established in righteousness.

See note on 17:3. As, by the removal of all dross from melted silver, there is produced that which suits the finer, so by the taking away of evil counselors and lawless men from before a king, his throne is established in righteousness. Notice, in Solomon's history, the many evildoers who had to be judged before he could occupy his throne in safety and in quietness. See 1 Kings 2 throughout.

The same principle abides in regard to the coming kingdom of our Lord Jesus Christ. The wicked shall be destroyed and all the transgressors rooted out of the land when He returns in triumph to usher in the great day of the Lord (2 Thess. 1–2; Rev. 19).

> 6 Display not thyself in the presence of the king,
>   And stand not in the place of great men.
> 7 For better is it that it be said unto thee—Come up hither,
>   Than that thou shouldst be put lower
>   In the presence of the prince whom thine eyes have seen.

Our Lord's parable in Luke 14:7–11 is the same in meaning and similar in language. Undoubtedly He set high value upon this precious collection of wise and helpful sayings.

That pride and love of approbation which leads one unduly to put himself forward in the presence of the great is almost certain to have a crushing rebuke. He who places his own estimate upon his importance and takes his place accordingly, will likely rate himself far higher than others would, and so be forced in shame to give place to abler and better men. The man who is content with the lowly seat may be called to a higher one if found to be deserving of such recognition. See David, chosen as king when but a shepherd lad (1 Sam. 16).

> 8 Go not forth hastily to strive,
>   Lest thou know not what to do in the end thereof,
>   When thy neighbor hath put thee to shame.

See notes on 24:5–6 and 27. Only when the matter is clearly of the Lord should one "go forth to strive." Too often saints are found like King Josiah, meddling in matters that do not concern them, to their shame and deep grief. How significant the words "after all this," by which the unhappy account of his failure in going out against Pharaoh-necho is introduced, after a lifetime of carefulness and of devotion to God; he "goes forth hastily" to take part in what he should never have interfered with, and so meets a dishonored death (2 Chron. 35:20–24).

Compare our Lord's words in Luke 12:57–59 and 14:31–33.

> 9 Debate thy cause with thy neighbor himself;
>   And discover not a secret to another:
> 10 Lest he that heareth it put thee to shame,
>   And thine infamy turn not away.

Much trouble and mischief might be avoided if people were careful to keep their differences to themselves, in place of spreading abroad information as to their shameful quarrels. If the simple scriptural rule, "Tell him his fault between thee and him *alone,*" were more generally acted upon, how many misunderstandings might be put right at once, in place of dragging on for long seasons and involving an ever-increasing circle of persons who should properly never even have heard of the case.

To go directly to one with whom there is danger of a quarrel, and debate the matter in a gracious spirit with him in secret, carefully keeping the matter from sharp ears and prying eyes—this is what the proverb commends. Nor is it only something commended. It is directly commanded by God Himself. Happy shall His people be when it is taken to heart and conscientiously acted upon! See Matthew 5:25–26.

> [11] As apples of gold in pictures of silver,
>   So is a word fitly spoken.

The imagery has puzzled most of the commentators. Just what apples of gold might be is a question with many. One supposes embroidery of golden apples among picture work of silver.

The explanation that seems most reasonable and commendable is that, by golden, we are to understand a rich yellow or orange color merely; not that the apples are actually of gold. It might be citron fruit, or oranges upon a silver platter; and many so understand it.

But the writer witnessed one day a most unusual occurrence in the chief orange-growing district of southern California; something, indeed, that none remembered as having taken place previously. A fairly heavy fall of snow occurred during the height of the orange harvest. The trees everywhere were covered with the silvery down, and as the lovely view spread out before me, and I noticed the great yellow globes hanging among the whitened boughs and leaves, I exclaimed involuntarily, "Apples of gold in pictures of silver!"

May not Solomon have gazed upon just such a scene? Oranges, in his time, were plentiful in Palestine; and the citron, a large fruit of the lemon variety, abounds there still. It is not unlikely that he had beheld a similar view, some wintry day, to that which I have attempted to describe.

The effect would be lovely beyond all powers of pen to make known, but equally lovely are right words spoken at the proper time. See the words of Boaz to Ruth, the Moabitess (Ruth 2:8–12).

¹² As an earring of gold, and an ornament of fine gold,
So is a wise reprover upon an attentive ear.

A rebuke kindly administered by a wise man should, in place of a rousing indignation, be esteemed as of greater value than a costly present. Such were the words of Oded the prophet to the host of Judah, and we find them acted upon as a message from God (2 Chron. 28:9–15).

¹³ As the cold of snow in the time of harvest,
So is a faithful messenger to them who send him:
For he refresheth the soul of his masters.

In ancient times, snow was used in Palestine very much as ice is among us. In winter it was carefully put away so as to be available for cooling drinks in the heat of summer. The simile therefore is very easy to understand. As the cold snow refreshes the reapers in the warm harvest days, so does a dependable messenger refresh the soul of his masters. See Jahaziel in 2 Chronicles 20:14–17.

¹⁴ Whoso boasteth himself of a false gift
Is like clouds and wind without rain.

See the contrast in 18:16. When clouds are seen in the sky in a period of drought, men hope for showers and are disappointed if they do not come. So when one talks of making gifts but fails to fulfill his promises, he disappoints in the same way.

But Jude refers to this passage in regard to those who profess to be gifted as teachers of the truth of God, but who in reality have nothing for the souls of their hearers. It is a common thing to see such men, self-confident and positive as to their abilities and spiritual insight, but who are bereft of all true godly discernment. See the full description of such false gifts in Jude 11–13.

¹⁵ By long forbearing is a prince persuaded,
And a soft tongue breaketh the bone.

Continued kindness and forbearance are powerful agents in overcoming obstinacy and angry passion, which seem as unyielding as a bone. The latter, is a hard, inflexible thing, but a soft tongue is said to break it; that is, mild persuasive language can overcome where heated terms and wrathful expressions would only arouse deeper resentment. See David's words to Saul after he had spared that monarch's life a second time (1 Sam. 26:17–25).

> [16] Hast thou found honey?
> Eat so much as is sufficient for thee,
> Lest thou be filled therewith, and vomit it.

See note on 24:13–14. To eat honey in moderation is good and healthful. Taken to excess it may be very deleterious. The same is true of what it signifies.

Throughout the Old Testament, honey seems to illustrate mere natural sweetness, hence it was forbidden to form part of the offering which typified Christ in His perfect sinless humanity (see Lev. 2). He never sought solace in natural things, however pleasant or agreeable. For us, they are permitted in their measure, but we need to beware of making them the chief object before our souls.

Wives and husbands need to watch lest their affection for each other, sweet and lovely as it is, crowds out the things of God. So with the various joys and pleasures of life. What is legitimate and wholly proper in its place, may prove very detrimental to all spiritual growth if it be permitted to become the supreme controlling power of the life. A little honey on the end of the pilgrim's rod is desirable and helpful. Its abuse is another thing altogether. See Jonathan (1 Sam. 14:27).

So too, from the very difficulties of the way, if met and overcome in the fear of God, may honey be extracted; but to go about searching for it is far different to receiving it thankfully, when found in the carcass of a lion slain in the power of faith. See Samson (Judg. 14:5–9, 14). Notice verse 27 below.

> [17] Let thy foot be seldom in thy neighbor's house;
> Lest he be weary of thee, and hate thee.

The lesson is simple and important, but one which many of us are slow to learn. The heart of the proverb is expressed in one of our own, "Familiarity breeds contempt." This is one form of the honey, a too free indulgence in which the verse above warns us. Even in the case of the best of friends it is well that there should be some delicacy as to continually visiting and intruding, for it is an easy thing to wear out one's welcome. Few of us can stand minute, daily inspection without its being very much to our disadvantage. It frequently happens that they who were the best of friends become the bitterest enemies, because of neglect of so simple a Scripture as this.

More time spent in secret with God, and less spent in gadding about among men, would result in far greater profit to our souls and bring much more glory to our Lord Jesus Christ. Consider the error to which "the younger widows" were prone, and be warned thereby (1 Tim. 5:13).

> ^{18} A man that beareth false witness against his neighbor
>   Is a battle-hammer [or, war club], and a sword, and a sharp
>   arrow.

How little the slanderer considers the grief oftentimes caused to the innocent objects of his vicious tongue! As warlike weapons, carrying pain and anguish in their wake, are the hateful and cruel words they recklessly utter, often destroying all peace of mind and arousing just indignation. On the other hand, it is well for the injured one to take all to the Lord Himself and leave it at His feet, accepting it as part of the discipline of the path. To remember that nothing can come to a believer but what divine love can use in blessing, is to rise triumphant above the tongue of slander and every other evil.

Nothing is harder for a wounded spirit and a sensitive soul than to endure uncomplainingly untrue accusations. Indignation against the false accuser, a determination to clear oneself at all costs, if possible; to avenge oneself on the evildoer—how natural are all these things to the human heart. But to go on, serenely looking to God for grace to so live that all shall see the falsity of the charge; to commit the keeping of my reputation to Him who permitted the trial for my humbling; to own the righteousness of His ways as I reflect on the many occasions upon which I have dishonored His name, however innocent I may be now; these are healthful exercises indeed. Thus I am kept from taking things into my own hand, and can count upon God to act for me, as of old He did for Job, for David, for Daniel, and a host of others who had learned to commit all to Him whose love is unchanging and who never permits a trial unless He discerns in the state of soul a "needs be" for the affliction which His government permits. See verse 23 below.

> ^{19} Confidence in an unfaithful man in time of trouble
>   Is like a broken tooth, and a foot out of joint.

What is more trying on the nerves and wearing on the spirit than a broken tooth, or a dislocated foot? Anxiety and inconvenience are ever present. So is it when dependence is placed upon a faithless man who deserts his post in time of trouble. See John Mark (Acts 13:13; 15:37–38).

20 As he that taketh away a garment in cold weather,
  And as vinegar upon soda [natron],
  So is he that singeth songs to a heavy heart.

The natron of the ancients is not the niter or saltpeter of our times, but was a native mineral soda of Palestine, which, when put in contact with an acid, would foam.

To take away a garment in cold weather would add to the person's discomfort, arousing indignation, even as vinegar poured upon natron would effervesce. So one who sang light frivolous songs to him who was of a heavy heart, would only increase his distress and cause his anger to be stirred.

There is a time for all things. The merry-hearted love to sing; the sad and grief-stricken prefer loving sympathy. See Judah by the waters of Babylon (Ps. 137:1–4).

21 If thine enemy be hungry, give him bread to eat;
  And if he be thirsty, give him water to drink:
22 For thou shalt heap coals of fire upon his head,
  And Jehovah shall reward thee.

These are the verses quoted, with the exception of the last clause, by the apostle Paul in Romans 12:20. He there takes them verbatim from the Septuagint.

It is certainly worthy of note that when a line of conduct suited to Christians, who have entered into the precious truths unfolded in Romans 3–8, is in question, the Holy Spirit should quote from this portion of the Old Testament. This but bears out the remark made in the introduction that here we have the behavior which becomes the man of God basking in the full blaze of present truth.

Vengeance is to be far from the thoughts of the saint. He is to show grace and compassion even to his enemies, losing no opportunity to minister to their need. By so doing, the fire of love will soften their angry feelings, and the Lord's reward will be upon the soul who thus imitates his Master, who said, "Love your enemies, bless them that curse you, do good to them that hate you, and pray for them which despitefully use you, and persecute you" (Matt. 5:44). It would be the greatest incongruity for one who was himself the object of grace to attempt to deal in judgment with those who had wronged him. See Stephen (Acts 7:60).

23 The north wind driveth away rain:
  So doth an angry countenance a backbiting tongue.

The receiver of stolen goods is as guilty as the thief. So is it with the one who gives encouragement to another to relate scandalous stories. Nothing is more conducive to strife and sorrow among the people of God than the repeating of matters that cannot profit, and that bring pain to the one of whom they are related. But there is no surer way to encourage the backbiter than by giving ear to his tales. If met by "an angry countenance," and reproved in the fear of God, the mischief might often be nipped in the bud.

When people come with unsavory tales about absent persons it would be well to meet them in the spirit that David manifested toward Rechab and Baanah, for such people are character assassins (2 Sam. 4:5–12).

> ²⁴ It is better to dwell in the corner of the housetop,
>   Than with a brawling woman in a wide house.

This is a repetition of 21:9. It is not by mere chance that the words are repeated, nor that several times the wretchedness of dwelling with an insubject and contentious woman is referred to. God has established an order in creation which is not broken with impunity. See Ephesians 5:22–24.

> ²⁵ As cold waters to a thirsty soul,
>   So is good news from a far country.

The glorious gospel of the blessed God is, above all else, that good news from a far country, which is to the thirsty soul like a draught of clear sparkling water from a cold spring. When, weary, famished, and ready to perish, the poor sinner quaffs the living water, it becomes in his inmost being a fountain springing up unto everlasting life. See the woman of Samaria (John 4:6–29).

> ²⁶ A troubled fountain, and a defiled well,
>   Is a righteous man giving way before the lawless.

To the thirsty traveler, a troubled fountain or an evil spring defiled with filth and impurities is a cause for grief and vexation. So will a godly and upright man be disappointed and pained to behold a righteous person set at naught, or oppressed by those who have no principle and who refuse to subject themselves to law, either divine or human. See Gedaliah and Ishmael (Jer. 41:1–3).[1]

²⁷ It is not good to eat much honey;
So to search after one's own glory is wearisome.

See note on verse 16 above. The immoderate use of honey is pernicious. Much more so is inordinate ambition. He who lives but to glorify himself will be wearied in the search after vanity. Of this the entire book of Ecclesiastes is witness. Also see God's message to Baruch the son of Neriah (Jer. 45:4–5).

²⁸ He that hath no rule over his own spirit
Is like a city that is broken down and without walls.

See note on 16:32. Self-control is ever important. This is the temperance of the New Testament. Paul made it his object to keep his body under, that thus he might make manifest the fact that he was not a reprobate or castaway (1 Cor. 9:26–27). Lack of this control of himself sadly dishonored Noah, and that shortly after world government had been committed to him (Gen. 9:20–21). Moses, too, of all men the meekest, failed in self-government when angered at Meribah (Num. 20). May we have grace given to hold our spirits in godly subjection, that thus we become not like a city exposed to the ready assaults of its enemies! Even when one is clearly in the right, nothing so prejudices his case as losing control of his temper, and uttering heated, hasty words. Others are prone to forget the minor points of the evidence at such a time, and to judge by the spirit manifested. Therefore the importance of exemplifying in our words and ways "the meekness and gentleness of Christ."

CHAPTER 26

PROVERBS 26

The frequently mentioned phrase, "the fool," furnishes the subject for the first twelve verses. It should be born in mind that the term as used here has no reference to one mentally weak or incapable through simplicity. Fool and folly are almost synonymous with sinner and sinfulness, though the added thought of willfulness is needed to fully understand many of the warnings and threatenings. Fools are those who make a mock at sin, rejoicing in iniquity, and refusing to heed the voice of wisdom.

> ¹ As snow in summer, and as rain in harvest,
> So honor is not seemly for a fool.

All are out of place and may cause serious inconvenience. Snow in summer is injurious because it retards growth. Rain during harvest greatly interrupts the reaper and may even ruin the crop. So a fool in the place of honor is unsuitable and may cause much damage. He knows not how to order his conduct and fulfills the passage, "Man being in honor abideth not, but is as the beasts that perish." See Nebuchadnezzar before his repentance (Dan. 4).

> ² As the sparrow in wandering, as the swallow in flying,
> So a curse causeless shall not come.

Fools are ever ready to curse and anathematize, often to the great anxiety of ignorant and timid souls who live in dread of the fulfillment of their maledictions. But as the sparrow and swallow cleave the air and pass quickly from view, so shall it be with a curse uttered without cause.

A second interpretation is suggested by some who conceive the meaning to be that no curse shall come upon anyone unless there be reason for it, but this really seems involved in what is suggested above. Compare Goliath's curse (1 Sam. 17:43).

> ³ A whip for the horse, a bridle for the ass,
>   And a rod for the back of fools.

See notes on 10:13 and 19:29. To some the order here will seem strange. We think of the horse as requiring the bridle to check it, and the ass, the whip to spur it on. But in Syria it is just the opposite. Horses are not much used and are often exceedingly stubborn, while the ass is apt to be too ready and needs to be held in by bit and bridle to keep it at a proper gait. The fool is likely to err on either side, and therefore must know the rod of correction for his willfulness. The psalmist warns against failing to render due obedience and therefore requiring bit and bridle guidance (Ps. 32:9).

> ⁴ Answer not a fool according to his folly,
>   Lest thou also be like unto him.
> ⁵ Answer a fool according to his folly,
>   Lest he be wise in his own eyes.

Though giving opposite directions, the two verses are too closely connected to allow even cavilers to raise the charge of contradiction. Time and manner need to be taken into consideration when one is in conversation with a fool. To answer him in the same scoffing and egotistical spirit that he manifests would be to sink to his level. If he rails, to rail in return would be but to follow his evil example. But on the other hand to allow foolish, unlearned statements to go unchallenged without rebuttal, will but strengthen him in his self-assurance and conceit. To expose his shallowness and reply convincingly to his folly may at least humble him and give him to feel the need of fuller investigation. When the men of Hezekiah answered not a word to the vapid blasphemies of Rab-shakeh, they obeyed the first of these instructions (2 Kings 18:36). When Nehemiah replied so brusquely to the wretched pretensions of Sanballat he acted according to the second (Neh. 6:8).

⁶ He that sendeth a message by the hand of a fool,
  Cutteth off the feet, and drinketh damage.
⁷ As the legs of the lame are not equal,
  So is a proverb in the mouth of fools.
⁸ As the binding of a stone in a sling,
  So is he who giveth honor to a fool.
⁹ As a thorn-branch in the hand of a drunkard,
  So is a proverb in the mouth of fools.

The same general subject is alluded to in each of these couplets. To entrust a fool with an important message is like cutting off the feet, or drinking a baneful draught. The purpose will be thwarted, for the messenger cannot be depended on. His feet might as well be amputated, so far as his carrying the word correctly is concerned. Or it may be that we are to think of the sender rather than the one sent. In that case it would be as sensible to cut off his own feet or to drink what is injurious as to entrust a message to a fool. Looked at from either standpoint, it conveys the thought of vexation and delay. Jonah played the part of such an envoy before he was brought to see his sin (Jonah 1).

The lame because of their unequal legs walk with a halting uncertain gait. When he who is not himself a child of Wisdom attempts to use her speech, he too halts and by his uncertain words and ways makes known his folly. Such was Saul among the prophets (1 Sam. 19:24).

The first part of verse 8 is somewhat ambiguous and has been variously rendered. The margin of our English Bibles suggests, "As he that putteth a precious stone into a heap of stones," which implies that to honor a fool is like casting a costly jewel among the common stones by the wayside—it is unvalued. Others read "putting into a purse a stone of the heap. That is, as it would be foolish to put carefully into one's purse a useless bit of stone, it is equally foolish to bestow honor upon one who does not deserve it.

Both the above would be true enough; but many scholars do not think that either of them is intended or implied here. The common version would seem to mean that it is as senseless to honor a fool as to bind a stone in a sling and then try to throw it. This seems well supported and appears to be the proper interpretation. See Herod (Acts 12:20–23).

A thorn branch when in the hand of a drunkard is almost certain to prove harmful to himself and others. The same is true when a fool sets up to teach. He will but destroy himself and those who give heed to him. Consider what God has said as to Shemaiah the Nehelamite (Jer. 29:30–32).

¹⁰ The great God that formed all things
  Both rewardeth the fool, and rewardeth transgressors.

Scholars are very far from agreement among themselves as to the exact meaning of the Hebrew in this text. For want of better authority we keep to the King James Version, which at least expresses a solemn truth that is often insisted on in the Word of God. Judgment, though it seem to tarry, is sure for all fools and transgressors. Nothing can turn this aside. God shall render to every man according to his deeds. Stuart and Muenscher read, "As an arrow that woundeth every one, so is he that hireth a fool, and he who hireth wayfarers." That is, to hire wicked or unknown persons is to invite disaster.

The rendering of the Revised Version is practically the same as this: "As an archer that woundeth all, so is he that hireth a fool and he that hireth them that pass by." There seems to be little clearness in the King James Version margin: "A great man grieveth all, and he hireth the fool, he hireth also transgressors."

J. N. Darby reads, "A master roughly worketh every one: he both hireth the fool and hireth passers by." He owns in a note that it is a "difficult verse." His rendering is ambiguous, but seems to convey the thought that, to a master, it is a small matter *whom* he hires, so long as he gets the work accomplished.

¹¹ As a dog returneth to his vomit,
  So a fool repeateth his folly.

The horrible habit of the dog that eats again the filthy food it has ejected from its stomach, is a suited picture of him who leaves his folly for a time, only to return to it with eager zest later.

The apostle Peter applies the proverb to those who, having professed to know the saving grace of Christianity, go on for a time in an upright way, but when exposed to their old temptations, not only fall into their former sins, but turn back to them with avidity and delight, thereby manifesting that the heart had not really been renewed. Such persons are often supposed to have been children of God, but now are considered to have lost the salvation they once enjoyed, and to have become again children of wrath, Such teaching as this is unknown in Scripture. All who come to Christ receive eternal life and shall never perish. They are forever linked up with Himself. The precious life such have received is *"eternal* life"—nonforfeitable.¹

Peter refers to persons who only had outwardly reformed their lives, but who were never truly converted to God, as a careful study of his words will make evident. He says, "For if after they have escaped the pollutions of the world, through the knowledge (or, acknowledgement) of the Lord and Savior Jesus Christ, they are again entangled therein and overcome, the latter end is worse with them than the beginning. For it had been better for them not to have known the way of righteousness, than, after they have known it, to turn from the holy commandment delivered unto them. But it is happened unto them according to the true proverb, The dog is turned to his own vomit again; and the sow that was washed to her wallowing in the mire" (2 Peter 2:20–22). Now if the previous part of the chapter be looked at, it will at once be seen that he has been writing of false teachers and false profession throughout: persons who would take up Christianity as a system, even with a view to pervert it, but who had never known its power. Such people might go on for a time as though really born of God, but their true state would at last be manifested. Giving up their unsatisfactory profession and relapsing into their old ways, they would become apt illustrations of the truth of this proverb.

Be it noted that a dog in Scripture never illustrates a believer, but is often used to picture a false teacher. See Paul's warning in Philippians 3:2 and notice Isaiah's description in 56:10–12 of his prophecy. It is these dogs who turn to their vomit again, even as a sow that has been washed goes back, when opportunity presents itself, to her wallowing in the mire. Had the sow been changed into a sheep (the type of a Christian) it would no longer delight in mud and filth. A sheep may fall into the mire, but if so, it will never be at rest again until it is free from it. A sow finds in it its natural element. This marks the difference between a real saint of God and a mere reformed hypocrite. Peter and Judas aptly picture the two classes. The look of Jesus broke Peter's heart and resulted in his restoration. Judas was controlled by his covetous spirit to the last, until remorse set in, but no repentance toward God. See the notes on 14:14.

> [12] Seest thou a man wise in his own eyes?
> There is more hope of a fool than of him.

See verse 5 above. Arrogant self-assumption and fancied superiority to all instruction place a man hopelessly beyond the reach of help. The out-and-out fool, who does not pretend to anything better than his folly and iniquity, is easier delivered than the pedantic egotist who makes a great profession of knowledge and piety but is thoroughly in love with his own ways. Against this wretched state we are warned in Romans 12:16.

Having considered the fool in various aspects, the sluggard is next held up to view, the four following verses having to do with him.

> [13] The sluggard saith, There is a lion in the way;
>   A lion is in the streets.
> [14] As the door turneth upon its hinges,
>   So doth the sluggard upon his bed.
> [15] The sluggard hideth his hand in the dish;
>   It is wearisome to him to bring it to his mouth.
> [16] The sluggard is wiser in his own eyes
>   Than seven men that can render a reason.

See notes on 13:4; 15:19; 19:15; 20:4; 21:25–26; and 24:30–34. The sluggard is the man we are all familiar with; one who means well, but accomplishes nothing because of continued procrastination. If there are no real difficulties, he will imagine them, and they then become as real to him as if actually existent. He cannot go out upon the streets because there is a lion in the way, though others see no danger. The man of determination would go forth in the strength of the Lord and rend the lion as Samson did; but not so with the slothful man. Any paltry excuse will keep him within doors. Compare 22:13.

In olden times doors were not hung upon hinges, but turned upon pivots, thus moving frequently, but never going anywhere. They turned on the pivot, but did not move from it. So with the sluggard; he is constantly expecting to be up and doing, but remains upon his bed, tossing from side to side.

Even when seated at the table, he is almost too lazy to carry his food from the dish to his mouth. It is the extreme of slothfulness, but in warm climates is not an untrue description. See 19:24.

Despite his lack of purpose and determination, he is wiser in his own eyes than any number of men who are characterized by tact and energy. He can invent excuses and plausible arguments in unlimited quantities to justify his disgraceful behavior; and neither the disgust nor the anger of better men than himself will affect him.

This lack of purpose is sometimes found among young saints and can only result in the breakdown of their testimony. Rather be overzealous than play the part of the sluggard. See Joash, king of Israel, and Elisha the prophet (2 Kings 13:14–19).

¹⁷ He that passeth by, and meddleth with strife belonging not
   to him,
   Is like one that taketh a dog by the ears.

To meddle with other people's quarrels is always foolish, and often dangerous. Dogs in Syria are wild and savage. To take one by the ears would be to
needlessly expose oneself to injury and suffering. It is the part of wisdom to let
them severely alone, a custom that is commonly followed. In the cities they
swarm in great packs and are useful as scavengers; but no one pretends to control
or interfere with them.

So when others are in strife, it is well for the passerby to avoid interference
and to let people settle their own differences between themselves, unless he be
appealed to by those who are disputing, when he may be able to act the part of
a peacemaker. Moses found his brethren bitterly to resent his unasked-for me-
diation when they strove together (Exod. 2:13–14).

¹⁸ As one who feigneth himself mad—
   Who casteth about darts, arrows and death;
¹⁹ So is the man that deceiveth his neighbor,
   And saith, Am not I in sport?

To wantonly perpetrate unkind tricks upon one, and then, after having caused
serious inconvenience, and perhaps heavy loss, to attempt to laugh it off as mere
amusement is to act like a man pretending to madness and finding his sport in
working injury upon others. Deceit in the name of pleasure is as much to be
decried as in anything else. Sobriety and a concern for the welfare of one's neighbors will cause such things to be sedulously avoided. Amusement at the expense
of another's suffering, none but a most thoughtless and selfish person will en-
gage in. See 10:23 and 2 Peter 2:13.

²⁰ Where no wood is, there the fire goeth out;
   So where there is no talebearer, contention ceaseth.
²¹ As coals are to burning coals, and wood to fire,
   So is a contentious man to kindle strife.
²² The words of a talebearer are as dainty morsels,
   And go down into the inner chambers of the soul.

See notes on 11:13 and 16:27–28. Already we have had our attention frequently directed to the evil of talebearing. But because we are so slow to learn, we have added instruction in regard to what has become in many places a blighting curse among the people of God. Happy is the assembly of saints that does not number a backbiter or talebearer among its members! As fire goes out for want of fuel when there is no wood to add to it, so many difficulties disappear when there is no whisperer to go about perpetuating strife. But, as when coals are added to burning coals, so is a contentious man to cause ill-feelings to be inflamed, and malice and hatred to burn more strongly than ever. It is a wretched business, going about from one to another, stirring up unholy passions, and making unhappy matters all the more difficult to adjust. For the words of a talebearer are by many devoured as though they were choice tidbits which go down into the depths of the being and are often ineradicable. See 18:8.

> ²³ Burning lips and a wicked heart
>   Are like a potsherd covered with silver dross.
> ²⁴ He that hateth, dissembleth with his lips,
>   And layeth up deceit within him;
> ²⁵ When he maketh his voice gracious, believe him not;
>   For there are seven abominations within his heart:
> ²⁶ His hatred is covered by deceit,
>   But his wickedness shall be disclosed before the
>   congregation.
> ²⁷ Whoso diggeth a pit shall fall therein:
>   And he that rolleth a stone, it will return upon him.
> ²⁸ A lying tongue hateth those who have been crushed by it;
>   And a flattering mouth worketh ruin.

One who makes fervent protestations of love and affection, while all the time his heart is bent on evil, is like a cheap earthen vessel that has been veneered with a coating of drossy silver. Such an article appears to be of value, but is really worthless. So with the hypocritical professions of the flatterer. His burning words are only uttered to cover the corruption of his purposes. Hating the object of his attentions, he will endeavor to deceive by fair speech; but his heart is full of abominations, and he is not to be trusted. He endeavors to cover his malice by falsehood, and for a time may succeed; but eventually his true character shall be manifested openly.

Having dug a pit for his neighbor, he shall fall into it himself, as did the fawning sycophant Haman, who by flattery and apparent zeal for the honor of Ahasuerus won from him permission to destroy all the Jews, but was discovered in his perfidy and hanged on the gallows he had made for Mordecai. He was as one who had rolled a stone up a hillside, which, breaking loose, returned with crushing force upon him. The courtiers who by similar means induced Darius to promulgate the decrees which they thought would result in Daniel's destruction, were brought, in the end, to the fate which they hoped would have been his.

The last verse expresses a truth which has long been recognized among all nations, and is preserved in proverbial form among many peoples. "It is common for men to hate those whom they have injured" is the English rendering of the saying of Tacitus. Conscious of having wronged another, and being determined not to confess it, the dissembler will store his heart with hatred against the object of his wrongdoing.

He who has debtors may graciously forgive them; but he who is in debt is very apt to cherish the bitterest animosity against the one from whom he has borrowed. One may readily overlook an injury, while he who has done another a favor will often be hated for his kindness, and ill-will be added to displeasure. This is so common among fallen men that it hardly needs comment.

To hide his wretched feelings, such a one will flatter with his lips while all the time he is plotting the ruin of his victim. It is the sin which in Judas Iscariot became, as it were, incarnate! May every Christian learn to avoid it as most revolting and disgusting, and altogether opposed to the transparency of the spirit of Christ.

CHAPTER 27

PROVERBS 27

Procrastination is a snare which often results in ruin. Against this error the first verse solemnly warns every reader.

> ¹ Boast not thyself of tomorrow;
>   For thou knowest not what a day may bring forth.

The present is given man in order that he may act in view of the future. To defer until the morrow what should be attended to today is the sad mistake which has destroyed untold thousands. The old Spanish proverb says, "The road of by and by leads to the house of never"; while another trite saying reads, "The way to hell is paved with good intentions." The English are fond of quoting, "Procrastination is the thief of time"; and it is likely that every nation has some maxim intended to remind one of the warning of our verse. Yet, alas, how prone we all are to leave for tomorrow matters which should be settled at once.

In nothing is this more manifest than in regard to the great question of the salvation of the soul. Again and again Scripture presses upon men the importance of an immediate settlement of this matter of tremendous moment. *"Today* if ye will hear His voice, harden not your hearts." "Behold, *now* is the accepted time; behold, *now* is the day of salvation." "Come *now,* and let us reason together, saith the Lord" (Heb. 3:7–8; 2 Cor. 6:2; Isa. 1:18). These are but a few of many such calls to instant decision. Yet what is more common than to find people putting off a final settlement until, like Festus, they have a "more convenient season," which in many instances is never found! The uncertainty of health, reason, and of life itself, all alike loudly cry, "Boast not thyself of tomorrow."

Pharaoh said "Tomorrow," when he should have said "Today," and the morrow found his heart as hard as the nether millstone, beyond the reach of repentance or concern (Exod. 8:10).

If the reader is unsaved, let me remind him of five important reasons why he should not delay in coming to Christ.

First—every day spent in sin is a day lost. The only true life is that which is lived for God. Those who are saved always regret not having turned to the Lord earlier, because they find such true joy and peace in the path of the just, which shines ever brighter and brighter unto the perfect day.

Second—every day spent in procrastination is adding to the terrible number of things you can never undo. It is often forgotten by the young that even though saved and forgiven at last, there are consequences of their sins which will never be blotted out. We have an influence on others, for good or ill, that a future change of ways can never utterly destroy. Then, sin leaves its effect upon our minds and bodies—an effect that lasts through all time. It was this a father meant to impress upon his son when he bade him drive a handful of nails part way into a clean, smooth post. With great delight the lad did as he was bidden. "Now, my boy," said the father, "draw them out." This was soon successfully accomplished. "Now take out the holes," was the next command. "Why, father," exclaimed the child, "that is impossible!" So we may think of the forgiveness of our sins as a drawing out of the nails, but, let us never forget, the marks remain. Therefore the wisdom of ceasing at once to do what can never be undone.

Third—it is possible that at any moment conviction of sin may pass away from the troubled soul, and that God may cease to speak to you any longer by His Holy Spirit. Many a man, or woman, has, by long resisting the Holy Spirit, reached a point where, like Pharaoh, the heart refused to respond to further entreaties or warnings. Such people are often said to be "gospel-hardened"; and the designation is all too correct.

Fourth—before tomorrow, death may claim you for his prey. Even as you read these lines, he may be feeling for your heartstrings. David said, "There is but a step between me and death "; and so it is with any of us. Before tomorrow, sinner, your lips may be silent, your heart be still, your form be cold, and your soul in hell!

Last of all, you should not forget that the Lord Jesus Christ is coming again.

He may return from heaven to call all His redeemed away (according to 1 Thess. 4:13–18) before you lay down this book. No event has to transpire, no prophecy to be fulfilled, before that great and solemn moment arrives. "In such an hour as ye think not," the day of grace may be brought to a close, and the days of vengeance begin for all who have rejected, or merely neglected, so great a salvation.

Knowing not what a single day may bring forth, it is surely the part of wisdom to turn at once to God, owning your sins and trusting His grace!

> ² Let another man praise thee, and not thine own mouth;
> A stranger, and not thine own lips.

Self-praise always bespeaks ill-breeding and a lack of realization of the fitness of things. If others extol, go on, humbly looking to God to keep you in a spirit of meekness and lowliness; for you know far more about your own failings than any other can. Boasting in your attainments or abilities is obnoxious and opens the door to criticism of a severe character. See the men of Ephraim and Manasseh (Josh. 17:14–15).

> ³ A stone is heavy, and the sand weighty;
> But a fool's wrath is heavier than them both.

It is because of its unreasonableness that a fool's wrath is so heavy. He will listen to no explanations and will view with malice and suspicion all attempts to appease him. Better far to leave such a man to himself than to strive with him, for he is incapable of sound judgment. Treat him as Hezekiah commanded his nobles to act toward Rab-shakeh (Isa. 36:21).

> ⁴ Wrath is cruel, and anger is outrageous;
> But who is able to stand before jealousy?

After all, wrath, of which the previous verse has spoken, is a brief tempest of the mind, and anger a passing emotion. Both are to be dreaded while they last; but jealousy far more, for it abides when all outward evidence of it has disappeared. "Jealousy is as cruel as sheol." See the brothers of Joseph (Gen. 37).

> ⁵ Open rebuke is better than secret love.
> ⁶ Faithful are the wounds of a friend;
> But the kisses of an enemy are deceitful.

True love will lead me to be faithful with my brother if his steps are declining from the path of rectitude. While avoiding a captious, faultfinding spirit, I will seek to recover his soul if he has gone astray. In so doing, I may have to wound, but such pains are faithful, and reproof in grace is better far than love kept concealed, which forbids my drawing his attention to his faults. An enemy may lavish kisses and tokens of affection at such a time, overlooking the evil and bolstering up the wrongdoer in his unrighteous cause, but they are deceitful manifestations, like the kiss of Judas. How faithful was Paul to Peter and Barnabas, and to the beloved Galatians, dear as all assuredly were to him! (Gal. 1–2).

> 7 The full soul tramples on a honeycomb;
> But to the hungry soul every bitter thing is sweet.

The verse has been paraphrased as follows: "The pampered glutton loathes even luxurious food; but he who is really hungry, will eat even indifferent food with a high relish." It is need that gives appetite and enjoyment for what would otherwise be despised. To many, the Word of God is one of these bitter things; but when the soul is hungry it becomes sweet as honey. See the little books eaten by Ezekiel and John (Ezek. 3:1–4; Rev. 10:9–10).

> 8 As a bird that wandereth from her nest,
> So is a man that wandereth from his place.

The Lord has given "to every man his work," and we may also say, to every man his place. "But now, hath God set the members everyone of them in the body, as it hath pleased Him" (1 Cor. 12:18). He who, in dependence on the Lord fills his appointed niche and maintains his proper place, shall find rich blessing; but as a bird that wanders from its nest exposes itself to danger and suffering, so is it with him who turns away from his sphere.

Looking at it in another way, we may apply the principle to assembly life. There is a place where God would have all His children gathered—to the peerless name of the Lord Jesus Christ. He who, having known the joy and blessedness of this, wanders from it because of fancied slights, or any cause whatever, is like a homeless bird that has forsaken its nest. See Demas (2 Tim. 4:10).

> 9 Ointment and perfume rejoice the heart;
> So doth the sweetness of a man's friend by hearty counsel,

> [10] Thine own friend, and thy father's friend, forsake not;
> And go not into thy brother's house in the day of thy
> calamity:
> For better is a friend that is near, than a brother far off.

Loving, solicitous counsel on the part of a true friend is as refreshing and stimulating to the soul as oil and perfume are to the body. In a warm, dry atmosphere and an enervating climate like that of Palestine, it was, and is, very soothing and invigorating to be anointed with oil; while sweet and stimulating perfumes are employed to rouse the dormant sensibilities and are found to be exceedingly grateful and refreshing. Happy is the man who has a friend of this character. It was such a one that David found in Jonathan.

When grief and calamity fall suddenly, it is far better to have a tried friend like this to turn to, than to be dependent on relations, however near, who may after all lack the heart and affection that marks the other. Time and distance are powerful forces for the weakening of family ties, as many have learned to their sorrow. Well it is for each to know that Friend who sticks closer than a brother! See notes on 17:17 and 18:24.

> [11] My son, be wise and make my heart glad,
> That I may give an answer to him that reproacheth me.

The obedience and careful behavior of a wise son will reflect glory upon his solicitous parent. When there is willfulness and disobedience the father will be reproached with not having properly trained his offspring. For us, who are "sons of God, through faith in Christ Jesus," the admonition is important. By walking worthy of Him who hath called us, we shall glorify before men our Savior-God and Father. How often do wicked men reproach Him for the follies of His children! David's sin gave occasion for the enemies of the Lord to blaspheme, and therefore it was that the child of Bathsheba had to die (2 Sam. 12:14).

> [12] A prudent man foreseeth the evil, and hideth himself;
> But the simple pass on and are punished.

It is a repetition of 22:3. See previous notes. How great must be the concern of the God you are neglecting, unsaved one, that again He should remind you of the importance of looking well to the future and hiding yourself in Christ before the evil fall, and there be no remedy! If after this second warning you pass carelessly on to your well-deserved doom, "What wilt thou say when He shall punish thee?" (Jer. 13:21).

> ¹³ Take his garment that is surety for a stranger,
>   And take a pledge of him for a strange woman.

This too is a repetition of a proverb given in the first great division of our book. See 20:16. We are not to suppose that it is mere chance that caused the friends of Hezekiah to duplicate several of Solomon's wise sayings in this way. It is rather that God would by this means bring home to our attention, in a special manner, the importance of the instruction they contain. He who neglects such full testimony is verily guilty, and deserves no sympathy when he has to reap as he sowed.

> ¹⁴ He that blesseth his friend with a loud voice, rising early in
>   the morning,
>   It shall be counted a curse to him.

There is a vein of easily perceived irony in these words. He who makes it a point to declare his protestations of affection and interest beneath one's window, with loud, garrulous tones early in the morning when the object of his attentions would fain rest, makes himself utterly obnoxious, and his blessing becomes rather a curse. Blatant uncalled-for words of praise are always to be dreaded. They generally manifest insincerity of heart and a lack of fine sensibilities that are most repugnant to a person of the opposite temperament. The Italians say, "He who praises you more than he is wont to do, either has deceived you, or is about to do it." See Absalom and the men of Israel (2 Sam. 15:1–6).

> ¹⁵ A continual dropping in a very rainy day,
>   And a contentious woman are alike;
> ¹⁶ Whosoever hideth her hideth the wind,
>   And the ointment of his right hand which betrayeth itself.

See notes on 21:9, 19. No better comment could be written on the first of these verses than Dr. Thompson's description of a Palestine rainstorm. He says: "Such rains as we have had thoroughly soak through the flat earthen roofs of these mountain houses, and the water descends in numberless leaks all over the room. This continual dropping—tuk, tuk—all day and all night, is the most annoying thing in the world, unless it be the ceaseless chatter of a contentious woman." He who endeavors to hide from others the annoying fact that such a disagreeable person shares his home, is like one who tries to hide the wind, or who seeks to keep people from detecting the fragrance when his right hand is anointed with perfumed oil. Ahasuerus considered Vashti as having offended in this way when she shamed him before all his nobles by defying his command (Esther 1:10–20).

> [17] As iron sharpeneth iron,
>   So a man sharpeneth the countenance of his friend.

As by friction, one iron instrument is sharpened and polished by contact with another, so we may be a help to each other by interesting and profitable intercourse and exchange of thought. A recluse is always a very one-sided man. He who would be a blessing to his fellows must mingle with them that he may learn to understand their needs and their sorrows, as well as that he may find gain by what in them is superior to his own knowledge or virtues. Among Christians, fellowship one with another is precious indeed, and becomes increasingly sweet as the days grow darker. How profitable to a Timothy the association with a Paul! (2 Tim. 3:10–11).

> [18] Whoso keepeth the fig tree shall eat the fruit thereof;
>   So he that regardeth his master shall be honored.

Fidelity, in whatever service one may be entrusted with, assures its reward in due time, even as the caretaker of the fig tree would be duly entitled to partake of its fruit. Let the Christian remember that his Master is in heaven, and that he who regards Him and keeps His Word in this the day of His rejection, shall be honored when the day of Christ has come. Meantime let him labor on, strong in faith, giving glory to God, and the reaping time is sure, as with the husbandman of 2 Timothy 2:6.

> [19] As in water face answereth to face,
>   So the heart of man to man.

Of all mirrors, clear water is perhaps the most primitive. As the reflected image answers to the face of him who is looking into it, so does one man's heart answer to another's. "There is no difference." However much men may seem to differ through hereditary characteristics, education, or the lack of it, environment, or experience; the fact remains, that all have the same evil corrupt heart, which is deceitful above all things and desperately wicked. No one has ground for boasting over another. All are sinners needing a Savior.

Therefore, if I would show a man his sinfulness, I need but to describe in a measure the evil of my own heart, and he is likely to think I have been privately informed as to his faults and am exposing him publicly! How often have men thus reasoned when some faithful preacher was declaring the terrible nature of the center of man's moral being, while yet altogether ignorant of the actual state and behavior of his auditors!

Blessed it is that, if all are alike sinners, for all a Savior has been provided. See the "No difference" gospel as expounded by the Holy Spirit in Romans 10:5–13.

> ²⁰ Sheol and destruction are insatiable,
> So the eyes of man are never satisfied.

This verse but helps to seal the truth of the previous one. In this all men are the same. The natural heart will not permit the eyes to be satisfied. There is in man a capacity likened to sheol and destruction. Let him get all he may, he still yearns for more. This is the great lesson of the book of Ecclesiastes. There, we find a man with a heart so large that all the world could not fill it. In the Canticles, on the other hand, we have an Object so great that the heart cannot hold it, but the cry goes up, "I am sick of love." It is Christ alone who can thus meet every craving of the soul, and more than satisfy all who find in Him the object of their deepest affections. See 30:15–16.

> ²¹ As the fining-pot for silver, and the furnace for gold,
> So is a man tried by his praise.

There is no hotter crucible to test a man than when he is put through a fire of praise and adulation. To go on through evil report, cleaving to the Lord, and counting on Him to clear one's name is comparatively easy, though many faint in such circumstances; but to humbly pursue the even tenor of his way, undisturbed and unlifted up by applause and flattery, marks a man as being truly with God.

Hundreds have prospered in soul when in adversity, who have failed grievously through prosperity. Gideon becomes a warning to all who are in danger of being carried away by undue appreciation (Judg. 8:22–27).

[22] Though thou pound a fool in a mortar among wheat with
a pestle,
Yet will not his foolishness depart from him.

Folly is bound up in the heart of the fool, and after long years of willfulness has become part of his very being. To beat him as one beats grain in a mortar will not deliver him from his wickedness. In childhood the correction properly administered might have had good effect (22:15), but having permitted his character to develop itself, it is now too late to seek to eradicate the foolishness by corporal punishment. Nor will moral suasion effect the desired result, for the fool is deaf to all entreaties and cares for nothing but doing his own pleasure. It is a dreadful state to be in. God alone can awaken such a one to a sense of his guilt and his danger, and turn him from his folly. See Jeremiah 13:23.

[23] Be thou diligent to know the state of thy flocks,
And look well to thy herds:
[24] For riches are not forever;
Not even the crown from generation to generation.
[25] The hay appeareth, and the tender herbage showeth itself;
And herbs of the mountains are gathered in.
[26] The lambs are for thy clothing,
And the goats are the price of the field:
[27] Thou shalt have goats' milk enough for thy food,
For the food of thy household,
And for the maintenance for thy maidens.

Faithful shepherd service results in suited provision for oneself and those dependent upon him. Wealth is fleeting and riches soon pass away. See note on 23:4–5. Therefore the importance of earnest persistent endeavor and careful adherence to duty. Even a crown endures not forever. Dynasties rise and fall in this world of changes. But he who plods on, husbanding his resources and wisely attending to the care of his flocks will have both food and clothing thereby; and what more does the wealthiest enjoy?

We may see in these verses also a picture of pastoral care among the sheep and lambs of Christ's flock. His word to Peter was "Feed my lambs," and "Shepherd my sheep." Wherever He has implanted the pastor's heart this will be the result. Such a one will look well to the state of the flock; not, however, with a view to pecuniary profit, nor as lording it over his own possessions, but out of pure love for the members of Christ. Nor will he be without reward. It is sure to come in the end, though he labor not for it. "When the chief Shepherd shall appear, ye shall receive a crown of glory that fadeth not away." See Peter's word to the elders in his first epistle, 5:1–4. In Jacob's defense to Laban we are reminded of what this shepherd-service may mean if carried out conscientiously (Gen. 31:40).

CHAPTER 28

PROVERBS 28

N one are so cowardly as those who are carrying about a guilty conscience.
Such are terrified by their own thoughts and take fright at a shadow. Of
them the first verse treats, and contrasts them with the righteous.

> ¹ The lawless flee when no man pursueth;
> But the righteous are bold as a lion.

Sin keeps men in continual dread; but the consciousness that one is seeking
to please God, and walk in righteousness before Him and before men, inspires
with holy confidence and almost superhuman courage. No lion was bolder in
facing his foes than have been naturally weak and timid men and women when
martyred for Christ's sake. Contrast the army of the Syrians with Elisha the
prophet (2 Kings 6:8–17; 7:6–7).

> ² For the transgression of a land many are its princes;
> But by a man of understanding and knowledge its stability
> shall be prolonged.

Transgression here seems to bear the sense of rebellion against lawful authority. When a people refuse to own the powers that be as ordained of God, they are

likely, in a disrupted state of society, to be exposed to the evil machinations of various leaders, each one jealous of the other; hence their princes or rulers are many, and continually changing.

In contrast to so unsettled a state, that land is happy indeed which is ruled over by a wise and understanding governor, who long occupies his seat of authority.

Among the Arabs, a dreadful malediction is implied in the words, "May God multiply your sheiks." No people or country can prosper when exposed to frequent alterations in the executive power. The state of Judah, after the carrying away of Zedekiah, is an apt illustration of this, as also much of the history of the Judges.

> ³ A poor man who oppresseth the poor,
>   Is like a sweeping rain that leaveth no food.

Obscure men, when suddenly elevated to positions of trust and confidence, are likely to be far harder on those of their own former class than one born in a different station of life. Such, often, seem utterly bereft of pity and compassion, and may well be likened to a sweeping rain, which instead of helping the crop to mature, washes away all the seed and leaves no food. It was this that made the publicans of our Lord's day to be so detested by the populace. Members of the chosen race themselves, hated and despised therefore by the Roman power; they yet took service under that very authority and used their positions as a means of oppressing their poor countrymen. See the protestation of Zaccheus, who declares he had not acted according to the ordinary custom (Luke 19:8).

> ⁴ They that forsake the law praise the lawless;
>   But such as keep the law contend with them.
> ⁵ Evil men understand not judgment;
>   But those who seek Jehovah understand everything.

It is natural that men who have themselves forsaken the law should praise those who follow in the same crooked path. When a man is always ready to excuse unrighteousness in others it generally bespeaks an uneasy conscience as to his own ways. They who walk uprightly are able to convict those who do not. There is a corresponding moral state which enables them to weigh matters aright.

Evil men are blind to true justice, because of the iniquity of their own lives. Those who put the Lord always before them, and who are exercised concerning His glory, are enabled to understand everything; that is not in an unlimited sense, but everything pertaining to rectitude of life and just judgment. See the Spirit-anointed ones of 1 John 2:20, 27.

> ⁶ Better is the poor that walketh in his uprightness,
> Than he that is perverse in his ways, though he be rich.

The honest poor may take comfort in the estimate that God puts upon them. In His sight they are far to be preferred to the perverse rich. Poverty is indeed a sore trial and often entails much sorrow, but it is not to be compared to the unhappiness of the godless wealthy man, who sows the wind to reap the whirlwind. Contrast the rich man and Lazarus (Luke 16:19–31).

> ⁷ He who keepeth the law is an intelligent son:
> But he that is a companion of riotous men shameth his
>   father.

Great is the joy a father finds when blessed with a careful, faithful son, who seeks to keep the commandments of God and the salutary ordinances of men for the Lord's sake. He thereby manifests true intelligence. The father of a wild, reckless lad who finds his companions among riotous men, is put to shame by his son's evil behavior. How rich the grace that led the father in Luke 15 to go out to meet such a son "while he was yet a great way off." It is a precious picture of the joy that fills the Father's heart above when one poor wanderer returns, who has long shamed the God who brought him into being by his wretched, sinful life.

> ⁸ He that by usury and unjust gain increaseth his substance,
> He shall gather it for him that shall pity the poor.

Extortion and covetousness are alike detestable in the sight of God. The putting of money out to usury, charging the needy a high and ruinous rate of interest, may seem to be good business in the eyes of unprincipled men; but treasure so earned will not profit the owners. Taken away in the midst of their days they shall leave it for those who are concerned about the poor. See God's Word to the rich men of the last days (James 5:1–6). Note also Jeremiah 17:11.

> ⁹ He that turneth away his ear from hearing the law,
> Even his prayer shall be an abomination.

God has never promised to hear prayer if the heart is not upright before Him. The psalmist says, "If I regard iniquity in my heart, the Lord will not hear me" (Ps. 66:18). This solemn fact, the verse we are now considering attests. It is in vain to look for answers to prayer when refusing to obey what God has caused to be written for our instruction. He has revealed His holy will in His Word. Everything necessary for the believer's instruction in righteousness is there made known. Where He is truly feared, that Word will have its due weight, and the subject soul will order his steps accordingly. When this is the case, prayer will be acceptable and will obtain a ready answer; but when the Word is refused or despised, what passes for prayer is but an abomination to the Lord. See Ezekiel's message to the self-willed elders of Israel who came to inquire of Jehovah (Ezek. 20:l-3).

> ¹⁰ Whoso causeth the righteous to go astray in an evil way,
>   He shall fall into his own pit:
>   But the upright shall have good things in possession.

See note on 26:27. To deliberately turn the steps of the righteous from the path of rectitude is to incur the divine displeasure in a most solemn and awful form. The Lord Jesus has said, "Whosoever shall stumble one of these little ones that believe in Me, it were better for him that a millstone were hung about his neck, and that he were drowned in the depth of the sea" (Matt. 18:6). How dreadful must be the iniquity of the heart when one could, with full intention, plot to turn any away from obeying the voice of the Lord! Yet many have so offended and been made to know the indignation of a holy God, who gives good things to the upright but metes out judgment to him who would lead them astray. Balaam was guilty of this heinous offense, and his doom was swift and sure (Num. 31:16; Rev. 2:14).

> ¹¹ The rich man is wise in his own eyes,
>   But the poor that hath understanding searcheth him out.

Pride and conceit often accompany great wealth. (See first clause of 10:15). It gives a certain sense of security and independence of God and environment that is ruinous to the unhumbled soul. But understanding is of far more value than great possessions. He who has it, though in poverty, is after all the superior of his well-to-do neighbor. It is not the great, the rich, the mighty, or the noble, that God has chosen; but "the poor of this world, rich in faith." See 1 Corinthians 1:26–29.

> ¹² When righteous men triumph, there is great glory:
> But when the lawless rise, men hide themselves.

See notes on 11:10; 29:2, and verse 28 below. The triumph of the righteous inspires joy and confidence in the breasts of those who are concerned about the stability and welfare of a state. But when the evildoers bear rule, there is a corresponding fear and anxiety, which leads even trustworthy men to conceal themselves, lest they become the objects of political hatred and enmity.

Long have men waited and groaned in pain for the coming triumph of the righteous One, whose kingdom shall be ushered in with great glory, when all the earth shall come into blessing. Until then, the kingdoms of this world must be subject to vicissitudes and overturnings, because of the rejection of the true King. Saul's wretched reign is a figure of the present time; the reigns of David and Solomon, of the coming glorious reign of Christ.

> ¹³ He that covereth his transgressions, shall not prosper:
> But whoso confesseth and forsaketh them shall obtain
> mercy.

It is the greatest mistake a soul can be guilty of, to attempt to cover sin and transgression. Yet men invariably shrink from coming out frankly with a confession of their true state and actions. It seems to be natural to fallen man (ever since the day that our first parents, by fig leaf aprons, sought to hide their nakedness) to endeavor to cover his shame, hoping thereby to avoid the just consequences of his sin. But God's Word clearly makes known the fact that he who justifies himself can only be condemned at last. It is the one who sides with God and condemns himself, who is justified from all things.

Confession is the divinely appointed method of securing conscience rest; confession not to some human mediator, but to God Himself. "If we confess our sins, He is faithful and just to forgive us our sins, and to cleanse us from all unrighteousness" (1 John 1:9). The ground upon which He can so act is the atonement of our Lord Jesus Christ. Because He, in rich grace, bore the sinner's judgment upon Calvary and shed His precious blood to put away sin, God can "be just and the justifier of him who believeth in Jesus."

Of course, by confession is not meant a general acknowledgment of sinfulness and wickedness of life, uttered as a kind of soul-ease. True confession involves genuine repentance and self-judgment. Therefore we are here told, "He that confesseth and forsaketh them shall have mercy." The repentant man no longer hugs the chains that bind him, but longs for full deliverance from them. He comes to God with real concern about his unholy ways and thoughts and words, earnestly seeking grace to cease from them, and to walk uprightly before the Lord. But this he cannot do in himself. It is only when he rests in simple faith in the finished work of Christ, and yields himself unto God as one now alive from the dead, that he is able to rise above the sins that have blighted his life and almost damned his soul.

David most preciously portrays the change that comes over a man when he ceases to hide, or cover, his iniquities, and comes out into the light of God's presence, confessing them before Him. It is only such a one who knows the blessedness of transgressions forgiven and sins covered. See Psalm 32.

When a man attempts to cover his own sin, he is but adding to the dreadful list, for he is refusing to heed the command which goes out to all men everywhere, calling upon them to repent.

But when God covers sin, it is done effectually and perfectly, and shall never be interfered with for eternity.

> ^{14} Happy is the man that feareth always,
> But he that hardeneth his heart shall fall into mischief.

See note on 23:17. This verse most appropriately follows the one we have just been considering. He who is forgiven, who rejoices in the knowledge of sins covered, is now responsible to act and walk ever in the fear of God. He who grows careless and prayerless, who neglects the Word of God or hardens his heart against discipline, persisting in taking his own way, will fall into grievous trouble and sorrow; for "whom the Lord loveth He chasteneth."

He who fears always will be delivered from vainglory and self-confidence. He will walk in accordance with God's revealed will. Fearing no longer to be judged for his sins, he will fear lest he grieve the Holy Spirit of God within him, and lest he dishonor the name of Him whom he delights to own as Savior and Lord. It was this salutary fear that kept Joseph when exposed to a temptation which would have overcome any who trusted in their own hearts (Gen. 39:9).

> ^{15} As a roaring lion, and a charging bear;
> So is a lawless ruler over the poor people.
> ^{16} The prince that wanteth understanding is also a great
> oppressor:
> But he that hateth covetousness shall prolong his days.

See verse 12 above and connected passages. A lawless ruler is one who, set in the place of authority, owns not the higher Power that has permitted him to occupy his honored position. He cares only to gratify his personal inclinations, as Ahab when he possessed himself so unrighteously of the vineyard of Naboth (1 Kings 21). Oppressing the poor and causing judgment to miscarry, such a prince is like a wild beast let loose among the populace.

Wanting true intelligence, he fails to see that the security of his throne is bound up with the welfare of his subjects; therefore he bears rule with a heavy hand until all hearts are alienated from him. It is covetousness and a desire for self-aggrandizement that is the root from which such conduct springs. He who hates and refuses to be controlled by this evil passion ensures the stability of his house and prolongs his days. Contrast Saul and David.

> [17] A man laden with the blood of any person shall flee to the
>   pit:
>   Let no man stay him.

To be consciously guilty of having willfully destroyed or abetted the destruction of an innocent man, is to bear on the conscience a fearful load that drives one on to suicide. This would be especially so in Israel. Unable to find a sheltering city of refuge, the guilty assassin would rather die by his own hand than meet the avenger of blood. The unhappy traitor Judas exemplified the proverb to the full.

> [18] Whoso walketh uprightly shall be saved:
>   But he that is perverse in his ways shall fall at once.

It is not the salvation of the soul that is here contemplated. None by walking uprightly can blot out past sin and be justified before God. This we have already noticed in our comments on verse 13. But it is salvation in a practical sense, day by day, from failure and sin, together with the sorrows resulting therefrom, that is referred to. The one who with purpose of heart cleaves to the Lord, walking uprightly before Him, will be saved from much that he would otherwise have to endure if taking his own way. He who refuses the correction of the Word of God and independently pursues his own course, walking in the pride and self-sufficiency of his heart, will have a sudden fall. His perverseness will result in unexpected disaster. How many a saint has proven this to his sorrow! But alas, how slow are we to learn, either from what God Himself has revealed, or from the failures of others! Among the prophets, Daniel and Jonah stand out in vivid contrast as illustrations of the two statements in this couplet.

> ¹⁹ He that tilleth his land shall have plenty of bread:
>   But he that followeth after vain persons shall have poverty
>   enough.

See notes on verse 7 above and 12:11. In the original Hebrew there is a striking parallelism here. Muenscher gives the rendering, "He who tilleth his land shall be *satisfied* with bread; but he who followeth vain persons shall be *satisfied* with poverty." The one, by diligence, shall be filled with what is needful to his building up; the other, because of his folly and neglect, shall be filled with woe, and be as needy as his neighbor is wealthy. It is not chance that thus makes one to prosper, while the other fails. It is simply the difference between patient, steady-going adherence to duty, and the casting off of restraint and following after the worthless. The two classes are everywhere about us.

In the spiritual realm they are likewise found. Two young men confess Christ. From the day of his conversion, one conscientiously separates himself from the world in its various forms, and devotes himself to faithful tilling of the fields of Scripture. The result is he grows in grace and in knowledge; his soul is fed; and, satisfied with bread himself, he has that which he can impart to the needy about him. The other, having the same opportunities, temporizes at first with the world, follows after its vain company, neglects his Bible, and becomes spiritually starved. At last he breaks down entirely in his discipleship and never amounts to anything for God. It is a grave question if he ever was saved at all. People wonder at the difference between the two; but there is nothing perplexing to the man of God who notes their respective courses. A semi-worldling never develops into a Timothy. It is the faithful, uncompromising young man who becomes a power for God and is satisfied with good things.

> ²⁰ A faithful man shall abound with blessings:
>   But he that maketh haste to be rich shall not be acquitted.

See notes on 22:1, 16; 23:4; and 27:24. A faithful man is not likely to accumulate vast wealth in a world like this; but he will be rich in heavenly treasure and shall abound with blessings even in a temporal sense, for he who acts for God can count on God to act for him. If the getting of riches is made his life's object he will not be acquitted when called to account for his methods and sharp practices. Fraudulent schemes may seem to triumph over steady-going industry, but the end will prove the value of the latter and the worthlessness of the former. To become rich quickly is almost certain evidence of injustice somewhere. The Christian may well shun such a course. It is far better to be comparatively poor but to maintain a good conscience, than to make haste to be wealthy and lose the sense of communion with God. See Isaiah's message to the conscienceless capitalists of his day, who seemed to know as much as money-lovers in our times, concerning the advantages to themselves, of the trust system (Isa. 5:8–10). Notice verse 22 below.

> ²¹ To have respect of persons is not good:
> Even for a piece of bread that man will transgress.

See notes on 18:5. Dishonest and thoroughly unprincipled, he who has respect of persons in judgment looks only to his own gain, and will defeat the ends of justice for the merest trifle, if it be for his apparent advantage. For "pieces of bread" the false prophetesses of the scattered Israelites were showing respect of persons in their messages when Ezekiel was commanded to prophesy against them (Ezek. 13:17–19).

> ²² He that hasteth to be rich hath an evil eye,
> And knoweth not that poverty shall come upon him.

See notes on 20:21 and verse 20 above. An evil eye is a covetous eye and bespeaks the state of the heart. Such a man, hasting to be rich, forgets the sure calamities which in God's righteous government are certain to overtake him. Ponder Micah 6:12 and Matthew 19:23–24.

> ²³ He that rebuketh a man shall afterwards find more favor
> Than he that flattereth with the tongue.

See notes on 19:25; 20:19; 26:28; and 27:6. For the moment, the flatterer may please the object of his praise; but one who is faithful in reproving will be more valued when there has been time for reflection. It is no kindness done a person when his faults are glossed over, and he is made to feel comfortable in his wrongdoing. He who goes to a wrongdoer in the fear of the Lord, meekly seeking to exercise him as to his unholy ways, may arouse anger and indignation at first; but he has time and conscience on his side. The result will be that he will find more favor than the other. Peter could write of "our beloved brother Paul" after the searching ordeal he underwent in Antioch (2 Peter 3:15).

> ²⁴ Whoso robbeth his father or his mother, and saith, It is no
>   transgression;
>   The same is the companion of a destroyer.

See notes on 19:13, 26. The youth who (pretending that he was entitled to the possessions of his parents, or that he had no responsibility toward their care when he became a wage-earner) spent all on himself and boldly declared his innocence of transgression was acting like the veriest criminal who destroys what belongs to others. The Pharisees, with all their religiousness, were violating the letter and spirit of this word by their Corban law (Mark 7:11).

> ²⁵ He that is puffed up in soul exciteth contention:
>   But he that putteth his trust in Jehovah shall be made fat.
> ²⁶ He that trusteth in his own heart is a fool:
>   But whoso walketh wisely shall be delivered.

See notes on 13:10 and 18:12. A man who is puffed up in soul readily stirs up strife. Haughty and self-confident, he boldly antagonizes persons more to be depended on than himself and will give them no rest unless he be permitted to have his own way. Proud, haughty and self-reliant, never having learned the lesson of no confidence in the flesh, by his unbending spirit and arbitrary ways, he will often cause untold mischief among the people of God. His course is the very opposite to that of one who has learned of Him who is meek and lowly in heart and who can therefore be trusted with prosperity and exemplifies in his life the fact that he is spiritually-minded and devoted to the Lord. He alone knows the human heart and He puts no reliance upon it whatever (Jer. 17:9–10). A man who walks humbly will walk wisely and will be delivered from many a snare. See the Lord's estimate of the heart as portrayed in John 2:23–25.

> ²⁷ He that giveth unto the poor shall not lack:
>   But he that hideth his eyes shall have many a curse.

See notes on 14:21; 21:13; and verse 8 above. It is one of the evidences of the interference of a benevolent providence in the affairs of men, that he who has pity upon the needy is never the loser thereby, while he who refuses to see their sad estate, and who hoards all his possessions for himself, finds them to be a cause of grief and anguish in the end. God makes Himself responsible to repay with interest all that is given to the poor. They are left in this world to test the hearts of those in more fortunate circumstances. A blessing is upon the philanthropic, and a curse upon the man who thinks only of his own enjoyment and leaves others suffer for need that he could relieve, had he the heart for it. See the rich young ruler (Luke 18:18–27). Compare with 11:25.

> [28] When the lawless rise, men hide themselves:
> But when they perish, the righteous increase.

See verse 12 above. When evil men are in the place of power, life and property are alike insecure, and men of peace and quietness conceal themselves, dreading to be brought into public notice. But when the unrighteous are overthrown, the upright are everywhere visibly increased, having confidence in the safety of their households and goods. See the condition of the Israelites in the days of the Philistine domination, and their altered estate when Jonathan overthrew their wicked oppressors (1 Sam. 13:6; 14:22).

CHAPTER 29

PROVERBS 29

Irrevocable and crushing judgment will be his portion who, despising all wise counsel and refusing all godly reproof, plunges on in his sin until the patience of the Lord is exhausted.

> [1] He that being often reproved hardeneth his neck,
>   Shall suddenly be destroyed, and that without remedy.

Hardening the neck is a figure taken from the manner in which a refractory bullock turns away from and avoids the yoke. In this way, men, in their obstinacy, persistently refuse to heed reproof, and set their wills stubbornly against what would be for their own best interests; thus insuring their destruction.

God is gracious and long-suffering, slow to anger, and doth not afflict willingly, nor grieve the children of men. Yet even *His* patience with the unrepentant comes to an end at last. He will plead, and strive, and warn, until it is manifest the heart is fully set upon having its own way. Then He leaves the hardened soul to its doom, giving it up to sudden destruction. Many are the scriptural examples of this, but I only remind the reader of Korah, Dathan, and Abiram, of Belshazzar and of Jezebel.

² When the righteous are increased, the people rejoice:
But when the lawless beareth rule, the people mourn.

See notes on 28:12, 28. However much men, as individuals, prefer sin to holiness, collectively, they rejoice when the righteous are in authority and mourn when evil is in high places. Even the vilest know the comfort of the protection to person and property enjoyed when the upright flourish. The unbeliever who hates Christianity and makes it the butt of his cheap ridicule, nevertheless prefers to live in a land where the teachings of the Bible are generally held and where the Christian faith is respected. In the measure that the principles of the New Testament control the minds of the men who administer civil government, peace and prosperity prevail; as none know better than the openly skeptical. The same was true in Israel in regard to the Law and the Prophets. The reign of a Josiah or a Hezekiah was much to be preferred to that of an Ahab or a Manasseh.

³ Whoso loveth wisdom rejoiceth his father:
But he that keepeth company with harlots spendeth his
substance.

See note on 28:7. Loose living is a snare to which young men are peculiarly exposed. He who is wise will shun it as he would a viper about to strike. Immorality is ruinous alike to body and soul. Its awful consequences beggar all powers of description. "Flee also youthful lusts" is a most salutary word. See 1 Corinthians 6:15–20.

⁴ The king by judgment establisheth the land;
But he that receiveth gifts overthroweth it.

When David sang of "a righteous ruler over men; a ruler in the fear of God," he had to own, "My house is not so." It is Christ who will be manifested as the king who, by judgment, will establish the land. A scepter of righteousness will be the scepter of His kingdom. Meantime it is the privilege of every earthly sovereign to endeavor to be a fitting type of God's anointed Ruler. The receiver of gifts or bribes is far from this. His evil example results in the corruption of the entire body politic. See this in Samuel's sons (1 Sam. 8:3).

⁵ A man that flattereth his neighbor
Spreadeth a net for his feet.

See notes on 28:23; and connected passages. True praise, the honest recognition of merit in another, is right and proper in its place, and may be the means of cheering and encouraging a deserving person when perhaps well-nigh cast down. But flattery—saying what the heart does not mean in order to mislead or to curry favor— is a net and a snare for the feet of the one who listens. Insincere remarks of an adulatory character are most dangerous. The lowly man will turn away in fear from any who approach him in this way. The heart is too prone to think well of self, as it is, without listening to the flattering words which are but as fuel to the fire of pride. How solemn the warning which the doom of Absalom would sound in our ears! None were so praised as he, and few princes have failed more terribly (2 Sam. 14:25).

> 6 In the transgression of an evil man there is a snare;
>   But the righteous shall sing and rejoice.
> 7 The righteous considereth the cause of the poor:
>   But the lawless regardeth not to know it.

The evil man is overthrown by his own transgressions. His very iniquities, in which he delighted, prove to be his undoing. When the upright shouts and sings for joy, the wicked is pierced through with many sorrows. The latter lives only for himself. He regards not the cry of the needy. The former, recognizing his own indebtedness to sustaining and preserving grace, is quick to show compassion to the indigent who cry for help. In this he becomes an imitator of Him who ever "went about doing good." Contrast the spirit of Peter and John with that of the unscrupulous Pharisees (Acts 3:1–8; Matt. 23:23–28).

> 8 Scornful men bring a city into a snare:
>   But wise men turn away wrath.

The first part of this couplet is rendered by J. N. Darby, "Scornful men set the city in a flame." When a crisis arises and the populace are stirred, the ruler who meets them with cold sarcasm or stinging scorn only adds to their anger and causes their passions to burn more fiercely than ever. Rehoboam's answer to the men of Israel is an exemplification of this(1 Kings 12:13–14). The counsel of the wise men, had it prevailed, would have conciliated the people and averted indignation.

> 9 If a wise man contendeth with a foolish man,
>   Whether he rage or laugh, there is no rest.

It is in vain to endeavor to convince a fool of his errors. Proud in heart, admiring himself and his opinions above all else, to strive with him will yield no good result. Whether he grow heated and wrathful, or whether he seem for the moment to accept advice cheerfully, laughing pleasantly or mocking in amused scorn, it all comes to the same thing: there will be no happy end to the affair because the fool will refuse to brook correction. Nehemiah's controversy with the sometimes affable but generally openly angry Sanballat illustrates well what is meant (Neh. 2:10, 19; 4:1–10; 6:1–9).

> [10] Men of blood hate the perfect:
>   But the just seek [or, care for] his soul.

Because of the very difference in their lives, bloodthirsty men hate those who are upright, even as "Cain, who was of that wicked one, and slew his brother . . . because his own works were evil, and his brother's righteous" (1 John 3:12). Holiness and godliness invariably provoke the malice of wicked men, who see in what is right and good the condemnation of their own vile ways.

The just, on the other hand, are glad to be what Cain was not—their brother's keeper—seeking to preserve his life and care for his soul. This concern for the blessing of those about him is one of the first and strongest evidences that a man has been born of God.

> [11] A fool uttereth all his mind [spirit]:
>   But a wise man keepeth it back.

Mind and spirit are used synonymously for the seat of intelligence. A fool readily pours forth all he knows, regardless of the effect it may have for good or evil. A wise man discreetly guards his tongue, knowing the impropriety of hasty speech.

It is not that the fool is more frank and open than he; but mere frankness, apart from care as to what is uttered, is not at all to be commended. It is what makes that pest of society, the gossip and the talebearer. Our Lord Himself, who knew all things, does not at once manifest His full acquaintance with the solemn events in which He had been the central figure; but asks the disciples, on their way to Emmaus, "What things?" when they express their wonder at His apparent ignorance. He wished to test their hearts; and all was for their blessing, as afterward so preciously proven (Luke 24:13–32). Joseph, in his dealings with his brethren, maintains the same reserve, until the moment arrives when the revelation, "I am Joseph!" will do its proper work (Gen. 42–45).

¹² If a ruler hearken to lies,
    All his servants are lawless.

In the apocryphal book of Ecclesiasticus there is a passage which seems to explain this proverb. "As the judge of the people is himself, so are his officers; and what manner of man the ruler of the city is, such are all that dwell therein." A corrupt ruler will surround himself with corrupt men, his own evil example acting powerfully upon the formation of the characters of his dependents. Therefore the importance of integrity and uprightness on the part of those who occupy positions of trust and honor. It was a sad period in the history of Judah when their pastors, or rulers, were their examples in disobedience to God (Jer. 2:8; 10:21).

¹³ The needy and the oppressor meet together:
    Jehovah enlighteneth the eyes of them both.
¹⁴ The king that faithfully judgeth the poor,
    His throne shall be established forever.

See notes on 22:2. It is greatly to be lamented that there are any to oppress the needy, seeing both are so dependent on the same common Benefactor, who "maketh His sun to rise on the evil and on the good, and sendeth rain on the just and on the unjust" (Matt. 5:45). His eye is over all His works, and He notes the need as well as the behavior of all His creatures. He makes the eyes of the poor and those who lord it over them alike to sparkle with life and intelligence.

A faithful king will be thoughtful of the weak, and will judge the poor in uprightness, thus patterning his actions after the Most High who rules over all in righteousness. Therefore his throne shall be established in peace. "Forever" is often used in what might be called a limited sense, as when, in law, we speak of transferring property "to him and his heirs forever"; that is, to perpetuity. See what is said as to the throne of Solomon, a type of the reign of Christ (Ps. 89:19–29).

¹⁵ The rod and reproof give wisdom;
    But a child left to himself bringeth his mother to shame.

See notes on 19:18 and 23:13–14. An undisciplined child will bring shame upon his mother and ruin upon himself. To refuse to chasten him because of personal repugnance to causing temporary pain is to manifest hatred instead of love. Correction and reproof, properly administered, are for the child's best

interests and open his heart to wisdom. Let the overindulgent parent be warned by
the fate of Adonijah. It is not for nothing that God has caused the unhappy fact to
be left on record that "his father had not displeased him at any time in saying,
Why hast thou done so?" No wonder he became a rebel! (1 Kings 1; 2:13–25).

> [16] When the lawless are multiplied, transgression increaseth:
> But the righteous shall witness their fall.

See verse 2 above, with connected passages. It is a principle in God's moral
government that although lawlessness may seem, like the flood, to prevail over the
highest mountains, it shall surely retreat and righteousness hold sway at last. When
the wicked are in power, transgression flourishes and uprightness is crushed; but
this can only be for a time. "The triumphing of the wicked is short, and the joy of
the hypocrite is but for a moment," as Zophar rightly observed, though he did
wrong in applying it to Job when he sought the cause of his affliction (Job 20:5).

Throughout the past and the present dispensations, in large measure the wicked
have been in power, permitted by God to try most severely at times the patience
of the righteous. But their overthrow is near, when God's King shall take to Him
His great power and reign, and the world kingdom of our God and His Christ
shall come. Then shall the upright "have dominion in the morning"—a morning without clouds, when righteousness and the knowledge of the Lord shall
cover the earth as the waters cover the sea (Isa. 11:9; Hab. 2:14).

> [17] Correct thy son, and he shall give thee rest;
> Yea, he shall give delight unto thy soul.

See verse 15 above. What wisdom does a parent need that correction may be
properly administered, and his household brought up in the fear of God! Nothing, perhaps, so causes one to realize his own failures and shortcomings as to see
them duplicated in his children; and nothing, therefore, makes one feel more
keenly the need of divine grace and wisdom in dealing with them. But the Word
is sure. Let the father and mother exercise a firm but kindly discipline, and God
has pledged Himself that it shall bear goodly fruit. The son corrected shall give
rest to the heart and delight to the soul. This was manifested in Isaac, whose
lovely obedience did not flinch when it meant to permit himself to be bound
upon the altar. And it is noteworthy that God had foreseen in Abraham the
ability to control his household before he made him the depositary of the promises (Gen. 18:19).

¹⁸ Where there is no vision, the people will become lawless:
But he that keepeth the law, happy is he.

By *vision* is meant spiritual enlightenment and insight into divine things. A reference to 1 Samuel 3:1 will make this clear. "The word of the Lord was precious in those days; there was no open vision." To meet this need God raised up Samuel, who was appropriately called "the Seer"—the man with opened eyes— as Balaam described himself.

It is of all importance that there be among the people of God in all ages this open vision. "Would God that all the Lord's people were prophets" (Num. 11:29), having the eyes of the heart enlightened, that they might discern clearly what is of God and what is opposed to His mind. It was this that the apostle Paul put before the carnal Corinthians when he wrote urging them to covet earnestly the best gifts, but rather that they might prophesy. The prophet is one who enters into what is of the Lord and gives it out in freshness and power, meeting the actual need of the time. He does not necessarily foretell future events, but he tells forth what reaches the conscience and quickens the affections.

When ministry of this nature is lacking among the people of God and the assemblies of His saints, they soon become lawless, substituting for the Spirit's energy the mere busy meddling of nature, and opening the door to what is simply of man in the flesh.

But we would not forget the second part of the couplet. Even let ministry of an edifying character be rarely known, yet where the Word of God controls there will be blessing. He who keeps it will be happy amidst the existing confusion, enjoying fellowship with Him who inspired it. When leaving the Ephesian elders at Miletus, it was not to gifted ministers that Paul commended them, in view of evil teachers soon to arise, but to God and the word of His grace, which was able to build them up. This abides today and remains to comfort and direct the saints in all circumstances. But the anointed eye is needed to discern what has been therein revealed. Lack of vision will be manifested in a cold, dry, theological or philosophical treatment of the Scriptures, as though given to exercise the intellect, rather than the heart and the conscience. Paul's prayer for the Ephesians is one applicable for all Christians while in this scene of trial and testing (Eph. 1:15–23).

¹⁹ A servant will not be corrected by words;
For though he understand, he will not answer.

The Septuagint reads, "a stubborn servant," which seems to convey the right thought. Correction by words alone would avail little with such a one if unprincipled and self-willed. Therefore strict discipline would be required if he be made to render proper service, which is here implied in answering. Is it not so with those of us who have been made servants of our Lord Jesus Christ? Have we not often failed to heed His Word, refusing its correction, therefore having to know the pains of chastisement? It is a lesson slowly learned. Most of us are more or less patterned on the order of Jonah, who was only rendered obedient by serious grief and trouble.

> 20 Seest thou a man hasty in his words?
> There is more hope of a fool than of him.

In 26:12 this statement is made concerning a man who is wise in his own eyes. The two things are likely to be found in the same person. He who is filled with self-conceit is very liable to be hasty in his words. Of God it is said, "He will not call back His words" (Isa. 31:2); and He needs not to do so, for "the words of the LORD are pure words: as silver tried in the fire, purified seven times" (Ps. 12:6). But the self-confident man is continually uttering words which he has to recall, because of his reckless impatience and his ready exaggeration. There is little hope of checking such a man, unless there be true self-judgment and repentance for what is a grave sin, though often treated as a mere infirmity for which he is to be pitied rather than blamed. Hasty speech betokens an unbroken spirit. It was characteristic of King Saul, and on a notable occasion would have caused the death of Jonathan had the people not interfered and rescued him (1 Sam. 14). Jephthah too is a solemn warning as to hasty speech (Judg. 11).

> 21 He that delicately bringeth up his servant from a child
> Shall have him become as a son in the end.

In a note, J. N. Darby states that "son" is, literally, "son of the house"; and explains it as meaning that he gets into possession of his master's goods. It was this that pained Abraham; for, much as he valued the service of Eliezer of Damascus, he could not bear the thought of a servant inheriting in the place of a son. God's servants are His sons, and so shall be His heirs, and joint heirs with the Lord Jesus Christ in glory.

²² An angry man stirreth up strife,
And a furious man aboundeth in transgression.

See note on 28:25. A man of unbridled temper provokes continual contention and had best be avoided. His fury can only spring from an evil nature unchecked, and therefore he abounds in violations of all law, human or divine. None can walk in communion with the Lord Jesus Christ and manifest a wrathful and passionate spirit. The two things do not go together. See the elder son in the parable, whose unreasonable anger was the only jarring note in the merriment occasioned by his brother's return (Luke 15:28).

²³ A man's pride shall bring him low;
But honor shall uphold the humble in spirit.

Pride precedes destruction. It is a sure precursor of coming judgment. But he who is of a meek and humble spirit shall obtain honor. Seeking it not, it shall be thrust upon him; while he who makes it his object shall fail miserably to obtain what he desires. Contrast Haman and Mordecai throughout the deeply interesting book of Esther.

²⁴ Whoso is partner with a thief hateth his own soul:
He heareth the adjuration, but will not confess.

To share the plunder with a robber is to make oneself partaker of his evil deeds, and draw down upon one's head the same sentence. He acts against his own best interests, even viewed from a worldly standpoint. Put under oath, he is afraid to testify the full truth, and therefore brings himself under condemnation for abetting and concealing a theft. See Leviticus 5:1.

It is a serious thing indeed to be thus a partaker of other men's sins. The Holy Spirit warns the believer against it, showing that association with evil, or condolence of it, necessarily defiles him who thus acts. See 2 John 10–11 and 1 Timothy 5:22. This is a principle often forgotten in our day, but one of vital importance for all who seek to maintain regard for the holiness of God's house on earth.

²⁵ The fear of man bringeth a snare;
But whoso putteth his trust in Jehovah shall be safe [or, set on high].

In the fourteenth verse of the preceding chapter we were reminded of the happiness of the man who fears always. Here we learn that there is a fear to be avoided as dangerous and soul ensnaring. The fear of God is most becoming to a saint. The fear of man is destructive of his spiritual life and testimony. How many a one has been ruined thereby!

Safety and security are his portion whose trust is in the Lord alone. He who fears God will not fear man. He who fears man does not fear God as he should. See Paul in Galatians 1:10; and compare Luke 12:4–5 and John 12:43.

> [26] Many seek the ruler's favor;
>   But a man's right judgment is from Jehovah.

This but adds to what the previous verse has brought to our notice. They who seek the ruler's favor are such as fear the face of man and will have to learn by sad experience the vanity of putting their trust in princes.

It is the Lord whose judgment is ever righteous. When Wolsey cried, "Had I but served my God as faithfully as I served my king, He would not have cast me off in my old age," he uttered a great truth.

While the man of God will be obedient to rulers, he will never fawn upon them. He sees in earthly potentates but the representatives and servants of the Most High, who rules in the kingdoms of men. Elijah is a splendid example of such a one, when confronting the ungodly Ahab, as narrated in 1 Kings 18.

> [27] An unjust man is an abomination to the just:
>   And he that is upright in the way is abomination to the
>   lawless.

The two families are forever opposed. The just detest what the wicked love, and vice versa. So it has ever been since Cain strove with Abel and slew him. So shall it be until the Devil and all who do his bidding are cast into the lake of fire. There can be no truce, no treaty of peace, between the hosts of good and evil. Incessant warfare must be waged until righteousness shall dwell undisturbed in the new heavens and the new earth, and God be all in all in the universe of bliss.

Until then, let those who know their God shrink not from the conflict; but, grasping the sword of the Spirit, clad in the panoply of heaven, go forth valiantly to meet the foe, depending upon His might who says, "All power is given unto Me in heaven and in earth. . . . And, lo, I am with you always, even unto the completion of the age" (Matt. 28:18–20).

This chapter concludes the collection of proverbs copied out, or collected, by the men of Hezekiah, and marks the end of the sayings distinctly attributed to Solomon. The next two chapters, which close the book, are credited to Agur, the son of Jakeh, and to King Lemuel. The latter, I judge, is but a pseudonym for the wise king; but Agur, as we shall see, is evidently a different personage.

The question of inspiration is not touched, whoever these men may be, for the very simple reason that in the times of our Lord Jesus Christ the book was composed of the various parts which now go to make it up; and when He said, "The Scripture cannot be broken," He necessarily included each portion of the Proverbs.

Whether Solomon himself, or a later editor, collected them into one volume, we have no means of knowing, save, of course, in regard to the five chapters we have just been considering: they never formed part of the book until the reign of the great reformer Hezekiah.

CHAPTER 30

PROVERBS 30

We now take up the study of the words of Agur, a wise man who keenly felt his ignorance, as is generally the case with the truly enlightened. In the first verse we learn all we are permitted to know as to his parentage.

> ¹ The words of Agur the son of Jakeh;
> The prophecy that man spake unto Ithiel,
> Even unto Ithiel and Ucal.

The first two proper names in this passage have been read by some as common nouns; in which case we would have to understand, "The words of a gatherer, the son of [the] pious." This might imply that the contents of the chapter have been gathered by an editor from various sources, that they might be preserved for our instruction. It is evident, however, that neither our translators nor the Masoretic scribes so understood it. In the Chaldee and Syriac translations the capitalized words are found as given in the text of our King James Bibles.

One learned Hebraist, Professor Stuart, by changing the vowel points, renders the whole verse thus: "The words of Agur, the son of her who was obeyed in Massa. Thus spake the man: I have toiled for God, I have toiled for God, and have ceased."

Some commentators have supposed Agur to stand for Solomon, and Jakeh for David; but the more sober accept what seems the most straightforward explanation, that Agur was an inspired man of whom we have no record elsewhere in Scripture, while his father's name gives no clue to his family or tribe in Israel. Ithiel, which is taken to mean "God is with me," and Ucal, "able," are apparently his companions, or possibly persons who received instruction from him.

He begins his oracle by declaring his own ignorance, apart from divine enlightenment—that "vision" of 29:18 which is essential to fit a man to be a teacher of holy things.

> ² Truly I am more stupid than any man,
>   And have not the understanding of a man.
> ³ I neither learned wisdom,
>   Nor have the knowledge of the Holy.

It is not affectation and prudery that causes him to use such language as this, but a deep sense in his soul of his limitations and lack of intelligence in the great matters about which he is exercised. He has been compared with Amos, who was no prophet, nor yet the son of a prophet, but was taken up by the Lord when engaged in his ordinary occupation and given the gift that enabled him to be even a rebuker of kings. Agur was a plain, simple man, of little natural ability, perhaps even below the average of human intelligence; yet the Lord opened his understanding, revealing to him great and precious things, and giving him the wisdom to impart them to, not only Ithiel and Ucal, but untold thousands who have found, and still find, them to be of great profit. He was one of those holy men of God of whom Peter tells us, who "spake as they were moved by the Holy Ghost." Inspiration is just God's taking up a poor, feeble instrument, and so controlling his mind, tongue, and pen as to cause him to give forth the very words of the Eternal One.

> ⁴ Who hath ascended up into heaven, or descended?
>   Who hath gathered the wind in His fists?
>   Who hath bound the waters in a garment?
>   Who hath established all the ends of the earth?
>   What is His name, and what is His Son's name?
>   [Tell me,] if thou knowest.

How vast the ignorance of the most learned man, when confronted with questions like these! We are at once reminded of the Lord's challenge to Job in chapters

38–39 of the wonderful book that bears his name. At the best, human knowledge is most circumscribed and contracted. No man, apart from divine revelation, could reply to the questions here asked. The first never found an answer until the words of our Lord concerning Himself, as recorded in John 3:13: "And no man hath ascended up to heaven, but He that came down from heaven, even the Son of Man which is in heaven." He it was who descended likewise, as it is written, "Now that He ascended, what is it but that He also descended first into the lower parts of the earth? He that descended is the same also that ascended up far above all heavens, that He might fill all things" (Eph. 4:9–10).

How much there is for the believer in the precious truth connected with the Lord's descent and ascension! Because of our sins He died upon the cross, bearing the righteous judgment of God. There He drank the dreadful cup of wrath which we could never have completely drained to all eternity. But because of who He was, He could drink the cup, and exhaust the wrath, leaving naught but blessing for all who trust in Him. He died and was buried, but God raised Him from the dead, and in triumph He ascended to glory. Enoch was translated that he should not see death. Elijah was caught up in a flaming chariot and carried by a whirlwind to heaven. But neither of these went up in his own power. Jesus, His work finished and His ministry on earth accomplished, ascended of His own volition, passing through the upper air as easily as He had walked upon the water.

The fact of His having gone up and having been received by the Shechinah—the cloud of divine Majesty—testifies to the perfection of His work in putting away forever the believer's sins. When on the tree, "Jehovah laid on Him the iniquity of us all." He could not be now in the presence of God if one sin remained upon Him. But all have been righteously settled for and put away, never to come up again: therefore He has gone in, in the power of His own blood, having accomplished eternal redemption. "Wherefore He saith, When He ascended up on high, He led captivity captive, and gave gifts unto men" (Eph. 4:8). He had "destroyed Him that had the power of death, that is, the devil," that He might "deliver them who, through fear of death, were all their lifetime subject to bondage" (Heb. 2:14–15).

The trembling, anxious sinner is pointed by the Holy Ghost, not to church or sacraments, not to ordinances or legal enactments, not to frames or feelings, but to a risen and ascended Christ seated in highest glory!

The righteousness which is of faith speaketh on this wise, Say not in thy heart, Who shall ascend into heaven? (that is, to bring Christ down from above:) or, Who shall descend into the deep? (that is, to bring up Christ again from the dead.) But what saith it? The word is nigh thee, even in thy mouth, and in thy heart: that is, the word of faith which we preach; that, if thou shalt confess with thy mouth the Lord Jesus, and shalt believe in thy heart that God hath raised Him from the dead, thou shalt be saved. For with the heart man believeth unto righteousness; and with the mouth confession is made unto salvation. (Romans 10:6–10)

Christ bore our sins on the cross. He died for them. He has been raised from the dead in token of God's infinite satisfaction in His work. He has ascended up to heaven, and His place on the throne of God as a Man in glory, is proof positive, that our sins are gone forever. This it is that, believed, gives deep and lasting peace.

When the believer realizes that all has been done in a way that suits God; that He who accomplished it is one with the Father; that man as a fallen creature had no part in that work save to commit the sins for which the Savior died: then, and not until then, does the majesty of the work of the cross dawn upon the soul.

The question, "What is His name, and what is His Son's name?" followed by the challenge, "Declare, if thou canst tell," finds its answer in the New Testament revelation of the Father and the Son.

> 5 Every word [or, saying] of God is pure [or, tried]:
>   He is a shield unto them that put their trust in Him.
> 6 Add thou not unto His words,
>   Lest He reprove thee, and thou be found a liar.

There are two great facts enunciated in these verses. The first is the perfection, and the second, the all-sufficiency of the words, or sayings of God. The Scriptures, as a whole, are called the Word of God. Any portion taken separately is a word, or saying of God. Now just, as "all Scripture is God-breathed," so is every part of it, yea, every jot and tittle, divinely inspired. It is therefore pure and perfect in itself. All who rest upon it find its great Author a shield and refuge for their souls from the enemy's assaults. He will be the protection of those who confide in Him; but no one really trusts Him who doubts, or casts reflections upon the integrity of His words.

To attempt to add unto what He has caused to be written is to deny the all-sufficiency of Scripture to meet and provide for every circumstance of life, and to enlighten as to all that belongs to the faith once delivered to the saints. There have not been wanting, in every age, visionaries and enthusiasts, as well as frauds and charlatans, who have sought to supplement the Bible with revelations and compilations of their own, claiming for their wretched productions divine authority. But as compared with all these poor attempts, the Holy Scripture shines forth like a diamond of beauty and value surrounded by worthless bits of glass and paste. It alone is the truth. All imitations are but lies that deceive and befog him who credits and follows them.

The apocryphal books to both Testaments are, at the best, but of this class; particularly is this the case in regard to the wild legends of Tobit and Judith, the apocalyptic visions of Hermes, and the ghostly records of the pseudo-gospels of the Infancy, St. Thomas, Nicodemus, and such like.

The Jewish Talmud and the vagaries of the Kabbalah belong to the same kind, "teaching for doctrines the commandments of men."

In the Christian era, especially in the last two centuries, many imitations have been palmed off on the credulous as of the same character as Holy Scripture, but judged by this text, we unhesitatingly declare them to be lies of Satan. Of this number are the pretended revelations and wild hallucinations of Emanuel Swedenborg; the Book of Mormon and kindred works of Joseph Smith and his followers; the Flying Roll of the Jezreelites; the prophecies and visions of Ellen White, regarded by the Seventh-day Adventists as of equal authority with the Bible; the unchristian and unscientific theories of Mary Baker Eddy, as set forth in *Science and Health,* which professes to be a key to the Scriptures; to which may be added any and every book or teaching that claims a divine origin, but has not been included in the Law, the Prophets, the Psalms, or the New Testament. In this grand collection, God has made known His holy will and revealed all that He will reveal as to Himself, His purpose, and His ways, until the ushering in of the glory for the saints and the day of doom for those who refuse His sure testimony, trampling it beneath their feet, or adding to it the poor thoughts of sinful man! Compare Psalms 12:6 and 119 in its entirety; as also Deuteronomy 4:2; 12:32; and Revelation 22:18–19.

> 7 Two things have I required of Thee;
>   Withhold them not from me before I die:
> 8 Remove far from me vanity and lies;
>   Give me neither poverty nor riches;
>   Feed me with food convenient for me:

⁹ Lest I be full, and deny Thee,
And say, Who is Jehovah?
Or, lest I be poor, and steal,
And take the name of my God in vain.

This prayer of Agur appeals to the heart of the saint in all dispensations. Like the touching prayer of Jabez recorded in 1 Chronicles 4:10, to which it has a strong resemblance, it is a suited utterance for any child of God, even though grace has taught the soul to say, "I have learned in whatsoever state I am, to be content. I know both how to be abased, and I know how to abound: everywhere, and in all things, I am instructed both to be full, and to be hungry, both to abound and to suffer need" (Phil. 4:11–12). It is only as the heart is occupied with Christ that one can thus triumph over all circumstances. He who knows himself understands well why Agur could pray for moderate circumstances, if it were the will of God. He did not distrust divine power to keep him in any state. He did distrust himself.

The first of the "two things" which he required of the Lord, was to be kept from iniquity. He desired that vanity and lies be far removed from him. The man of God fears sin and hates it. The new nature within him makes it impossible that he should be happy while walking in an evil way. Holiness is his joy and delight, therefore he groans for full deliverance from the flesh, that lawless principle within his breast that wars against the new nature. He who, professing to be a Christian, yet finds pleasure in vanity and lies, manifests thereby his true condition, and makes it plain to every Spirit-taught soul that he is still a stranger to the new birth. This detestation of iniquity and yearning to be delivered, not only from its power, but from its very presence, is one of the surest evidences that a work of God has been wrought in the soul, even though there may be great darkness and little understanding of the precious, peace-giving truths of the gospel. The youngest saint, and the oldest, may therefore very properly take up the cry of Agur, "Remove far from me vanity and lies."

The second petition has to do with temporal things and is worthy of careful notice. We can well understand a man praying against poverty, but it is most unusual to find one who dreads wealth and prays to be kept from riches. He dreaded abject poverty, lest in his weakness, it afford occasion for the working of the flesh, causing dishonesty, and bringing reproach upon the name of his God. But riches, too, were equally to be feared, because it is a common thing for men to grow more and more independent of God as their worldly goods are increased: "Jeshurun waxed fat, and kicked" (Deut. 32:15). The wealthy are exposed to many a snare that those in moderate circumstances know little of. This, Agur had observed; therefore he would not desire to revel in luxury, but would be fed with food befitting his station in life, and would choose, if such were the will of God for him, to occupy a middle position between the two extremes of deep need and overflowing abundance. The wisdom and piety behind such a petition become increasingly evident, the more it is considered.

> ¹⁰ Accuse not a servant to his master,
>   Lest he curse thee and thou be found guilty.

The lot of a servant in the East, who was often a slave, was hard enough at the best. Therefore he who took it upon himself to accuse such an one to his master, whether the accusation were true or false, was likely to be hated by the poor wretch he had informed upon; and if he were proven to have had no just grounds for his charge, he should be put to shame by one of inferior station. Applying the principle to Christians, we are reminded of the impertinence and lack of thoughtfulness and care, one for another, which would lead one saint to judge the service of his fellow laborer. "Who art thou that judgest another man's servant? To his own Master he standeth or falleth. . . . Let us not therefore judge one another any more; but judge this rather, that no man put a stumbling-block or an occasion to fall in his brother's way" (Rom. 14:4, 13).

> ¹¹ There is a generation that curseth their father,
>   And doth not bless their mother.
> ¹² There is a generation that are pure in their own eyes,
>   Yet are not washed from their filthiness.
> ¹³ There is a generation—oh how lofty are their eyes!
>   And their eyelids are lifted up.
> ¹⁴ There is a generation, whose teeth are as swords,
>   And their jaw-teeth as knives,
>   To devour the poor from off the earth,
>   And the needy from among men.

The word *generation* is here used, as in many other parts of Scripture, to describe a particular class of mankind having certain characteristics in common; as when our Lord spoke of the Jews as an evil and adulterous generation, and declared that that generation should not pass away prior to His return from heaven. To suppose He meant a generation of thirty to forty years is to throw the entire prophecy into confusion. The so frequent use of the word in the sense indicated above, might have suggested to any sober reader the true teaching of the passage.

It is the generation of the children of pride that Agur so graphically sketches for our instruction and warning. Self-sufficient, they recognize no indebtedness to father and mother, but curse the one and do not bless the other. Contaminated with the horrible pollution of their sins, they are nevertheless pure in their own sight, declaring every one his own goodness. See 20:6.

Lifting up their eyes and elevating their eyebrows, they manifest their supercilious insolence and haughtiness; while, if any seek to correct them, or make them conscious of their true condition in the sight of God, they turn angrily upon him, as wild beasts, ready to rend with their teeth, which are like swords and knives. Even where there is no provocation, they can be cruel and treacherous, devouring the poor and the needy. See 6:17 and 21:4.

It is the generation afterward headed up in the typical Pharisee, cold and proud, outwardly correct and pious, while secretly devouring widows' houses and heeding not the cry of the poor.

Such is man in his self-righteousness. Such would be characteristic of all, had not the matchless grace of God made some to differ!

> ¹⁵ The horse-leech hath two daughters;
> Give! Give! [are their names].
> There are three things that are never satisfied,
> Yea, four things say not, It is enough:
> ¹⁶ Sheol; and the barren womb;
> The earth that is not filled with water;
> And the fire that saith not, It is enough.

Proud and self-sufficient though he be, yet the heart of man is never satisfied. "Like a leech voracious of his food," he never feeds to satiety. The two daughters are perhaps simply a symbolical way of declaring this characteristic of the bloodsucker of Arabia. But I have followed Professor Noyes and Professor Stuart in regarding the words "Give! Give!" as their names. The name is the index to their wretched habits.

Notice the peculiar yet exact use of the numbers three and four. Three things are never satisfied, namely, the unseen world, into which disembodied spirits are constantly descending; the barren womb; and the earth upon which rain falls incessantly somewhere. But four things say not, "It is enough." Therefore to the three already given, he adds the fire. It devours until all that it can reach has been destroyed, when it has to cease, and is, in a sense, satisfied, but only because it must be; for were there more material to feed upon, it would go on destroying still.

All of these are but pictures of the restless yearning, implanted in man's bosom by the Fall. The world and all that it contains is not enough to fill and satisfy it. "Thou hast made us for Thyself," said Augustine of Hippo, "and our hearts will never be at rest, until they rest in Thee." How slow we are to learn the lesson!

> [17] The eye that mocketh at his father,
> And despiseth to obey his mother,
> The ravens of the valley shall pick it out,
> And the young eagles shall eat it.

See verse 11 above. It is a well-known fact that ravens, eagles, and many other birds of carrion and of prey begin their attack upon either a carcass or a living animal, or person, by plucking out the eyes. Instinct seems to tell them that, the power of sight gone, their victims are quite disabled. "The crow shall one day pick out thine eyes!" is an Eastern imprecation of dire import, which may indeed be founded upon this very proverb.

The disobedient mocker shall come to grief in a similar way to what is here described. Suddenly, but surely, he shall be bereft of the power of vision, and stumble in the darkness, vainly trying to beat off the foes that have destroyed his happiness and would further ruin his life. It is the law of retribution which all have to bow to. How many a parent, when shamed and heartbroken because of the waywardness of an unfilial son or daughter, has remembered in an agony of remorse similar disobedience on his own part, when parents, long since departed, were harassed and distressed by his refusal to be controlled. These things come back in later years with crushing force.

> [18] There be three things too wonderful for me,
> Yea, four which I know not:
> [19] The way of an eagle in the air;
> The way of a serpent upon a rock;
> The way of a ship in the midst of the sea;
> And the way of a man with a maid.
> [20] Such is the way of an adulterous woman,
> She eateth, and wipeth her mouth,
> And saith, I have done no wickedness.

Again we have a three and a four carefully distinguished. All the causes of wonder are beyond a man's ability to explain, but only three are impossible for him. The several ways or paths of an eagle in the air, a serpent on a rock, or a ship in the sea, he cannot trace. The way of a man with a maid—completely controlling her mind and will—though none may explain it, there are yet too many examples of it, to permit its being considered as too wonderful for him.

Such is the way of an adulterous woman. Hardened in conscience, she lives in her sin, but like the eater who wipes his mouth, and removed all evidence of his eating, she hides her guilt and boldly says, "I have done no wickedness."

"Lest any of you be hardened by the deceitfulness of sin" is a word to be profitably kept in mind. Sin is often excused as though it were something for which men were not morally accountable. People are fond of considering it more as a mental and physical disease, than as iniquity for which the wrongdoer shall be called to account. But God has declared plainly, He will "bring every work into judgment, with every secret thing, whether it be good, or whether it be evil" (Eccl. 12:14).

> [21] For three things the earth is disquieted,
>   And for four, which it cannot bear:
> [22] For a servant when he reigneth;
>   And a fool when he is filled with meat;
> [23] For an odious woman when she is married;
>   And a handmaid that dispossesseth her mistress.

The first three of these obnoxious things are very disquieting. The fourth completely overturns the order of the household.

A servant reigning is like the sweeping storm of 28:3. It was not an infrequent occurrence in the East for a slave or a servant to be, through some remarkable turn of events, suddenly elevated to great power; sometimes through treachery, as in the case of Zimri (1 Kings 16:1–20), or through favoritism as in that of the undeserving Haman. Persons of low birth so exalted are often far harder on the populace than those born in high station. One has said that a servant ruling becomes "the most insolent, imperious, cruel, and tyrannical of masters." Equally disquieting is a fool or a churl who is filled with meat; that is, has all that heart can wish. Rolling in plenty, he despises the needy and considers that his possessions entitle him to respect, though he be bereft of every virtue, as was Nabal the husband of Abigail to whom we have before referred.

A fitting completion to this wretched trinity is an odious woman when married. Unamiable and vindictive in her disposition, she destroys the peace and happiness of her husband and dependents.

The fourth instance, however, is more to be dreaded than all, so far as interfering with the order of the home is concerned. The Septuagint renders the clause "A handmaid when she hath supplanted her mistress." When it happens that one taken into the home as a menial wins the husband's affections, alienating his wife and children, utter ruin has come in. Unhappily, such instances are far from rare, and have wrecked thousands of families.

How important it is to watch for the first beginnings of an unholy familiarity that may result so fatally!

> [24] There are four things which are little upon the earth,
>   But they are exceeding wise:
> [25] The ants are a people not strong,
>   Yet they prepare their meat in the summer;
> [26] The conies are but a feeble folk,
>   Yet make they their houses in the rocks;
> [27] The locusts have no king,
>   Yet go they forth all of them by bands;
> [28] The lizard taketh hold with her hands,
>   And is in kings' palaces.

In these four wise things, as many have long since noticed, we have a beautiful gospel picture.

We have already remarked the provident habits of the grain-eating ant of Palestine, in the notes on 6:6–8. We are therefore prepared at once to recognize the fact that its wisdom consists in making due preparation for the future. Taught by instinct to make use of present opportunities in order to supply coming needs, it carefully stores away that which will be its food when the bright days of summer are past and gone and the cold of winter renders it too late to go out and search for provision to sustain life.

In material things, man readily shows the same wisdom as this tiny creature. He, too, provides against the coming days when ill health or old age will forbid his going forth to labor. But is it not an amazing thing that men who display remarkable foresight in regard to matters that pertain to this life, will yet forget altogether to make due preparation for that unending eternity to which every moment bears them nearer?

Forgetful of the ages to follow this short life on earth, they allow golden opportunities to slip by, never to return, and rush carelessly on, ignoring the need of their souls and the fearful danger that lies just beyond death. "As it is appointed unto men once to die, but after this the judgment; so Christ was once offered to bear the sins of many; and unto them that look for Him shall He appear the second time, without sin, unto salvation" (Heb. 9:27–28). Here we learn of the fast approaching danger, as also of the One who alone can give deliverance from it. But the majority of mankind are so insanely concerned about the fleeting present that they utterly ignore the everlasting future.

To all such, the insignificant little ant preaches loudly, crying in the ears of any who will listen, "Flee from the wrath to come; prepare to meet thy God!" It is a practical preacher too, for it teaches by action. Refusing to idle away the golden hours of summer, like human triflers on every hand who allow childhood, youth, and middle age to slip by, leaving them still unprepared for eternity, the ant faithfully uses the present in view of the future.

This is wisdom indeed and pictures what all may well take to heart. If the reader is unsaved, if he has not yet settled his eternal matters by coming to Christ, let me shout in his ears the cry of the shipmaster to the runaway prophet: "What meanest thou, O sleeper? Arise, call upon thy God!" (Jonah 1:6). If you are not awakened soon, you will be aroused too late; only to learn that preparation days are over and eternity has begun with your soul still unsaved, and to abide Christless forever!

To him who desires to escape coming judgment the "coney" has also a message telling of the only safe refuge. Properly speaking, the little animal of the twenty-sixth verse is not a coney at all, but a very timid defenseless creature of the marmot type, known to naturalists as the Syrian hyrax. The true coney belongs to the rabbit family and does not seek a habitation in the rocks. But the hyrax does. It is described as a small animal found in Lebanon, Palestine, Arabia Petra, Upper Egypt, and Abyssinia. It is about the size, figure, and brownish color of the rabbit, with long hind legs adapted to leaping, but is of a clumsier structure than that quadruped. It is without a tail, and has long bristly hairs scattered over the general fur; as to its ears (which are small and roundish instead of long, like the rabbit), its feet, and snout, it resembles the hedge-hog. From the structure of its feet, which are round, and of a soft, pulpy, tender substance, it cannot dig, and hence is not fitted to live in burrows like the rabbit, but in the clefts of the rocks. It lives in families; is timid, lively, and quick to retreat at the approach of danger; and hence is difficult to capture. In its habits it is gregarious, and feeds on grain, fruits and vegetables. In the Hebrew it is called *shaphan,* and is included in the lists of unclean animals in Leviticus 11:5 and Deuteronomy 14:7, because though its jaws work with a cud-chewing motion, it does not divide the hoof. In Psalm 104:18 the same fact is referred to that is brought to our attention here in the Proverbs: "The high hills are a refuge for the wild goats, and the rocks for the conies."

Feeble and defenseless in the presence of its enemies, unable too to burrow and make a house for itself, the hyrax finds in the clefts of the rocks a suitable dwelling place where it is safe from the power of the marauder and protected from the fury of the elements. Surely the picture is plain. "That Rock was Christ," says the apostle, when writing of the rock from which flowed the living water in the wilderness. Here too the rock speaks of Him; for He alone is the sinner's refuge. The little unclean hyrax, weak and feeble, flees to the rocks and is safe. So, too, the helpless unclean sinner, awakened to a sense of his dire need and aroused by the signs of the storm that is soon to break over the heads of all who neglect God's salvation, flees for refuge to the Lord Jesus Christ, and finds in Him a safe and blessed shelter where no foe can ever reach him and judgment can never come.

It is in the clefts of the rock that the hyrax hides, and it is in a Savior, pierced for our sins and bruised by the awful vengeance of the Holy One, that the believing soul finds a hiding place.

> On Him almighty vengeance fell,
> Which would have sunk a world to hell;
> He bore it for a chosen race
> And thus became their hiding place.

Has my reader found a refuge in Him? Oh, be persuaded, I pray you, if still exposed to the wrath of God, to cease from all effort to save yourself (which can only result in bitter disappointment in the end) and flee to Jesus while He still sounds out the peace-giving invitation, "Come unto Me, all ye that labor and are heavy-laden, and I will give you rest" (Matt. 11:28).

The third of these wise things is the locust. Having no visible head, no leader, yet they go forth by bands, like soldiers in their respective regiments. So methodical are they that they seem to be acting under definite instructions and in strictest discipline. To those who have found a refuge in Christ they furnish an example of that subjection one to another, and to our unseen Head in heaven, that might well shame us as we contemplate the broken, scattered condition of the people of God, and reflect upon our share in the terrible ruin.

To the world and the world church, the body of Christ must seem like a heterogeneous, miscellaneous company, with no leader and no bond of union; but the same Jesus who died for His people's sins is now seated in highest glory, and made by God the Head of all who have been redeemed by His precious blood. The Holy Spirit, sent down from heaven upon His ascension there as Man, is now indwelling every believer, thus binding all together in one great company, every one "members one of another."

This is most blessed, and when the soul enters into it, will lead to judgment of all that is opposed to the truth of the church as revealed in Scripture. If "there is one body," and the Word of God knows no other, I should own my membership in that alone, and by obedience to the truth, walk worthy of the vocation wherewith I am called.

The locusts all act together, and this it is that declares their wisdom. So should it be with the body of Christ. Divisions and schisms are declared plainly to be sinful and works of the flesh. "For ye are yet carnal; for whereas there is among you envying, and strife, and divisions, are ye not carnal, and walk as men?" (1 Cor. 3:3).

Earnestly the saints are exhorted to walk together in love and fellowship, "striving together for the faith of the gospel." Throughout the letter to the Philippians this precious unity is ever insisted on; and in 1 Corinthians likewise. In 1:10 of the latter epistle, the apostle writes: "Now I beseech you, brethren, by the name of our Lord Jesus Christ, that ye all speak the same thing, and that there be no divisions among you; but that ye be perfectly joined together in the same mind and in the same judgment." Such is the lesson of the locusts. May we have grace to learn it in the presence of God.

It is now pretty generally acknowledged that the Hebrew word *shemameth* in verse 28 refers not to the spider, but to a little house lizard called the gecko, which is very common in Palestine and has a peculiar idiosyncrasy for fine hangings and palatial homes. It uses its forefeet very much as though they were indeed "hands," catching its food, chiefly flies and spiders, therewith, and securely holding them while it devours them. On the underside of each toe is a tiny spongelike sac, containing an adhesive liquid. As it runs up marble walls, or out upon tessellated ceilings, this substance oozes out and enables it to "take hold with its hands" upon the smooth, slippery surfaces, whence it is not easily dislodged.

May it not speak to us of the power of faith, which is indeed the hand by which the believing sinner takes hold of the precious truth of God, thus entering into the blessing He would have all His own enjoy? This it is that gives us to be at home in the King's palace, and ensures an eternal abode in the Father's house.

Amazing is the grace which gives to all who believe on the Lord Jesus Christ a place by faith even now in "the heavenlies"; yet such is our happy portion. For "God who is rich in mercy, for His great love wherewith He loved us, even when we were dead in sins, hath quickened us together with Christ, (by grace are ye saved;) and hath raised us up together, and made us sit together in heavenly places in Christ Jesus: that in the ages to come He might show the exceeding riches of His grace, in his kindness toward us, through Christ Jesus" (Eph. 2:4–7). Now we are there *in* Him. He has gone up on high as our representative. Soon we shall be there *with* Him, to enjoy His companionship for eternity!

Happy is the soul who has learned aright the message of these four wise things![1]

Passing on from them, we next are instructed as to the Christian's walk and behavior, in the four comely things that follow:

> [29] There be three things that go well,
>   Yea, four that are comely in going:
> [30] A lion, that is strongest among beasts,
>   And turneth not away for any;
> [31] A [beast] girt in the loins; a he-goat also;
>   And a king, against whom there is no rising up.

It is quite proper to speak of the first three creatures as going well, or excelling in going; though it would hardly apply to a king. Majestic and glorious, he is comely in his goings forth, and therefore comes under the second head.

The lion is characterized by unflinching boldness, and speaks of that holy courage which should mark the Christian soldier as he contends earnestly for the faith once delivered to the saints. In his faith, he is to have virtue (true courage), that he may withstand in the evil day, and turn not aside for any. It is not mere natural forwardness, or dogged determination, that is contemplated, but "the irresistible might of weakness" that leans upon God, that led Paul to write, "When I am weak, then am I strong."

The second in the series has been variously understood as the greyhound, the girded horse, the zebra, and even the cock! The latter is preferred in the Septuagint, Syriac, Vulgate, and Chaldee versions. But the word simply means, "girded as to the loins," according to the best authorities, and may therefore be applied to any slender creature characterized by swiftness. The translators of the King James Version preferred greyhound, as most fully expressing the idea of an animal adapted to running. It matters little what beast is signified. The lesson for us is clear enough. As a loin-girt animal rests not until it reaches its prey, or the goal to which it is running, so the saint is to press swiftly on, refusing to be turned aside by the attractions of this world. It is as the racer he is viewed in Philippians 3: "Brethren, I count not myself to have apprehended: but this one thing I do, forgetting those things which are behind, and reaching forth unto those things which are before, I press toward the mark for the prize of the calling of God on high in Christ Jesus" (vv. 13–14). This should ever be the Christian's attitude. Having here no continuing city, he halts not to dally with the trifling things of earth, but, with girded loins and the eye fixed on Christ, he hastens on to the judgment seat where the prize is to be awarded. "Wherefore, seeing we also are compassed about with so great a cloud of witnesses, let us lay aside every weight, and sin which doth so easily beset us, and let us run with patience the race that is set before us, looking unto Jesus the author and finisher of faith; who for the joy that was set before Him endured the cross, despising the shame, and is set down at the right hand of the throne of God" (Heb. 12:1–2). He was the great pattern pilgrim, ever "girt in the loins," passing through this world as a stranger; finding here only sorrow and grief, but whose joy is now full in glory!

The he-goat is the "climber." Refusing the low and often unhealthful valleys, he mounts up, higher and higher, to the rocky hills and the peaks of the mountains, as we have already been reminded in the psalm (104:18). Breathing the exhilarating air of "the top of the rocks," he finds both pleasure and safety in his retreat. The lesson is simple. It is the Christian who, like Habakkuk, walks upon the high places, that will be able to rejoice in the day of trouble and joy in the God of his salvation when everything of earth seems to fail (Hab. 3:17–19). From the soul of the climbing saint there will ever be melody "for the Chief Singer on the stringed instruments."

Heavenly-mindedness lifts the soul above all the mists of this poor world, and enables one to view all from God's standpoint. "If ye then be risen with Christ, *seek those things which are above,* where Christ sitteth on the right hand of God. Set your mind on things above, not on things on the earth. For ye have died, and your life is hid with Christ in God" (Col. 3:1–3). This is the lesson of the he-goat. Would that every believer did enter into it!

The last in the list of these comely things is the king going forth in his might, against whom there is no rising up. It is the overcomer, the man of faith, made unto God a king, whose dignity is never greater than when he walks in lowliness and meekness through this scene, drawing his supplies from above, not from below. Great is the honor conferred upon all who have been redeemed. No longer children of the night, but of the day, they are called to overcome the world in the power of the truth made good to the soul by faith. Such a "king" was Abraham as he went from Melchizedek's presence to meet Sodom's fawning monarch, whom he vanquished in a different way from that in which he had defeated the confederacy headed by Chedorlaomer (Gen. 14). Such would God have every saved one to be; but if we would enter into it, we must take sides with Him, counting the richest treasures of earth as dung and dross. "This is the victory that over-cometh the world, even our faith" (1 John 5:4). Strong in faith, the man of God views the present in the light of the future, and so, even though accounted as sheep for the slaughter, can exclaim, "Nay, in all these things we are more than conquerors, through Him that loved us" (Rom. 8:37).

> ³² If thou hast done foolishly in lifting up thyself,
>   Or if thou hast thought evil, lay thy hand upon thy mouth.
> ³³ Surely the churning of milk bringeth forth butter,
>   And the wringing of the nose bringeth forth blood:
>   So the forcing of wrath bringeth forth strife.

Having depicted in parable the dignity of the saint and the behavior that becomes him, Agur's last word is an exhortation to self-judgment, in case any have so far forgotten their holy calling as to foolishly exalt themselves, or have spoken or acted with evil intent. If the thoughts be not pure, speech is exceedingly dangerous; it is better far to lay the hand upon the mouth than to persist in what is unrighteous.

It is so easy to force wrath; that is, to provoke another to anger. To do so betrays a soul out of communion with God, and a spirit insubject to His Word. As butter is produced by churning, and blood by pressing the nose, so strife results from unnecessary provocation. "The servant of the Lord must not strive." He is exhorted to meekness and that fine courtesy which marked all that Jesus said and did. Coarse, ungenerous words and ways are very unbecoming in one who is a subject of divine clemency, and who is therefore expected to manifest toward even his enemies the compassions of Christ.

With this message Agur's ministry for us comes to a close. Unknown though he be, save for this precious collection of wise sayings preserved for our edification in this one chapter, how much should we have lost if the Spirit of God had not included his ministry in the sacred volume!

CHAPTER 31

PROVERBS 31

The final chapter of the book is occupied with what is designated as

¹ The words of King Lemuel,
The prophecy that his mother taught him.

That Lemuel was his mother's name for Solomon is generally believed, and seems likely to be true. There was no King Lemuel among those who sat on the thrones of either Judah or Israel; nor do we have any record of one of that name among the surrounding nations. It occurs only in this chapter, and is probably intended for the son of David and Bathsheba. The word simply means "Unto God," or, "With God."

It is most interesting and deeply affecting to be permitted to listen to a part of the instruction given by his mother to the young prince. Precious is it also to note how grace had wrought in her soul, if she be indeed identical with Bathsheba, so that she, whose history had been so sadly blotted, could be her son's guide and counselor in matters of such great importance. No doubt the loss of her first-born, taken away in the Lord's discipline, made him who had been called Jedediah, "Beloved of Jehovah," all the dearer to her heart (2 Sam. 12:24–25). He was probably brought up to be much in her company, learning to value greatly her instruction and her loving care. How much he was indebted to her for that

281

godliness which marked his early reign, will never be known until the records are read out at the judgment seat of Christ. The influence of a God-fearing mother is beyond all telling.

The opening verse of her prophecy, or oracle, seems to imply her deep concern that she give just the counsel needed.

> ² What, my son? and what, O son of my womb?
> And what, O son of my vows?

The thrice-repeated "what" has the force of "what shall I say?" She desired to have the mind of God as to that which she endeavored to impress upon his young heart. Words, with Lemuel's mother, were sacred things. She felt keenly the need of instructing her son aright, and feared lest she in any way should mislead him.

The expression, "son of my vows," speaks volumes. Like Hannah, she had doubtless been much in prayer for her child both before and after his birth. Humbled and repentant, deeply exercised over the so-recent sin in which she had participated, there would be cause for much concern as to the future of the child whose mother had so sadly failed. This she would feel keenly, and it would seem to have resulted in pious vows concerning the one to be entrusted to her. That the vows themselves would not be in keeping with the Christian revelation does not touch the point. They were right and proper in the dispensation of law, and expressed the purpose of her heart to bring up her child in the fear of God.

Some might seek to use such a passage as authority for making vows now, and especially baptismal and confirmation pledges. But all this is wide of the mark, though none can doubt the sincere piety and the good intentions of many who thus bind themselves. Such a practice, however, is thoroughly opposed to the letter and spirit of the New Testament. In a legal age, when God was dealing with the responsible man as such, it was quite in keeping with His ways, and He gave full instruction concerning vows and the necessity of paying them; making known also how a wife or a minor might be released from them, if on the day of the promise the husband, or father, disallowed them. See Leviticus 27. But nothing like this is known in the Epistles written to unfold the doctrine and practice pertaining to the church of God.

Undoubtedly, Christian parents can, and should, bring their children to God in prayer, seeking divine wisdom to bring them up in the nurture and admonition of the Lord. This answers, in the present age of grace, to the vows and pledges made by godly parents of old.

Before dismissing this subject of vows, I just remind the reader that if one has been, through ignorance and legality, betrayed into making a vow which he afterward learns is unscriptural and opposed to the truth of God, he should go at once to the Lord in contrition of heart, confessing his error. To go on as though he had really bound his soul thereby would be a grave mistake. For instance, a Romish priest takes a vow of celibacy. Should he in after years, discerning more clearly the will of God, leave the apostate system wherewith he has been connected, his bad vow is in no sense binding once he repents. Such a case is contemplated in 1 Corinthians 7:25–28, 36. He who has pledged himself to perpetual virginity, if he finds later that he has made a mistake and put himself under grievous bondage, is free to marry, and the word says, "He sinneth not." The solemn words of Ecclesiastes 5:4–6 do not affect the question at issue, as what is there contemplated is a vow made in accordance with the law, in the legal dispensation. "Ye are not under law, but under grace."

> ³ Give not thy strength unto women,
> Nor thy ways to that which destroyeth kings.

Faithfully was Lemuel warned against the snare of licentiousness. How well would it have been for Solomon if he had ever persevered in the path of temperance and sobriety here indicated, remembering the word, "He shall not multiply wives to himself" (Deut. 17:17). His early life seems to have been marked by obedience to this command of God and heeding his mother's warning, but in his later years he cast discretion to the winds, and the sad result was "his wives turned away his heart."

> ⁴ It is not for kings, O Lemuel,
> It is not for kings to drink wine,
> Nor for princes to desire strong drink:
> ⁵ Lest they drink and forget the law,
> And pervert the judgment of any of the afflicted.
> ⁶ Give strong drink unto him that is ready to perish,
> And wine unto those that be of heavy hearts:
> ⁷ Let him drink, and forget his poverty,
> And remember his misery no more.
> ⁸ Open thy mouth for the dumb
> In the cause of all such as are appointed to destruction.
> ⁹ Open thy mouth, judge righteously,
> And plead the cause of the poor and needy.

He who would rule well over a nation must first be master of himself. It was here that Noah failed when set over the renewed earth. Earnestly Bathsheba warns her son of the evil effects that follow intemperate indulgence in wine and strong drink. It is not for kings to be given to inebriation; for drunkenness befogs the mind and benumbs the faculties. Drinking immoderately, they are likely to forget the law, and thus be rendered unfit to try a case in righteousness.

The king of old was the representative not merely of the executive power but, in a large sense, of the judicial and the legislative sides of government. The afflicted and the oppressed would not receive justice from a besotted king, therefore the importance of temperance and the clearness of mind that accompanies abstinence from what would inflame the brain and cloud the understanding.

If any drink to intoxication, let it be those who are ready to perish and those who are disheartened and bitter of soul. There is a tinge of undisguised irony in the sixth and seventh verses that must not be overlooked. Strong drink might help the despondent to forget their poverty and to remember their misery no more; but the true remedy is for the judge of the oppressed to hear their cause patiently and render a decision in righteousness, as he cannot do if under the power of wine. He is to open his mouth for those who cannot speak for themselves and deliver any who would be in danger of destruction which has not been deserved. See 24:11–12.

From verse 10 to the end of the chapter, the subject is the virtuous woman. This section is an acrostic poem, each verse beginning, in the original, with one of the letters of the Hebrew alphabet as indicated in the text here used, though not seen in our King James Bibles. It was a favorite form of composition among the Hebrews, and is used frequently in the Psalms and in the Lamentations of Jeremiah.

> ¹⁰ *(Aleph)* Who can find a virtuous woman?
> For her price is far above rubies.
> ¹¹ *(Beth)* The heart of her husband doth safely trust in her,
> So that he shall not lack gain.
> ¹² *(Gimel)* She will do him good and not evil
> All the days of her life.

Virtuous is used in the sense of thrifty and devoted. The thought of chastity is of course included, because the devoted wife would be faithful to her husband; but it is not that which is particularly before the mind. The virtuous woman is a dependable woman; one who can be counted on in every emergency. Capable and energetic, with a high sense of the dignity and importance of administering the affairs of the home, her worth is not to be compared with that of jewels, however valuable.

In such a wife the heart of her husband may safely confide, for he finds in her love and unselfish affection treasure so vast, that, let his circumstances be as they may, he can never be in poverty. Her influence is for good and not evil all the days of her life. It is a lovely picture of the mutual relationship of Christ and the church: the latter owning Him as Head and delighting to love and serve Him; while *He* finds His joy in her and beholds in her an inheritance of untold value!

¹³ *(Daleth)* She seeketh wool and flax,
    And worketh willingly with her hands
¹⁴ *(He)* She is like the merchants' ships,
    She bringeth her food from afar.
¹⁵ *(Vau)* She riseth also while it is yet night,
    And giveth meat to her household,
    And a portion to her maidens.

Finding her deepest joy in loving service, the virtuous wife takes delight in weaving with her own hands the wool and the flax which are to be the clothing for her household. The picture is an Eastern one, but nonetheless lovely to Western eyes. Kitto says, "In the state of society to which this description belongs, every kind of drapery for the person, the tent, or the house, is manufactured at home by the women, who make it a matter of pride to be able to boast that their husbands and children are entirely clad by the labor of their hands; and the man's robe clings the more sweetly to him—is warmer in winter, and cooler in the heat, from his knowledge of the dear hands by which every thread has been prepared."

Dainty delicacies or coarse fare when provided by her hands become sweet indeed to the objects of her solicitude. She is not content with slipshod service but is constantly bringing forth "things new and old," as the ships of the merchants bring to our doors the treasures of distant lands.

Slothfulness she shames by her early rising, even before the first beams of the sun begin to light the horizon. In Syria, the women are up long before the dawn to prepare the morning meal, "grinding at the mill," according to our Savior's description, in order that the men may go forth early to labor, and thus be enabled to rest during the sultry part of the day.

It is only love that can render service like this sweet and delightful. Where that is lacking, it must be the veriest drudgery. So Paul could write of himself and his fellow laborers as bondservants of Jesus Christ. This should be the church's happiness—to serve the living and true God, while waiting with eager expectancy for His Son from heaven.

The wife here described serves in the consciousness of her true estate. Unless that be settled all would be fear and anxiety. So with the Christian. Service springs from the knowledge of an established relationship. It is not as a price paid to win the favor of an unreconciled God. But believers, on their part, having been reconciled to Him, who needed not to be reconciled to them, serve in newness of the spirit, not in the oldness of the letter. Thus all uncertainty is gone, and willing hands work as a result of the power of Christ's constraining love.

> [16] *(Zain)* She considereth a field, and buyeth it:
>   With the fruit of her hands, she planteth a vineyard.
> [17] *(Cheth)* She girdeth her loins with strength,
>   And strengtheneth her arms.
> [18] *(Teth)* She perceiveth that her merchandise is good:
>   Her candle goeth not out by night.

Unlike the unfaithful servant, who wrapped his talent in a napkin and hid it away where he could not use it, the prudent wife is continually, by her economy and foresight, adding to her husband's possessions. Like Jabez, she enlarges her coast and becomes also keeper of a vineyard, a joyful service; for the fruit of the vine throughout Scripture speaks of gladness. The bride in the Canticles has to acknowledge, "mine own vineyard have I not kept," but it is blessedly otherwise with her whose varied labors we are here called to contemplate with admiration.

The girding of the loins for service may well remind us of that subjection to the truth of God which ever marks out the devoted soul; for it is with the truth the loins are to be girded; and this both for strength and fitness to take up the daily tasks. No believer can render proper service unless the loins of the mind are thus controlled by the unerring Word of the Lord. The virtuous woman girds her loose flowing garments tightly about her, drawing them up to leave the feet free, as she goes about her work, doing with her might what her hands find to do.

In her labor she finds profit, nor does her lamp go out by night, for she realizes the importance of being ever watchful as well as energetic. How many a soul has sadly failed because, while there was great activity, the corresponding watchfulness was not maintained! The lamp of testimony has been allowed to burn very dimly, or to die out; and forgetting the place and portion of children of light, the careless soul has been found, as though a child of darkness, sleeping among the dead.

¹⁹ *(Yod)* She layeth her hands to the spindle,
  And her hands hold the distaff.
²⁰ *(Caph)* She stretcheth out her hand to the lowly,
  Yea, she reacheth forth her hands to the needy.
²¹ *(Lamed)* She is not afraid of the snow for her household,
  For all her household are clothed with scarlet.

The nineteenth verse has reference to the ancient custom, which is still prevalent among some Eastern peoples, of spinning without the use of a wheel. They hold the distaff in one hand and twirl their long wool spindles with the other, stopping to wind the thread upon them as fast as it is drawn out. Thus, by diligence and economy, the virtuous woman is able to minister, with loving care to the lowly and the needy. Nor is hers the charity which fails to begin at home, for she watches solicitously for the comfort of her family; by her own skill making scarlet garments of the warm wool for their covering in time of cold and snow.

Some prefer the rendering "double garments" to "scarlet," as they do not see what the color has to do with keeping out the cold; but the word is never so translated elsewhere in Scripture. It is the scarlet obtained from the Tola, a cochineal-like insect, which, being crushed, produces a fine deep red, or rich crimson dye, much admired by the Orientals. It is the "worm" of Psalm 22:6, to which our Lord likens Himself, He who was bruised and slain that all His redeemed might be clothed in splendor for eternity.

It is noteworthy that, to the present day, the mountain Nestorians and other Eastern tribes clothe their households in a scarlet or striped stuff, much like Scotch tartan in texture and material. It is to garments such as these that the text refers. Even in the smallest details the Word of God is absolutely correct.

²² *(Mem)* She maketh herself coverings of tapestry,
  Her clothing is fine linen and purple.
²³ *(Nun)* Her husband is known in the gates,
  When he sitteth among the elders of the land.
²⁴ *(Samech)* She maketh linen [garments], and selleth [them],
  And delivereth girdles unto the merchant.

The King James Version reads "silk" in describing the clothing of verse 22, but it is now well-known that not until the reign of Justinian was silk brought to the Levant from China. Fine, white linen, glistening like silk, such as the bride is arrayed with in Revelation 19, is what is undoubtedly intended; as elsewhere in Scripture purple and fine linen are used together as the attire of the well-clothed. See Luke 16:19.

The purple was obtained from "the juice of a certain species of shell-fish found on the eastern shores of the Mediterranean Sea. The juice of the entire fish was not used, but only a little of its liquor, called the flower, contained in a white vein, or vessel, in the neck."

Typically, the fine linen and purple picture, as in the tabernacle hangings, practical righteousness and royal glory. In the rich man referred to above, we see how one could be outwardly covered with what spoke of uprightness and privilege, while actually "poor, and wretched, and blind, and miserable, and naked." The virtuous wife is robed in what bespeaks her true character and dignity.

Her husband too is honored and esteemed. His place as sitting among the elders of the land implies that he occupied a seat in the gate of the city, as a judge, or a magistrate. See notes on 22:22 and 24:7. His wife's thrift and good judgment reflect credit upon him, adding to the esteem in which he is held. Such a spouse is indeed "a help meet for him."

Not only has she sufficient to clothe her household and herself, but her unwearying industry enables her to produce linen garments and girdles for the caravan merchants, who readily purchase the work of her hands, to carry them to distant places. Thus she is "bearing fruit in good works," and her abundant labors provide clothing for those far-removed from her own dwelling.

The spiritual lesson is easily seen. She who is faithful in ministering at home and clothes herself in a garment of practical godliness and righteousness, will have enough and to spare for the blessing of others in "the regions beyond."

> ²⁵ *(Ayin)* Strength and honor are her clothing;
>   And she shall rejoice in time to come.
> ²⁶ *(Pe)* She openeth her mouth with wisdom;
>   And on her tongue is the law of kindness.
> ²⁷ *(Tsaddi)* She looketh well to the ways of her household,
>   And eateth not the bread of idleness.

Every clause here is of the deepest importance. The fine linen and purple are really explained symbolically in verse 25: "Strength and honor are her clothing." That is, of course, strength of character, or, as already noted, uprightness of heart and conduct, coupled with that gracious dignity which belongs to one who walks with God. No wonder it is written, "She shall rejoice in time to come." Godliness and joyfulness are inseparable. "The joy of the LORD is your strength." There is no real happiness apart from righteousness, and vice versa. Where the conscience is at rest, the heart sings for joy. When David sinned, he lost, not salvation, but the joy of it, which was never his again until all was out in the presence of God, and he became once more "a man in whose spirit there is no guile." Then he could call upon the upright in heart to join with him in songs of rejoicing. Contrast Psalms 32 and 51.

As long as the soul has any controversy with God—if persisting in any known sin, refusing to confess evildoing, or failing to walk in any truth revealed in the Word—there will be only unrest and lack of peace and joy. The secret of a happy Christian life is very simple. It consists in walking in the power of an ungrieved Spirit. Let there be any compromise with unholiness, and the Spirit of God, who dwells in every believer, is grieved. In such a case, it is impossible that there should be either peace of mind or joy of heart. But when all that is contrary to His holy will is dragged out into the light and judged, then it is that the confiding saint, arrayed in clothing of "strength and honor," can lift up the voice in song and make accompanying melody unto the Lord in the heart. Nor will this gladness fade away while daily reckoning oneself to be "dead indeed unto sin, but alive unto God in Christ Jesus our Lord."

Fittingly the next verse shows that into the lips of such a one grace is poured; nor is the salt of righteousness lacking. Like Priscilla instructing Apollos, she opens her mouth with wisdom, and the law of kindness is on her tongue. What a contrast to the shrewish and contentious woman, several times contemned in the earlier chapters. See notes on 21:19 and 27:15–16. Because of the pureness of her heart, her tongue delights to utter words of grace and truth. See 22:11. Who does not prize a season of fellowship with such a rare saint as this! When, instead of petty complaints and wretched, slanderous tales, the lips pour forth words of loving-kindness and declare their joy in the precious truth that possesses the reins and the soul, conversation becomes profitable indeed; when, by such well-directed wisdom and tenderness, the hearers are edified and refreshed.

The twenty-seventh verse emphasizes something which in a wife and mother is unspeakably precious. She looks well to the *ways* of her household. Solicitously she notices the habits and actions, as well as marking the speech, of her children. Without nagging and ill-temper, she yet exercises a firm but loving discipline over each one; checking here and encouraging there, as she sees either to be needed. Never too busy to seek to win an erring one from the snares of worldliness and pride, she eats not the bread of idleness, but by both example and precept endeavors to guide her offspring in the way of peace. Having a mother like this, how poignant must be the grief of heart, how strong the reprovings of conscience, if the feet of any of her household go astray for a time in paths of sin!

> [28] *(Koph)* Her children rise up, and call her blessed;
> Her husband also, and he praiseth her, [saying,]
> [29] *(Resh)* Many daughters have done virtuously,
> But thou excellest them all.

Realizing in later life (what may not always be so clear to them in childhood or early youth) the wisdom and love manifested in her firm but tender discipline, her children arise up and shower encomiums upon her, attributing their well-being and blessing to her godly training and instruction; while her husband, rejoicing in such a partner of his joys and sorrows, exclaims in honest praise, "Many daughters have done virtuously, but thou excellest them all!" He has found in her what the heart ever craves—one whose comeliness of soul and mind excel even beauty of face and form.

May we not see in his admiration and delight a picture of the tender love with which our heavenly Bridegroom shall regard His bride, the church, when He presents her to Himself, in the soon coming day of glory, "not having spot, or wrinkle, or any such thing!"

> [30] *(Schin)* Favor is deceitful, and beauty is vain:
> But a woman that feareth Jehovah, she shall be praised.
> [31] *(Tau)* Give her of the fruit of her hands;
> And let her own works praise her in the gates.

Here we have the secret of her devoted, virtuous life. She fears the Lord. This, which our book has declared to be the beginning of wisdom, is her abiding characteristic. Her words, her ways, her dress, and her household discipline, are all ordered as in His presence.

Others may pride themselves on their beauty, or endeavor to obtain favor by winning words and pleasing manners; but if there be no true *character* behind such charms, the day will soon come when praise will give place to contempt; while she who fears Jehovah will be honored by all who appreciate virtue and excellence of spirit. Her beneficent labors too will receive their public and well-merited recognition.

But we who have the light of New Testament revelation can see in this last verse more than a hint of the coming manifestation at the judgment seat of Christ. When the mists of earth have gone forever, when its pride and folly and iniquity are eternally past, such a one as the mother of Lemuel has been describing shall appear in her Lord's own presence with rejoicing, bearing her sheaves with her. At His feet she will cast down the fruit of her hands and the works His grace has wrought in and through her, to have all surveyed by Himself. How sweet to hear His words of approbation in the gate, "Well done, good and faithful servant! Enter thou into the joy of thy Lord."

Who then will regret days of toil and nights of watching? Who then would exchange the saint's path and portion, with all its responsibilities as well as privileges, for a place of ease and careless enjoyment of a few fleeting hours on earth? Not one.

Living in view of that sacred hour when all our works shall be inspected and passed upon by Him who has won our deepest affections, may we have purpose of heart and earnestness of soul to cleave to Himself, holding fast His faithful word, and not denying His name, while waiting here for His return.

If these notes and meditations shall assist any so to do, they will have accomplished the author's most cherished desire.

PART 2

SONG OF SOLOMON

PREFACE

The little volume now before the reader consists of revised notes, considerably abbreviated, of addresses delivered in the Moody Memorial Church, Chicago, during a part of the winter of 1931–32. Many of those who listened to them professed to find blessing and edification, and there were hundreds of requests for their publication in book form, to which I have been pleased to respond. Their preparation for publication has brought added joy to my own soul while meditating afresh on this singularly delightful portion of the Word of God. The attentive reader will realize at once that there has been no attempt to fully expound the Song, but, rather to stress in each address some one or more of the outstanding features of the particular portion discussed. I hope none will charge me with intentional plagiarism if they find a reemphasis of precious truths on which others have dwelt before me. I am glad to acknowledge my indebtedness to many to whom this book has proven a wellspring of spiritual refreshment, and undoubtedly I have incorporated much that they have written into my own addresses. I have profited particularly from the reading of *The Song of Solomon,* by Adelaide Newton; *Meditations on the Song of Solomon,* by Andrew Miller; *The Canticles,* by J. G. Bellett; *The Song of Songs,* by J. B. Jackson; *The Song of Solomon,* by H. Friend, and an excellent work on the same subject by Dr. A. C. Gaebelein. All of these I can most heartily recommend to any wishing fuller exposition than I have attempted to give in these fragmentary discourses.

If God be pleased to own this attempt to create a greater yearning for fellowship with Himself and to lead the way into a deeper knowledge of the love of Christ, the labor expended will be well worthwhile.

H. A. Ironside

CHAPTER 1

SONG OF SOLOMON 1

We will be glad and rejoice in thee, we will remember thy love more
than wine. (Song of Solomon 1:4)

The Song of Solomon is a little book which has had a peculiar attraction for
many of the people of God all through the centuries, and others of them
have had great difficulty in understanding just why such a book should have a
place in the canon of Holy Scripture at all. Frequently I have heard those who, it
seemed to me, ought to have known better, say that as far as they were concerned
they could see nothing of spiritual value in this little book, and that they ques-
tioned very much whether it were really entitled to be considered as part of the
inspired Word of God. As far as that is concerned, it is not left to the church in
our day to decide which books should belong to the canon of Scripture and
which should be omitted. Our blessed Lord Jesus Christ has settled that for us,
at least as far as the Old Testament is concerned. When He was here on earth He
had exactly the same Old Testament that we have, consisting of the same books,
no more and no less.

Those that are sometimes called the Apocryphal books did not belong to the
Hebrew Old Testament which He valued and fed upon, and which He commended to His disciples, and, more than that, upon which He placed His divine

imprimatur when He referred to the entire volume and said, "The Scripture cannot be broken." Therefore we do not have to raise any question as to the inspiration of the Canticles. He declared the Hebrew Bible to be the Word of the Living God, and there are many figures from this little book in various parts of the New Testament; for instance, "the well of living water" (John 4); "the veiled woman" (1 Cor. 11); "the precious fruit" (James 5:7); "the spotless bride" (Eph. 5:27); "unquenchable love" (1 Cor. 13:8); "love strong as death" (John 15:13); "ointment poured forth" (John 12:3); "draw me" (John 6:44); "the Shepherd leading His flock" (John 10:4–5, 27); and "the fruits of righteousness" (Phil. 1:11). Who can fail to see in all these allusions the Song of Solomon?

If we grant that it is inspired, what then are its lessons? Why do we have it in Holy Scripture? Many of the Jewish teachers thought of it simply as designed of God to give a right apprehension of conjugal love. They thought of it as the glorification of the bliss of wedded life, and if we conceived of it from no higher standpoint than this, it would mean that it had a right to a place in the canon. Wedded life in Israel represented the very highest and fullest and deepest affection at a time when, in the nations surrounding Israel, woman was looked upon as a mere chattel, as a slave, or as the object of man's pleasure to be discarded when and as he pleased. But it was otherwise in Israel. The Jewish home was a place where love and tenderness reigned, and no doubt this little book had a great deal to do with lifting it to that glorious height.

But down through the centuries, the more spiritually minded in Israel saw a deeper meaning in this Song of Solomon; they recognized the design of God to set forth the mutual love subsisting between Jehovah and Israel. Again and again, in other Scripture passages, Jehovah is likened to a bridegroom, Israel to His chosen bride, and so the spiritual in Israel, in the years before Christ, came to look at the Song in this way. They called it "the Book of Communion." It is the book that sets forth Jehovah and His people in blessed and happy communion. And then all through the Christian centuries those who have had an insight into spiritual truth have thought of it from two standpoints. First, as typifying the wondrous relationship that subsists between Christ and the church, the glowing heart, the enraptured spirit of our blessed Lord revealing Himself to His redeemed people as her Bridegroom and her Head, and the church's glad response. And then, looking at it from a moral standpoint, as setting forth the relationship between an individual soul and Christ, how many a devoted saint has exclaimed with gladness, "Oh, I am my Beloved's, and His desire is toward me."

Rutherford's meditations were evidently based on this little book when he exclaimed:

Oh, I am my Beloved's,
  And my Beloved's mine,
He brings a poor vile sinner
  Into His house of wine;
I stand upon His merit,
  I know no safer stand,
Not e'en where glory dwelleth
  In Immanuel's land.

Therefore we may think of the book from four standpoints. Looking at it literally, we see the glorification of wedded love. Looking at it from a dispensational standpoint, we see the relationship between Jehovah and Israel. Redemptively, we find the wonderful relationship between Christ and the church. And studying it from the moral or spiritual standpoint, we see it as the book of communion between an individual soul and the blessed, glorified, risen Lord.

It is a bit difficult to get the exact connection of the different portions of the book. It is not a drama, as the book of Job is; it does not present to our consideration any continued story. It consists rather of a series of love lyrics, each one complete in itself. It is the lover with heart enraptured setting to music the thrill of the soul, and thus you have this cluster of song flowers, each one setting forth some different phase of communion between the beloved and the one so loved. And yet, back of it all, there must be some kind of story. What is this background?

Something like a hundred years ago, Ewald, the great German critic, who has been called the father of higher criticism, suggested that the story was something like this. In the hill country north of Jerusalem there was a family in charge of a vineyard belonging to King Solomon. The young shepherdess had been won by a shepherd who had drawn her heart to himself, and their troth had been plighted. But King Solomon, as he rode along the lane one day, saw this young shepherdess in the vineyard, and his heart went out to her. He determined to win her for himself, and so tried by blandishment to stir up her affections. But she was true to her sylvan admirer. By-and-by the king actually had her kidnapped and taken to his palace, to the royal harem, and there again and again he pressed his suit and tried to alienate her from her shepherd lover in the hills. Sometimes she was almost tempted to yield, for her case seemed a hopeless one, but then she would remember him, her former lover, and she would say, "No, I cannot turn from him. 'I am my beloved's, and his desire is toward me.'" Eventually King Solomon set her free and she went back to the one she loved.

That view of things has been accepted by a great many Bible students, and I have been a little surprised at times to hear some of my fundamental brethren set it forth, apparently without realizing its source. Personally, I reject it. I do not think it at all likely that a man like Ewald, who had no real spiritual insight, ever understood this little book of communion. A man who could be called the father of higher criticism, who gave the start to the present modern trend of handling the Bible, refusing to recognize its true inspiration, does not seem to me to be such an one as the Spirit of God would use to open up this little book to us.

There are several other reasons why I refuse this view. First and foremost, it would make King Solomon "the villain of the piece," and when we turn to the Word of God, we find that Solomon is viewed by the Holy Spirit of God as a type of the Lord Jesus Christ. You will find that in the Psalms Solomon is portrayed as the prince of peace succeeding David after years of warfare, and setting forth Christ's coming again to reign as Prince of Peace. In the New Testament the Lord Jesus says, "The queen of the south shall rise up in the judgment with this generation, and shall condemn it: for she came from the uttermost parts of the earth to hear the wisdom of Solomon; and, behold, a greater than Solomon is here" (Matt. 12:42). When I say that Solomon is a type of Christ, I do not mean Solomon personally. Whenever any man is spoken of as a type of Christ, you are not to think of what the man is in himself, but what he is officially. David officially was a type of Christ; David personally was guilty of very grievous sin, but the Lord is the sinless One. Solomon was guilty of very serious departure from God during certain periods of his life, but officially he represented our Lord Jesus Christ as the Prince of Peace. It is not the way of the Spirit of God to present a character, or some other animate or inanimate object, as a type of Christ in one place and a type of that which is wicked and unholy in another; and if we were to take Ewald's suggestion as the real story behind this book, we would have to think of Solomon as the type of the world, the flesh, and the Devil, trying to win the heart of this young woman away from the shepherd who represents the Lord Jesus Christ.

Another reason why I reject this is that it would mean that we would have to understand some of the most lovely and tender passages of this little book in which the king addresses himself to the shepherdess, as mere blandishment instead of a sincere and holy love. These very passages are those which all down through the centuries have thrilled the heart of the people of God. They have reveled in them, they have delighted in them, and fed their souls upon them. It is not likely that they have been misled, that the Holy Spirit who came to guide into all truth has thus deceived, or allowed to be deceived, so many of God's most spiritual people throughout the centuries, and therefore, I refuse to take the story that I have given you from Ewald as the explanation of the Song of Solomon.

Let me give you another story, the one that came to me one day when I was alone on my knees. I had to teach this little book and was a bit perplexed about it. I did not like the story of Ewald, and so I went to the One who wrote the book and asked Him to tell me what was behind it. "Oh," you say, "did you know the Author of the book?" Yes, I have known Him for a long time. At that time I had known Him about thirty years, now it is forty-one years. "Well," you say, "the book is rather a recent thing if you know the author." No, not at all, it is a very old book; but the Author is the Ancient of Days and I have known Him ever since in grace He saved my soul. And so I took Him at His word and reminded Him of His promise that when the Holy Spirit came, He would take of the things of Christ and show them unto us; and I said, "Blessed Lord, I am all perplexed about this little book; by Thy Spirit show it to me so that I will really understand its meaning." I am going to give you the story that it seemed He gave to me. You may not think I am correct. Very well, you go to Him and ask Him about it, and if He tells you something different, come and tell me, and I will be glad to correct my story if you can show me that I am wrong.

This is what I thought I could see behind it all. Up there in the north country, in the mountain district of Ephraim, King Solomon had a vineyard (we are told that in the eleventh verse of the last chapter), and he let it out to keepers, to an Ephraimite family. Apparently the husband and father was dead, but there was a mother and at least two brothers, two sons. We read, "My mother's children were angry with me." In Hebrew it is, "My mother's sons." There may have been more sons, but there were at least two. And then there were two daughters, two sisters, a little one spoken of in the eighth chapter: "We have a little sister." She was a little undeveloped one. And then there was the older daughter, the Shulamite. It would seem as though this one was the "ugly duckling," or the "Cinderella" of the family. Her brothers did not appreciate her and foisted hard tasks upon her, denying her the privileges that a growing girl might have expected in a Hebrew home. "My mother's sons were angry with me." That makes me wonder whether they were not her half-brothers, if this were not a divided family.

"My mother's sons were angry with me; they made me the keeper of the vineyards; but mine own vineyard have I not kept." They said to her, "No; you can't loll around the house; you get out and get to work. Look after the vineyard." She was responsible to prune the vines and to set the traps for the little foxes that spoiled the vines. They also committed to her care the lambs and the kids of the flock. It was her responsibility to protect and find suitable pasture for them. She worked hard and was in the sun from early until late. "Mine own vineyard have I not kept." She meant, "While working so hard in the field, I have no opportunity to look after myself." What girl is there that does not value a few hours in front of the looking glass, the opportunity to fix her hair and to beautify herself in any lawful way? She had no opportunity to care for her own person, and so she says, "My own vineyard have I not kept." I do not suppose she ever knew the use of cosmetics of any kind; and yet as she looked out on the road she would see the beautiful ladies of the court riding on their palfreys and in their palanquins, and as she got a glimpse of them, or as she bent over a woodland spring and saw her own reflection, she would say, "I am sunburned but comely, and if I only had the opportunity, I could be as beautiful as the rest of them." That is all involved in that expression, "Mine own vineyard have I not kept."

One day as she was caring for her flock she looked up, and to her embarrassment there stood a tall and handsome stranger-shepherd, one she had never seen before, gazing intently upon her, and she exclaimed, "Look not upon me, because I am black, because the sun hath looked upon me." And then she gives the explanation, "My mother's children were angry with me; they made me the keeper of the vineyards; but mine own vineyard have I not kept." But he answers quietly without any offensive forwardness, "I was not thinking of you as swarthy and sunburned and unpleasant to look upon. To my mind you are altogether lovely; behold, thou art fair, my love; there is no spot in thee." Of course that went a long way toward a friendship, and so little by little that friendship ripened into affection, and affection into love, and finally this shepherd had won the heart of the shepherdess. Then he went away, but before he went, he said, "Some day I am coming for you, and I am going to make you my bride." And she believed him. Probably no one else did. Her brothers did not believe him, the people in the mountain country felt she was a poor simple country maiden who had been deceived by this strange man. She had inquired of him where he fed his flock, but he put her off with an evasive answer, and yet she trusted him. He was gone a long time. Sometimes she dreamed of him and would exclaim, "The voice of my beloved," only to find that all was quiet and dark about her. But still she trusted him.

One day there was a great cloud of dust on the road and the country people ran to see what it meant. Here came a glorious cavalcade. There was the king's bodyguard and the king himself, and they stopped just opposite the vineyard. To the amazement of the shepherdess, the royal outriders came to her with the announcement, "The king has sent us for you." "For me?" she asked. "Yes, come." And in obedience she went, and when she looked into the face of the king, behold, the king was the shepherd who had won her heart, and she said, "I am my beloved's, and his desire is toward me."

One great reason why I think this is the story of the Canticles is because all the way through this wondrous volume, from Genesis to Revelation, we have the story of the Shepherd who came from heaven's highest glory down into this dark world that He might woo and win a bride for Himself. And then He went away, but He said, "I will come again, and receive you unto Myself." And so His church has waited long for Him to come back, but someday He is coming to fulfill His Word, and,

> When He comes, the glorious King,
> All His ransomed home to bring,
> Then anew this song we'll sing,
>   "Hallelujah, what a Savior!"

And so I think that is the background of the expression of loving communion in this little book, the Song of Songs. You notice that very title reminds you of the holy of holies; it is the transcendent song. The Jews did not allow a young man to read the book until he was thirty years of age, lest he might read into it mere human voluptuousness and misuse its beautiful phrases, and so we may say it is only as we grow in grace and in the knowledge of Christ that we can read this book understandingly and see in it the secret of the Lord.

I think the first chapter divides itself into three parts. The first four verses give us the soul's satisfaction; it is the expression of the bride's delight in her bridegroom. She exclaims, "The Song of songs, which is Solomon's. Let Him kiss me with the kisses of His mouth: for Thy love is better than wine." I remember a dear servant of God saying at one time, "I have sometimes wished there were only one masculine personal pronoun in the world, so that every time I say, *'Him,'* everyone would know I mean the Lord Jesus Christ." You remember Mary Magdalene saying, "They have taken away my Lord, and I know not where they have laid Him." Then, looking up to the one she supposed to be the gardener, she said, "Sir, if thou have borne Him hence, tell me where thou hast laid Him, and I will take Him away." She did not think it necessary to use the name Jesus. There was only One to her, and that was the Lord who had saved her; and so the enraptured soul says, "Oh, to enjoy His love, His communion; to enjoy the blessedness of finding satisfaction in Himself." "Because of the savor of Thy good ointments Thy name is as ointment poured forth, therefore do the virgins love Thee." We are reminded how the house was filled with the odor of the ointment when Mary broke her alabaster box and poured it upon His head.

> How sweet the name of Jesus sounds
>> In a believer's ear!
> It soothes his sorrows, heals his wounds,
>> And drives away his fear.

And now the heart cries out, "Draw me, we will run after Thee: the King hath brought me into His chambers: we will be glad and rejoice in Thee, we will remember Thy love more than wine: the upright love Thee." The shepherdess has been brought from the hill country into the royal palace, as you and I from the distant country into the very presence of the Lord Himself, and how often our hearts have sung,

> I am Thine, O Lord, I have heard Thy voice,
>> And it told Thy love to me;
> But I long to rise in the arms of faith,
>> And be closer drawn to Thee.

> Draw me nearer, nearer, nearer, blessed Lord,
>> To the cross where Thou hast died;
> Draw me nearer, nearer, nearer, blessed Lord,
>> To Thy precious bleeding side.

"We will run after thee: the king hath brought me into his chambers: we will be glad and rejoice in thee, we will remember thy love more than wine." She has been claimed by the King. What a wonderful picture we have here of real communion. No one has ever entered into the truth of communion with Christ until He Himself has become the all-absorbing passion of the soul. His love transcends every earthly joy, of which wine is the symbol in Scripture. Why is it so used? Because of its exhilarating character. Wine speaks of anything of earth which stimulates or cheers. When a worldling is cast down and depressed, he says, "Give strong drink unto him that is ready to perish, and wine unto those that be of heavy hearts. Let him drink and forget his poverty, and remember his misery no more" (Prov. 31:6–7). And so wine speaks of the joys of earth to which we once turned before we knew Christ. But after we know Him, we say,

"We will remember Thy love more than wine." For that reason I am always grieved in spirit when some young Christian comes to me with the old, old question, "Do you think there is any harm in this or that?—any harm in the theater, in dancing, in a game of cards, in the social party that has no place for Christ?" I say to myself, "If they only really knew Him, they would never ask such questions." "We will remember Thy love more than wine." One minute spent in fellowship with Him is worth all the joys of earth. That is what this book is designed to teach us.

There is a fullness in His love, a sweetness found in fellowship with Christ, of which the worldling knows nothing. If you are in Christ, these things fall off like withered autumn leaves. I often hear people singing,

> Oh, how I love Jesus,
> Oh, how I love Jesus,
> Oh, how I love Jesus,
>   Because He first loved me!

And yet the same people who sing those things sometimes never spend half-an-hour a day over the Bible; never spend ten minutes alone with God in prayer; have very little interest in the coming together of the Lord's people to wait on Him. Invite them to a prayer meeting and they are never there, but invite them to a social evening and they are all present. It is evident that the love of Christ is not yet the controlling passion of the heart. The surrendered soul exclaims, "We will remember Thy love more than wine." And in Ephesians we read, "Be not drunk with wine, wherein is excess, but be filled with the Spirit." The Spirit-filled believer never craves the follies of the godless world. Christ is enough to satisfy at all times.

The next section takes in verses 5–11. Here you have that little retrospect that I have already given you. It looks back to the time when she first met her lover and inquired of him as to where he fed his flock. He answered, "If thou know not, O thou fairest among women, go thy way forth by the footsteps of the flock, and feed thy kids beside the shepherds' tents." In other words, it is as when the disciples of John came to Jesus and said, "Master, where dwellest Thou?" And He said, "Come and see." And so the soul cried out, "O Thou shepherd of my heart, where feedest Thou?" And he said to her, "Just go along in the shepherds' path, feed your flock with the rest, and you will find out." If you take the path of devotedness to Christ, you will soon know where He dwells. If you walk in obedience to His Word you cannot fail to find Him.

In verses 12–17 we have a wonderful picture of communion with the king. There he and his beautiful bride are together in the royal palace, and she says, "While the king sitteth at his table"—and the table is the place of communion— "my spikenard sendeth forth the smell thereof. A bundle of myrrh is my well-beloved unto me." In other words, "He is to me like a fragrant nosegay in which my senses delight." And so as we enter into communion with Christ, He becomes all in all to us and the heart goes out in worship and praise, like Mary, as already mentioned, in the house of Bethany bringing her alabaster box of ointment and pouring it on the head of Jesus. The king sat at the table that day, and her spikenard sent forth its fragrance and the house was filled with the odor of the ointment. That is the worshipper. There can be no real worship excepting as the heart is occupied with Him.

It is common nowadays to substitute service for worship, and to be more taken up with hearing sermons or with ritual observances than with adoration and praise. God has said, "Whoso offereth praise glorifieth Me." He tells us He dwells amid the praises of His people. It is the satisfied heart that really worships. When the soul has been won for Christ there will be appreciation of Himself for what He is; not merely thanksgiving (important as that is) for what He has so graciously bestowed upon us. "Whom having not seen, ye love; in whom, though now ye see Him not, yet believing, ye rejoice with joy unspeakable and full of glory." This causes the spirit to go out to Him in worship and praise.

"The Father," Jesus told the Samaritan woman, "seeketh such to worship Him." He yearns for the adoring love of devoted hearts. May we indeed respond to His desire and ever "worship Him in spirit and in truth."

CHAPTER 2

SONG OF SOLOMON 2

He brought me to the banqueting house, and his banner over me was love. (Song of Solomon 2:4)

The figure of the bride and the bridegroom is used very frequently in Scripture. Isaiah in the Old Testament says, "As the bridegroom rejoiceth over the bride, so shall thy God rejoice over thee." It is used of the church in the New Testament, "Christ loved the church and gave Himself for it; that He might sanctify and cleanse it with the washing of water by the Word." And when the apostle Paul speaks of the divine institution of marriage he says, "For this cause shall a man leave his father and mother, and shall be joined unto his wife, and they two shall be one flesh. This is a great mystery: but I speak concerning Christ and the church." And then writing to the Corinthian believers, he says, "I have espoused you to one husband, that I may present you as a chaste virgin to Christ." Therefore, this delightful figure of the sweet and intimate marriage relationship is used throughout Scripture to set forth our union and communion with the Eternal Lover of our souls.

I have said that the Song of Solomon is the Book of Communion. We have that beautifully set forth in the first seven verses of this second chapter. The bride and the bridegroom are conversing together. We delight to speak with those whom we love. One of the wonderful things about love is that when some-one has really filled the vision of your soul, you do not feel that any time that is taken up communing with him is wasted. Here then you have the lovers out in the country together and she exclaims, for it is evidently she who speaks in verse 1, "I am the rose of Sharon, and the lily of the valleys." Generally we apply those words to the blessed Lord; we speak of Him as the Rose of Sharon. We sing sometimes, "He's the Lily of the Valley, the Bright and Morning Star." It is per-fectly right and proper to apply all of these delightful figures to Him, for we cannot find any figure that speaks of that which is beautiful and of good report that cannot properly be applied to the Lord. But the wonderful thing is that He has put His own beauty upon His people. And so here the bride is looking up into the face of the bridegroom saying, "I am the rose (really, the narcissus, a blood-red flower) of Sharon, and the lily of the valleys"—the lily that thrives in the hidden place, not in the town, not in the heat and bustle of the city, but out on the cool countryside, in the quiet field. Does it not speak of the soul's separa-tion to Christ Himself?

It is when we draw apart from the things of the world, apart to Himself, that we really thrive and grow in grace and become beautiful in His sight. I am afraid that many of us do not develop spiritually as we should, because of the fact that we know so little of this heart-separation to Himself. One of the great griefs that comes to the heart of many a one who is seeking to lead others on in the ways of Christ, is to know the influence that the world has upon them after they are converted to God. How often the question comes from dear young Christians, "Must I give up this, and must I give up that, if I am going to live a consistent Christian life?" And the things that they speak of with such apparent yearning are mere trifles after all as compared with communion with Him. Must I give up eating sawdust in order to enjoy a good dinner? Who would talk like that? Must I give up the pleasures of the world in order that I may have communion with Christ? It is easy to let them all go if the soul is enraptured with Him; and when you get to know Him better, when you learn to enjoy communion with Him, you will find yourself turning the question around; and when the world says, "Won't you participate with us in this doubtful pleasure or in this unholy thing?" your answer will be, "Must I give up so much to come down to that level? Must I give up communion with Him? Must I give up the enjoyment of His Word? Must I give up fellowship with His people in order to go in the ways of the world?" That would be the giving up. Dear young Christian, do not think of it as giving up anything to go apart with Him and enjoy His blessed fellowship. It is then the separated soul looks into His face and says, "I am like the narcissus of

Sharon, and the lily of the valleys," and He at once responds, "As the lily among thorns, so is My love among the daughters." It is the heart-satisfaction that He has in His people.

See the contrast between the beautiful, fragile, lovely lily and the rough, un-pleasant, disagreeable thorn. The thorn speaks of those who are still under the curse, walking in the ways of the world, and the lily sets forth His sanctified, devoted people, those who have turned from the world to Himself. This is His estimate of His saints, and as this little colloquy goes on—for it is just the soul speaking to Him and He responding, a beautiful holy dialogue—the bride looks up and says, "As the apple-tree among the trees of the wood, so is My Beloved among the sons. I sat down under His shadow with great delight, and His fruit was sweet to my taste." He says to her, "You are like a lily to Me in contrast to the thorns." And she says, "And You to me are like a beautiful fruit tree in contrast to the fruitless trees of the wood." Scholars have wondered just what word should be used here to translate the name of this tree. Is it the apple tree that we know, or is it the citron, a tree of a beautiful, deep green shade, producing a lovely fruit, like a cross between our grapefruit and orange, a most refreshing fruit? But the thought that the bride expresses is this: You are so much more to me than any other can possibly be. I have shade and rest and refreshment in your presence. "I sat down under His shadow with great delight, and His fruit was sweet to my taste."

How often the Spirit of God employs the figure of a shadow. To understand it aright you have to think of a hot eastern clime, the tropical sun shining down upon a wayfarer. Suddenly he sees before him a place of refuge, and exclaims as David does in the seventeenth Psalm, "Keep me as the apple of the eye, hide me under the shadow of Thy wings." Again in Psalm 36:7, "How excellent is Thy lovingkindness, O God! Therefore the children of men put their trust under the shadow of Thy wings." Isaiah speaks of "the shadow of a great rock in a weary land." The figure is used very frequently in the Bible in speaking of rest and of comfort found alone in communion with Christ.

There is no drudgery here. You married folk who are here today, do you remember when you first fell in love with the one who afterward became your life companion? Did you find it hard to spend half an hour with him? Did you try to find an excuse for staying away from that young lady? Did you always have some other engagement so that you would not be at home when that young man called on you? No; but you tried to put everything else out of the way so as to have the opportunity to became better acquainted with the person who had won your heart. So it is with the believer. The more we get to know of Christ the more we delight in His presence. So the bride says, "I sat down under His shadow with great delight, and His fruit was sweet to my taste." Her bliss was complete.

"Delight thyself also in the Lord, and He shall give thee the desires of thine heart." You cannot delight in Christ if you are going after the things of the world. "No man can serve two masters: for either he will hate the one, and love the other; or else he will hold to the one, and despise the other. Ye cannot serve God and mammon" (Matt. 6:24). And so you cannot enjoy Christ and the world at the same time.

Then we go a step farther in this scene of communion. "He brought me to the banqueting house, and His banner over me was love." This is the place of the soul's deep enjoyment when all else is shut out, and Christ's all-satisfying love fills the spirit's vision, and the entire being is taken up with Himself. This is indeed the "house of wine," the rest of love. In verses 5–6 you have the soul so completely enthralled by the one who has won her heart that she does not care to think of anything else. Then in verse 7 we have his tender answer, for it is the bridegroom speaking now: "I charge you, O ye daughters of Jerusalem, by the roes, and by the hinds of the field, that ye stir not up, nor awake my love, till she please," not "till he please." The word is in the feminine, and the point is this: He sees such joy in His people when they are in communion with Him that He says, "Now do not bring in anything to spoil this until she herself please." We have that illustrated in the Gospels. Jesus had gone to the house of Mary, Martha, and Lazarus, and Martha served and was cumbered about her serving. But Mary took her place at the feet of Jesus and listened to His words. She was in the banqueting house and His banner over her was love. He was enjoying communion with her. But Martha said, "I have something more important for Mary than that; it is more important that she put the dishes on the table and get the dinner ready." But Jesus said, as it were, "Martha, Martha, I charge you that ye stir not up, nor awake my love till she please." In other words, "As long as she is content to sit at My feet and commune with Me, this means more to Me than the most enjoyable repast."

When the poor Samaritan woman came to Him at the well outside the city of Sychar, His disciples came and wondered if He were not hungry, but He said, "I have meat to eat that ye know not of." It meant more to Him to have that poor sinner listening to His words and drawing near to Him and entering into the love of His heart, than to enjoy the food that they had gone to the city to get. Service is a wonderful thing; it is a great thing to labor for so good a Master. But oh, there is something that comes before service, something that means more to Him and should mean more to us, and that is fellowship with Himself!

A husband and father was bereft of his precious wife and had just a darling daughter left to him. In those lonely days after the wife had passed away, he found his solace and his comfort in this beautiful girl she had left behind, and evening after evening when he came home from work, they would have their quiet little meal together, and then after the dishes had been put away they would go into the sitting room, and talk or read, and enjoy each other's company. But now it was getting on toward the holiday season, and one evening after doing up the dishes, the daughter said, "Now, Father dear, you will excuse me tonight; I have something to occupy me upstairs. You can read while I go up." So he sat alone, and the next night the same thing happened, and night after night for about two weeks he sat alone each evening. On Christmas morning the girl came bounding into his room saying, "Merry Christmas, Father dear," and handed him a beautiful pair of slippers she had made for him. He looked at them, and then kissed her and said, "My darling, you made these yourself?" "Yes, Father." "Is this why I have been denied your company the last two weeks?" he asked. "Yes," she said, "this is my secret." Then he said, "That is very lovely, but next time I would rather have you than anything you can make for me." Our blessed Lord wants ourselves. Our heart's affection means far more to Him than service. And yet there will be service, of course, but service that springs out of communion, and that accomplishes a great deal more than when we are too busy to enjoy fellowship with Him.

Another section of the chapter is from verse 8–13, and that we may call "Love's Expectation." In this section he is absent from her and she is waiting for him to return. Suddenly she thinks she hears his voice, and she springs up saying, "The voice of my beloved! Behold, he cometh leaping upon the mountains, skipping upon the hills." You and I who know His grace realize something of what this means. He has saved us, won our hearts, as this shepherd lover won the heart of this shepherdess, and He has gone away, but He said, "I will come again, and receive you unto Myself," and when He comes, He will be the glorious King. It was the shepherd who won her heart; it was the King to whom she was wedded. And so Jesus, the Good Shepherd, has won us for Himself, but He will be the King when we sit with Him upon the throne.

Does it not stir your soul to think that at any moment we may hear His voice saying, "Arise, My love, and come away?" Listen to the way she depicts it here. "My beloved spake and said unto me, Rise up, my love, my fair one, and come away. For, lo, the winter is past, the rain is over and gone; the flowers appear on the earth; the time of the singing is come and the voice of the turtle [dove] is heard in our land; the fig tree putteth forth her green figs, and the vines with the tender grape give a good smell. Arise, my love, my fair one, and come away." It is not merely the singing of birds, as you have it in the King James Version, but "the time of singing," when He will sing and we shall sing, and we shall rejoice together, when earth's long winter of sorrow and trial and perplexity is ended and the glorious spring will come with our blessed Lord's return. You see this is just a little poem in itself, a complete love lyric in anticipation of the bridegroom's return. How soon all this may be fulfilled for us, how soon He may come for whom our hearts are yearning, we do not know. We have waited for Him through the years; we have known the cold winters, the hard and difficult days; we have known the trying times, but oh, the joy, the gladness when He comes back! He has said, "A little while and He that shall come will come and will not tarry."

> "A little while"—the Lord shall come,
>   And we shall wander here no more;
> He'll take us to His Father's home,
>   Where He for us is gone before—
> To dwell with Him, to see His face,
>   And sing the glories of His grace.

We shall then share the glory that He went to prepare. What will that mean for us and for Him! He will have the joy of His heart when He has us with Him.

The closing verses speak of that which should be going on during all the time of His absence. In the first place, we ought to be enjoying Him anticipatively, and then there should be self-judgment, putting out of the life anything that would grieve or dishonor Him. The bridegroom speaks; may He speak to our souls. "O My dove, that art in the clefts of the rock." That is where we are resting, in the cleft of the rock.

> Rock of Ages, cleft for me,
> Grace hath hid me safe in Thee.

"O My dove, that art in the clefts of the rock, in the secret places of the stairs," or, "in the hidden places of the going up." We are moving upward from day to day, soon to be with Himself. "Let Me see thy countenance, let Me hear thy voice; for sweet is thy voice, and thy countenance is comely." Have you heard Him saying that to you, and have you sometimes turned coldly away?

Probably when you arose in the morning you heard Him say, "Let Me see thy countenance before you begin the work of the day; spend a little time with

Me, let Me hear thy voice; talk with Me before you go out to speak to other people; let Me enjoy a little time with you, the one for whom I died, before you take up the affairs of the day." And you have just turned coldly away, looked at your watch, and said, "I am sorry, but I cannot spare any time this morning; I must hasten to the office or the shop," and so all day He waited for you. When evening came, He spoke again and said, "Let Me see thy countenance, let Me hear thy voice," and you said, "Oh, I am so tired and weary tonight, I have to hurry off to bed." Have there not been many days like that? Are there going to be many more? Or will you seek by grace to respond to the love of His heart and let Him see your face and hear your voice a little oftener?

Then we have her response, "Take us the foxes, the little foxes, that spoil the vines: for our vines have tender grapes." You see, her brothers had driven her out to be the vinedresser. Now she thinks of that, and sees a figure there, and says, "I know how I had to watch the vines so carefully, and now I have to watch the growth of my own spiritual life. As I set traps for the little foxes, so now I have to judge in myself anything that would hinder fellowship with Him, that would hinder my spiritual growth." What are the little foxes that spoil the vine? I can tell you a good many. There are the little foxes of vanity, of pride, of envy, of evil speaking, of impurity (I think this though is a wolf instead of a little fox). Then there are the little foxes of carelessness, of neglect of the Bible, of neglect of prayer, of neglect of fellowship with the people of God. These are the things that spoil the vine, that hinder spiritual growth. Deal with them in the light of the cross of Christ; put them to death before they ruin your Christian experience, do not give them any place. "Take us the foxes, the little foxes, that spoil the vines."

And now we have the closing words, "My beloved is mine, and I am his: he feedeth among the lilies." We need to be reminded of this again and again. The most intimate, sweet, and unsullied spiritual relationship is brought before us here. And this is to continue, "Until the day break, and the shadows flee away." When will that be? When our blessed Lord returns. "Turn, my beloved, and be thou like a roe or a young hart upon the mountains of Bether," that is, the mountains of separation. He is the object of her soul as she abides upon the mountains of separation until he comes back.

Oh, that these things were more real with us all! We profess to "hold" the truth of our Lord's near return. But does it hold us in such a way that we esteem all earthly things but loss for Him who is so soon to claim us wholly for Himself? "Let us search and try our ways," and make sure that we allow nothing in our lives that destroys the power of this "blessed hope" over our souls.

CHAPTER 3

SONG OF SOLOMON 3

I sought him whom my soul loveth; I sought him, but I found him not.
(Song of Solomon 3:1)

The third chapter of this exquisite book is divided into two parts; the first comprises verses 1–5, and the second, the balance of the chapter, verses 6–11. The opening section which we now consider sets before us communion interrupted and renewed.

We are not told just what it was that had disturbed the fellowship of the lovers. It may have been the absence of the beloved, resulting in a temporary lethargic condition on the part of his espoused one. Possibly the entire section is to be treated as a dream. In fact, this seems the most likely explanation. But dreams often reflect the disturbed state of the heart. "A dream cometh through the multitude of business" (Eccl. 5:3).

The opening verse depicts the restlessness of one who has lost the sense of the Lord's presence. What saint has not known such experiences? David once exclaimed, "LORD, by Thy favor Thou hast made my mountain to stand strong; Thou didst hide Thy face, and I was troubled" (Ps. 30:7). This withdrawal of the light of His countenance is not necessarily in anger. Sometimes it is admonitory. It is love's way of bringing the soul to a realization of something cherished or

314

allowed that grieves the Holy Spirit of God. Or it may be the testing of faith to see whether one can trust in the dark as well as in the light. Rutherford's experience is depicted thus:

> But flowers need night's cool sweetness,
>   The moonlight and the dew;
> So Christ from one who loved Him,
>   His presence oft withdrew.

To His disciples He said, when He announced His going away, "Ye believe in God, believe also in Me." That is to say, "As you have believed in God whom you have never seen, so when I am absent believe in Me. I will be just as real—and just as true—although to sight unseen." For though the soul lose the sense of His presence, nevertheless He still abides faithful. He never forsakes His people though He seems to have withdrawn and He does not manifest Himself. This is indeed a test of faith and of true-hearted devotion. We say, "Absence makes the heart grow fonder," but there is often greater truth in the old proverb, "Out of sight, out of mind." When the Lord as a boy stayed in the temple, even Mary and Joseph went on "supposing Him to be in the company," not realizing the true state of affairs.

Here the bride feels her loss. She seeks for him; he is not there. There is no response to her cry. For her, rest is impossible with this awful sense of loneliness upon her. She must seek until she finds; she cannot be contented without him. Would that this were always true of us! But, alas, how often we go on bereaved of the assurance of His presence, yet so insensate that we scarcely realize our loss. Here there is energy—determination—action! She *must* find him who is all in all to her. Love abhors a vacuum. Only the sense of his presence can fill and satisfy her heart.

In her dream—or possibly in reality—she leaves her mountain home and goes forth in search of the object of her deep affections. To the city she wends her way, and wanders about its streets and peers into every hidden place, looking only for him! But at first her search is unrewarded. In fact it is not until she bears witness to others of his preciousness that he gladdens her vision. Note the terms used: "I sought him; I found him not; I will seek him; I found him not."

The watchmen, guarding the city at night, are surprised to see a lovely and yet apparently respectable woman going about at such an hour. But she turns eagerly to them before they can reprove her, crying in the distress of her soul, "Saw ye him whom my soul loveth?" The abrupt question conveyed little information indeed. To the prosaic guardians of the peace, it must have sounded almost incoherent. But to her it was all that was necessary. There was only one for whom her soul yearned. Surely they too would know his worth! But from them she gets no response.

Leaving them, she has scarcely gone from their sight before she comes upon the object of her search. In an ecstasy of rapture she lays hold of him, and clinging to him as to one who might again vanish away, she brings him into her own home where she first saw the light of day.

The more the passage is pondered, the more evident it seems to be that all this happened in a dream. But it tells of the deep exercises of her soul. She misses him; she cannot be happy without the sense of his presence. Her only joy is found in abiding in his love. She finds him when she seeks for him with all her heart.

This is what gratifies him. And so again we have the refrain of satisfied love. "I charge you, O ye daughters of Jerusalem, by the roes and by the hinds of the field, that ye stir not up, nor wake my love, until she please" (v. 5), for, as previously mentioned, the expression here is in the feminine in the original. Nothing gives our Lord more delight than to find a heart that joys in Him for what He is in Himself. Too often we think rather of His gifts, the gracious favors He bestows. It is right and proper that these should stir us to thanksgiving; but it is as we get to know Himself and to joy in His love that we really worship in blissful communion.

> The bride eyes not her garments,
>   But her dear Bridegroom's face;
> I will not gaze at glory,
>   But on my King of Grace!
> Not at the crown He giveth,
>   But on His pierced Hand;
> The Lamb is all the glory
>   Of Immanuel's land.

The latter part of the chapter is of an entirely different character, and sets forth the truth of union rather than of restored communion. It is a little gem, complete in itself. The espoused one has waited long for the return of the shepherd whose love she has prized above all else. His promise to return for her has been cherished and relied upon, even though at times his continued absence has made the heart sick with yearning and even overwhelmed the drooping spirit with fear. But never has she really lost confidence in his plighted word. Eagerly she has awaited the fulfillment of his promise.

One day all the simple folk of the countryside are astir and filled with interest and wonder as they behold a grand procession wending its way along the highway up from the glorious city of God. Outriders and trumpeters on prancing chargers herald the approach of a royal equipage. "Who is this that cometh?" This is the question raised by every onlooker. Whose progress is this? Who travels in such grandeur and splendor? One can imagine the scene, and none can blame the curious conjectures as the peasants of the hills gaze with wonder upon the advancing cavalcade. In the Hebrew the question is really, "Who is she that cometh?" It is a bridal procession. But who is the honored maiden called to share the love of the king? Evidently at first they look in vain for a sight of her. Everything proclaims a nuptial parade, but no bride is really seen.

The bridegroom, however, is clearly in evidence. It is the son of David himself. In excited admiration the wondering people exclaim: "Behold his palanquin, which is Solomon's!" The royal conveyance is recognized. Sixty valiant soldiers guard their king as he journeys through the country. Clad in armor, each with his sword ready to defend his sovereign against any lurking traitorous foes, they move on in orderly array, as the excitement among the shepherds and vinedressers grows ever more intense. Not often have their eyes been regaled by such a scene as this! Perhaps they will never see its like again!

How magnificent, how costly is that royal palanquin! It is the king's provision for the comfort of his bride. And that bride is half-hidden among the rest of the country folk, not daring to believe that such honor is for her. All eyes are on the king. It is his crowning day—his nuptial hour—the day of the gladness of his heart. He has come forth to seek and claim his spouse whom he won as the shepherd, and to whom he now reveals himself as the king.

There is no actual mention of the claiming of the bride and bringing her to the king, it is true. But it is clearly implied. He has come to fulfill his promise to make her his own. With deep and chastened joy she responds to the royal summons and takes her place at his side, and so the procession sweeps on, leaving the bewildered onlookers gasping with startled amazement at the sudden change in the estate of her who had been through the years but one of themselves. It is a worthy theme for a Song of Songs! And most graphically it portrays the glorious reality which the bride of the Lamb shall soon know when the Shepherd-King comes to claim His own.

He is coming as the Bridegroom,
　　Coming to unfold at last
The great secret of His purpose,
　　Mystery of ages past;
And the bride, to her is granted,
　　In His beauty now to shine,
As in rapture she exclaimeth,
　　"I am His, and He is mine!"
Oh, what joy that marriage union,
　　Mystery of love divine;
Sweet to sing in all its fullness,
　　"I am His, and He is mine!"

How short then will seem the waiting time; how trifling the follies of earth which we gave up in order to be pleasing in His sight! How slight too will the sufferings of the present time appear, as compared with the glory then to be enjoyed.

If some fancy we have drawn too much upon imagination as we have sought to picture the real background of these lovely lyrics, let me ask, Is it possible to mistake the picture when all Scripture tells the same story? What was the marriage of Adam and Eve intended to signify? What shall be said of the servant seeking a bride for Isaac, and what of the love of Jacob as he served so unweariedly for Rachel? Of what "great mystery" does Asenath, the Gentile wife of Joseph, speak? And what shall be said of the love of Boaz for Ruth? Hosea who bought his bride in the slave-market gives a darker side of the picture, yet all is in wonderful harmony. All alike tell the story that "Christ . . . loved the church, and gave Himself for it; that He might sanctify and cleanse it by the washing of water by the Word, and present it unto Himself a glorious church, not having spot, or wrinkle, or any such thing" (Eph. 5:25–27). "All fair" indeed will she then be in His eyes, and one with Him forever, for, it is written, "For this cause shall a man leave his father and mother, and shall be joined unto his wife, and they two shall be one flesh. This is a great mystery: but I speak concerning Christ and the church" (Eph. 5:31–32).

Surely all this should speak loudly to our hearts, we who through grace have been won for One we have never yet seen, but of whom we read, "Whom having not seen, ye love; in whom, though now ye see Him not, yet believing, ye rejoice with joy unspeakable and full of glory." What will it be when we behold Him coming in royal array to claim us as His very own, when we discern in the King of kings, the Good Shepherd who gave His life for the sheep, and who, before He left this scene, gave the solemn promise, "If I go . . . I will come again and receive you unto Myself." That glad nuptial hour draws on apace. Well may our hearts be stirred and our spiritual pulses quickened as we join the wondering cry, "Who is this that cometh?"

When the bride is caught away, what will the astonishment be on the part of those who had never understood that she was the loved one of the Lord Most High? When they realize that the church is gone and the heavenly procession has passed them by, what will be their thoughts in that day?

But we must pause here for the present. The next chapter gives us the glad recognition and the happy response.

CHAPTER 4

Song of Solomon 4:1–11

> Thou art all fair, my love; there is no spot in thee. (Song of Solomon 4:7)

It is not strange that as we think of our Lord Jesus Christ, the heavenly Bridegroom, our souls are moved to their deepest depths, but it is hard for us to realize that He has a greater love for us than we could ever possibly have for Him. And so here in this fourth chapter of the Song of Solomon, we hear the bridegroom expressing to his loved one the feelings of his heart toward her, and as we read these words, as we listen to these heart-breathings, we should remember that the speaker is really our Lord Jesus Christ, and that the bride may be looked at in various ways, as we have already seen. Prophetically, we may think of the bride as Israel, and Jehovah rejoicing over her in that coming day; individually, we may think of the bride as representing any saved soul, and the Lord expressing His delight in the one He has redeemed to Himself by His precious blood; or as that church which Christ loved and for which He gave Himself.

So we may see in these utterances His delight in His church. In verses 1–7 of this fourth chapter, you will notice that He addresses Himself directly to the bride, and He speaks of her beauties as He sees them in a very wonderful way.

The imagery, of course, as throughout this book, is strictly oriental, and goes considerably beyond what we prosaic occidentals are in the habit of using. And yet as we read it, we see that there is nothing coarse, nothing that would bring the blush to the cheek of modesty. It is the fullest, most rapturous delight of the bridegroom in the bride, but every expression is in keeping with the holiness of this blessed little book.

First, he speaks of her general appearance. Four times over in this chapter, he tells her of her fairness. Twice he declares it in verse 1. He says, "Behold, thou art fair, my love; behold, thou art fair." In verse 7 we read, "Thou art all fair, my love; there is no spot in thee." Again in verse 10, "How fair is thy love, my sister, my spouse! How much better is thy love than wine!" And yet she had no fairness in herself, as we had no beauty in ourselves. In an earlier chapter we heard her say, "I am black as the tents of Kedar, as the curtains of Solomon." But he says, as he looks at her through love's eyes, "Thou art all fair." Does it not bring before us the wondrous thing that our Savior has done for every one of us who have been redeemed by the precious blood of Christ? We would never have been saved at all if we had not realized in some measure our own wretchedness, our own sinfulness, our unlovely character. It was because of this that we fled to Him for refuge and confessed that we were anything but fair, anything but beautiful. We took our places side by side with Job and cried, "I have heard of Thee by the hearing of the ear: but now mine eye seeth Thee. Wherefore I abhor myself, and repent in dust and ashes" (Job 42:5–6). We knelt beside Isaiah and exclaimed, "I am a man of unclean lips, and I dwell in the midst of a people of unclean lips" (Isa. 6:5). We took part with Peter and cried, "Depart from me; for I am a sinful man, O Lord" (Luke 5:8). But when we took that place of repentance, of acknowledgement of our own natural deformity and unloveliness, He looked upon us in His grace and said, "Thou art perfect in Mine eyes by the comeliness which I have put upon thee." And now as those who have been washed from our sins in His own precious blood, He addresses us in the rapturous way that we have here, "Thou art all fair, My love; there is no spot in thee." What! No spot in us, when we were stained by sin, when we were polluted by iniquity? Once it could be said of us, "From the sole of the foot even unto the head there is no soundness in it; but wounds, and bruises, and putrifying sores: they have not been closed, neither bound up, neither mollified with ointment" (Isa. 1:6). And now His holy eyes cannot find one spot of sin, nor any sign of iniquity. Let this give us to understand what grace hath wrought.

> Amazing grace, how sweet the sound,
> That saved a wretch like me!

It is only God's matchless grace that has thus made us accepted in the Beloved.

Then you will notice that the bridegroom looking upon his bride speaks of her person in the most glowing terms, referring to seven different things. First, he speaks of her eyes and says to her, "Thou hast doves' eyes within thy locks." What does that mean? The dove was a clean bird, the bird of love and sorrow, the bird offered in sacrifice upon the altar, and thus typifies our Lord Jesus as the heavenly One. And now he sees reflected in his bride that which speaks of himself. "Thou hast doves' eyes." We may not have stopped to realize it, but the dove is very keen of sight. Recently in an eastern city, a poor carrier pigeon fell exhausted on one of those high buildings, and somebody working on the roof of the building caught it utterly unable to rise. They found attached to it a message that had come over three thousand miles, and that little dove had seen its way all along the miles, and had flown on and on until at last it had brought the message to that eastern city. When our blessed Lord says to us, "Thou art fair, My love; behold, thou art fair; thou hast doves' eyes within thy locks," it means not only that we have eyes of beauty, but eyes quick to discern the precious and wonderful things that are hidden for us in His holy Word. Do we respond to this, or do these doves' eyes sometimes take to wandering, going out after the things of a poor godless world?

He says, "Thy hair is as a flock of goats, that appear from Mount Gilead." He refers to the Syrian goat with its long silken hair. One can imagine the beauty of the scene, a flock of goats up yonder on the mountainside. The bridegroom says, "Your hair reminds me of that." Hair, in Scripture, is a woman's glory. That is one reason why she is not supposed to follow the styles of the world and cut away her beauty and glory. You remember the woman of old who loved Jesus and knelt at His feet and washed them with her tears and wiped them with her hair. She was using that which spoke of her beauty and her glory to minister to Him, the loving, blessed Savior. Some of my sisters will forgive me if I say that it would be difficult for them to dry anyone's feet with their hair! Yes, her hair is a woman's glory and beauty, and, incidentally, that is exactly the reason why the Word of God tells the woman to cover her head when she comes into the presence of the Lord. When she comes in before Him whose glory fills the heavens, to join with His worshipping people, she is to cover her own glory that no one's attention may be distracted, but fixed on Christ Himself. When you get the inwardness of these things, you find there is a beauty and a privilege in them that does away with all legality, and also does away with leaving us free to follow our own judgment. In Scripture, some things are commanded because they are right, and other things are right because they are commanded. When He makes known His will, the subject Christian bows to His Word, assured that there is a reason for it, though he does not always understand it. How He delights to behold His obedient people; how He glories in their moral beauty!

Then, in the third place, he speaks of her teeth, and we may think that strange, but there is nothing more beautiful than a lovely set of pearls half-hidden in the mouth. "Thy teeth are like a flock of sheep that are shorn, which came up from the washing; whereof every one bear twins, and none is barren among them." The two sets of teeth answer to the twins in their cleanliness and sparkling beauty, so attractive in his eyes. And how important the teeth are, spiritually speaking, because they speak to us of mastication, of the ability to properly lay hold of and digest our food. I am afraid there are a number of toothless Christians from that standpoint. Some say, "I do not know how it is, but other people read their Bibles and find such wonderful things, when I do not find much in mine." The trouble is you have such poor teeth, you do not masticate your spiritual food properly. It is by meditation that we appropriate our daily provision. David said, "My meditation of Him shall be sweet" (Ps. 104:34). Until He gives you a new set of spiritual teeth, you had better use some secondhand ones. Thank God for what others have found; read their books, and get something that way! By-and-by, if you will wait on Him, the Lord will give you back your teeth, even if you have lost them, and you will be able to enjoy the truth for yourself.

The third verse is most lovely: "Thy lips are like a thread of scarlet, and thy speech is comely." This is different from that abominable custom of today that leads so many women, of course not consistent Christian women, but those of the world and Christians living on the edge of the world, to put that filthy stuff upon their lips that makes them look like a cross between poor, low women of the street and circus performers. Here it is the red lip of health, of spiritual health. "Thy lips are like a thread of scarlet, and thy speech is comely." Why? Because it is speech that has to do with Him! The bride loves to speak of the bridegroom, as the Christian loves to speak of Christ, and her lips are like a thread of scarlet, for she exalts that blood by which she has been brought nigh to God. Every real Christian will have lips like a thread of scarlet, for he gladly confesses that he owes everything for eternity to that precious atoning blood of the Lord Jesus Christ. It is not only when we gather at the table of the Lord, when we bow in worship as we take the bread and cup as from His blessed pierced hand, that we love to sing and speak and think of the blood; but always, everywhere, at all times, the believer delights to remember that he has been redeemed to God by the precious blood of Christ. You will find the scarlet thread running right through this book.

God has said, "The life of the flesh is in the blood, and I have given it to you upon the altar to make an atonement for your soul; it is the blood that maketh an atonement for the soul." "When I see the blood, I will pass over you." "We have been redeemed to God by the precious blood of Christ, as of an unblemished spotless lamb, foreknown indeed from the foundation of the world, but manifest in these last times for you." "The blood of Jesus Christ, God's Son, cleanseth us from all sin." And when at last we get home to heaven, our lips will be like a thread of scarlet still, for we will join in that new song and sing our praises to Him who was "slain and has loosed us from our sins in His own blood," and we will render adoration unto the Lamb whose blood was shed, that we might be made kings and priests unto God. O Christian, make much of the blood, speak often of the blood. Do not be satisfied with the namby-pamby, bloodless religion of the day. When you ask the question, "Are you a Christian?" and you get the ready answer, "Oh, yes; I belong to the church," then see that your lips are like a thread of scarlet and ask, "Are you trusting in the precious blood of the Lord Jesus alone for salvation?" So often you will find that the idle profession made a moment ago was only an empty thing. They are Christians in name only. There are thousands about us who know nothing of the cleansing value of the blood of Jesus.

"Thy temples are like a piece of a pomegranate within thy locks." You know the temple speaks of the dome of thought, and so the bride's thought is about her bridegroom. She loves to think of him, to meditate upon the treasures found in his word. Then he delights in her as she delights in him.

In the next verse we have the strength of her character, given her by divine grace. "Thy neck is like the tower of David builded for an armory, whereon there hang a thousand bucklers, all shields of mighty men." David's tower, you see, is the place of defense, the place of strength, and the bride here is one of those who can stand up straight and boldly look the world in the face, assured of the love and protection of her matchless bridegroom. And so we are called upon to be "strong in the Lord, and in the power of His might." The head won't be hanging down like a bulrush when our hearts are taken up with Him. There will be a boldness that is never known when out of communion with Him.

Then, last of all, in the seventh place he speaks of that which tells of affection. "Thy two breasts are like two young roes that are twins, which feed among the lilies." Her heart is his, her whole being belongs to him, and he rejoices in her. We may well sing:

Jesus, Thou art enough
   The mind and heart to fill;
Thy patient life—to calm the soul;
   Thy love—its fear dispel.
O fix our earnest gaze
   So wholly, Lord, on Thee;
That, with Thy beauty occupied,
   We elsewhere none may see.

As we joy in Him, we will find that He will joy in us. You remember what Faber wrote:

That Thou should'st so delight in me
   And be the God Thou art,
Is darkness to my intellect,
   But sunlight to my heart.

I cannot understand why He should say, "Thou art all fair, My love; there is no spot in thee." I cannot comprehend such matchless grace, but my heart can rejoice in it, and so I love Him in return because He first loved me.

Following this section in which we have the bridegroom's joy in the bride, in verses 8–11 we have his summons to companionship with himself. The bridegroom would call his bride away from everything else that has occupied her in order to find in him her all in all. "Come with me from Lebanon, my spouse, with me from Lebanon: look from the top of Amana, from the top of Shenir and Hermon, from the lions' dens, from the mountains of the leopards. Thou hast ravished my heart, my sister, my spouse; thou hast ravished my heart with one of thine eyes, with one chain of thy neck. How fair is thy love, my sister, my spouse! how much better is thy love than wine! and the smell of thine ointments than all spices!" He sees her upon the mountainside. And, you know, the mountain is the place of privilege, the place of beauty, of worldly grandeur and glory, but it is also the place of danger. The leopard's lair is there and the lion's den, and as he beholds her there alone, he cries, "Come with me from Lebanon . . . from the lions' dens, from the mountains of the leopards." Our blessed Lord wants the companionship of His redeemed people. How sweet those words, "Come with Me!" He never calls His people from anything, either the beautiful things of the world or the dangerous things (and after all, the beautiful is often the most dangerous), simply to take a path alone, but it is always, "Come with Me," and you cannot afford, you who love His name, to draw back, to say, "There are other things so lovely, so beautiful, that my soul must have; I cannot leave them to go with Thee." He who died for you, He who left heaven's glory in order to redeem your soul, calls to you and says, "Come with Me." Can you draw back and say, "No; it is too much to ask; I cannot leave these surroundings; I cannot leave these worldly follies; I cannot quit this place of danger for Thy sake, Lord Jesus." Surely there is not very much love there. You need to get down before Him and confess the sin of your cold-heartedness and indifference, and ask for a fresh vision of the love that He manifested in the cross that your heart may be weaned away from everything else. Dr. Watts has put it:

> He calls me from the lion's den,
> From this wild world of beasts and men,
> To Zion where His glories are,
> No Lebanon is half so fair.
> Nor dens of prey, nor flowery plains,
> Nor earthly joys, nor earthly pains,
> Shall hold my feet or force my stay,
> When Christ invites my soul away.

Does your heart respond to that? What He desires above everything else is to see His people finding satisfaction in His company.

And then in the closing two verses of this section, verses 10–11, we read, "How fair is thy love, my sister, my spouse! how much better is thy love than wine! and the smell of thine ointments than all spices! Thy lips, O my spouse, drop as the honeycomb; honey and milk are under thy tongue; and the smell of thy garments is like the smell of Lebanon." You remember in the first chapter it is she who said, looking up to him, "We will remember thy love more than wine." Now it is he who responds to her and says, "How much better is thy love than wine! and the smell of thine ointments than all spices! Thy lips, O my spouse, drop as the honeycomb: honey and milk are under thy tongue; and the smell of thy garments is like the smell of Lebanon." His people should be fragrant with the sweetness of Christ. It is said of the disciples of old, "They took knowledge that they had been with Jesus," and if we are in His company, there will be a rich fragrance of holiness, of heavenliness, about us wherever we are found.

A minister tells of riding with another preacher on top of a bus in London, England. As they came down a poor-looking street with a big factory on one side, they were halted, and they noticed the doors of the factory had opened and hundreds of girls were pouring out and making their way across the street to a lunch room; suddenly the air was filled with a sweet delightful fragrance. The visitor said, "Isn't that remarkable in a factory district here in London?—such wondrous fragrance! It seems like the odor of a great garden. You would not think of finding such fragrance in this district." "Oh, you don't understand," said his friend, "this is one of the largest perfume-factories in all the British Isles, and these young people are working constantly among the perfumes, and everywhere they go the fragrance remains upon their garments."

Beloved, if you and I are living in fellowship with Christ, if we keep in touch with Him, everywhere we go His fragrance will be manifested in our lives.

CHAPTER 5

SONG OF SOLOMON 4:12–5:1

A garden inclosed is my sister, my spouse; a spring shut up, a fountain sealed. Thy plants are an orchard of pomegranates, with pleasant fruits; camphire, with spikenard, spikenard and saffron; calamus and cinnamon, with all trees of frankincense; myrrh, and aloes, with all the chief spices: a fountain of gardens, a well of living waters, and streams from Lebanon. Awake, O north wind; and come, thou south; blow upon my garden, that the spices thereof may flow out. Let my beloved come into his garden, and eat his pleasant fruits. I am come into my garden, my sister, my spouse: I have gathered my myrrh with my spice; I have eaten my honeycomb with my honey; I have drunk my wine with my milk: eat, O friends; drink, yea, drink abundantly, O beloved. (Song of Solomon 4:12–5:1)

We have been noticing in chapter after chapter how the blessed Lord puts before us our privileges as those who are permitted to enter into communion with Himself, and now in this little section we have the believer (if you think of it as the individual), or Israel, or the church, whichever you will, pictured as a watered garden set apart for our Lord Himself to bring forth fruit that will be to His delight. It is a lovely figure, one used on a number of other occasions in Scripture. In the fifty-eighth chapter of the prophet Isaiah, God pictures His people as such a garden. In verse 11, He says, "The Lord shall guide thee continually, and satisfy thy soul in drought, and make fat thy bones: and thou shalt be like a watered garden, and like a spring of water, whose waters fail not." This is a beautiful picture. Primarily it refers to Israel, and morally it speaks of any believer, of that which God would see in all His saints as they walk with Him. In Jeremiah 31:12, we read, "Therefore they shall come and sing in the height of Zion, and shall flow together to the goodness of the LORD, for wheat, and for wine, and for oil, and for the young of the flock and of the herd: and their soul shall be as a watered garden; and they shall not sorrow any more at all." It is the Risen Christ Himself from whom we draw abundant supplies of mercy and grace; but did you ever think of your own heart as a garden in which He is to find His joy? Your very life is as a garden which is to be for His pleasure. That is the figure you have here. It is the bridegroom looking upon his bride with his heart filled with delight as he says to her, "You are to be for me, you are like a lovely garden yielding its fruit and flowers for me, set apart for myself."

"A garden inclosed is my sister, my spouse; a spring shut up, a fountain sealed." We in America like open gardens that anybody can enjoy, but in Syria and in other parts of the old land, they have many enclosed gardens, gardens that are walled in. This is necessary in some of those countries, as otherwise they would be destroyed by marauding creatures and robbers. It is as though the Lord says, "That is what I want My people to be, separated to Myself; I want them to have about them the wall of holiness, for I have marked them off as My own." In the Psalms we read, "The Lord hath set apart him that is godly for Himself." Some Christians shrink from the idea of separation. If it is only a legal thing, it may become mere Pharisaism with no heart to it, but if it is to Himself, if it is the soul going out to Him, if one turns away from the world for love of Him, then separation is a very precious thing indeed, and one does not need to think of it as legal bondage, for it is being set apart for God Himself. Could one think of a higher privilege on earth than that He might find His joy in us and we might find our joy in Him?

"A garden inclosed is my sister, my spouse." How Satan likes to break down the wall, to destroy that principle of holy separation which would keep our hearts for the Lord alone; but what a loss it is to our own souls, and what a loss it means to Him, when His people become like a garden trodden underfoot, as it were, by every wayfarer. That is what the Christian becomes who does not keep the path of separation.

Then notice the next figure, "A spring shut up, a fountain sealed." Pure water is a very precious thing in the Far East and so often, when a spring is discovered, it is walled about, covered, and locked, and the owner of it keeps the key so that he can go and drink when he will, and the water is kept from pollution and waste. That is what our Lord would have in His people. He has given His Holy Spirit to dwell in us, and the Holy Spirit is Himself the Fountain of Water within every believer's heart, that we might be to His praise and to His glory. This living water within the garden will, of course, result in abundant fruit and flowers.

"Thy plants are an orchard of pomegranates, with pleasant fruits; camphire, with spikenard." The orchard suggests more than a mere garden of beautiful flowers; not only something fair to look at, or something that is fragrant to the senses, but something fruitful as well. What precious fruit is borne by the believer; what precious fruit is found in the heart of the one who is shut up to God! In Philippians 1, the apostle tells those dear saints that he is sure that God who has begun the good work in them will perform it until the day of Jesus Christ. In verses 9–11 of this chapter, he says, "And this I pray, that your love may abound yet more and more in knowledge and in all judgment; that ye may approve things that are excellent; that ye may be sincere and without offense till the day of Christ; being filled with the fruits of righteousness, which are by Jesus Christ, unto the glory and praise of God." It seems to me that everyone ought to understand that a life that is lived for God is one bringing forth the fruits of righteousness. Love, purity, goodness, sweetness, kindness, compassion, consideration for others, all of these things are the beautiful fruits that grow in this garden when the living water is properly fructifying the soil. In Galatians 5:22 we have a long list of the fruit of the Spirit. Challenge your own heart by asking, "Am I producing this kind of fruit for Him, 'Love, joy, peace, longsuffering'?" It is that patience, you know, that makes you willing to endure. Then there is "gentleness, goodness, faith, meekness, temperance." This is the delightful fruit that our Lord is looking for in the lives of His people. He would have every one of us as a garden that produces fruit like this.

That word translated "orchard" is really similar to the Persian word for "paradise," and it may suggest that as God has a paradise above for His own people, where they shall share His joy for all eternity, so a believer's heart when it is producing fruit like this, is for God a paradise where He finds His joy and His delight. I wonder if we think enough of that side of it. Are we not likely to become self-centered and merely think of God as serving us, the blessed Lord Jesus giving Himself for us, dying for us, rising again for us, nurturing our souls, guiding us through the wilderness of this world and bringing us at last to glory?

Some of the hymns we sing are almost entirely occupied with the blessings that come to us, but these do not rise to the height of the Christian's communion at all. It is when we are through thinking about what God is doing for us, and are seeking by grace to adore the One who does all this for us, and are letting our lives go out to Him as a thank offering in praise and adoration, that we truly rise to the height of our Christian privileges. Then it is that He gathers these sweet and lovely fruits in His garden. It is not only fruit upon which He feeds, but it is that which gives satisfaction in every sense. "Camphire, with spikenard, spikenard and saffron; calamus and cinnamon, with all trees of frankincense; myrrh and aloes, with all the chief spices." Some of these plants give forth their fragrance as the rain and dew fall upon them; some of them send forth a subtle aroma when the rays of the sun are warming them. Others never exude, never give out their fragrance, until they are pierced and the sap flows forth. So is it with our lives. We need all kinds of varied experiences in order that we may manifest the graces of Christ in our behavior, and it is not only that we are to be for His delight in the sense in which I have been speaking, but we are to be for His service too, in making known His grace to a lost world.

In the next verse we read, "A fountain of gardens, a well of living waters, and streams from Lebanon." Let us see if we can correlate that. There is Lebanon, that backbone mountain range of Palestine, with Mount Hermon to the north covered with snow. The streams coming down from Lebanon sink into the ground, and as they do so, springs rise here and there in vales and dells to the surface of the earth, and so the living water flows forth to refresh the thirsty soil. The living water represents, as we know from John's gospel, the blessed Holy Spirit. Our Lord Jesus said, "If any man thirst, let him come unto Me and drink. He that believeth on Me, as the Scripture hath said, from within him shall flow rivers of living water. But this spake He of the Spirit, which they that believe on Him should receive: for the Holy Ghost was not yet given; because that Jesus was not yet glorified" (John 7:37–39).

Now the Spirit of God descending from above enters into our inmost being and then we have the living water springing up unto everlasting life. Our own hearts are refreshed and gladdened, and the living water in abundance flows out from us for the blessing of a lost world around. Is this not a beautiful picture? My brother, my sister, what do you know of this life in the fullness of the Holy Spirit? Far too many of us seem to be content to know that our sins have been forgiven, that we have a hope of heaven based upon some testimony that we have received from Holy Scripture. But it is more than this. We are not merely to have the assurance of our own salvation, but every one of us should be as watered gardens for Him, with streams flowing out for the refreshment of dying men and women all about us.

In what measure is your life touching others? In what measure are you being used of God to win other souls for Christ? If we have to confess, as many of us would, that we have never had the privilege of winning one soul, that so far as we know we have never yet given a testimony to any one that has really been blessed in his or her coming to Christ, let me suggest that there must be something that is hindering the outflow of the living water. Can it be that great boulders of worldliness, selfishness, pride, carnality, sinful folly or covetousness are literally choking the fountain of living water, so that there is just a little trickling when there should be a wonderful outflowing? If this is the case, seek by grace to recognize these hindrances and deal with them one by one. Away with worldliness, away with pride. Who am I to be proud? What have I to be proud of? "What hast thou that thou hast not received?" Away with carnality, away with self-seeking, away with covetousness, away with living for my own interests, and let me henceforth live alone for Him who shed His precious blood for me and redeemed me to Himself. As I thus deal with these things that hinder the outflow of the living water, I will myself enter into a new, living, blessed and wonderful experience, and my testimony then will count in blessing to those about me, and my life will be at its best for Him.

There has been some question as to the identity of the first speaker in verse 16. It is very evident that the one who speaks in the last sentence is the bride, but is it the bride or the bridegroom in the first part of the verse? "Awake, O north wind; and come, thou south; blow upon my garden, that the spices thereof may flow out." If it is the bridegroom who is speaking, then he it is who is calling on the winds to blow upon what he calls, "my garden," the heart of his bride, in order that she may be at her best for him. If, on the other hand, as I am personally inclined to believe, it is the bride who is speaking, then it indicates her yearning desire to be all that he would have her to be. Dear child of God, is that your desire? Do you yearn to be all that Christ would have you to be, or are you still actuated by worldly and selfish motives that hinder communion with Him? Listen to these words again, as we think of them as coming from the lips of the bride, "Awake, O north wind." That is the cold, bitter, biting, wintry blast. Naturally she would shrink from that as we all would, and yet the cold of winter is as necessary as the warmth of summer if there is going to be perfection in fruit bearing. It is as though she says, "Blessed God, if need be, let Thy Spirit breathe upon me through trial and sorrow, and difficulty and perplexity; take from me all in which I have trusted from the human standpoint; bereave me of everything if

Thou wilt; leave me cold, naked, and alone except for Thy love, but work out Thy will in me."

The best apples are grown in northern climes where frost and cold have to be faced. Those grown in semi-tropical countries are apt to be tasteless and insipid. It takes the cold to bring out the flavor. And it is so with our lives. We need the north winds of adversity and trial as well as the zephyrs of the south so agreeable to our natures. The very things we shrink from are the experiences that will work in us to produce the peaceable fruits of righteousness. If everything were easy and soft and beautiful in our lives, they would be insipid; there would be so little in them for God that could delight His heart; and so there must be the north wind as well as the south. But, on the other hand, we need the south wind also, and our precious Lord tempers the winds to every one of us. "Awake, O north wind; and come, thou south; blow upon my garden, that the spices thereof may flow out." It is a blessed thing to be in that state of soul where we can just trust ourselves to Him.

Charles Spurgeon tells of a man who had the words, "God is love," painted on his weather vane. Someone said, "That is a queer text to put there. Do you mean to say that God's love is as changeable as the wind?" "Oh, no," said the other; "I mean that whichever way the wind blows, God is love." Do not forget that. It may be the north wind of bereavement when your dearest and best are snatched from you, but "God is love." It may be that the cold wind of what the world calls ill-fortune will sweep away like a fearful cyclone all that you have accumulated for years, but "God is love," and it is written, "The Lord hath His way in the whirlwind and in the storm, and the clouds are the dust of His feet" (Nah. 1:3).

Perhaps you have been asking questions like this, "Why has God allowed the sufferings we have had to undergo? Why has He allowed these weeks and months with no employment and everything slipping away, the savings of years gone?" Dear child of God, He gives not account of any of His matters now, but,

> When you stand with Christ in glory,
> Looking o'er life's finished story,

then He will make it clear to you, and you will know why He allowed the cold wind to blow over His garden as well as the south wind, and if you would bow to Him now, and recognize His unchanging love, perhaps He would be able to trust you with more zephyrs from the south than you ordinarily experience. We are not subject enough to the will of God. We need to learn the lesson that, "All things work together for good to them that love God, to them who are the called according to His purpose" (Rom. 8:28).

"Awake, O north wind; and come, thou south; blow upon my garden, that the spices thereof may flow out." In other words, "Anything, Lord, that will make me a better Christian, a more devoted saint; anything that will make me a more faithful child of Thine, so that Thou canst find Thy delight in me." Is that your thought? And then she looks up into the face of her bridegroom and says, "Let my beloved come into his garden, and eat his pleasant fruits." How He delights to get such an invitation as that from His people. He responds to her immediately, for the first verse of chapter 5 really belongs to this section. She no sooner says, "Come," than he replies, "I am come into my garden, my sister, my spouse: I have gathered my myrrh with my spice; I have eaten my honeycomb with my honey; I have drunk my wine with my milk: eat, O friends; drink, yea, drink abundantly, O beloved."

It closes with a scene of rapturous communion. And when you look up to the Beloved of your heart and say, "Come into Thy garden and eat Thy pleasant fruits," He will immediately respond, "I am come." You will never have to wait; you will never have to give Him a second invitation. If you have any time for Him, He always has time for you.

CHAPTER 6

SONG OF SOLOMON 5:2–8:5

I sleep, but my heart waketh: it is the voice of my beloved that knocketh, saying, Open to me, my sister, my love, my dove, my undefiled: for my head is filled with dew, and my locks with the drops of the night. I have put off my coat; how shall I put it on? I have washed my feet; how shall I defile them? My beloved put in his hand by the hole of the door, and my bowels were moved for him. I rose up to open to my beloved; and my hands dropped with myrrh, and my fingers with sweetsmelling myrrh, upon the handles of the lock. I opened to my beloved; but my beloved had withdrawn himself, and was gone: my soul failed when he spake: I sought him, but I could not find him; I called him, but he gave me no answer. The watchmen that went about the city found me, they smote me, they wounded me; the keepers of the walk took away my veil from me. I charge you, O daughters of Jerusalem, if ye find my beloved, that ye tell him, that I am sick of love. (Song of Solomon 5:2–8)

We have a very long section before us beginning with the second verse of chapter 5 and concluding with the fifth verse of chapter 8. In this entire portion we have traced out for us in a very wonderful way the interruption of communion and its final restoration. We have already had one similar picture in this book where the bridegroom's absence produced a temporary sense of estrangement. We have that dealt with more fully in this section, where the bridegroom's advances are coldly spurned. If we will remember that the bride speaks of any regenerated soul and that the bridegroom is our blessed Lord Jesus Christ, I am sure we shall have no difficulty in getting the spiritual lesson of these chapters.

We have all experienced interrupted communion. We have all known such periods of glad joy in the Lord as those brought before us in the previous chapter. But how often have we found that, following almost immediately on a period of great blessing and delightful fellowship with the Lord, there may come a time of spiritual dearth and broken fellowship. You recall that in Israel's history they were scarcely through rejoicing over the wonderful victory at Jericho before they were wringing their hands in despair because of the defeat at Ai. How often in our Christian lives we have similar experiences. Perhaps you go to an edifying meeting where your whole soul is stirred by the singing, by the prayers, and by the ministry of the Word, and you feel as though you would never again lose sight of your blessed Redeemer's face; and yet the spirit is willing but the flesh is weak, and within a very short time you find yourself inquiring,

> Where is the blessedness I knew
> When first I saw the Lord?

And everything seems dark and cloudy and you no longer discern your Savior's presence. Is there any one who has had uninterrupted communion with the Lord throughout all the years? I am sure there is not. Even if we imagined so, it would simply be because we lacked that sensitiveness which would enable us to apprehend the fact that He was in some sense grieved because of our behavior.

We have a wonderfully beautiful picture here. The bride has retired and she is drowsing, just about asleep, and yet a bit restless, when there comes a knock at the door. It is the knock of the beloved one who has returned from a distant journey and he cries, "Open to me, my sister, my love, my dove, my undefiled; for my head is filled with dew, and my locks with the drops of the night." We have the same picture in the New Testament in the third chapter of the book of Revelation, in which we see the Lord Jesus waiting outside the door of the Laodicean church. He says, "Behold, I stand at the door and knock: if any man hear My voice, and open the door, I will come in to him, and will sup with him, and he with Me." But what lethargy there is! How few respond to His gracious request! And so here the bride exclaims, "I have put off my coat; how shall I put it on? I have washed my feet; how shall I defile them?" There is a fretfulness about it. Why am I disturbed at this hour? Why did you not come at some other time? I have taken off my coat; why should I put it on now? I have washed my feet; why should I defile them? This refers to the Eastern custom of washing the feet before seeking repose, for in that land they wore sandals and the upper part of the foot Had no covering. In other words, she did not want to bestir herself even so much as to open the door to him. Have you never known similar experiences?

Have you never been so much concerned with your own affairs, with seeking your own ease, with self-pleasing, that when His voice called you for an hour of communion and fellowship with Him, you really repelled His advances, instead of gladly throwing open the door and saying, "Blessed Lord, nothing else is worthwhile but to enjoy the sunshine of Thy smile, to enjoy fellowship with Thyself"?

In this instance, we may see in the bride's behavior evidence of just such a state of soul. But then, as she lies there drowsing, neither actually asleep nor awake, she discerns something that moves her heart. She says, "My beloved put in his hand by the hole of the door." We will not understand the simile unless we are familiar with those Eastern doors and locks. The lock was on the inside of the door, and there was an opening where the owner could, if he had the key, reach in and use the key from the inside to open the door. He comes, but he does not open the door in that way. He has asked admission and wants her to rise and open for him. She sees that hand come through the opening and the moment she does so, her heart is stirred and she cries, "Oh, I must let him in." And now she rises and hurries to the door and even as she lays hold of the lock, she ex- claims, "My hands dropped with myrrh, and my fingers with sweet-smelling myrrh, upon the handles of the lock." That refers to another Eastern custom. When a lover came to visit the one who had won his heart and found that she was not at home, or if at home, she did not respond to his advances, he covered the lock of the door with sweet-smelling ointments and left flowers as a token of his affection. And so the bride says, "My hands dropped with myrrh, and my fingers with sweetsmelling myrrh." It was not a dream then; he had really been there and had gone. But she threw the door open to enable him to hear her cry, "Come, come in!" but there was no answering response. "My beloved," she said, "had withdrawn himself and was gone."

Love is very sensitive. The trouble with many of us is that we fail to recognize this. We have an idea that the beloved one should be ready whenever we are for a time of gladness together, but it is not always so. And so, sometimes when He comes to the heart's door we practically say, "No; it is inconvenient. I do not want to drop things right now." But later when we would enjoy His presence we find He has gone. Have you never had such experiences? Has He come to you and said, "I want you to sit down with Me over My Word; I want you to spend a little time in prayer; to dismiss other things from your mind and commune with Me," and you have said, "Oh, but I have so much to occupy me; I cannot do it now." Plenty of time for self but very little for Him. And then some wonderful token of His loving-kindness came to you, and you said, "Oh, I must respond to His heart," and you threw open the door as it were and called, but He was not there. And did you ever know what it was to go on for days and weeks without any real sense of His presence? "My beloved had withdrawn himself." If you do not respond to His voice when He comes to you in tender grace, you may seek Him for a long time before you will enjoy fellowship with Him again. Such is the sensitiveness of love. He wants to make you feel that His love is worthwhile, and wants to test you as to whether you are really in earnest when you profess to desire fellowship with Him.

And so as the story goes on, she leaves the house and goes out into the city seeking after him, and as she makes her way from street to street, perchance calling his name and looking here and there and wondering where he has hidden himself, she says, "The watchmen that went about the city found me, they smote me, they wounded me; the keepers of the walls took away my veil from me." You will always have to suffer if you refuse obedience to the voice of Christ when He calls you. You will always have to be tested before communion is restored.

There is a word in the New Testament that has troubled some of our sisters. In 1 Corinthians 11 we are told that a Christian woman, when she is engaged in worship with the people of God or in public prayer or testimony, is to cover her head with a veil. And people say, "Why the veil?" The Bible says that the veil is her "power." Is not that a strange thing? In the margin of our Bible we have a rather peculiar interpretation of that. I think it must have been suggested by a man. It says, "Power, a sign that she is under the power of her husband." But I do not think that is it, at all. This verse, I believe, explains what it means. The covering on her head is her power. In what sense? Look at it this way. As long as her head was veiled that was her power, but when the keepers saw her going about the streets at night, they misunderstood her motive and character, and they took away her veil. The unveiled woman was marked out as one who was unclean and unchaste; but the covering on her head was the sign of the chaste and modest wife or maiden.

Years ago I was a Salvation Army officer. I remember that our Army girls could go anywhere with those little blue bonnets. I never knew but one in all the years I was connected with them, who was insulted by anyone in any place as long as she had that little bonnet on. I have been seeking the lost in the lowest kind of bars on the Barbary Coast of San Francisco, and have seen the Army girls come in with their papers and go from one rough ungodly man to another, and ordinarily no one ever said an unkind or a wicked word to them. But once a drunken sailor dared to say something insulting to one of them, immediately practically the entire crowd jumped on him and knocked him down and gave him such a trouncing as he had never had before; and then threw him into the street for the police to pick up. The little blue bonnet was the power of the Salvation Army lassie. Just so the covered head of the women in that oriental land. The uncovered head bespoke the immoral woman, while the covered head was her power, and told that she was seeking to live a life of goodness and purity. So here, because the bride has lost the sense of her bridegroom's presence, she is branded as though she were impure and unholy. This shame has come upon her because she did not immediately respond to her bridegroom's call.

She turns for help to the daughters of Jerusalem as the morning dawns and she sees them coming down the street. "I charge you, O daughters of Jerusalem, if ye find my beloved, that ye tell him, that I am sick of love." In other words, Tell him my heart is yearning for him; tell him I repent of my indifference, of my cold-heartedness and my unconcern, and want him above everything else. Christian, is that what your heart says? Are you a backslidden believer? Do you remember times when you enjoyed communion with your Lord, when life with Him was sweet and precious indeed? But alas, alas, that fellowship has been broken, and you are saying with Job, "Oh, that I knew where I might find Him!" Does your heart say today, "Tell Him that I am sick of love, that my whole being is yearning after Him; I want to be restored to Him, to the sweetness of communion?" The daughters of Jerusalem say, "What is thy beloved more than another beloved, O thou fairest among women? What is thy beloved more than another beloved, that thou dost so charge us?"

This one that you say means so much to you, why is he more to you than you might expect another to be to us? The world says, "Why is Christ more to you than any other?" Why does Jesus mean so much more to us than the things that you and I have known in the world? "Tell us that we may seek him with thee." Then at once she begins to praise him and laud him. From verse 11 to the end of the chapter in wonderful oriental imagery she praises his kindness, his graciousness, his aptness to help, his strength, and his tenderness. She cries, "My beloved is the chiefest among ten thousand." And when she thus praises him they turn again and say, "Where has he gone? How is it that you have let him slip out of your sight if he is so much to you?" Is that not a proper question? If Christ is so precious to you, if He means so much to you, why is it that you so easily allow fellowship to be broken? Why do you so readily permit other things to come in and hinder communion?

"Whither is thy beloved gone, O thou fairest among women? Whither is thy beloved turned aside? that we may seek him with thee." And then instantly as she bears testimony to him, she recalls the last words he said to her before that eventful night, "I am come into my garden," and her own heart was the garden, and she says, "I know where he is. My beloved is gone down into his garden, to the beds of spices, to feed in the gardens, and to gather lilies." And instantly he speaks; he is right there. He had been waiting and watching for her to come to the place where he was everything to her soul, and at once he exclaims, "Thou art beautiful, O my love, as Tirzah, comely as Jerusalem, terrible as an army with banners." And then through all the rest of the chapter he praises her; he expresses his appreciation of her as she had expressed hers of him. In chapter 7, verses 1–9, he uses one beautiful figure after another to tell all his delight in her. It is a wonderful thing to know that the Lord has far more delight in His people than we ourselves have ever had in Him. Someday we shall enjoy Him to the fullest; someday He will be everything to us; but as long as we are here, we never appreciate Him as much as He appreciates us. But as she listens to his expression of love, her heart is assured; she has the sense of restoration and fellowship. In verse 10 she says, "I am my beloved's, and his desire is toward me." In other words, he has not turned against her. When we turn from Him, the natural thought of our hearts is that He has turned against us, but He has not. If He allows us to go through trial, it is like Joseph testing his brethren in order to see if there was genuine repentance of sin.

Three times in this little book we have similar expressions to this, "I am my beloved's and his desire is toward me." In chapter 2, verse 16, we read, "My beloved is mine, and I am his." That is very precious. Are you able to say, "My beloved is mine, and I am His?" In other words, Have you given yourself to Him? Have you trusted Him as your Savior? If you have, He has given Himself to you. Just the very moment you give yourself to Him in faith, that moment He gives Himself to you and comes to dwell in your heart. This is the assurance, then, of salvation. "My beloved is mine, and I am His." And then in chapter 6, verse 3, she says, "I am my beloved's, and my beloved is mine." That is communion. I belong to him and he belongs to me, that we may enjoy one another together. And then in verse 10 of chapter 7, we read, "I am my beloved's, and his desire is toward me." Every doubt and every fear is gone. She has found her satisfaction in him and he finds his in her. What a wonderful picture! Shall it be only a picture, or is it to be a reality in our lives? Is it not a fact that so often we do the very things the Shulamite did? So often we turn a deaf ear to the Bridegroom's voice. We can be so busy even with Christian work that we do not take time for Him. I can be so occupied with preaching that I do not have time for prayer. I can be so taken up with preparing sermons that I do not have time to feed on the Word. You may ask, "Why, how can you prepare sermons without feeding on the Word?" It is one thing to study the Bible in order to prepare an address which I am to give to other people, but it is another thing to sit down quietly in the presence of the Lord and say, "Blessed Savior, as I open Thy Book I want to hear Thy voice speaking to my heart. I want Thee to talk to me, to express Thyself to me in tones of tender love." As I read in that attitude, He speaks to my soul, and as I lift my heart to Him in prayer, I talk with Him. That is communion.

Do not be content with the knowledge of salvation; do not be content to know that your soul is eternally secure; do not be content to know that you are serving Him in some little measure. Remember, there is something that means more to Him than all your service, and that is to sit at His feet and delight your soul in His love. As you read this description in the sixth chapter it will remind you of the fullness there is in Christ. It seems as though every figure is exhausted to show His wonder.

> Join all the glorious names
>   Of wisdom, love, and power,
> That angels ever knew,
>   That mortals ever bore;
> All are too mean to speak His worth,
>   Too mean to set the Saviour forth.

Oh, to have the heart so occupied with Him that we shall lose sight of everything else, and Christ alone will satisfy every longing of our souls!

CHAPTER 7

SONG OF SOLOMON 8:6–7

Set me as a seal upon thine heart, as a seal upon thine arm: for love is strong as death; jealousy is cruel as the grave: the coals thereof are coals of fire, which hath a most vehement flame. Many waters cannot quench love, neither can the floods drown it: if a man would give all the substance of his house for love, it would utterly be contemned. (Song of Solomon 8:6–7)

It is, of course, the love of the bridegroom for his bride that is thus spoken of. We have been tracing the manifestations of it throughout this little book, from the time when the shepherd first looked upon the shepherdess and his heart went out to her until the time when they were united in marriage. It is a beautiful picture, first of the love of Christ reaching us in our deep, deep need, and then that glorious union with Him which will be consummated at the marriage supper of the Lamb.

Now you hear the bride exclaiming, "Set me as a seal upon thine heart, as a seal upon thine arm." The seal speaks of something that is settled. One draws up a legal document and seals it and that settles it. And so Christ and His loved ones have entered into an eternal relationship, and He has given us the seal, the Holy Spirit. "Upon believing, ye were sealed with that Holy Spirit of promise."

This is "the earnest of our inheritance until the redemption of the purchased possession." That seal is the pledge of His love, and you will notice that in the words that follow we have love spoken of in four ways, at least we have four characteristics of love.

First, there is the strength of love. "Love is strong as death." Second, the jealousy of love. In our King James Version we read, "Jealousy is cruel as the grave," and of course that is often true of human love. It may be a very cruel thing indeed, but actually the word translated "cruel" is the ordinary Hebrew word for "firm" or "unyielding." It may be translated, "Jealousy is unyielding as the grave." "The coals thereof are coals of fire, a vehement flame," and this expression, "a vehement flame," in the Hebrew text is "a flame of Jah." That is the first part of the name of Jehovah and it is one of the titles of God. In the third place we have the endurance of love. "Many waters cannot quench love, neither can the floods drown it." And then lastly, the value of love. "If a man would give all the substance of his house for love, it would utterly be contemned."

First let us meditate on the strength of love; and we are thinking, of course, of the love of our God as revealed in the Lord Jesus Christ, for Christ is the Bridegroom of our souls. "Love is strong as death." This He has already demonstrated. "Christ loved the church and gave Himself for it." And that giving Himself meant going into death to redeem His own. "Love is strong as death." We might even say in His case, "It is stronger than death," for death could not quench His love. He went down into death and came up in triumph that He might make us His own, and it is of this we are reminded as we gather at the Lord's Table. It is this which He wishes us to cherish in a special way when we come together to remember Him. He knows how apt we are to forget; He knows how easy it is to be occupied with the ordinary things of life, and even with the work of the Lord, and forget for the moment the price He paid for our redemption; and He would call us back from time to time to sit together in sweetest and most solemn fellowship, and meditate on that mighty love of His which is "strong as death." Nothing could turn Him aside.

Love that no thought can reach,
Love that no tongue can teach,
Matchless it is!

Because there was no other way to redeem our souls, "He stedfastly set His face to go to Jerusalem." When He went through that Samaritan village, they did not receive Him because they realized that there was no desire upon His part to remain among them at that time, but they saw "His face as though He would go to Jerusalem," and they said as it were, "Well, if He prefers to go to Jerusalem rather than remain here with us, we are not going to pay attention to His message. We are not interested in the proclamation that He brings." How little they understood that it was for them, as truly as for the Jews in yonder Judea, that He "set His face stedfastly to go to Jerusalem." If He had not gone to Jerusalem and given Himself up to the death of the Cross, there could be no salvation for Samaritan, Jew, or Gentile. But oh, the strength of His love! He allowed nothing to divert Him from that purpose for which He had come from heaven. Before He left the glory, He said, "Lo, I come (in the volume of the book it is written of Me,) to do Thy will, O God" (Heb. 10:7). And to do the will of God meant for Him laying down His life on the cross for our redemption. Do we think of it as much as we should? Do we give ourselves to meditation, to dwelling on the love of Christ, a love that passes knowledge, and do we often say to ourselves, "The Son of God loved me, and gave Himself for me"? Oh, the strength of His love!

Then we think of the jealousy of love. I know that jealousy in these poor hearts of ours is often a most contemptible and despicable thing. Jealousy on our part generally means utter selfishness. We are so completely selfish, we do not like to share our friends with any one else; and what untold sorrow has come into many a home because of the unreasonable jealousy of a husband, of a wife, of parents, or of children. But while we deprecate a jealousy which has selfishness and sin at the root of it, there is another jealousy which is absolutely pure and holy, and even on our lower plane someone has well said that, "Love is only genuine as long as it is jealous." When the husband reaches the place where he says, "I do not care how my wife bestows her favors on others; I do not care how much she runs around with other men; I am so large-hearted I can share her with everybody," that husband does not love his wife, and if you could imagine a wife talking like that about her husband, you would know that love was gone, that it was dead.

Love cannot but be jealous, but let us see that it is a jealousy that is free from mere selfishness and unwarranted suspicion. When we think of it in connection with God we remember that one of the first things we learned to recite was the Ten Commandments, and some of us were perplexed when we read, "I the LORD thy God am a jealous God, visiting the iniquity of the fathers upon the children unto the third and fourth generation of them that hate Me." We shrank back from that because we were so used to thinking of jealousy as a despicable human passion, that we could not think of God having it in His character. But it is He who has a right to be jealous. God's jealousy is as pure as is His love, and it is because He loves us so tenderly that He is jealous. In what sense is He jealous? Knowing that our souls' happiness and blessing alone will be found in walking in fellowship with Himself, He loves us so much He does not want to see us turning away from the enjoyment of His love and trying to find satisfaction in any lesser affection, which can only be for harm and eventual ruin. "The end of these things is death."

Paul writing to the Corinthian church says, "I am jealous over you with a godly jealousy, for I have espoused you to one husband, that I may present you a chaste virgin to Christ." And then he gives the ground of his jealousy. "But I fear, lest by any means, as the serpent beguiled Eve through his subtlety, so your minds should be corrupted from the simplicity that is in Christ." You see Paul was a true pastor. He loved the people of Christ's flock and knew that their only lasting joy was to be found in living in communion with their Savior; and His heart was torn with a holy jealousy if he saw them turning aside to the things of the world, following after the things of the flesh, or being ensnared by the Devil. Every God-anointed pastor will feel that way.

Young believers sometimes imagine that some of us who try to lead the flock of God are often needlessly hard and severe, and they think us unsympathetic and lacking in compassion and tenderness when we earnestly warn them of the folly of worldliness and carnality. They say, "Oh, they don't understand. That old fogy preacher, I have no doubt, had his fling when he was young, and now he is old and these things no longer interest him, and so he wants to keep us from having a good time!"

Let me "speak as a fool," and yet I trust to the glory of God. As a young believer coming to Christ when I was fourteen years old, the first lesson I had to learn was that there is nothing in this poor world to satisfy the heart, and by the grace of God I sought to give it all up for Jesus' sake. The only regret I have today is that there have ever been times in my life when I have drifted into carnality and fallen into a low backslidden state, and so allowed myself something which afterward left a bad conscience and a sense of broken fellowship, and I never was happy until it was judged, and I was once more in communion with the Lord. If sometimes we speak strongly to you about going in the ways of the world, reminding you that God has said, "Come out from among them, and be ye separate, and touch not the unclean thing," it is because we have learned by years of experience that there is no peace, there is no lasting joy, there is no true unspoiled happiness for those who walk in the ways of the world. If you want a life of gladness, a life of enduring bliss; if you want to be able to lie down at last and face death with a glad, free spirit, then we beg of you, follow the path that your blessed Lord Jesus took. Oh that we might not be turned aside but that we might rouse our souls to a godly jealousy.

I wonder if you have ever noticed that the blessed Holy Spirit who dwells in every believer is Himself spoken of as jealous. There is a passage found in James 4:4–5, that I am afraid is not often really understood, because of the way it is translated in our King James Version, but it is a very striking one: "Ye adulterers and adulteresses, know ye not that the friendship of the world is enmity with God? Whosoever therefore will be a friend of the world is the enemy of God. Do ye think that the Scripture saith in vain, The Spirit that dwelleth in us lusteth to envy?" Take that home, dear young Christian. Do not be seduced by the world and its folly; do not be turned aside from the path of faithfulness to Christ by the mad rush for worldly pleasure and amusement; do not allow the flesh to turn you away and rob you of what should be your chief joy. "The friendship of the world is enmity with God. Whosoever therefore will be a friend of the world is the enemy of God." It is the next verse that perhaps we might not understand. "Do ye think that the Scripture saith in vain, The Spirit that dwelleth in us lusteth to envy?" One might gather that this expression, "The Spirit that dwelleth in us lusteth to envy," was a quotation from Scripture, as though He were asking, "Do you think the Scripture, that is, the Old Testament, saith in vain, 'The Spirit that dwelleth in us lusteth to envy'?" But you can search the Old Testament from the beginning of Genesis to the end of Malachi, and you will not find those words or anything that sounds like them. So it is clear that that is not what is meant. In fact, there are really two distinct questions in the Greek. First there is the question, "Do ye think that the Scripture speaketh in vain?" Do you? Do you think that the Scripture speaks in vain? Having read its warnings and its admonitions against worldliness, against the unequal yoke, against the pleasures of sin, against following the path of the flesh, do you sometimes say in your heart, "I know it is all in the Bible, but after all, I am not going to take it too seriously?" Do you think that the Scripture speak in vain?

Why has God put these things in His Word? Is it because He does not love you, and desires to keep you from things that would do you good? That is what the Devil told Eve in the beginning. He insinuated that God did not love her. He said, "God doth know that in the day ye eat thereof, then your eyes shall be opened, and ye shall be as gods, knowing good and evil" (Gen. 3:5). And Eve said, "I am going to eat of it; I will try anything once." Is that what you have been saying too? If you can only do this or do that, you think you will have an experience you have never had before. The whole world is looking for new thrills today. Before you act, put the question to yourself, "Does the Scripture speak in vain?" It tells you that the end of all these things is death and you may be assured the Scripture does *not* speak in vain.

Then there is a second question, "Doth the Spirit that dwelleth in us jealously desire?" And the answer is, "Yes." The Holy Spirit dwelling in the believer jealously desires to keep us away from the world and to keep our hearts true to Christ. Do you realize that you never tried to go into anything that dishonored the Lord, you never took a step to go into the world, but the Spirit of God within you was grieved, and sought to exercise you because He jealously desired to keep you faithful to Christ? I am talking to Christians. If you are not a Christian, the Spirit does not dwell in you, and you do not know what this is.

Our blessed Lord wants you all for Himself. People say sometimes, "Well, I want to give the Lord the first place in my heart," and they mean that there will be a lot of places for other things. The Lord does not merely want the first place; He wants the whole place; He wants to control your whole heart, and when He has the entire control, everything you do will be done for His glory.

A striking little incident is told by Pastor Dolman. Before the world war he was in Russia holding some meetings in the palace of one of the Russian nobility. Among those who attended the meetings was a grand duchess. She was a sincere evangelical Christian. Dr. Dolman was talking one day about a life devoted to Christ, about separation and unworldliness, and when he finished, the Grand Duchess stepped forward and said, "I do not agree with everything Pastor Dolman said."

"What did I say with which you do not agree, Your Imperial Highness?" asked Dr. Dolman.

"You said it is wrong to go to the theater. I go to the theater, but I never go without first getting down on my knees and asking Him to go with me, and He does."

Pastor Dolman said, "But, Your Imperial Highness, I did not say a word about the theater."

"I know; but you meant that."

"Your Imperial Highness," said Dr. Dolman, "are you not turning things around? Who gave you or me authority to decide where we will go or what we will do, and then to ask the Lord to be with us in it? Instead of getting down on your knees and saying, 'Lord, I am going to the theater, come with me,' why don't you wait until He comes to you and says, 'Grand Duchess, I am going to the theater, and I want you to go with Me?'"

She threw up her hands and was honest enough to say, "Pastor Dolman, you have spoiled the theater for me. I cannot go again."

"Where He leads me, I will follow," but don't you start and ask Him to tag along. Let Him lead. Because He knows that your real, lasting happiness and joy are bound up in devotion to Him, He is jealous lest you should be turned aside.

Now we notice the endurance of love. "Many waters cannot quench love, neither can the floods drown it." How precious that is! How blessedly it was proven in His case. He went down beneath the floods of divine judgment. He could say, "Deep calleth unto deep at the noise of Thy waterspouts: all Thy waves and Thy billows are gone over Me" (Ps. 42:7). But it did not quench His love, and through all the years since His people have had to endure many things; they have had to pass through deep waters, to go through great trials, but He has been with them through it all. "In all their affliction He was afflicted, and the angel of His presence saved them" (Isa. 63:9). In Isaiah 43:2 we read, "When thou passest through the waters, I will be with thee; and through the rivers, they shall not overflow thee: when thou walkest through the fire, thou shalt not be burned; neither shall the flame kindle upon thee." Don't you love to have somebody to whom you can go with all your troubles and know He will never get tired of you?

Some years ago I became acquainted with a poor little old lady in a place where I was ministering the Word. She was going through all kinds of sorrow, and she came to me and said, "I would just like to tell you about my troubles." I felt like saying, "Dear sister, I wish you would tell them to the Lord." But I sat down and listened, and now for over ten years I have been getting her troubles by mail, and I try to send her a little encouraging and sympathetic word in reply. Recently I met her again and she said, "You must be getting awfully tired of my troubles," and if I had told the truth, I would have had to say, "Yes, I am," but I said, "What is troubling you now?" "Oh," she said, "it is not anything new, but it is such a comfort to find somebody who will enter into them and understand!" And she was so effusive in her gratitude I was ashamed that I had not entered into things more deeply. Ah, we have a great High Priest who never wearies of our trials. We weary of hearing of them sometimes because they stir our hearts and we would like to do that which we cannot do; but He has power to see us through. No trial, no distress, can quench His love. "Having loved His own which were in the world, He loved them unto the end" (John 13:1). Somebody has translated it this way, "Having loved His own which were in the world, He loved them all the way through." Through what? Through everything. He even loved Peter through his denial, through his cursing and swearing, and loved him back into fellowship with Himself. His love is unfailing. Having taken us up in grace, He loves to the end.

Let us look now at the value of love. Can you purchase love? Can you pay for it? I was in a home at one time where a very rich man of seventy years of age, worth millions, had married a girl of eighteen. Her ambitious, worldly-minded mother had engineered the marriage. I could not help noticing that young wife off in a corner sobbing to herself and crying bitterly, but I tried never to interfere, for I did not want her to tell me what was in her heart. But one day the husband said, "Do you notice how downhearted my wife is?" I said, "She must have had some great sorrow."

"I am her sorrow," he said. "She was a poor girl, very beautiful and talented, and, as you know, I have been very successful, and I just thought that I could give her every comfort and could surely make her love me. I know that we do not seem to be suited; she is so much younger than I. But she can have everything, all the beautiful clothes and jewels she wants, and surely any girl ought to be happy in a home like this. But, you know, it is all in vain; I cannot seem to buy her love."

Of course not. He ought to have known that he did not have that in his heart to which she could respond. They belonged to two different ages, as it were. "Many waters cannot quench love, neither can the floods drown it: if a man would give all the substance of his house for love, it would utterly be contemned." You cannot buy love, but oh, His love to us creates love in us. It is not the wonderful things that He has done for us, it is not the fact that He has enriched us for eternity, but it is because of what He is. "We love Him because He first loved us."

> His is an unchanging love,
> Higher than the heights above;
> Deeper than the depths beneath,
> Free and faithful, strong as death.

What a blessed thing to know Him and love Him and be loved by Him! Oh, to be kept from wounding such a Lover, from grieving His Holy Spirit! For we read, "The love of God is shed abroad in our hearts by the Holy Spirit which is given unto us."

CHAPTER 8

Song of Solomon 8:8–14

What shall we do for our sister? (Song of Solomon 8:8)

This question was put by the bride to the bridegroom after she had been brought into the full enjoyment of the privileges that he delighted to lavish upon her. He had found her a shepherdess there in the hill country, and loved her and won her heart in those trying days when she felt herself so despised and neglected. Brought to the palace and united in marriage to the king, enjoying to the full his tender consideration and surrounded by the evidences of his affection, she could not keep from thinking of the little mountain home from which she had come.

She thought of the dear old mother who had raised her and cared for her after the father's death, for it is evident that the mother was a widow, and the family by superintending the king's vineyard earned a precarious living; and then she thought of the little sister, much younger than she, who had none of the privileges that she was enjoying. And as she thought of her, she seemed to say, "This bridegroom of mine, my king, the one who has loved me and brought me into these privileges, cannot but take an interest in my family, in my household, and I am going to speak to him about that sister of mine." And so she turned to him in the most tender and confiding way, and said, "I have a little sister, a little undeveloped sister, up there in the vineyard. I am concerned about her. Is there not something we could do for her? What shall we do for our sister?" And he responds at once, "If she be a wall, we will build upon her a palace of silver: and if she be a door, we will inclose her with boards of cedar." You see, this is just the oriental way of saying, "I am so glad you spoke to me about that little sister of yours; I am so glad that you have not forgotten her and her needs. It will be a real privilege for me to show my love for you by what I do for her." And so he uses the striking figures of the wall and the door as he asserts his willingness to help. It was as though he said, "Whatever her circumstances are, and whatever her needs are, I will be delighted to minister to them and I will make you my agent in doing it."

It seems to me this expresses one of the very first evidences of union with Christ. We are no sooner saved ourselves, no sooner rejoicing in the knowledge of Christ as our Redeemer, as the Lover of our souls, as our heavenly Bridegroom, than we begin to think of others less privileged, and our hearts cry out with longing, "What about my little sister? What about my brother? What about those who are still in their sins and still in their deep deep need, who do not know, do not understand this incomprehensible love of Thine which means so much to me?" And it is the Holy Spirit Himself who puts that yearning into our hearts that leads us to manifest an interest in the souls of others. In other words, every real Christian feels within him something that impels him to missionary service.

Are you saved yourself? Then have you been to the Lord about that little sister, or about that neglected brother? Perhaps it is a little sister or a brother you have never seen, and maybe, strange to say, of an altogether different color from yours! Perhaps that little sister of yours is away yonder, a child widow in India, perhaps a downtrodden native woman in Central Africa, or a degraded Indian in the wilds of South America, but yet your little sister; for we read, "God hath made of one blood all nations that be upon the face of the earth." And while you may say, "But she is so sinful, so undeserving," you must remember that you too were sinful and undeserving, and the grace that is lavished upon you came from His heart of love. He delights to give to the undeserving, and the very need of that little sister of yours is the reason why you should be going to the Lord about her.

The bride here is really praying about her sister. Do you often go to the blessed Lord in prayer for that little sister of yours? Perhaps it is a brother. My brother, you who rejoice in Christ Jesus, do you think very often of that poor, ignorant, under-privileged, degraded, sinful brother of yours, living perhaps in heathen darkness today, or dwelling in the slums of one of our great cities, or, it may be, enjoying all that this life has to offer and yet not knowing Christ? Have you been to Him about that degraded one? Somebody has said, "A selfish Christian is a contradiction in terms," and yet we do hear people talking about selfish Christians. Christianity is the manifestation in the life of the love of Christ, and that same love which was lavished upon you He would now have you lavish upon others in their need. What wonderful pictures we have along this line!

In the beginning of John's gospel we read how the Lord revealed Himself to one and another, and everyone who got that divine revelation went after someone else. Each said, "I have a brother, a friend, a dear one in need, and I must go to that one and tell the story of Jesus; tell him that we have found Him." The privileges, the blessings that God has given to us in Christ, are not given to us for ourselves alone. We may say in connection with them all: You must either use them or lose them. "What," you say, "are you telling us that we may lose our souls after having been truly converted?" That is not a blessing. Your soul is you. Of course you cannot lose that if it is saved. I recognize the fact that having life eternal, you shall never perish, but I am talking about the blessings that the Lord lavishes upon you from day to day. They are in order that you may share them with others. To what extent do you enter into that?

I would have you think of three things. First, to what extent do you use your time for the blessing of other people? When I find Christians who need so much physical recreation and have so little time to seek to win souls, I do not quite understand it. I was speaking with a young man some months ago, and I said, "Do you do anything to win others for Christ?" He said, "I would like to, but it doesn't seem to be my gift. I work hard all day, and when Saturday comes I have to go off and get some physical exercise." I think his great invigorating exercise was throwing horseshoes at a little stick. I said, "Did it ever strike you that you could get wonderful exercise by taking a bundle of tracts and going out on a country road and visiting the homes along the way, telling people about their souls? Walking is wonderful exercise."

"But," he said, "you see, I am thinking of serious things all week, and I cannot be serious on Saturday afternoon." Time is given us to use in view of eternity. I quite recognize that we need a certain amount of physical exercise or we would go to pieces, but you will find you can get on beautifully if you give more of your time to God. I was saved forty-one years ago, and I can honestly say my best times ever since have been those in which I have spent my days trying to help other people to a knowledge of Christ, and it is the greatest exercise in the world. I was visiting a preacher some time ago, and he asked, "What do you do for physical exercise?" I replied, "I preach." "But I mean when you want to get a rest," he said. "I preach some more and that rests me," I answered; "the more you do in the work of the Lord, the better you feel." "Brother," he said, "you will have a nervous breakdown if you are not careful." "But I am trying to be careful," I said. It isn't the Lord's work that gives people nervous breakdowns; it is getting into debt, getting mixed up in questionable things, and then you get worried and upset. Just keep at solid service for the Lord Jesus Christ, and you will not have a nervous breakdown. Paul was at it for thirty years. They tried to kill him again and again; he was half-drowned several times, and was thrown to wild beasts, but the old man, when about seventy years of age, had much more vigor than a lot of worldly preachers that I meet, who have to go on a prolonged vacation every once in a while. Your time belongs to the Lord Jesus, and He gives it to you in order that you may use it to bless and help other folk. "Look not every man on his own things, but every man also on the things of others" (Phil. 2:4).

Some time ago, I knew a dear man, one of the greatest men for physical exercise I ever saw. He worked hard on the street railroad. I would see him down on his knees, a great big covering over his eyes to shield them from the brilliant light, as he welded the steel rails. By Saturday noon, he was just worn out, and he would get a bundle of books and off he would go for exercise, over the hills and far away, hunting up poor needy souls, maybe in the county hospital, possibly in the jails, and to poor families. Sometimes he would hear of somebody lying sick and poor and miserable, and he would go to see that one. And you know he had a remarkable way of preaching the gospel. He would often lay down a five-dollar bill at the side of the bed, if he found out that they had no money to pay the bills. On Sunday he would say, "My! I was worn out yesterday, but I had a wonderful time Saturday afternoon, and I am all rested up." He was living for others.

> Live for others while on earth you live,
> Give for others what you have to give.

Then you will find the secret of a really happy Christian life. Your time is to be spent in the service of Christ for the blessing of others, for the blessing of the little sister, of that poor brother.

And then there is something else. He has entrusted you with your talents. "Oh, but," you say, "I haven't any." Oh, yes; you have. You would not like it if others said you had none. But who are you using them for? For Christ, for the blessing of that brother, of that sister in need? It is the investment that you make of your talents here for the glory of the Lord Jesus Christ that is going to bring you a reward at His judgment seat. You remember what He said, "Unto every one that hath shall be given . . . but from him that hath not shall be taken away even that which he hath."

You are to use the talents God has given you for Jesus' sake. Is it the ability to speak? Use it for winning souls to Christ. Is it that you know how to be a kindly sympathetic friend? Then surely you have a wonderful sphere for service. Is it looking up the shut-ins, the sick and needy, and giving them a tender loving word? You would bless and help so many you never think of now, if you would only begin to use those talents for Him. It is not all the work of the man on the platform. I never see souls coming to Christ in a meeting but I wonder what started them. Years ago, when I was young and ignorant, I would go home to my wife and say, "I won six souls tonight," and she would look at me and say, "Are you sure *you* did it?" I would say, "No," of course, "but the Lord used me." But you know it really began away back of that. Perhaps it was a dear Sunday school teacher who had been sowing the seed in the heart of that young man or woman. It was lying there dormant for days, months, or years, and as the Word of God came anew, something was said that just caused it to fructify and burst into life, and that boy or girl came to Jesus. Perhaps it was the lesson the mother taught as the child knelt at her knee long ago. Perhaps it was the father's word dropped into the heart. There is seldom a soul who comes to Christ but there were a lot of folk who had to do with it. It is not just the preacher and the preached message. God give us to use our talents for Christ. Paul planted, Apollos watered, "but God gave the increase."

Then there is my privilege not only to use my time and my talents but my money, to help and bless that little sister, that neglected brother. What a wonderful thing consecrated money is! There never would have been a dollar bill, a piece of silver money, a gold, copper or nickel coin in the world, if it had not been for sin. That is why Jesus calls it the mammon of unrighteousness. Every coin in your pocket is a witness that sin has come into the world. If men and women had remained as they were when God created them, there would have been no money. People would not have sought to build up fortunes, and buy and sell things. We would still be living in a glorious state on this earth, and we would not have had to go out and earn our bread by the sweat of our brow. And now Jesus says, "Make to yourselves friends of the mammon of unrighteousness; that, when ye fail, they may receive you into everlasting habitations" (Luke 16:9). Since the money is here, and we cannot get along without it, do not live for it; do not let it get a hold on you ("The love of money is the root of all evil"), but use it now in reference to the everlasting habitations; use it to meet, of course, your own needs and those of your family, but then use it as God enables you, to bless and help others in their deep spiritual need and in their temporal need too. Then, by-and-by, when at last you reach the glorious habitation, you will see a throng running down the golden street to meet you, and they will say, "Welcome," and you will ask in amazement, "Who can these be?" And one will answer, "We are so glad to welcome you here, for it was your dollar that paid for that Testament that brought me the message of Christ." Another, "You met my need when in such distress I thought nobody cared for me, and then you gave me the money for a good dinner, and I could not help but think of the God of all grace who had put it in your heart to do that for me"; and another, "I came to Jesus because of the kind deed you did for me." Then we will feel it was worthwhile that we spent and were spent for others. "What shall be done for our little sister?" Let us share with her the good things we have.

The king says, "If she be a wall, we will build upon her a palace of silver." A wall speaks of security. If she has already entered into the blessings of Christ, we will build upon her a silver palace. We will add to that which is already hers. We will try to help and lead her on and build her up in the things which be in Christ. "If she be a door, we will inclose her with boards of cedar." A door speaks of responsibility, or opportunity for service. "A great door," says the apostle, "and effectual is opened unto me, and there are many adversaries" (1 Cor. 16:9). "Behold, I have set before thee an open door, and no man can shut it: for thou hast a little strength, and hast kept My word, and hast not denied My name" (Rev. 3:8). But what use is a door if it has no side posts to swing from? "If she be a door, we will inclose her with boards of cedar." If she wants an opportunity for service, we will help to make it possible, and we will assist her in whatever is required, that she may work the better for the Lord Jesus Christ.

Then as the chapter closes and the little book closes, the bride, her heart content to think she has come into blessing and that her little sister too has come into blessing, goes over the past and talks about the vineyard days, the love that has been shown and the bliss now hers, and then she turns to her beloved one and says, "Make haste, my beloved, and be thou like to a roe or to a young hart upon the mountains of spices." "Till the day break and the shadows flee away." The consummation of all bliss will be when we are at home forever with Him. Until then, let us seek to spend and be spent for His glory.

You have heard of the missionary offering that was being taken, and as the box was handed to a very wealthy man, he brushed it to one side and said, "I do not believe in missions." "Then," said the usher, "take something out; this is for the heathen." How can you be a real Christian and not be concerned about those who are less privileged than you are? God stir our hearts to think of the millions still in their great, great need. If we can do nothing else for them, we can bring their case to Him; we can be prayer helpers; we can intercede on their behalf. The wonderful thing is that when you begin to pray, the rest follows. Men who pray devise ways and means for giving.

A lady said to me one time, "You know my husband is unsaved, and he never lets me have any money. He says he wouldn't for the world give me a dime to put in the missionary offering. But I started praying about missions, and as I prayed, there came such a burden on my heart to do something. I had two or three chickens that I had bought with a little money I received from doing some sewing for a neighbor. It was all mine, and I said, 'I am going to devote one chicken to the Lord, and every egg that this chicken lays will belong to Him.' It has been wonderful to me to see that the other chickens lay every once in a while, but my husband growls and says, 'That missionary chicken of yours lays nearly two eggs a day.' Of course that is an exaggeration, but every little while I have another dozen eggs, and I take them to the corner store and get my money, and that goes for missions." I believe that the Lord will take that money and do with it what He did with the five loaves and two fishes: multiply, and multiply, and multiply them. Maybe one way in which He will multiply it will be to start some of you giving, and then, you see, the Lord will turn to this lady and say, "You are the woman that had that chicken the preacher told about. I am going to give you a part of the reward, for these folks just copied from you!"

Let us seek by grace to make every day count for the blessing of others. Loving Him truly we cannot be selfish or indifferent to the needs of those for whom He died, "until the day break and the shadows flee away."

ENDNOTES

Chapter 1: Proverbs 1

1. Emphasis has been added by the author in this and all subsequent Scripture quotations throughout this book.

2. These words must ever possess a tender and precious interest for the writer. It was through having learned them as a lad in the Sunday school that I was, when fourteen years of age, truly awakened by the Spirit of God to see the awful result of rejecting the call of the gospel. Unable to shake off the vivid impression of God's righteous wrath if I longer refused His grace, I fell down before Him confessing myself a lost, undone sinner, and found in John 3:16 the solace my conscience needed: "For God so loved the world, that He gave His only begotten Son, that whosoever believeth in Him should not perish, but have everlasting life." It was a night to be remembered forever!

Chapter 8: Proverbs 8

1. F. W. Grant, *The Crowned Christ* (New York: Loizeaux, n.d.), a marvelous unfolding of the truth as to the person and varied offices of the Lord Jesus.

Chapter 11: Proverbs 11

1. Those who have paid little attention to the moral instruction contained in the book referred to might find profit in consulting H. A. Ironside, *Notes on the Book of Esther* (New York: Loizeaux, n.d.).

Chapter 14: Proverbs 14

1. A gospel address on this solemn passage can be found in H. A. Ironside, *The Only Two Religions* (New York: Loizeaux, n.d.).

Chapter 20: Proverbs 20

1. For an exhaustive treatment of the Scripture doctrine as to the spirit and soul, I know nothing better than the erudite and painstaking work of the late F. W. Grant, *Facts and Theories As to a Future State* (New York: Loizeaux, n.d.).

2. In so writing I do not forget the Scripture declaration that "there is none that seeketh after God." The savage gropes after Him because of his fear, and desires to propitiate His supposed anger and hatred. He has no desire to love and serve Him because of what He has done and is.

Chapter 25: Proverbs 25

1. For a full exposition consult H. A. Ironside, *The Weeping Prophet: Reflections on the Prophecy and Lamentations of Jeremiah* (New York: Loizeaux, n.d.).

Chapter 26: Proverbs 26

1. See H. A. Ironside, "Concurrent Blessings," in *The Only Two Religions* (New York: Loizeaux, n.d.).

Chapter 30: Proverbs 30

1. J. B. Gottshall, *The Ant, the Coney, the Locust, and the Lizard,* in Nature in the Light of Scripture series (New York: Loizeaux, n.d.). This title contains much that is helpful and suggestive.